FAIRY TAIL

フェアリーテイル

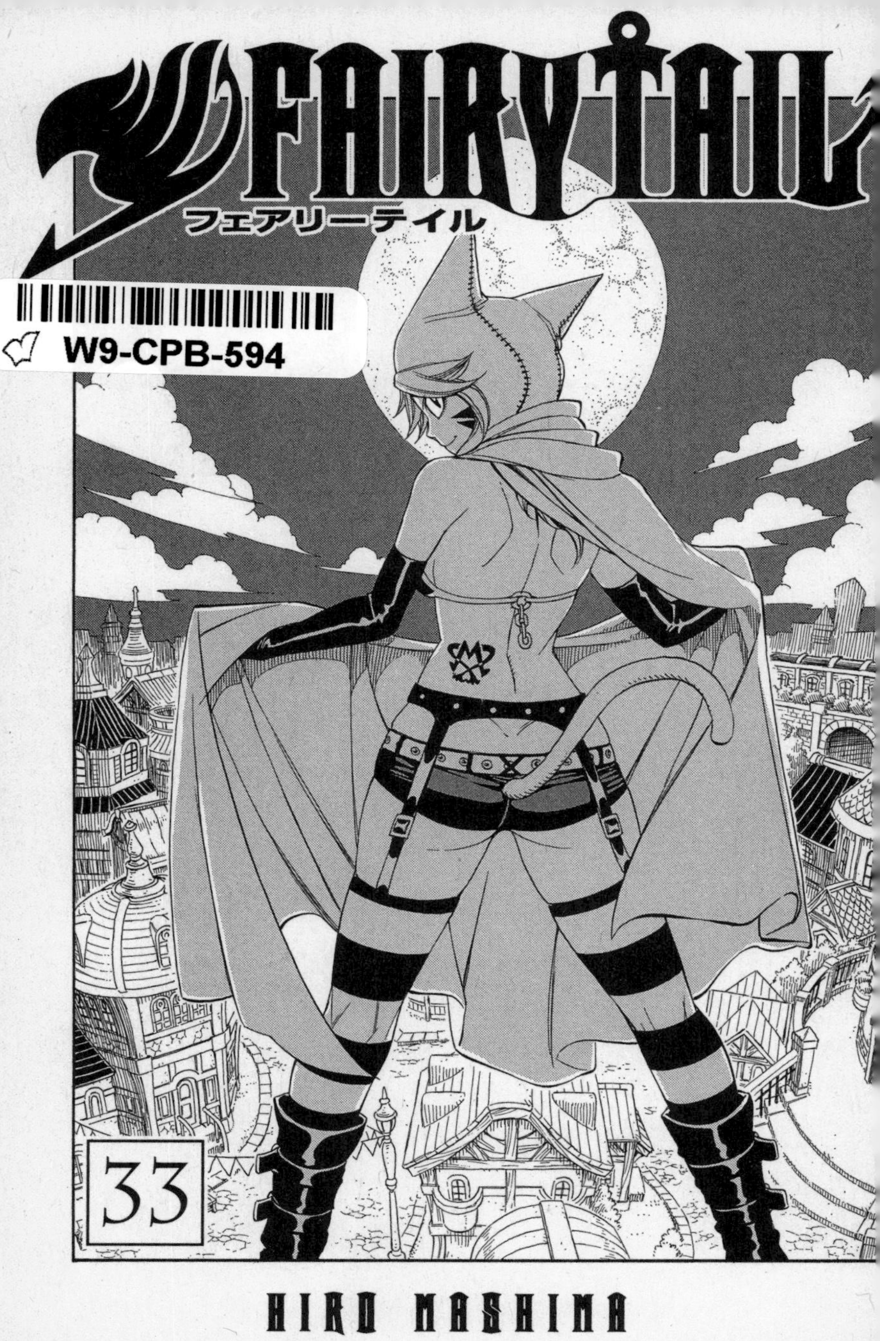

33

HIRO MASHIMA

FAIRY TAIL 33

What's inside!

CONTENTS

Chapter 275: Drunken Hawk ⌁ ⌁ ⌁ 3

Chapter 276: Chariot ⌁ ⌁ ⌁ 23

Chapter 277: Socks ⌁ ⌁ ⌁ 43

Chapter 278: Elfman vs. Bacchus ⌁ ⌁ ⌁ 63

Chapter 279: A Door Sunken into Darkness ⌁ ⌁ ⌁ 91

Chapter 280: Kagura vs. Yukino ⌁ ⌁ ⌁ 121

Chapter 281: Grudges Wrapped in the Curtain of Night ⌁ ⌁ ⌁ 141

Chapter 282: Ten Keys and Two Keys ⌁ ⌁ ⌁ 161

Translation Notes ⌁ ⌁ ⌁ 195

Preview of Vol. 34 ⌁ ⌁ ⌁ 197

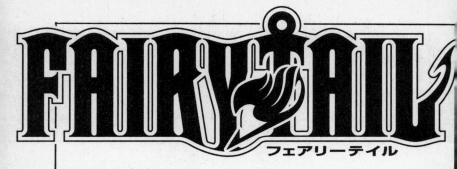

FAIRY TAIL

フェアリーテイル

Grand Magic Games: First Day Results

Competition Section

1. Saber Tooth
2. Raven Tail
3. Lamia Scale
4. Blue Pegasus
5. Mermaid Heel
6. Quatro Cerberus
7. Fairy Tail B
8. Fairy Tail A

Battle Section

☐	FTA Lucy	vs.	RT Flare	☒
☒	BP Ren	vs.	HM Araña	☐
☐	QC Warcry	vs.	ST Olga	☒
☐	FTB Mystogan	vs.	LS Jura	☒

Point Ranking

1. Saber Tooth	20P
2. Raven Tail	18P
3. Lamia Scale	16P
4. Blue Pegasus	14P
5. Mermaid Heel	3P
6. Quatro Cerberus	2P
7. Fairy Tail B	1P
8. Fairy Tail A	0P

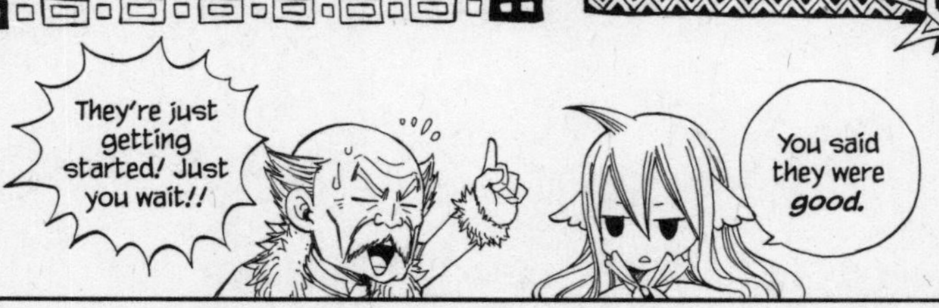

You said they were *good.*
They're just getting started! Just you wait!!

Chapter 275: Drunken Hawk

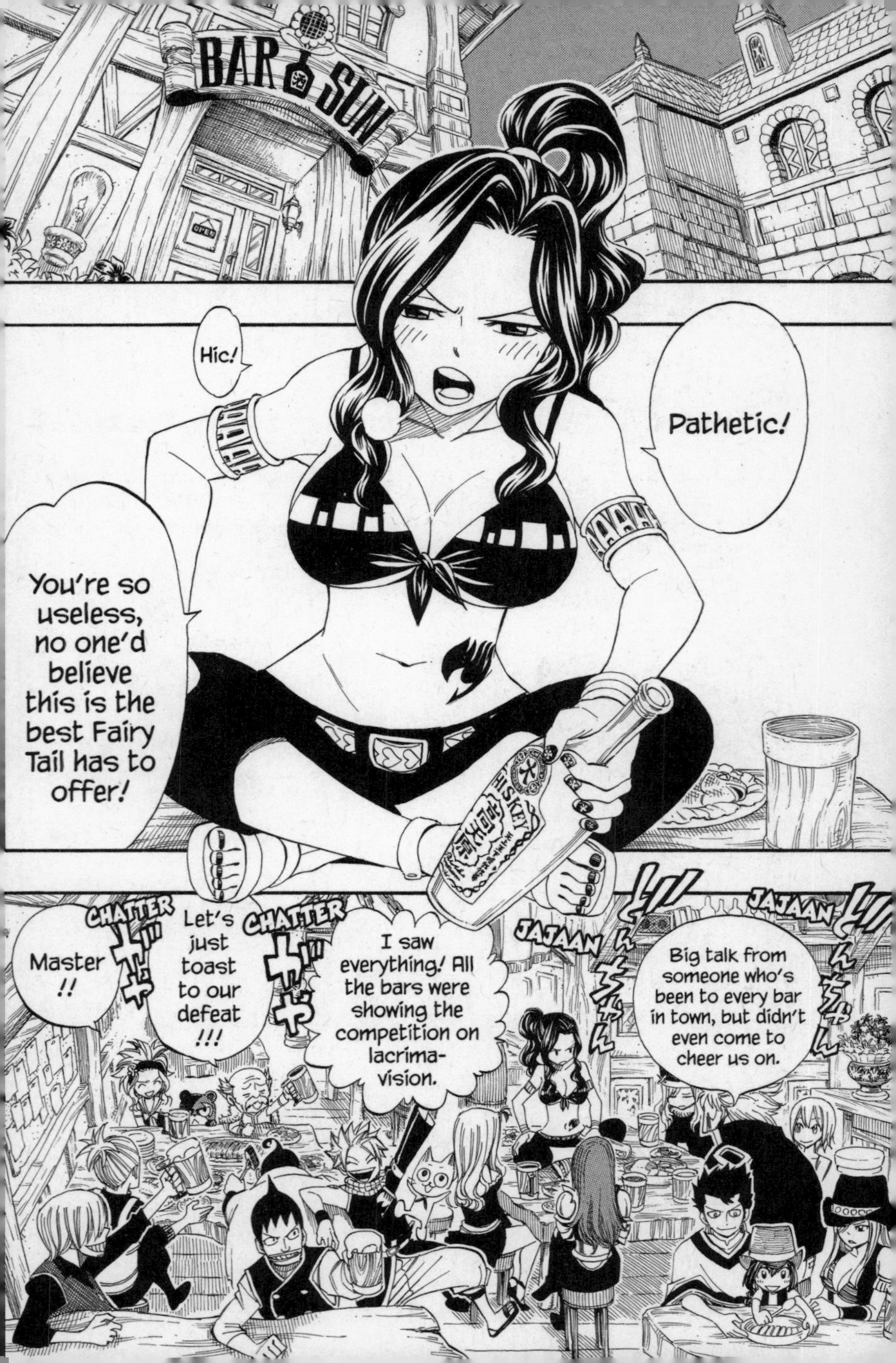
BAR SUN
OPEN
Pathetic!
Hic!
You're so useless, no one'd believe this is the best Fairy Tail has to offer!
JAJAAN
Big talk from someone who's been to every bar in town, but didn't even come to cheer us on.
JAJAAN
I saw everything! All the bars were showing the competition on lacrima-vision.
CHATTER
Let's just toast to our defeat!!!
CHATTER
Master!!

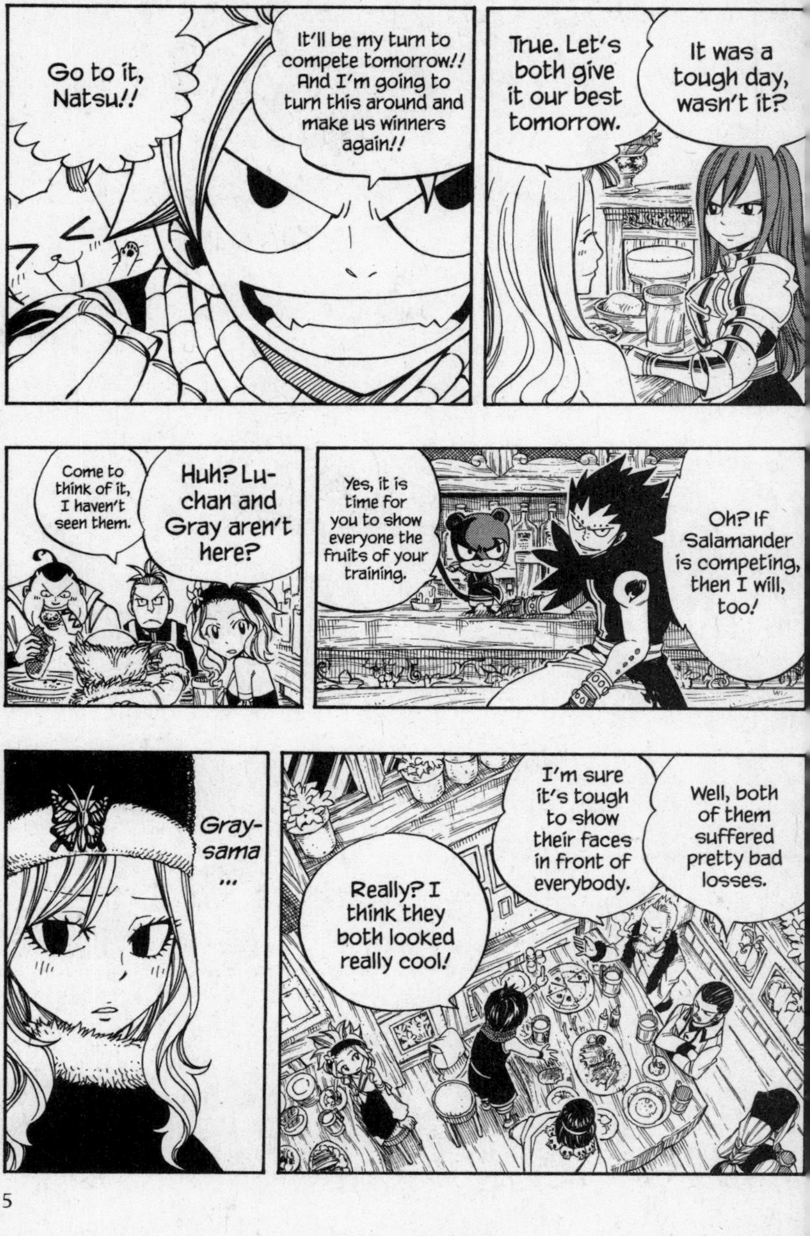

It was a tough day, wasn't it?
True. Let's both give it our best tomorrow.
It'll be my turn to compete tomorrow!! And I'm going to turn this around and make us winners again!!
Go to it, Natsu!!
Oh? If Salamander is competing, then I will, too!
Yes, it is time for you to show everyone the fruits of your training.
Huh? Lu-chan and Gray aren't here?
Come to think of it, I haven't seen them.
Well, both of them suffered pretty bad losses.
I'm sure it's tough to show their faces in front of everybody.
Really? I think they both looked really cool!
Gray-sama ...

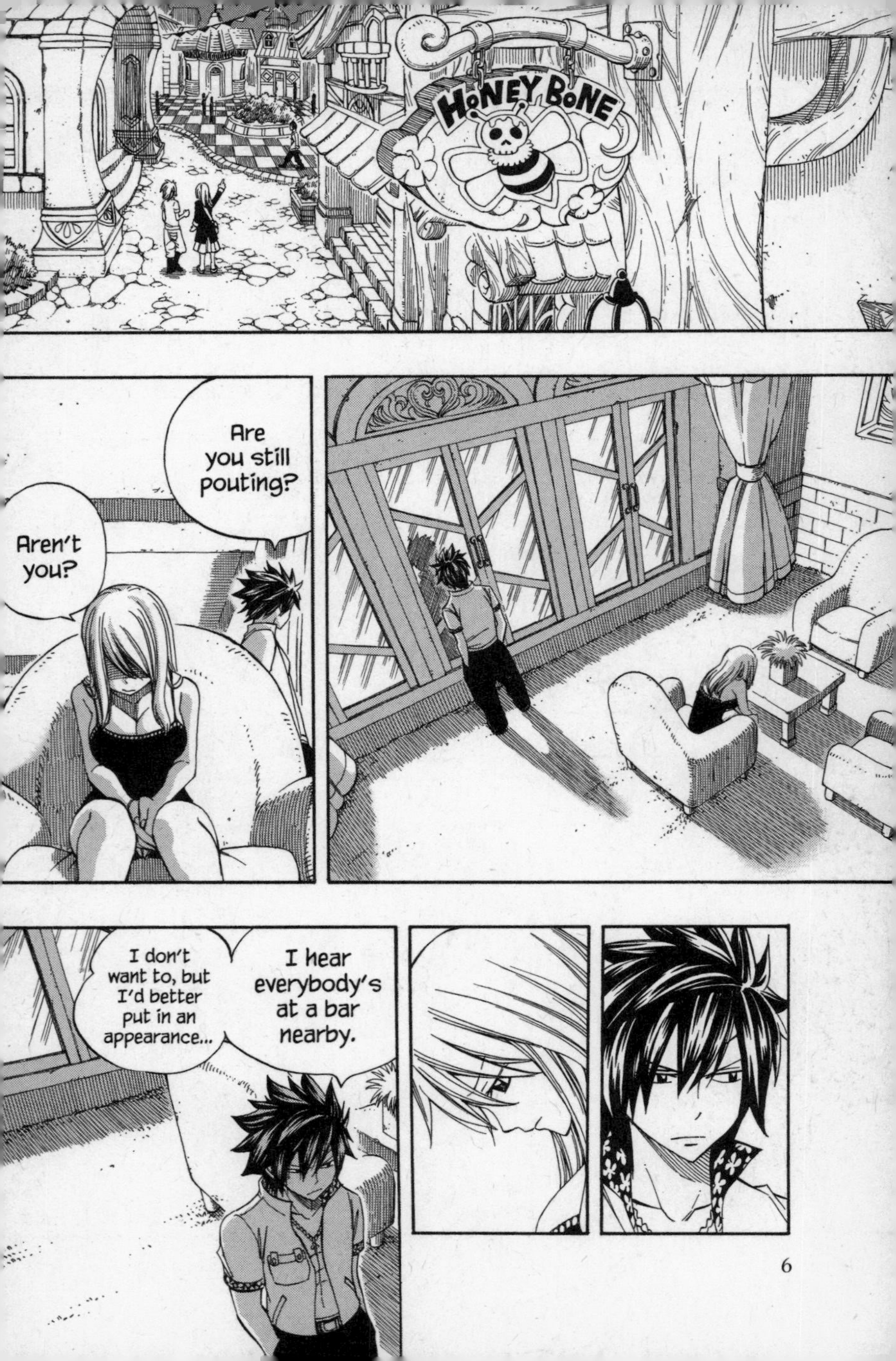
HONEY BONE
Are you still pouting?
Aren't you?
I hear everybody's at a bar nearby.
I don't want to, but I'd better put in an appearance...

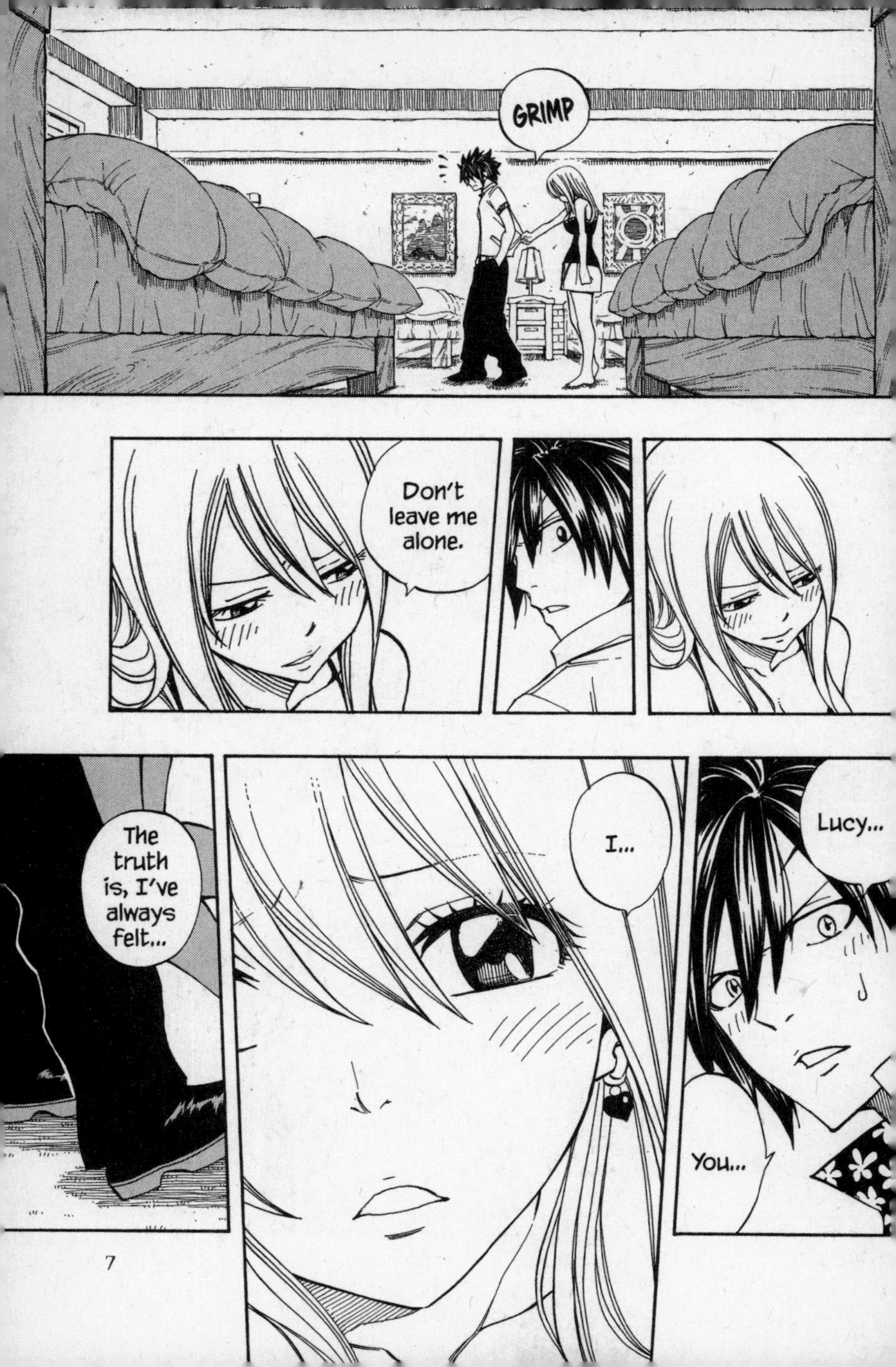
GRIMP
Don't leave me alone.
Lucy...
You...
I...
The truth is, I've always felt...

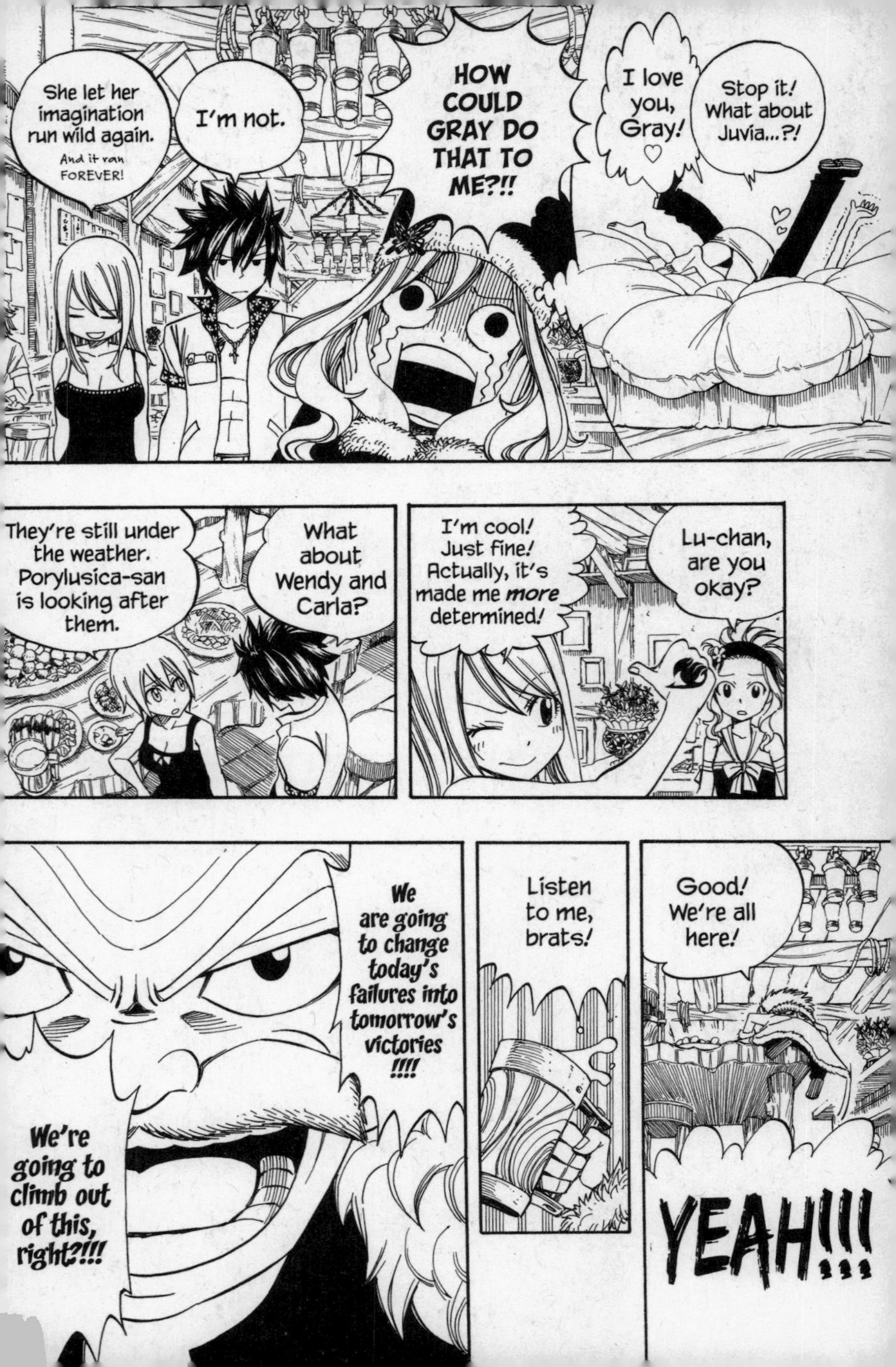
Stop it! What about Juvia...?!
I love you, Gray!
HOW COULD GRAY DO THAT TO ME?!!
I'm not.
She let her imagination run wild again.
And it ran FOREVER!
Lu-chan, are you okay?
I'm cool! Just fine! Actually, it's made me *more* determined!
What about Wendy and Carla?
They're still under the weather. Porylusica-san is looking after them.
Good! We're all here!
YEAH!!!
Listen to me, brats!
We are going to change today's failures into tomorrow's victories!!!!
We're going to climb out of this, right?!!!

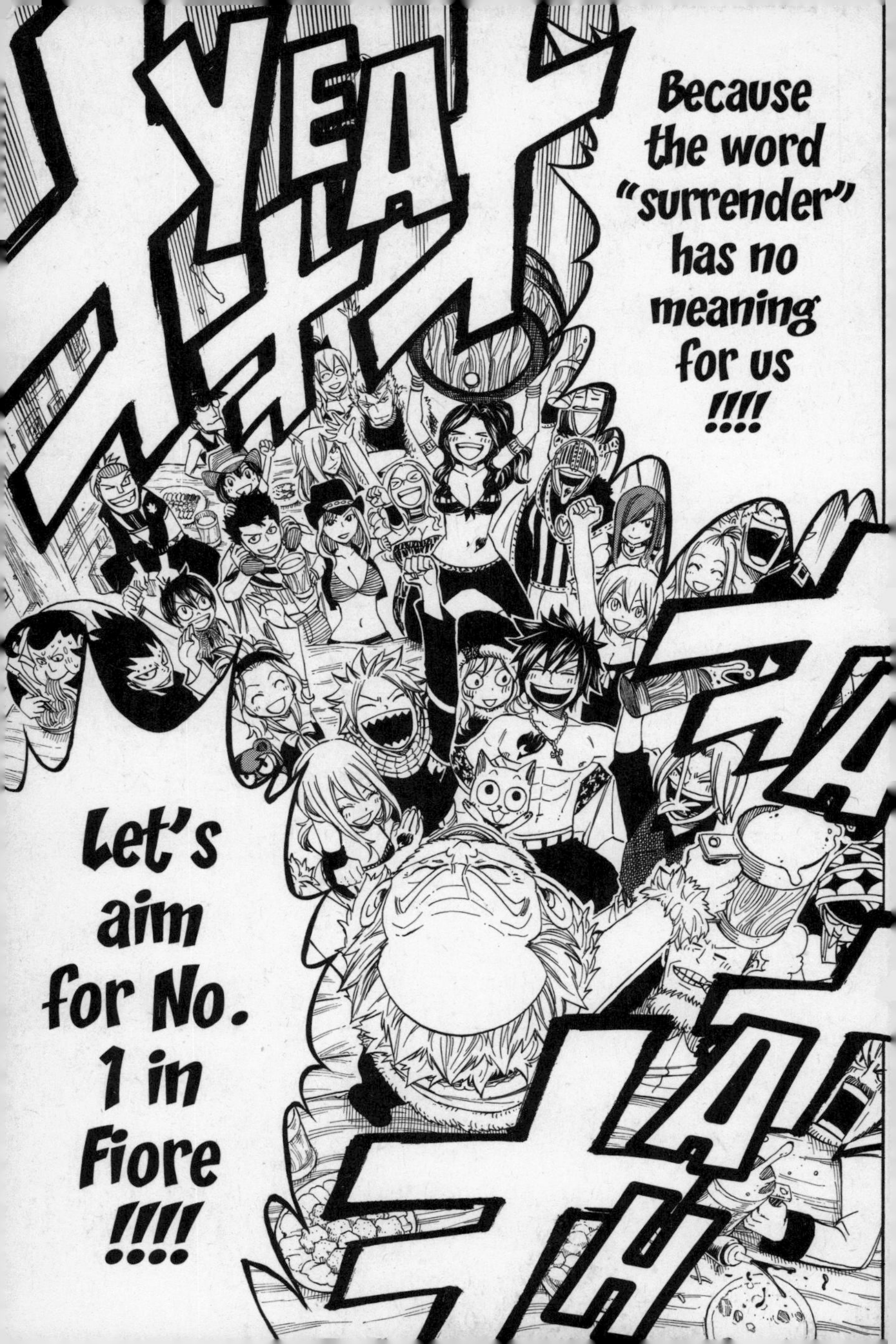
Because the word "surrender" has no meaning for us !!!!
Let's aim for No. 1 in Fiore !!!!

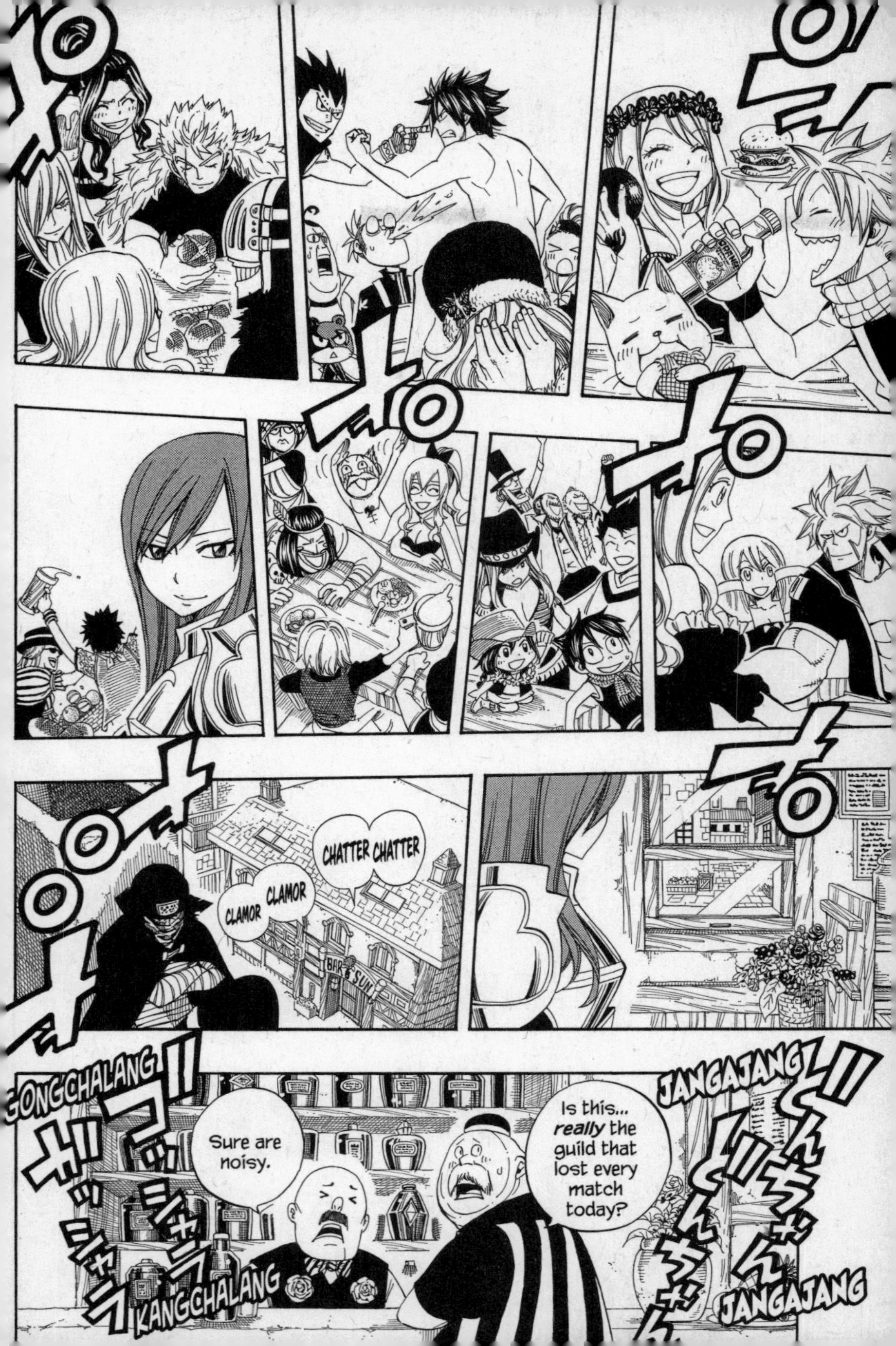

CHATTER CHATTER
CLAMOR CLAMOR
JANGAJANG
Is this... *really* the guild that lost every match today?
Sure are noisy.
GONG CHALANG
KANGCHALANG
JANGAJANG

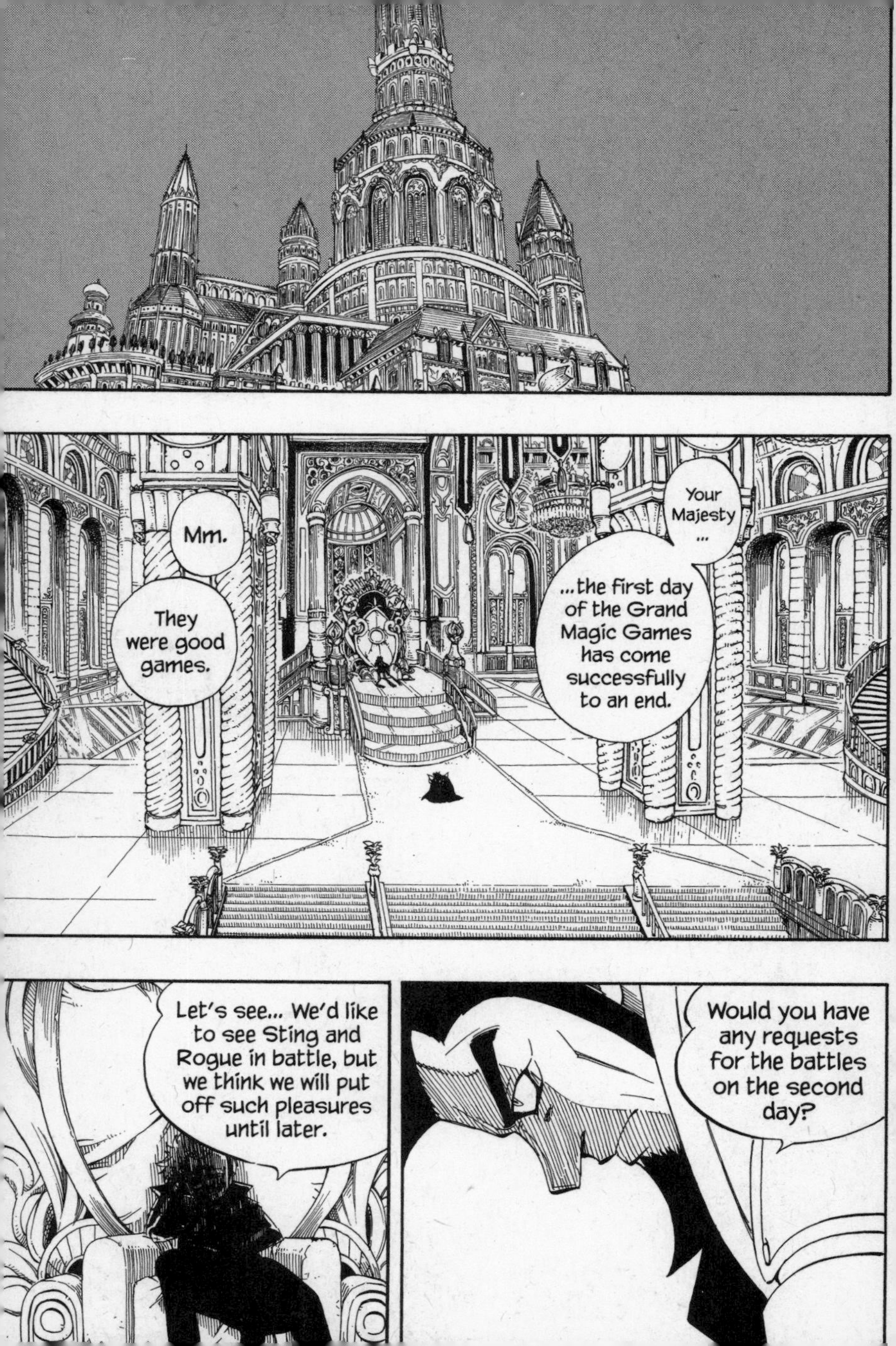
Your Majesty ...
...the first day of the Grand Magic Games has come successfully to an end.
Mm.
They were good games.
Would you have any requests for the battles on the second day?
Let's see... We'd like to see Sting and Rogue in battle, but we think we will put off such pleasures until later.

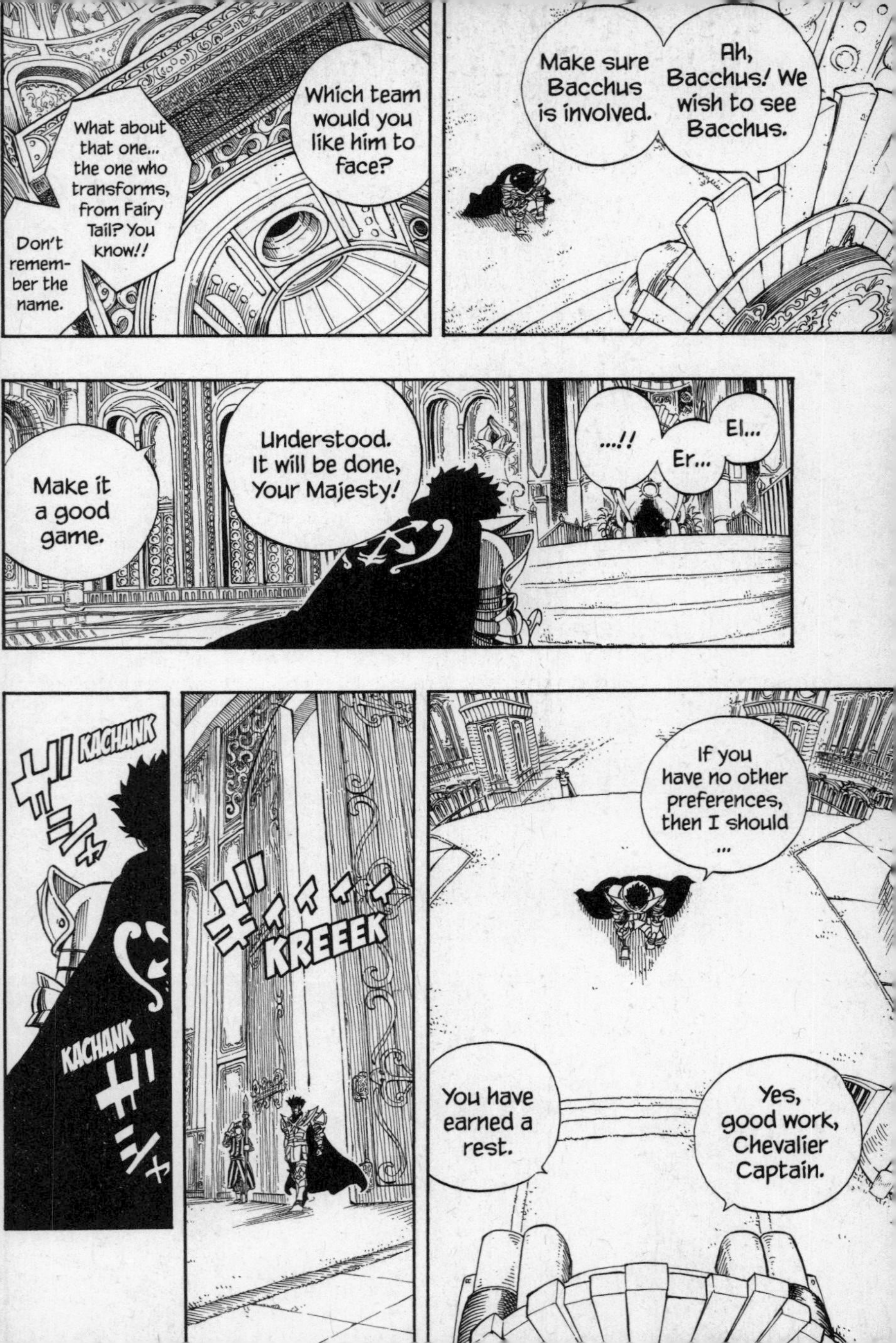

Ah, Bacchus! We wish to see Bacchus.
Make sure Bacchus is involved.
Which team would you like him to face?
What about that one... the one who transforms, from Fairy Tail? You know!!
Don't remem-ber the name.
El...
Er...
...!!
Understood. It will be done, Your Majesty!
Make it a good game.
If you have no other preferences, then I should ...
Yes, good work, Chevalier Captain.
You have earned a rest.
KREEEK
KACHANK
KACHANK

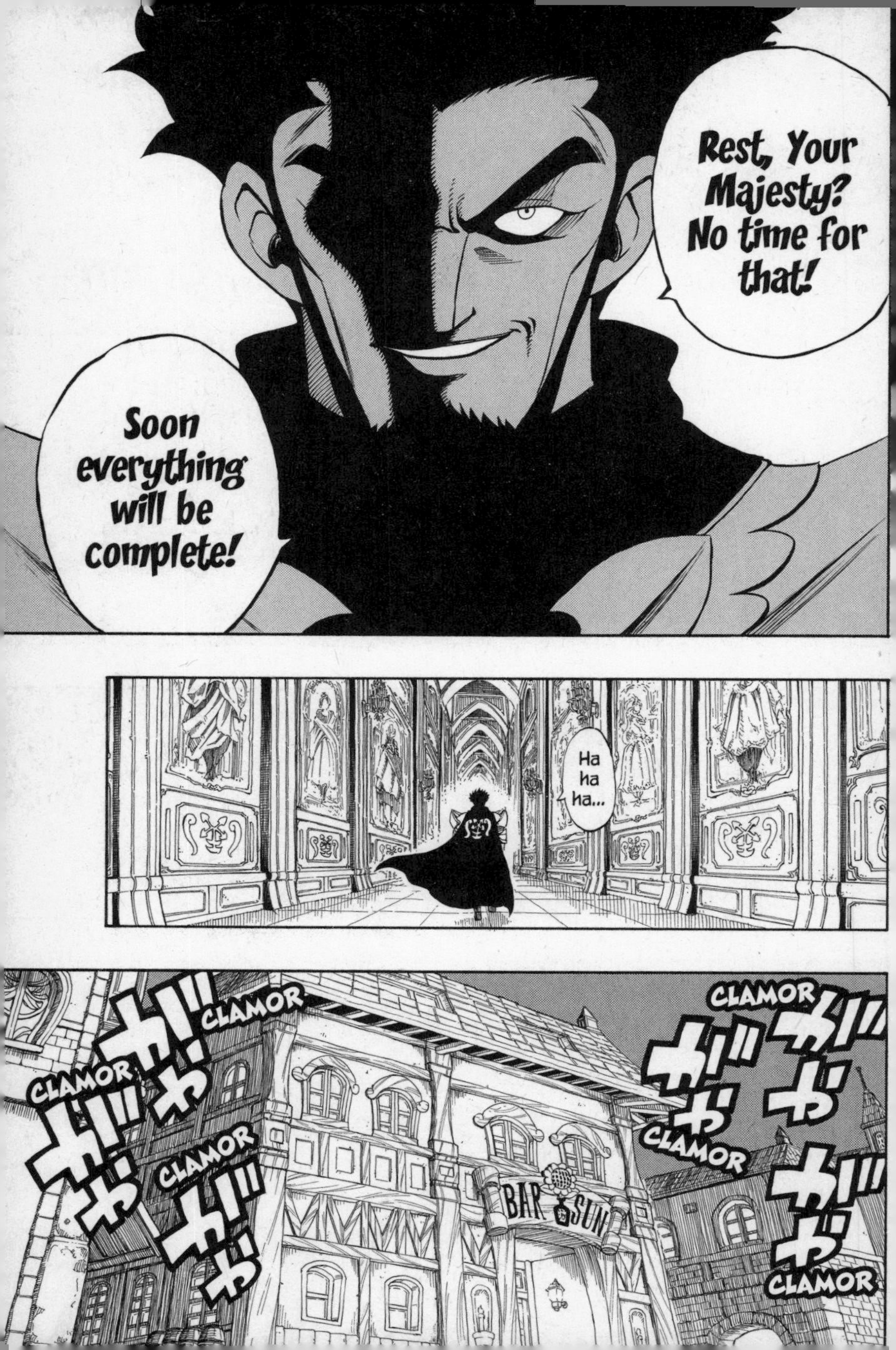
Rest, Your Majesty? No time for that!
Soon everything will be complete!
Ha ha ha...
CLAMOR
CLAMOR
CLAMOR
BAR SUN
CLAMOR
CLAMOR
CLAMOR

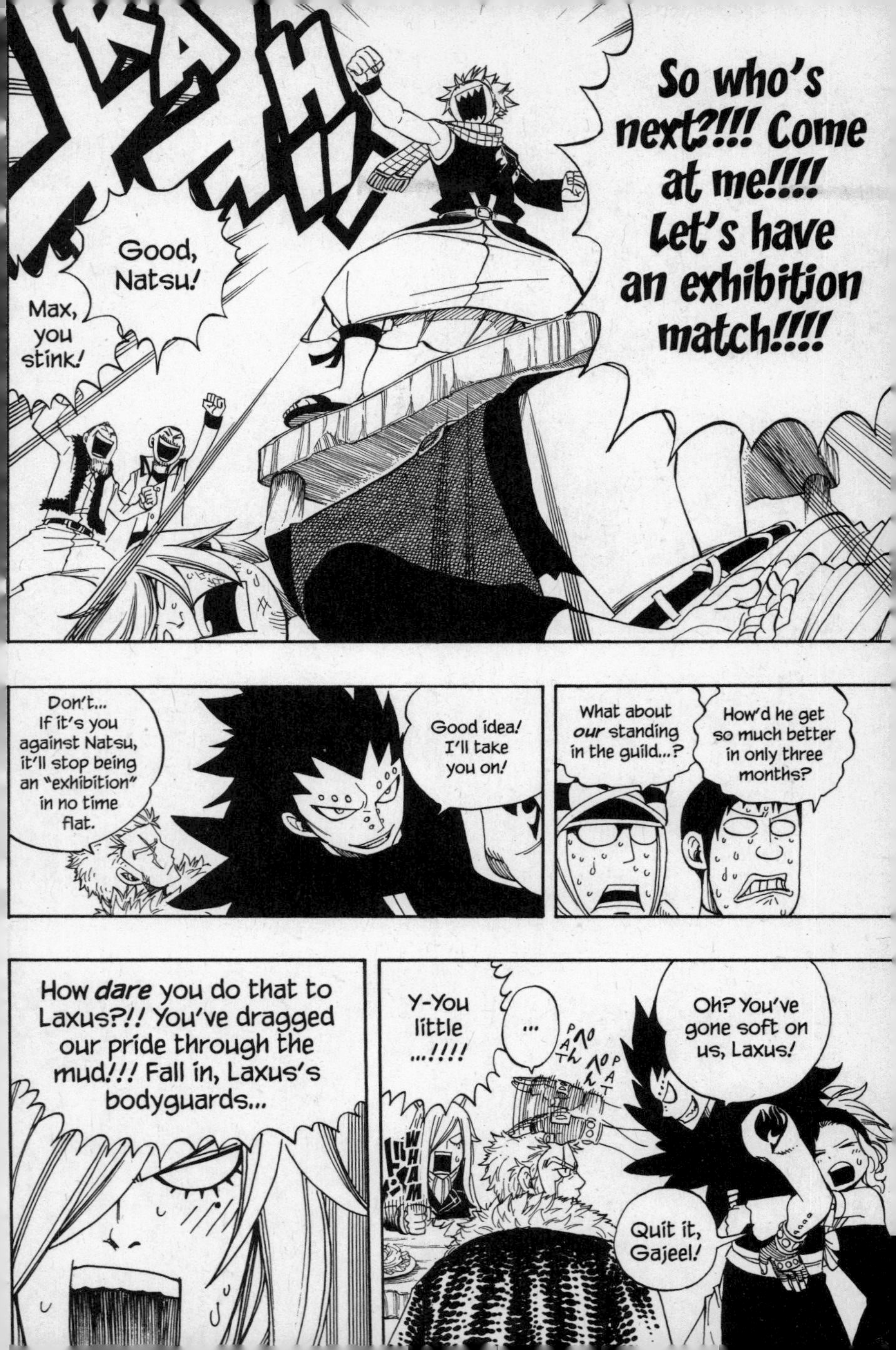
So who's next?!!! Come at me!!!! Let's have an exhibition match!!!!
Good, Natsu!
Max, you stink!
How'd he get so much better in only three months?
What about *our* standing in the guild...?
Good idea! I'll take you on!
Don't... If it's you against Natsu, it'll stop being an "exhibition" in no time flat.
Oh? You've gone soft on us, Laxus!
PAT
PAT
...
Y-You little ...!!!!
Quit it, Gajeel!
How *dare* you do that to Laxus?!! You've dragged our pride through the mud!!! Fall in, Laxus's bodyguards...

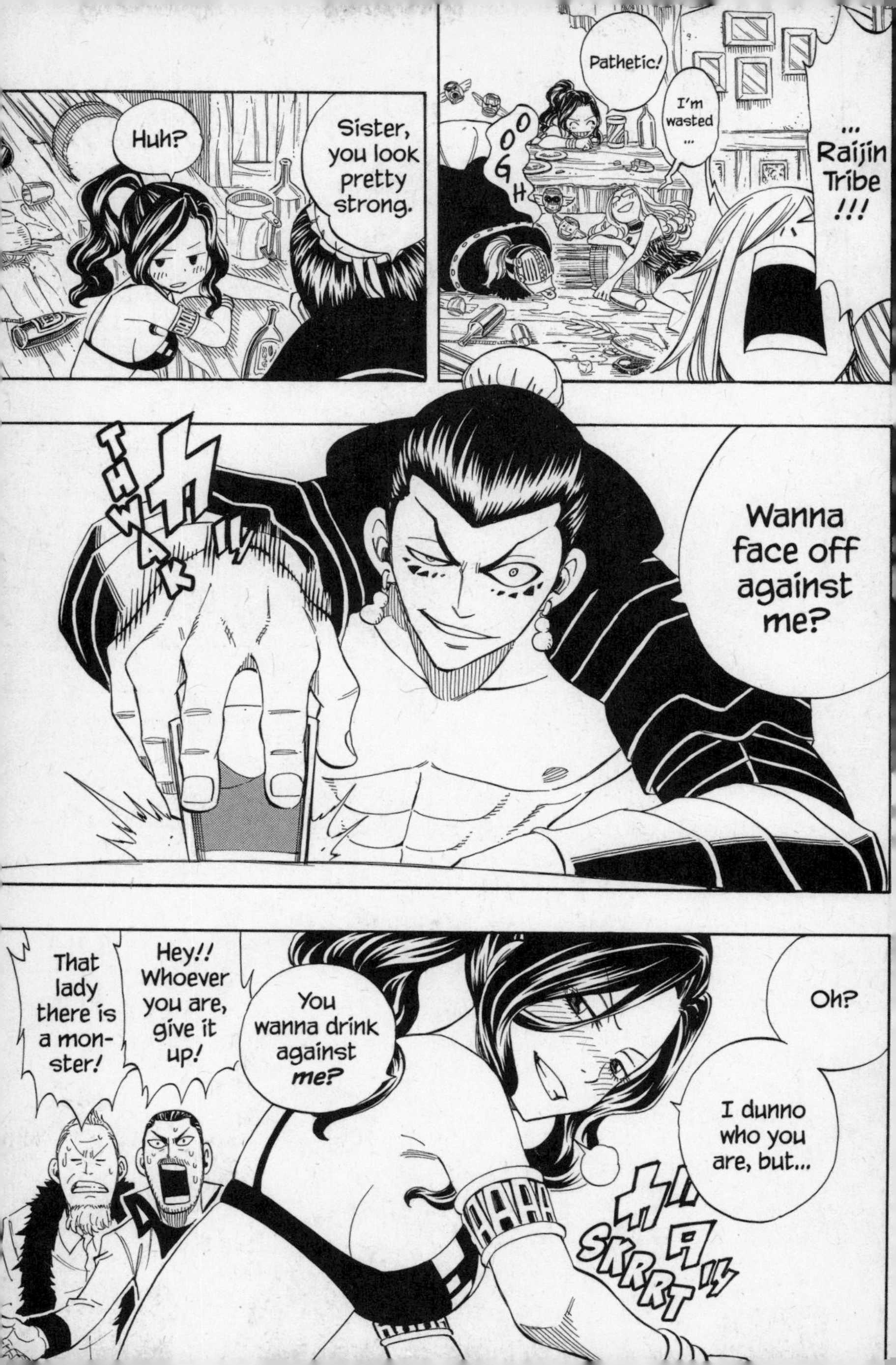
Pathetic!
I'm wasted ...
OOGH
... Raijin Tribe !!!
Sister, you look pretty strong.
Huh?
Wanna face off against me?
THWAKK
Oh?
I dunno who you are, but...
SKRRT
You wanna drink against *me?*
Hey!! Whoever you are, give it up!
That lady there is a mon-ster!

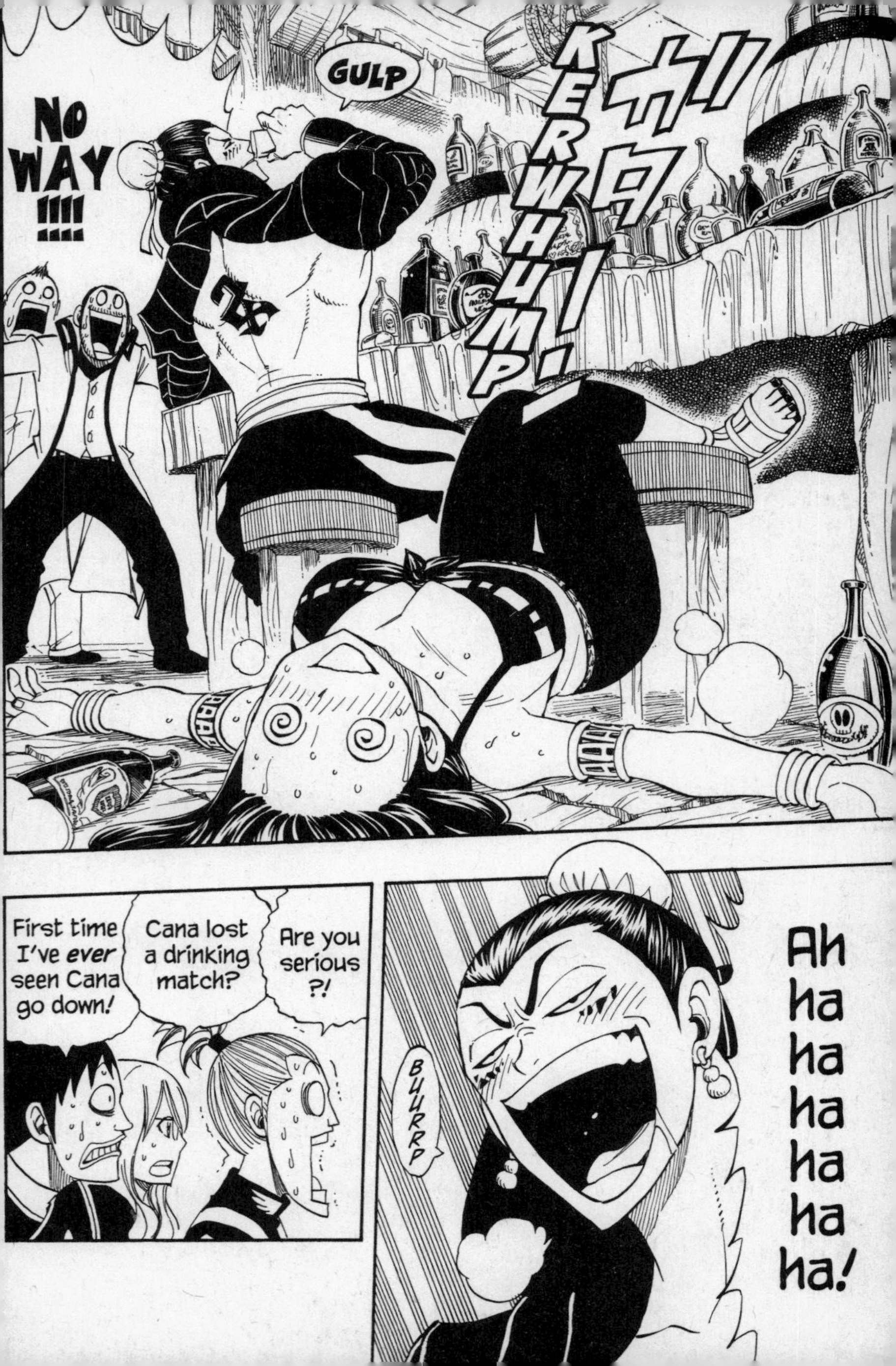
KERWHUMP!
GULP
NO WAY!!!!
Ah ha ha ha ha ha ha!
BUURRP
Are you serious?!
Cana lost a drinking match?
First time I've *ever* seen Cana go down!

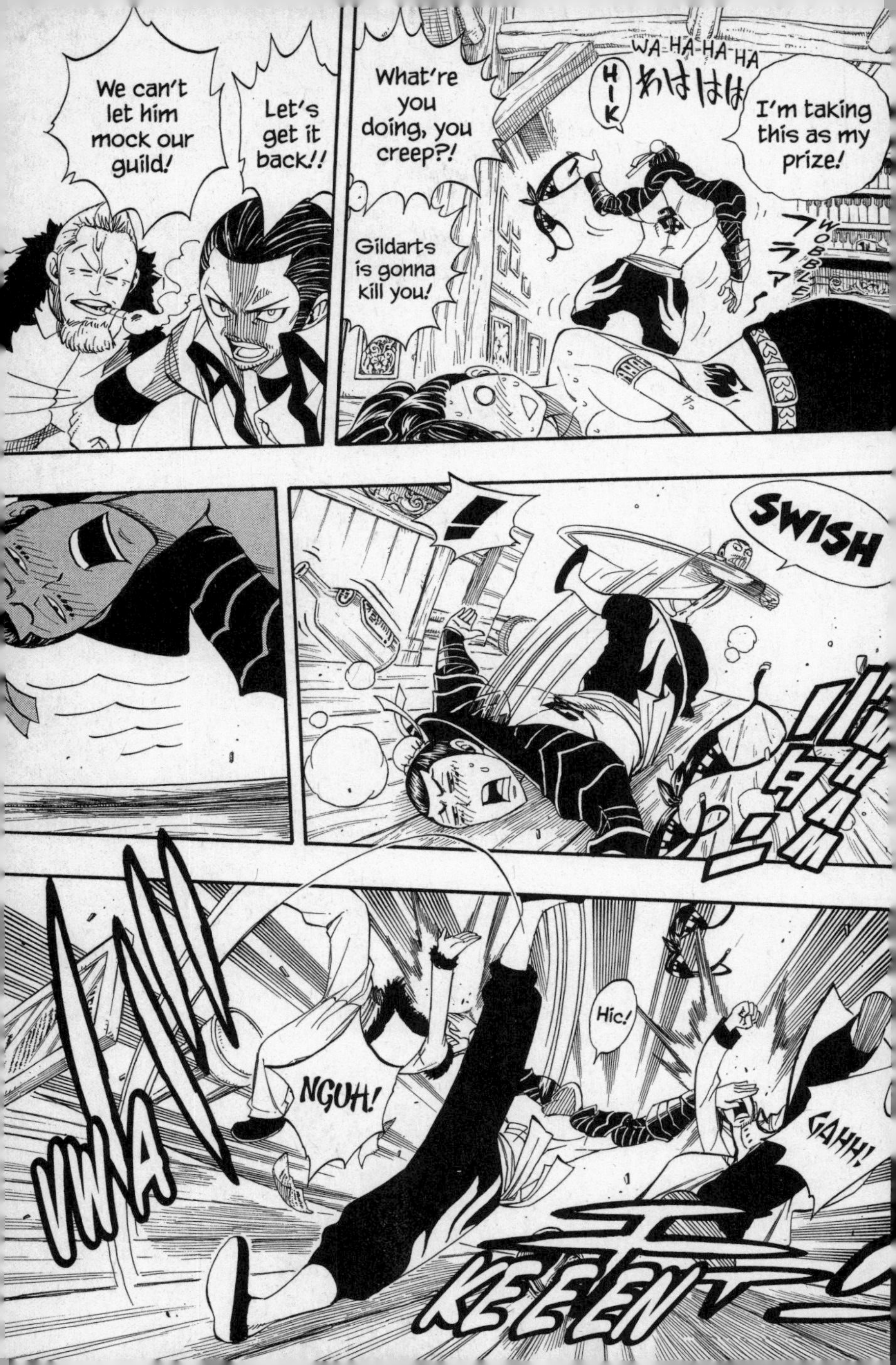

I'm taking this as my prize!
WA-HA-HA-HA
わははは
HIK
What're you doing, you creep?!
WOBBLE
フラァ~
Gildarts is gonna kill you!
Let's get it back!!
We can't let him mock our guild!
SWISH
!
WHAM
Hic!
GAHH!
NGUH!
KEEEN
UWA

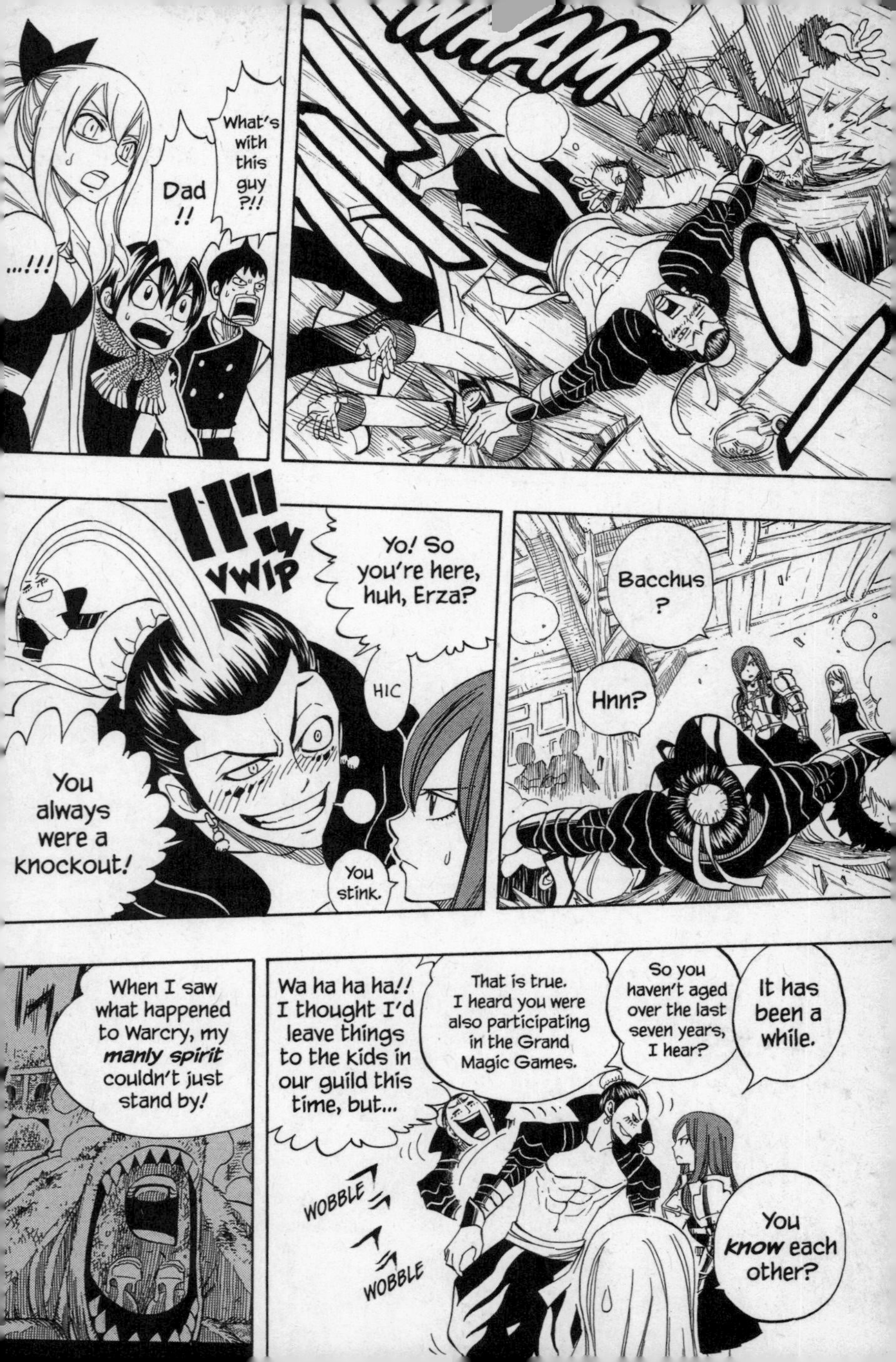
WHAM
What's with this guy?!!
Dad!!
...!!!
Bacchus?
Hnn?
Yo! So you're here, huh, Erza?
VWIP
HIC
You always were a knockout!
You stink.
It has been a while.
So you haven't aged over the last seven years, I hear?
That is true. I heard you were also participating in the Grand Magic Games.
Wa ha ha ha!! I thought I'd leave things to the kids in our guild this time, but...
WOBBLE
WOBBLE
You *know* each other?
When I saw what happened to Warcry, my *manly spirit* couldn't just stand by!

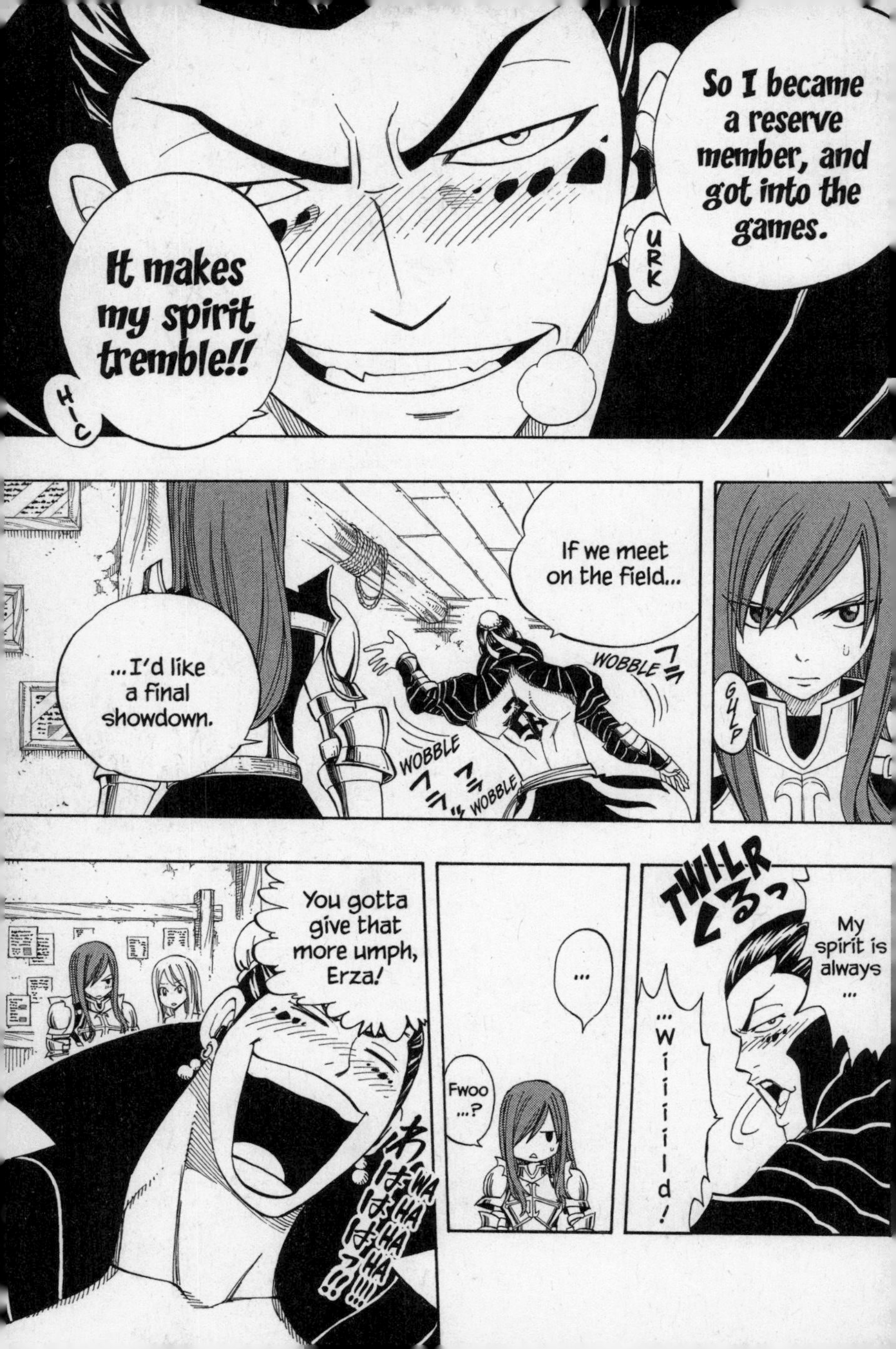
So I became a reserve member, and got into the games.
URK
It makes my spirit tremble!!
HIC
GULP
If we meet on the field...
WOBBLE
...I'd like a final showdown.
WOBBLE
WOBBLE
TWILR くるっ
My spirit is always ...
...Wiiiiild!
...
Fwoo ...?
You gotta give that more umph, Erza!
わはははっ!!!
WA HA HA HA

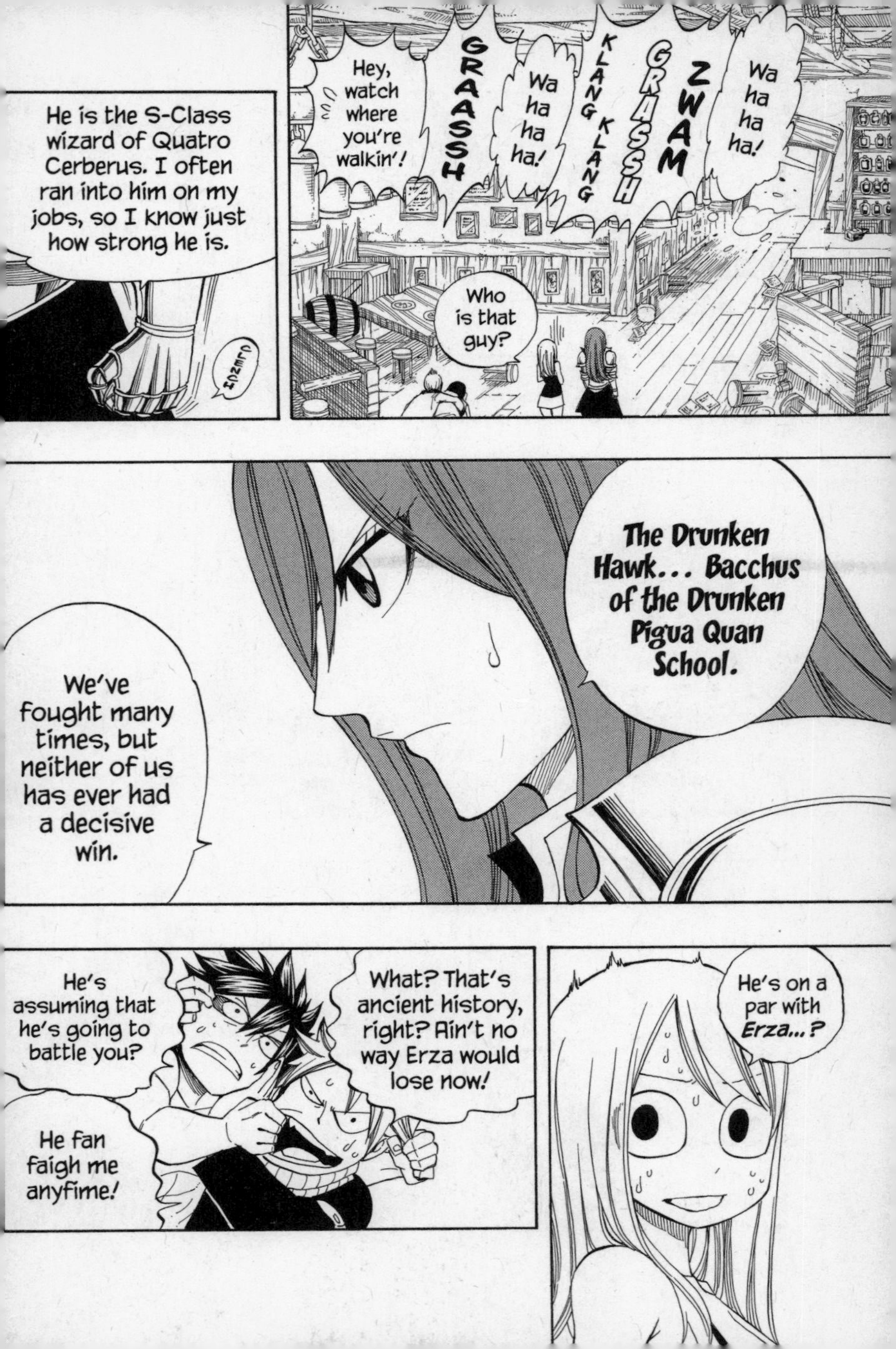

Wa ha ha ha!
ZWAM
GRAASSH
KLANG KLANG
Wa ha ha ha!
GRAASSH
Hey, watch where you're walkin'!
Who is that guy?
He is the S-Class wizard of Quatro Cerberus. I often ran into him on my jobs, so I know just how strong he is.
CLENCH
The Drunken Hawk... Bacchus of the Drunken Pigua Quan School.
We've fought many times, but neither of us has ever had a decisive win.
He's on a par with Erza...?
What? That's ancient history, right? Ain't no way Erza would lose now!
He's assuming that he's going to battle you?
He fan faigh me anyfime!

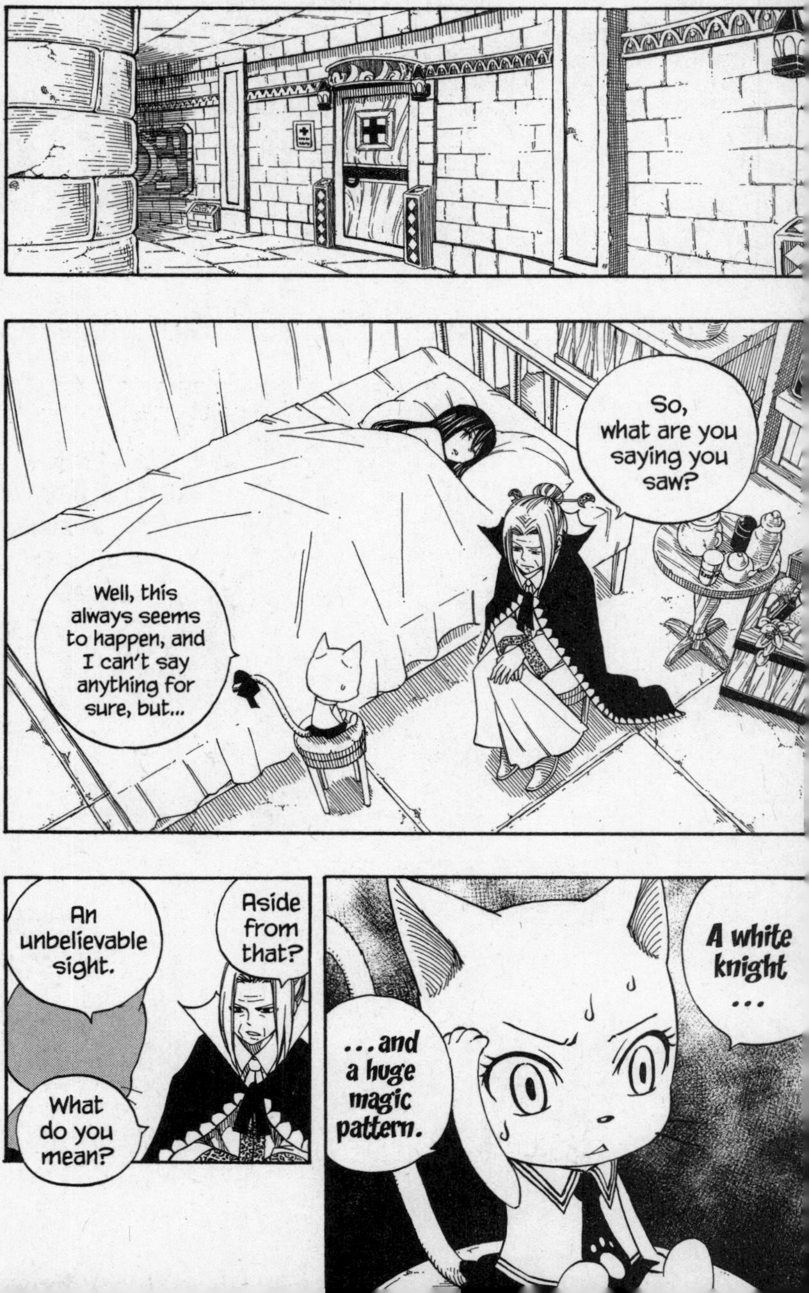
So, what are you saying you saw?
Well, this always seems to happen, and I can't say anything for sure, but...
A white knight ...
...and a huge magic pattern.
Aside from that?
An unbelievable sight.
What do you mean?

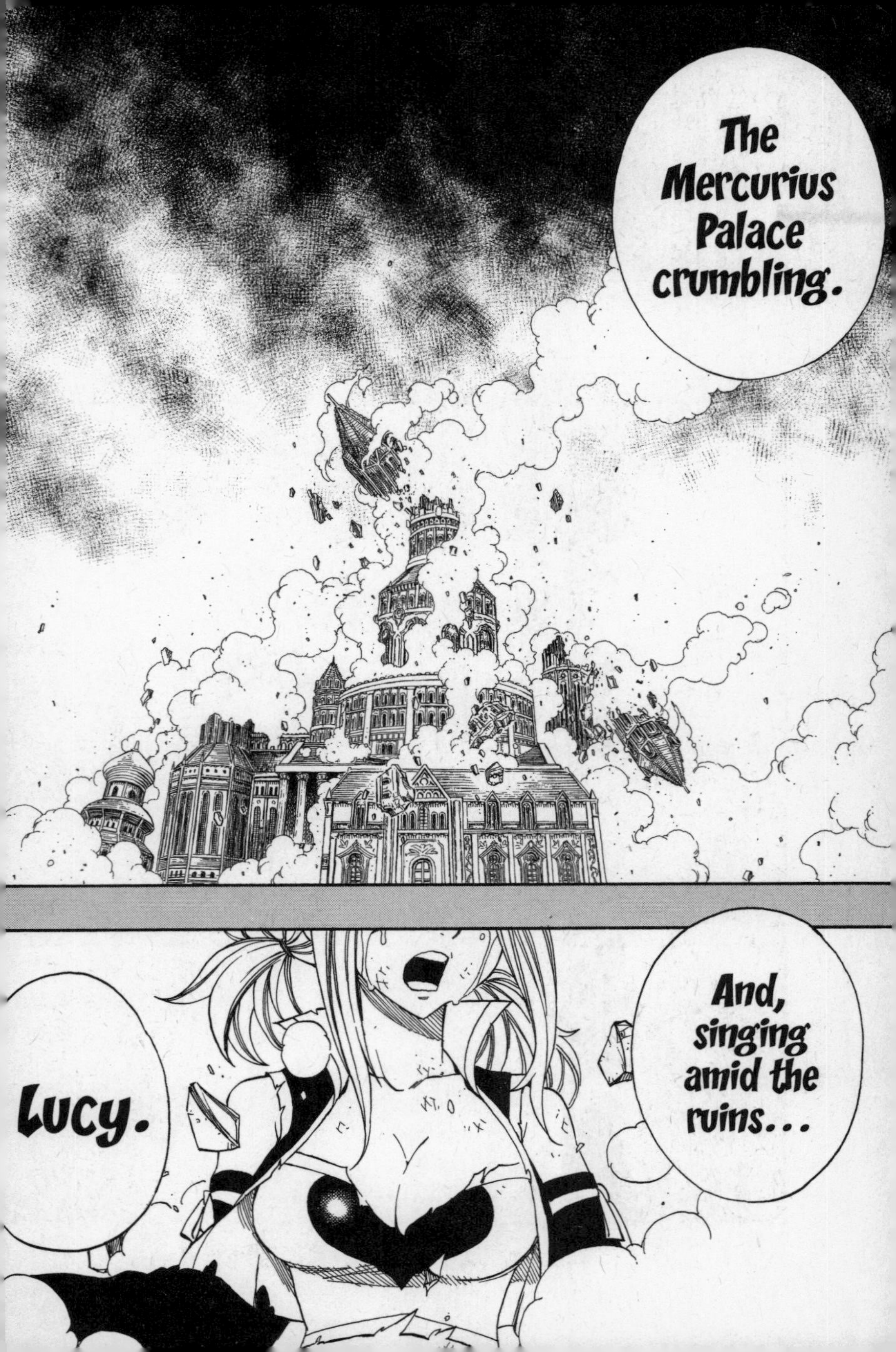

The Mercurius Palace crumbling.
And, singing amid the ruins...
Lucy.

FAIRY TAIL

フェアリーテイル

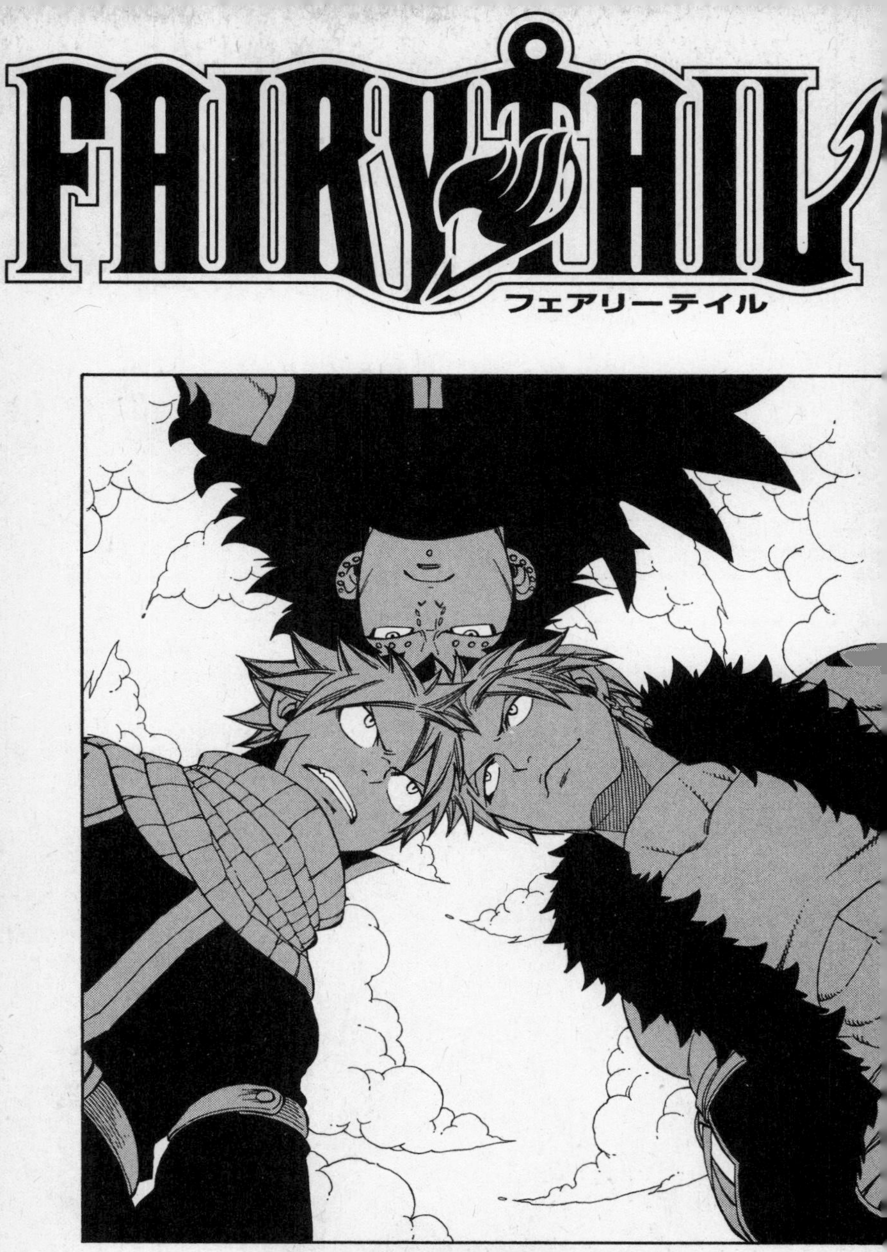

Chapter 276: Chariot

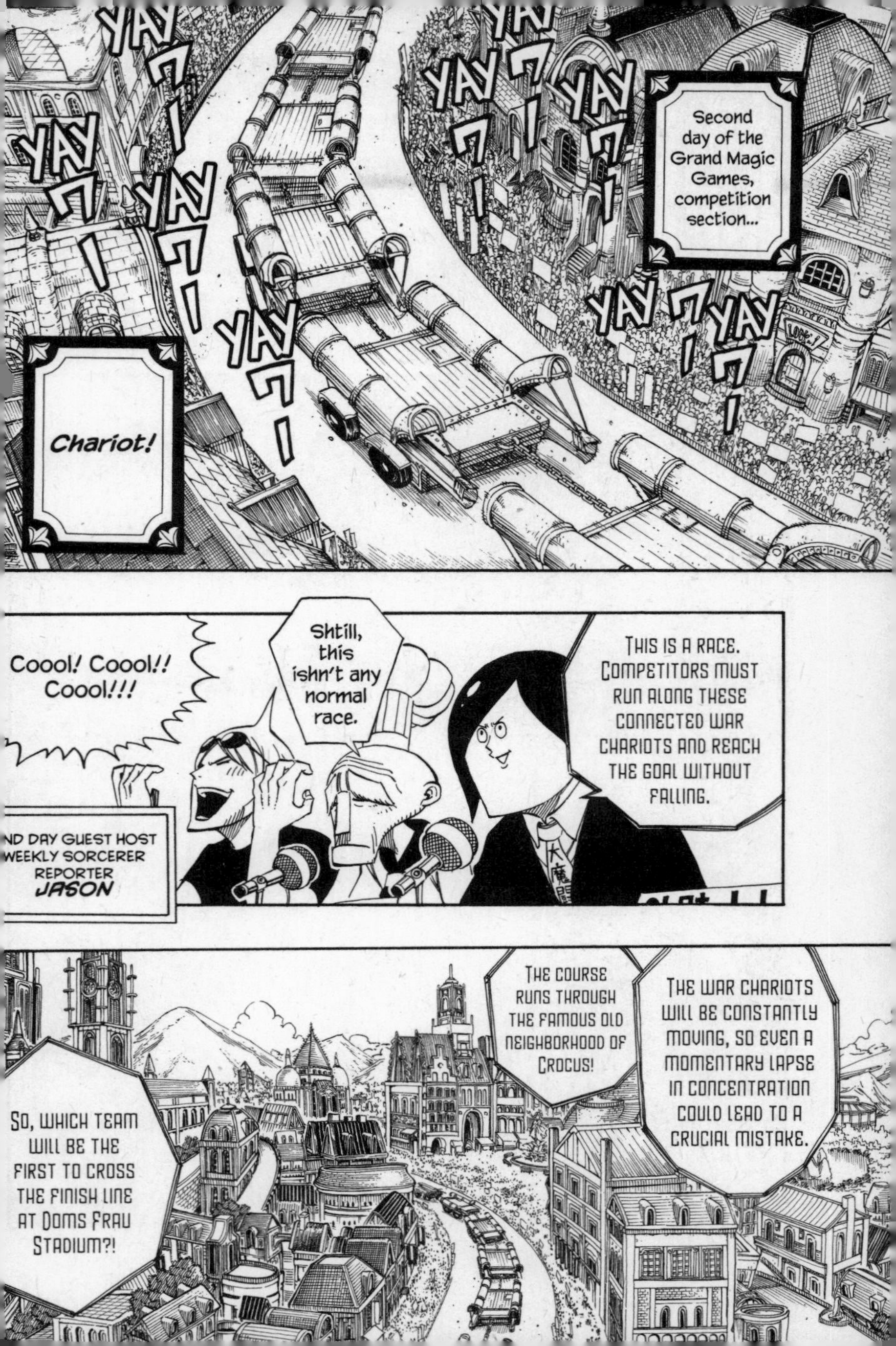
Second day of the Grand Magic Games, competition section...
YAY
YAY
YAY
YAY
YAY
YAY
YAY
YAY
YAY
Chariot!
THIS IS A RACE. COMPETITORS MUST RUN ALONG THESE CONNECTED WAR CHARIOTS AND REACH THE GOAL WITHOUT FALLING.
Shtill, this ishn't any normal race.
Coool! Coool!! Coool!!!
ND DAY GUEST HOST WEEKLY SORCERER REPORTER JASON
THE WAR CHARIOTS WILL BE CONSTANTLY MOVING, SO EVEN A MOMENTARY LAPSE IN CONCENTRATION COULD LEAD TO A CRUCIAL MISTAKE.
THE COURSE RUNS THROUGH THE FAMOUS OLD NEIGHBORHOOD OF CROCUS!
SO, WHICH TEAM WILL BE THE FIRST TO CROSS THE FINISH LINE AT DOMS FRAU STADIUM?!

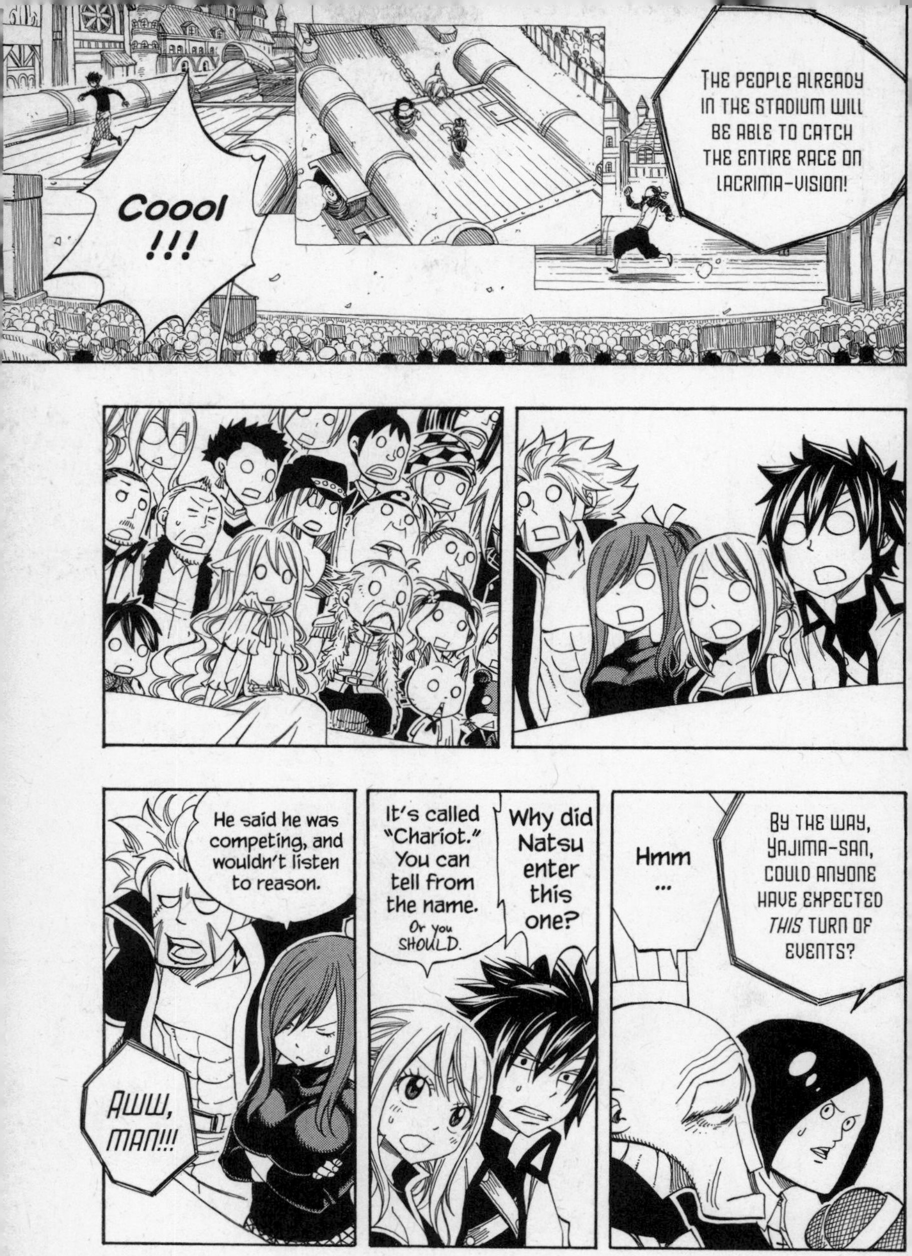

THE PEOPLE ALREADY IN THE STADIUM WILL BE ABLE TO CATCH THE ENTIRE RACE ON LACRIMA-VISION!
Coool !!!
BY THE WAY, YAJIMA-SAN, COULD ANYONE HAVE EXPECTED *THIS* TURN OF EVENTS?
Hmm ...
Why did Natsu enter this one?
It's called "Chariot." You can tell from the name.
Or you SHOULD.
He said he was competing, and wouldn't listen to reason.
AWW, MAN!!!

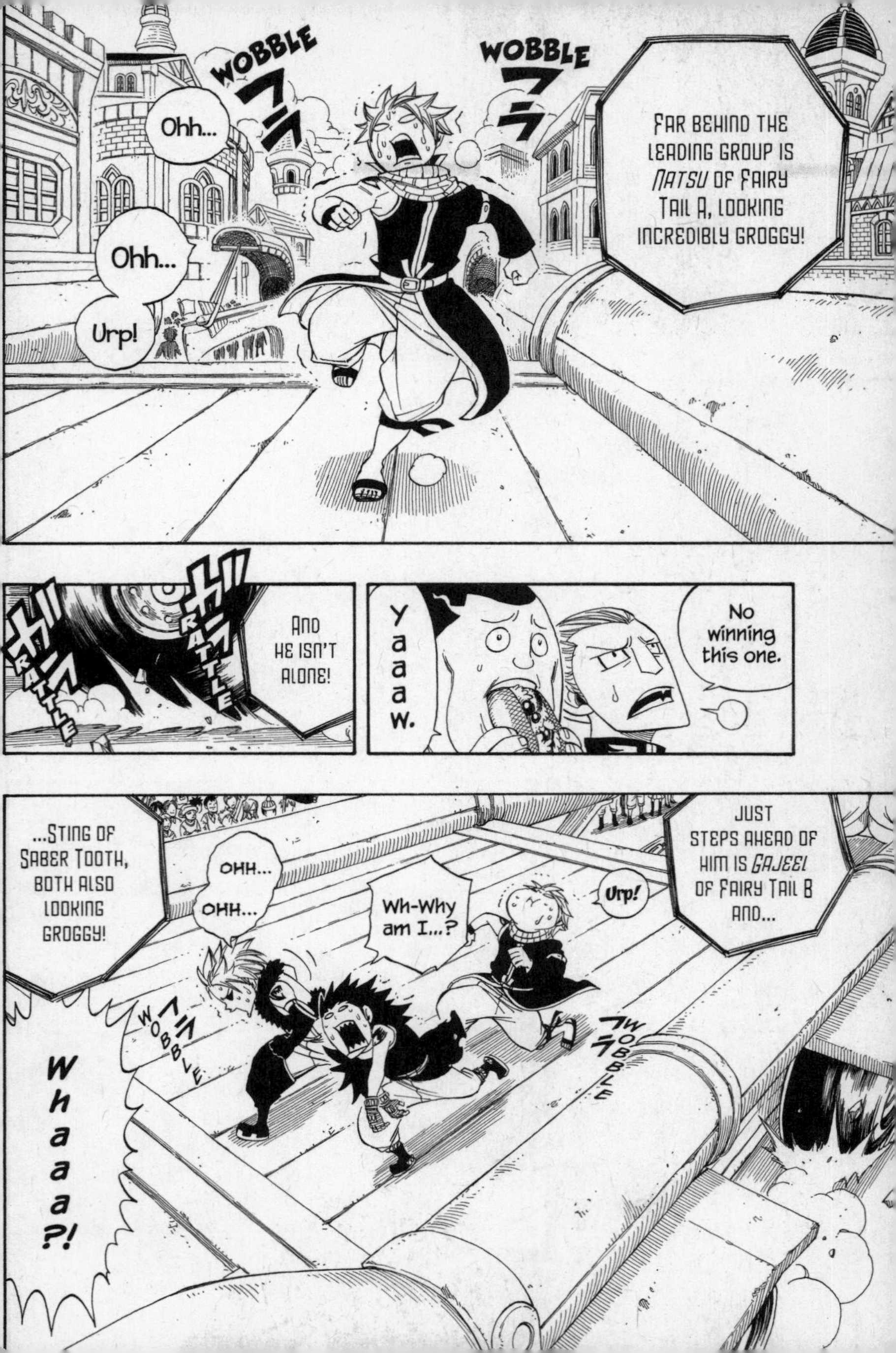
FAR BEHIND THE LEADING GROUP IS NATSU OF FAIRY TAIL A, LOOKING INCREDIBLY GROGGY!
WOBBLE
WOBBLE
Ohh...
Ohh...
Urp!
No winning this one.
Yaaaw.
RATTLE
AND HE ISN'T ALONE!
RATTLE
JUST STEPS AHEAD OF HIM IS GAJEEL OF FAIRY TAIL B AND...
Urp!
WOBBLE
Wh-Why am I...?
OHH...
OHH...
...STING OF SABER TOOTH, BOTH ALSO LOOKING GROGGY!
WOBBLE
Whaaaa?!

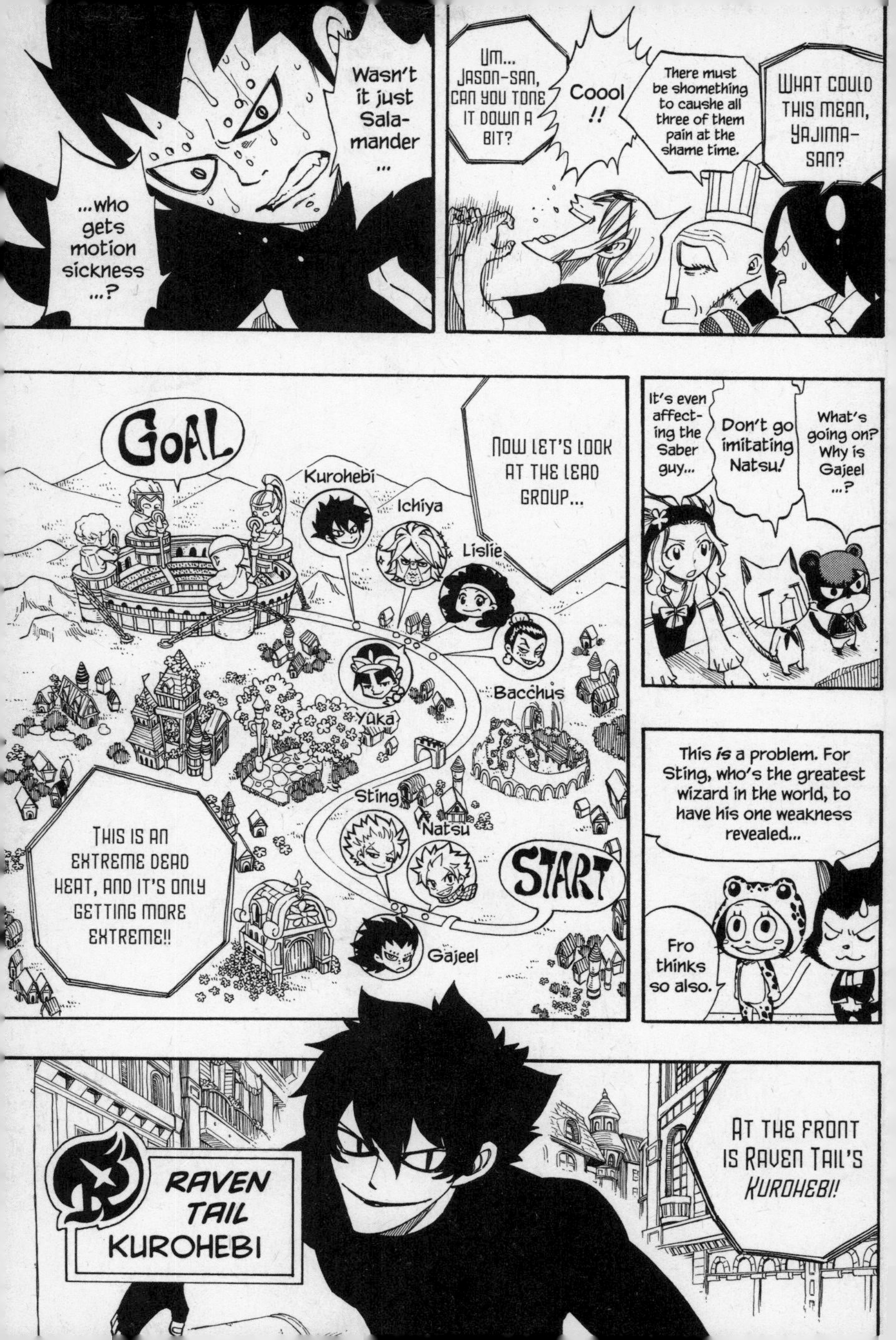
WHAT COULD THIS MEAN, YAJIMA-SAN?
There must be shomething to caushe all three of them pain at the shame time.
Coool!!
UM... JASON-SAN, CAN YOU TONE IT DOWN A BIT?
Wasn't it just Salamander...
...who gets motion sickness...?
What's going on? Why is Gajeel...?
Don't go imitating Natsu!
It's even affecting the Saber guy...
This *is* a problem. For Sting, who's the greatest wizard in the world, to have his one weakness revealed...
Fro thinks so also.
NOW LET'S LOOK AT THE LEAD GROUP...
GOAL
Kurohebi
Ichiya
Lislie
Bacchus
Yûka
Sting
Natsu
START
Gajeel
THIS IS AN EXTREME DEAD HEAT, AND IT'S ONLY GETTING MORE EXTREME!!
AT THE FRONT IS RAVEN TAIL'S *KUROHEBI!*
RAVEN TAIL
KUROHEBI

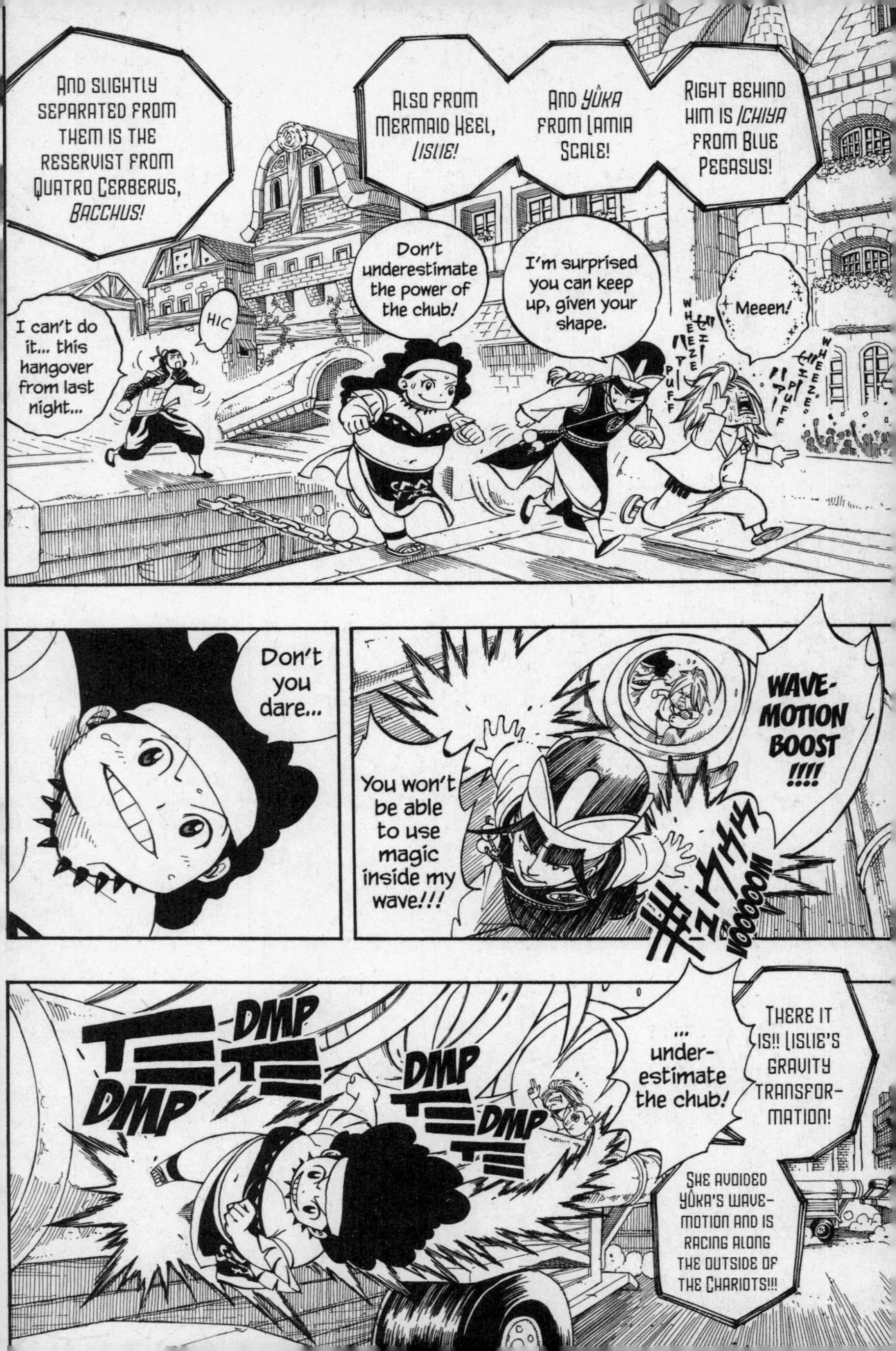

Right behind him is Ichiya from Blue Pegasus!
And Yûka from Lamia Scale!
Also from Mermaid Heel, Lislie!
And slightly separated from them is the reservist from Quatro Cerberus, Bacchus!
Meeen!
WHEEZE
PUFF
WHEEZE
PUFF
I'm surprised you can keep up, given your shape.
Don't underestimate the power of the chub!
HIC
I can't do it... this hangover from last night...
WAVE-MOTION BOOST!!!!
You won't be able to use magic inside my wave!!!
Don't you dare...
There it is!! Lislie's gravity transformation!
She avoided Yûka's wave-motion and is racing along the outside of the Chariots!!!
... under-estimate the chub!
DMP
DMP
DMP
DMP

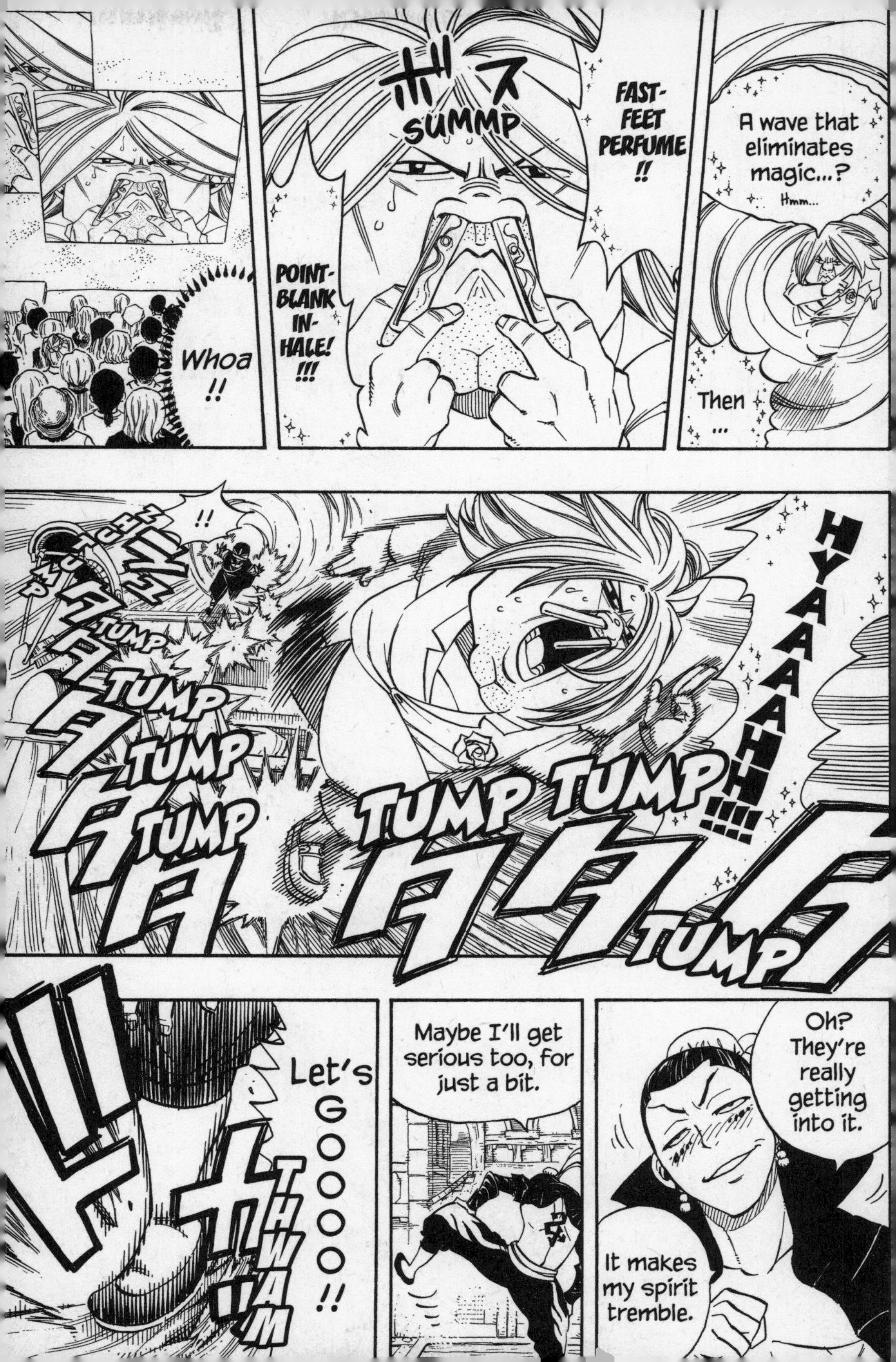
A wave that eliminates magic...?
Hmm...
Then ...
ポス
SUMMP
FAST-FEET PERFUME!!
POINT-BLANK INHALE!!!
Whoa!!
HYAAAAAHH!!!!
!!
TUMP
TUMP
TUMP
TUMP
TUMP
TUMP TUMP
TUMP
Oh? They're really getting into it.
It makes my spirit tremble.
Maybe I'll get serious too, for just a bit.
Let's GOOOO!!
THWAM

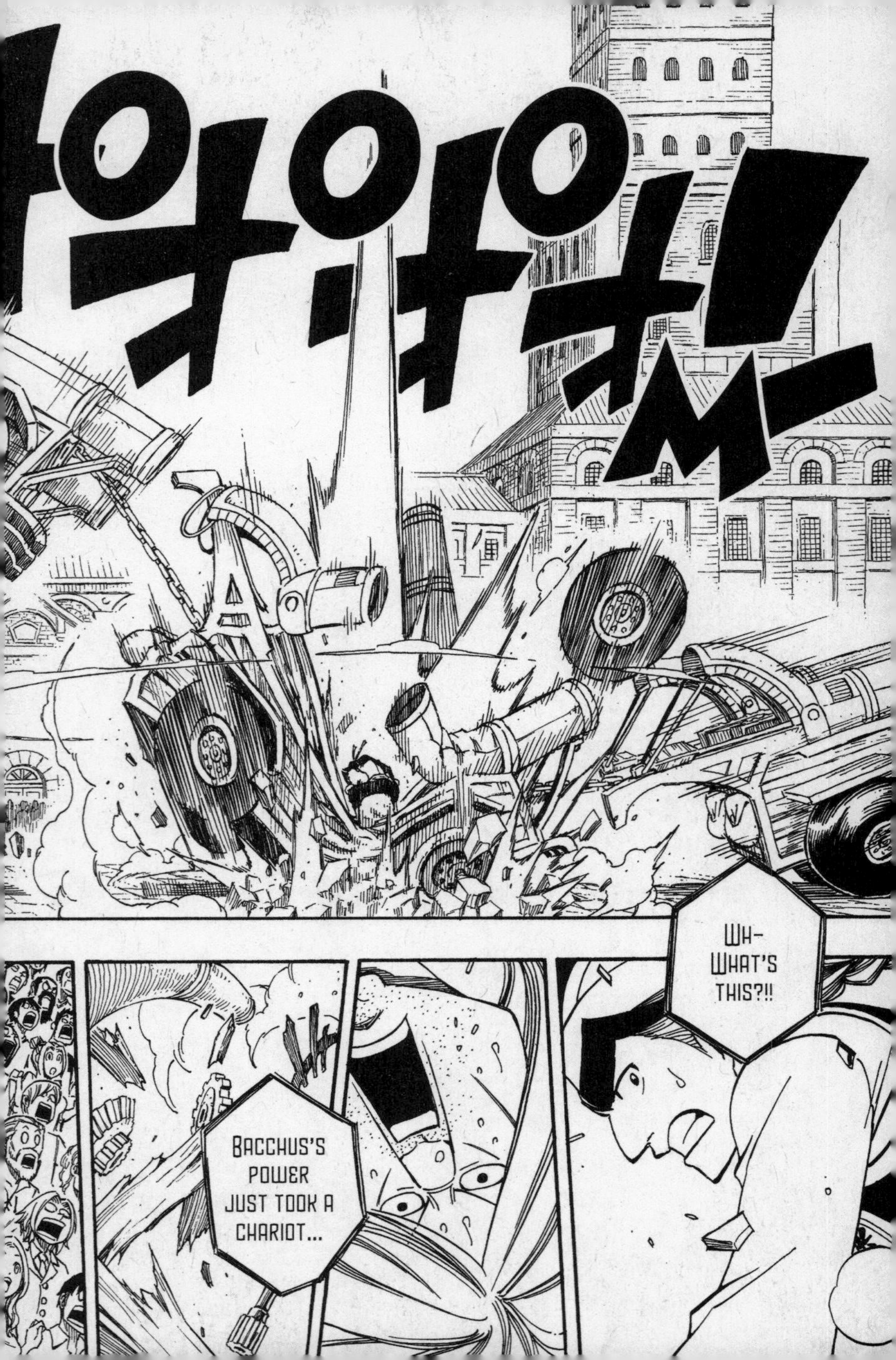
WH-WHAT'S THIS?!!
BACCHUS'S POWER JUST TOOK A CHARIOT...

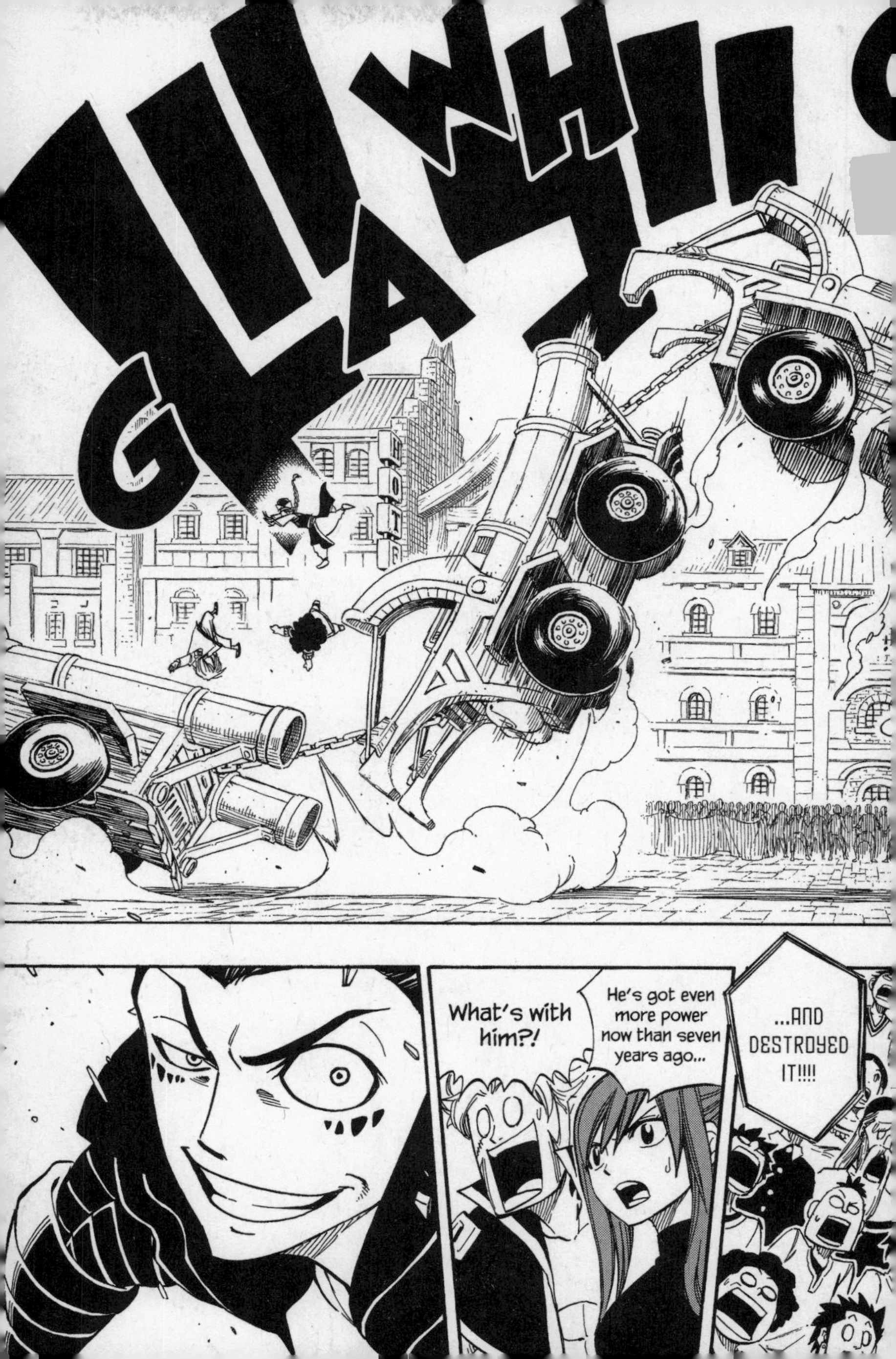
...AND DESTROYED IT!!!!
He's got even more power now than seven years ago...
What's with him?!

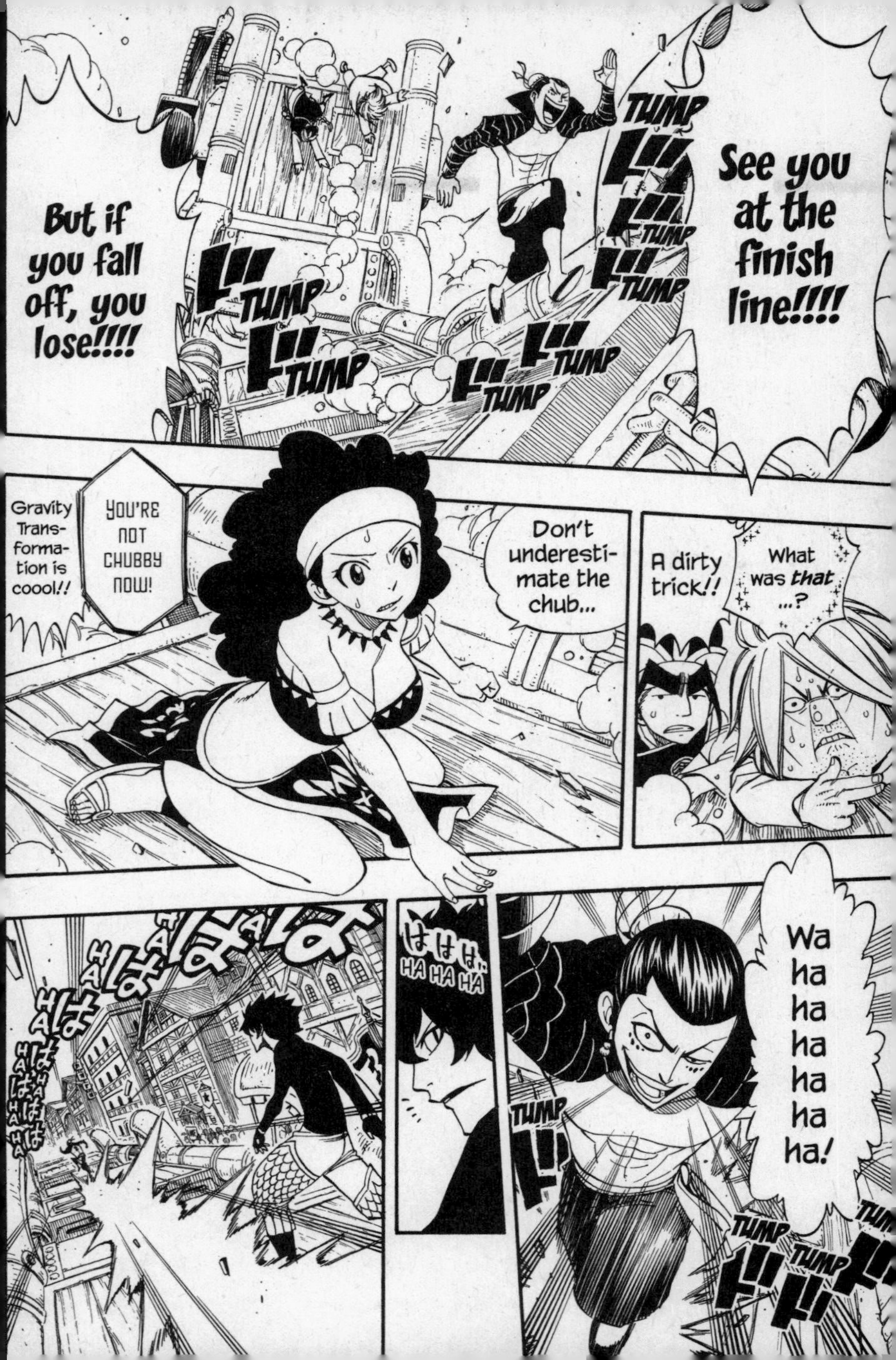

See you at the finish line!!!!
TUMP TUMP TUMP
But if you fall off, you lose!!!!
TUMP TUMP TUMP TUMP TUMP
What was that ...?
A dirty trick!!
Don't underestimate the chub...
YOU'RE NOT CHUBBY NOW!
Gravity Transformation is coool!!
Wa ha ha ha ha ha ha!
TUMP
TUMP TUMP TUMP
ははは、 HA HA HA
ははははは HA HA HA HA HA

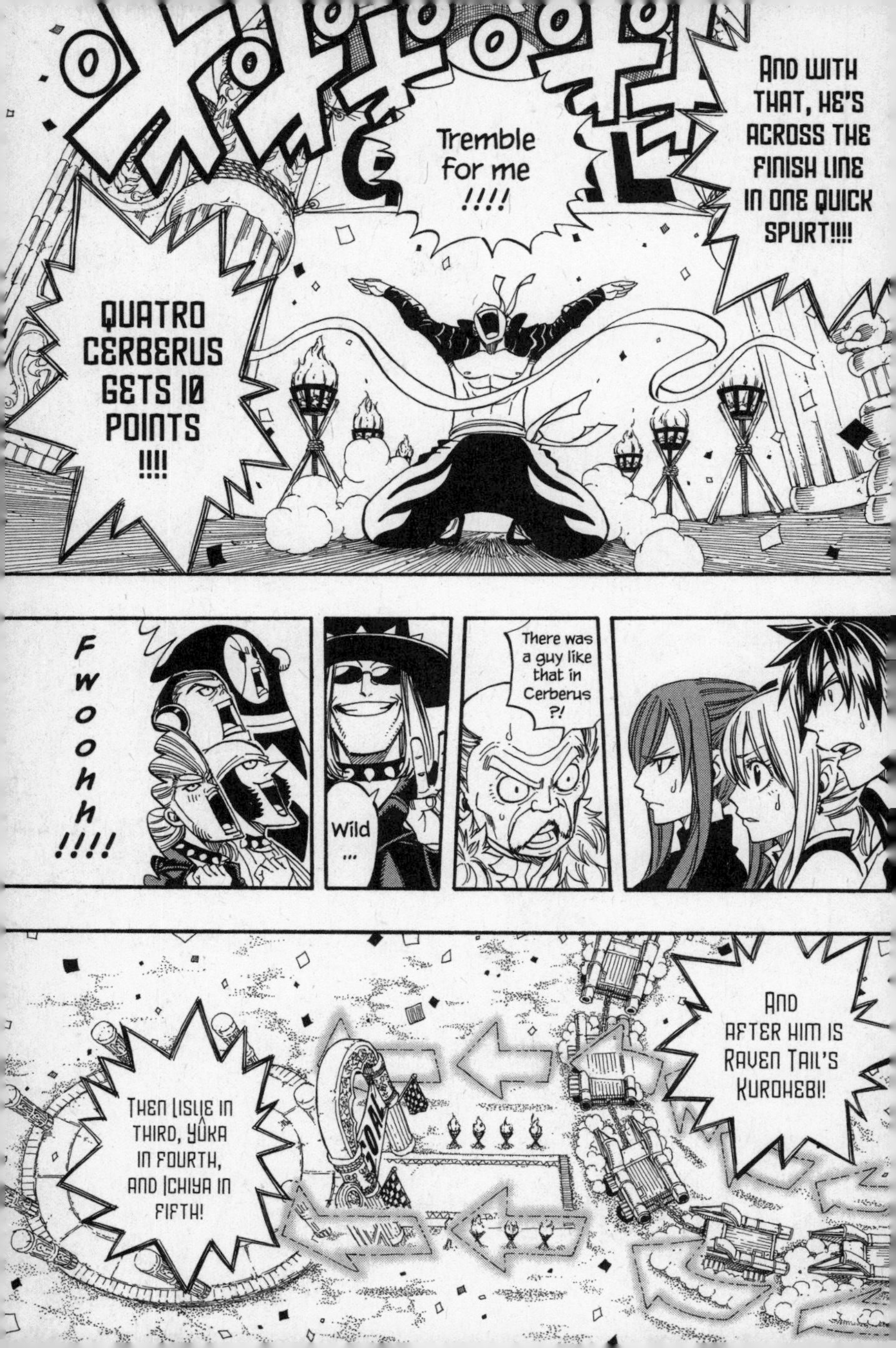
And with that, he's across the finish line in one quick spurt!!!!
Tremble for me !!!!
Quatro Cerberus gets 10 points !!!!
There was a guy like that in Cerberus ?!
Wild ...
Fwooohh!!!!
And after him is Raven Tail's Kurohebi!
Then Lislie in third, Yûka in fourth, and Ichiya in fifth!

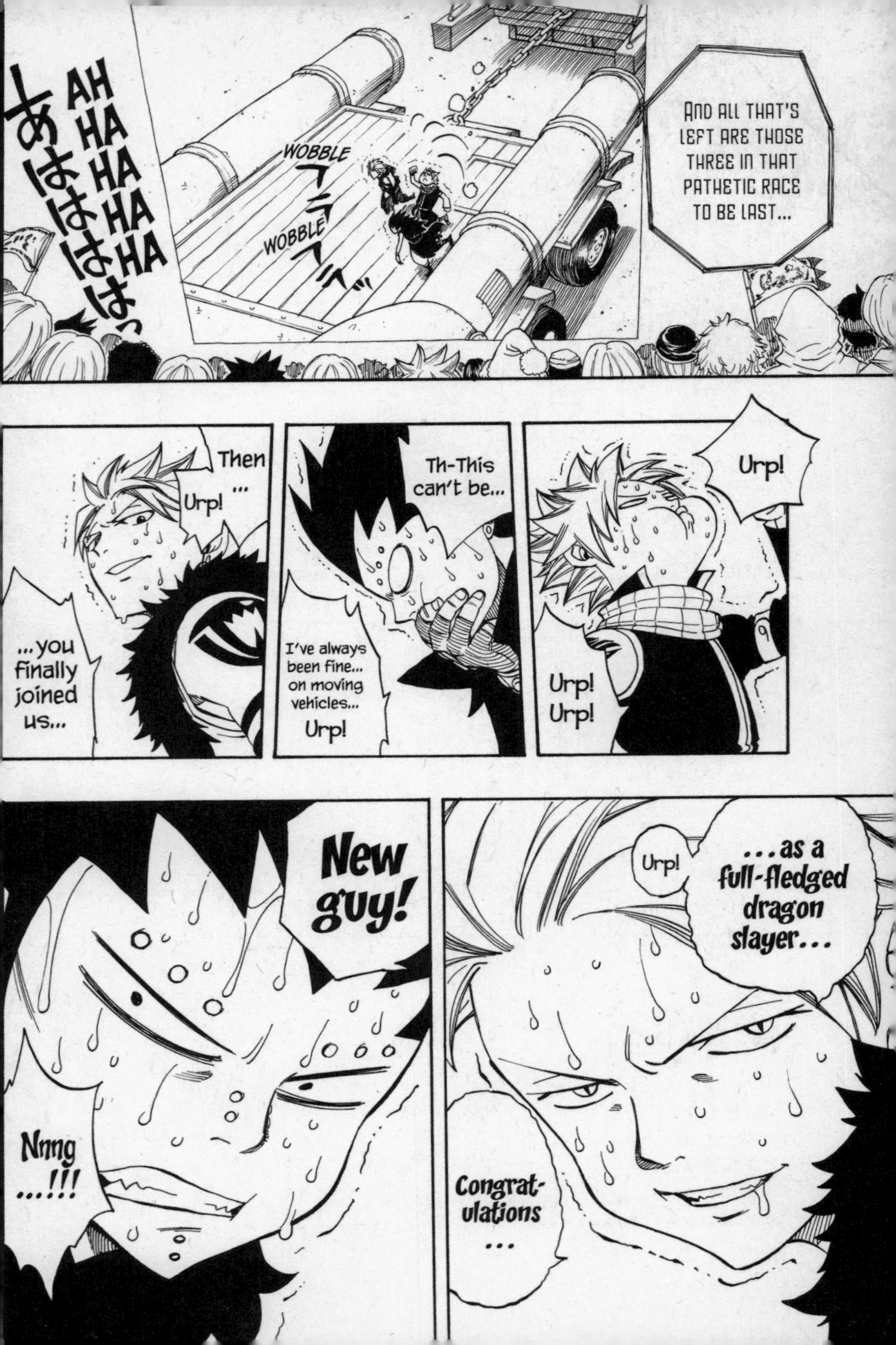
AND ALL THAT'S LEFT ARE THOSE THREE IN THAT PATHETIC RACE TO BE LAST...
AH HA HA HA HA HA
あはははは っ
WOBBLE
WOBBLE
Urp!
Urp! Urp!
Th-This can't be...
I've always been fine... on moving vehicles...
Urp!
Then ...
Urp!
...you finally joined us...
...as a full-fledged dragon slayer...
Urp!
Congrat-ulations ...
New guy!
Nnng ...!!!

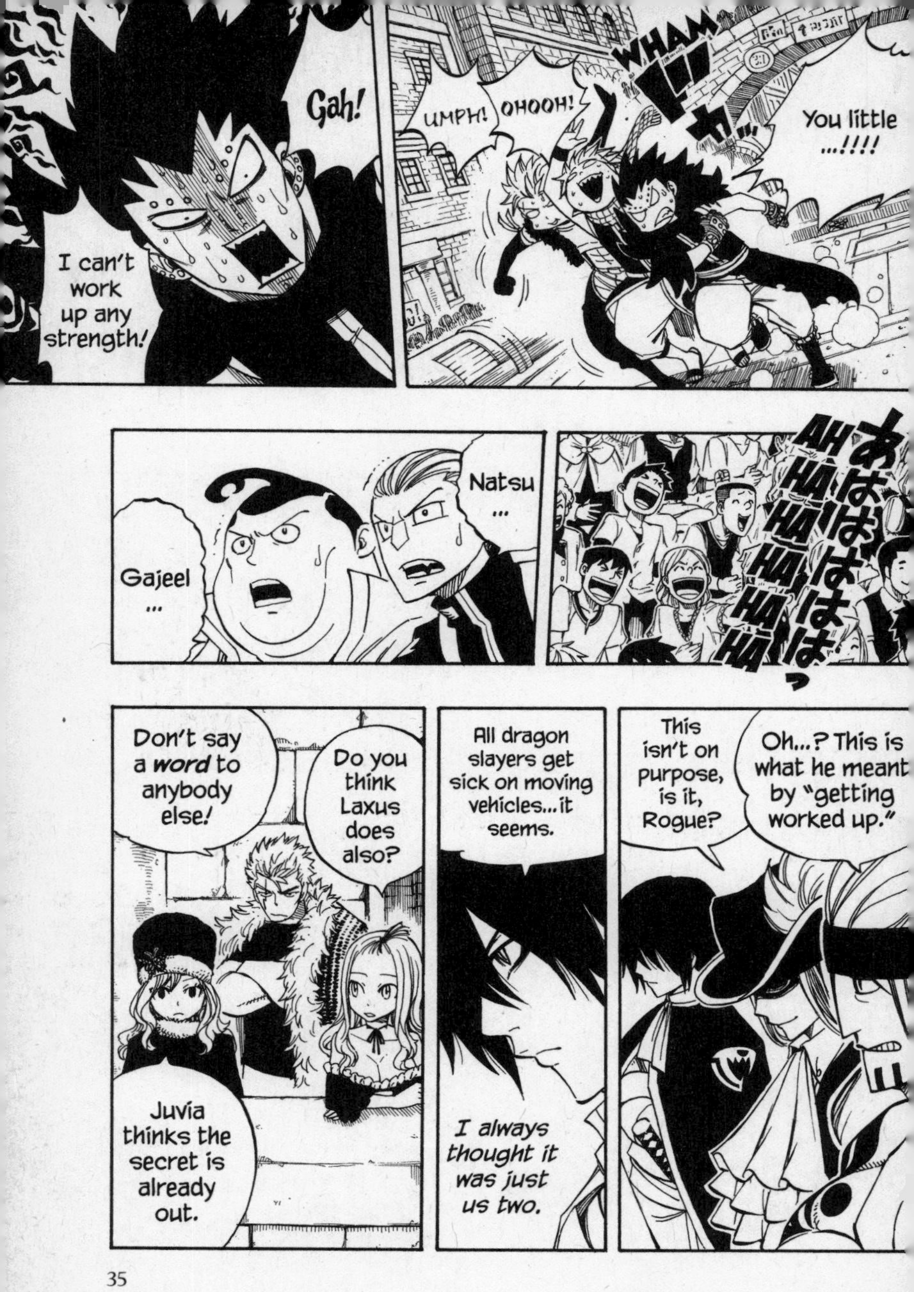
WHAM
You little ...!!!!
OHOOH!
UMPH!
Gah!
I can't work up any strength!
AH HA HA HA HA HA
あはははは
Natsu ...
Gajeel ...
Oh...? This is what he meant by "getting worked up."
This isn't on purpose, is it, Rogue?
All dragon slayers get sick on moving vehicles...it seems.
I always thought it was just us two.
Do you think Laxus does also?
Don't say a *word* to anybody else!
Juvia thinks the secret is already out.

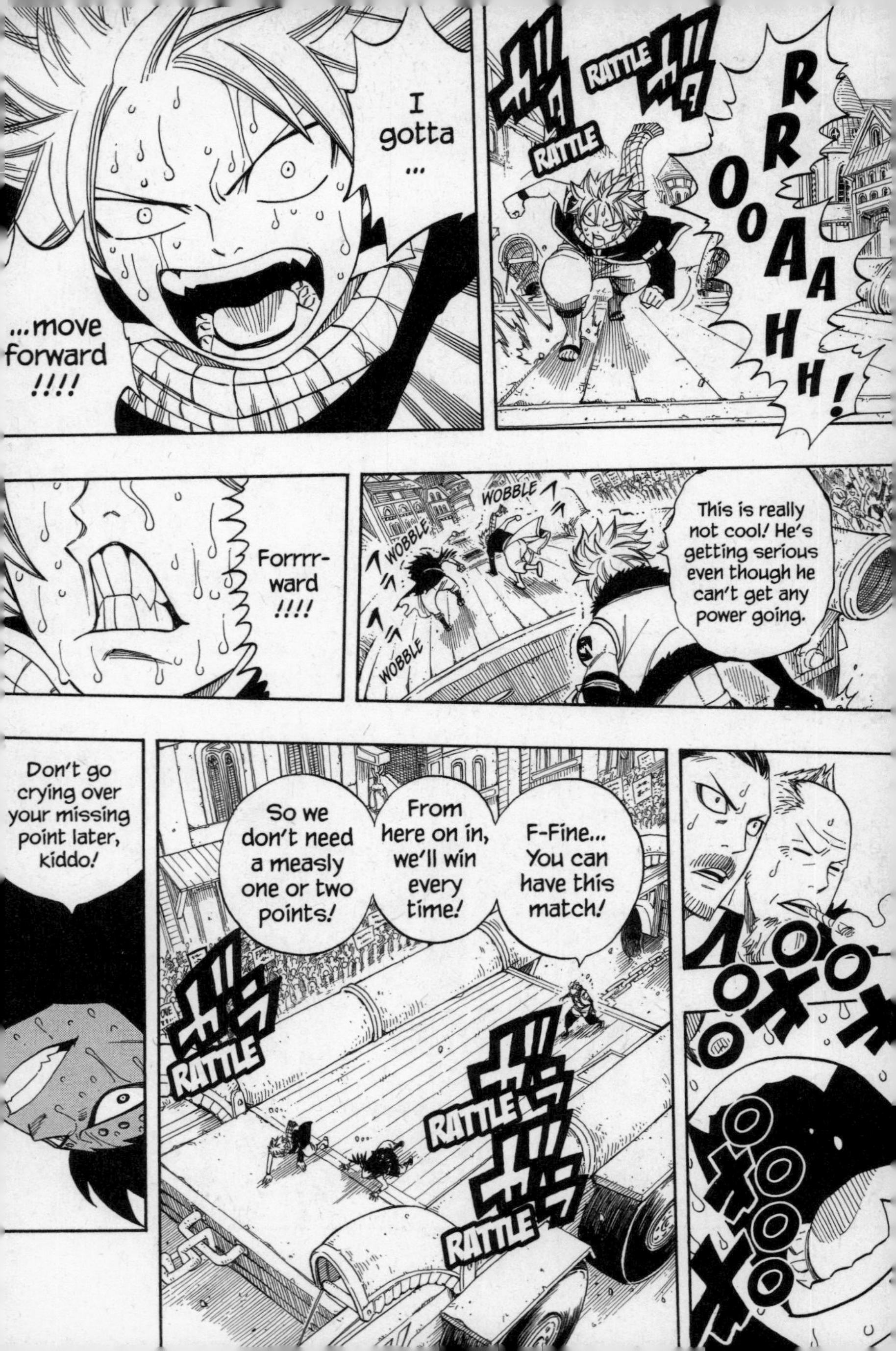
RATTLE
RATTLE
RROOAAHH!
I gotta ...
...move forward !!!!
This is really not cool! He's getting serious even though he can't get any power going.
WOBBLE
WOBBLE
WOBBLE
Forrrr-ward !!!!
F-Fine... You can have this match!
From here on in, we'll win every time!
So we don't need a measly one or two points!
RATTLE
RATTLE
RATTLE
Don't go crying over your missing point later, kiddo!

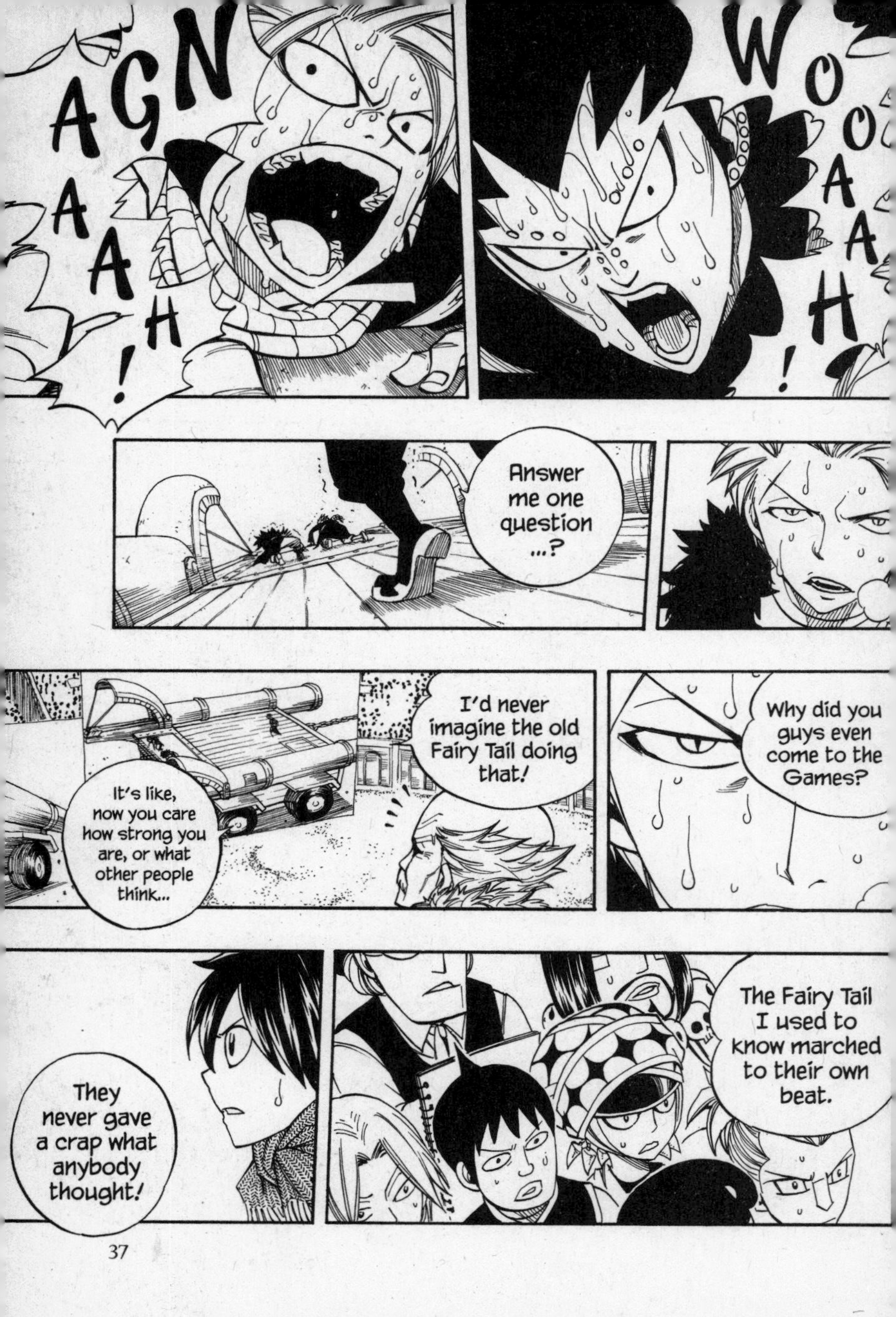
WOOAAH!
AGNAAH!
Answer me one question...?
Why did you guys even come to the Games?
I'd never imagine the old Fairy Tail doing that!
It's like, now you care how strong you are, or what other people think...
The Fairy Tail I used to know marched to their own beat.
They never gave a crap what anybody thought!

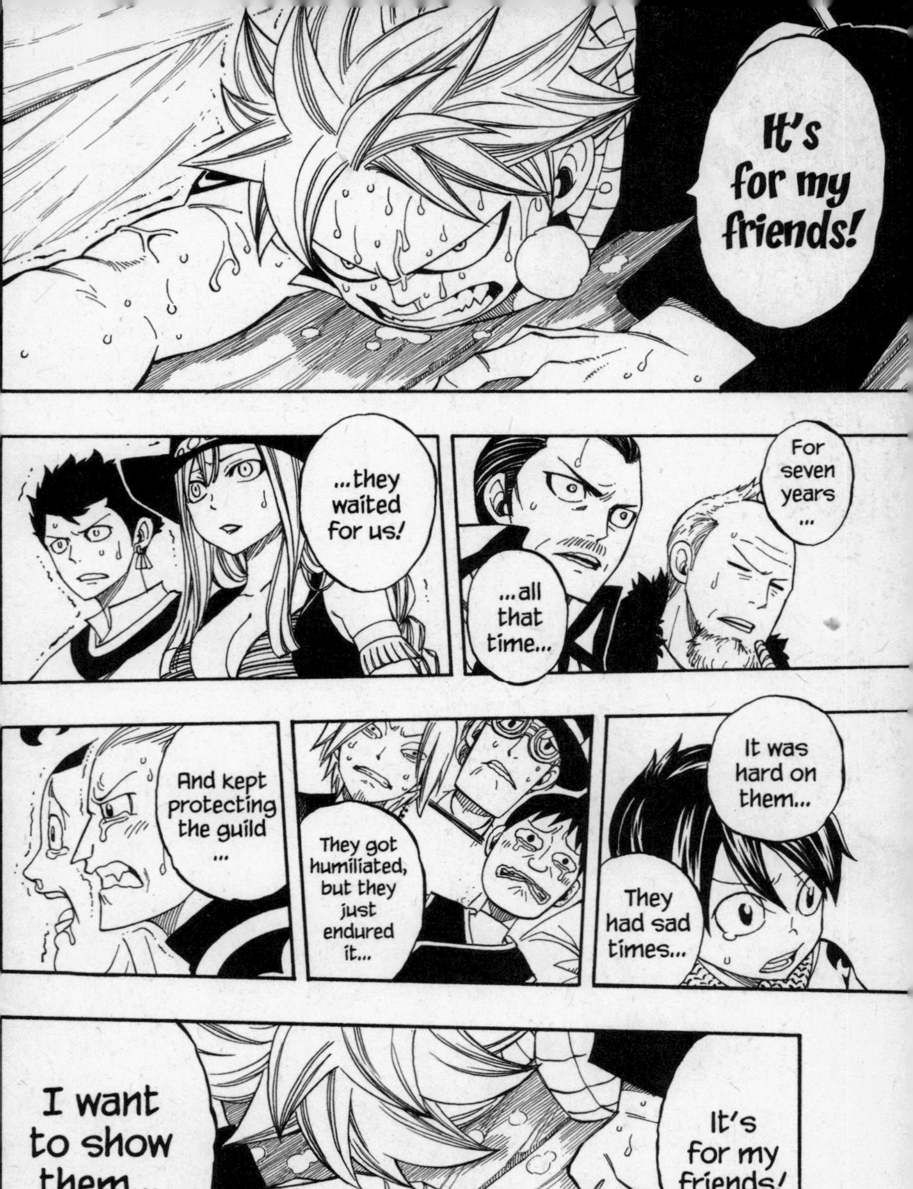

It's for my friends!
For seven years ...
...all that time...
...they waited for us!
It was hard on them...
They had sad times...
They got humiliated, but they just endured it...
And kept protecting the guild ...
It's for my friends!
I want to show them...

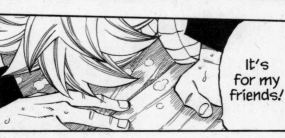

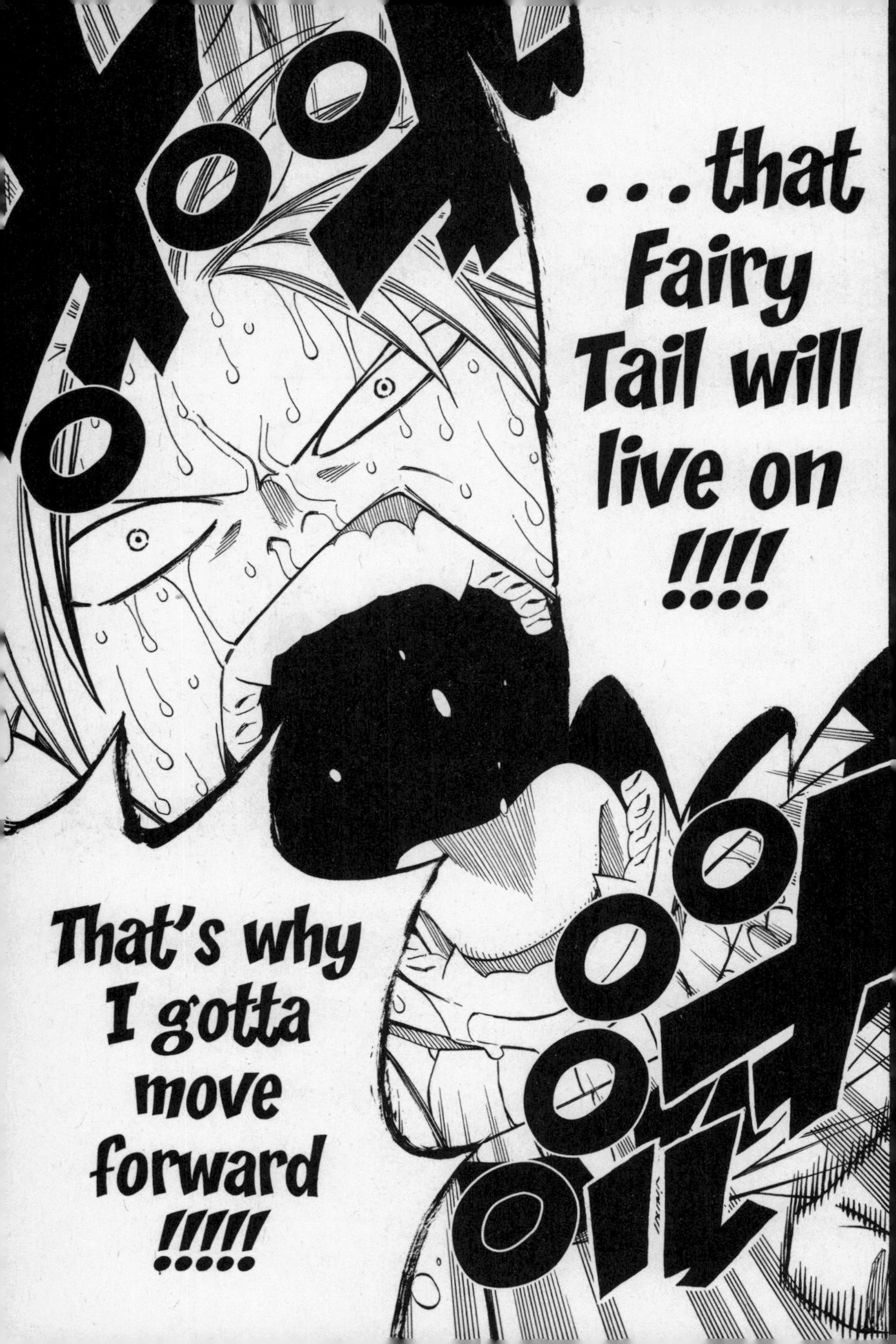
...that Fairy Tail will live on!!!!
That's why I gotta move forward!!!!!

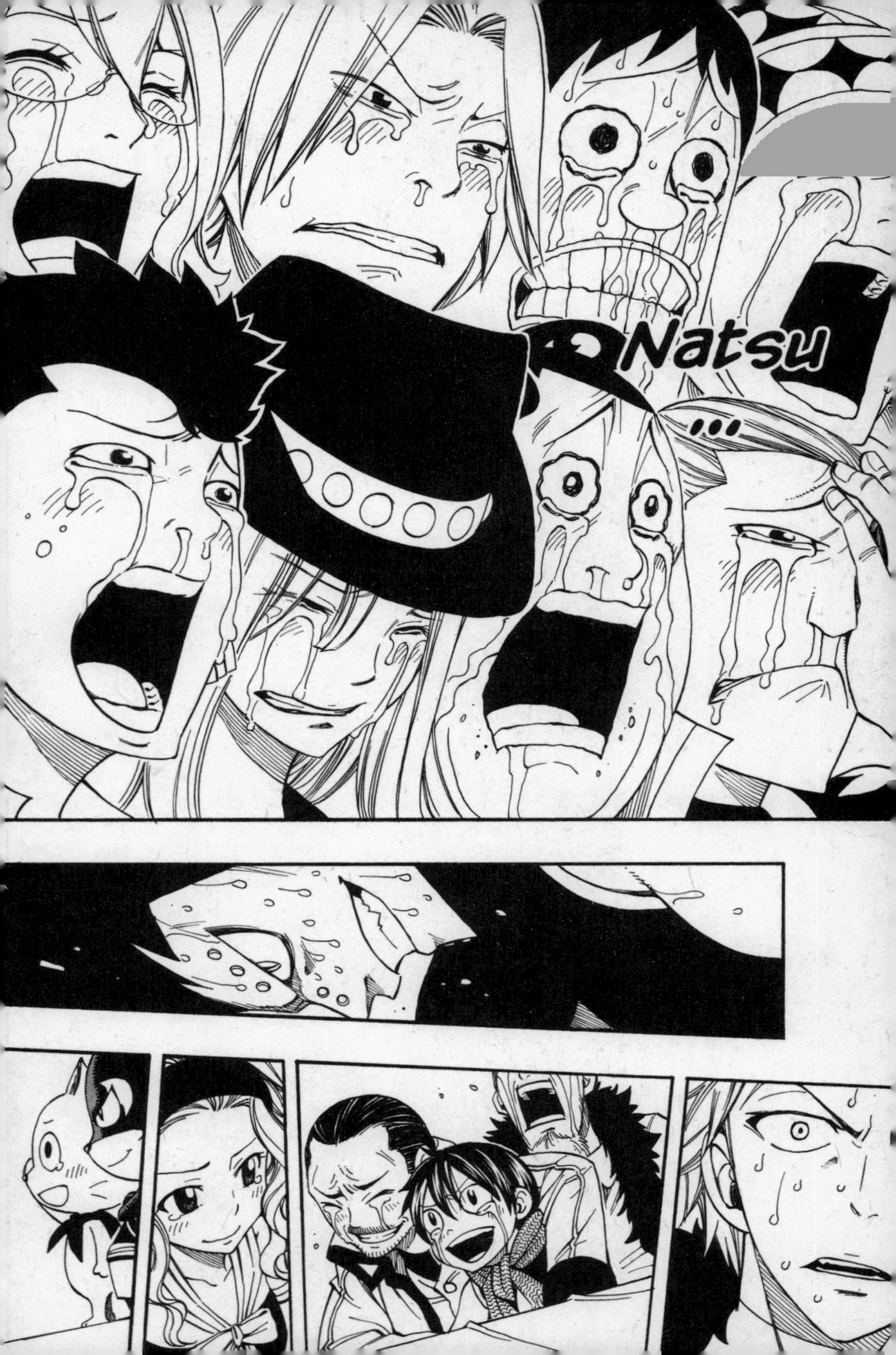
Natsu
...

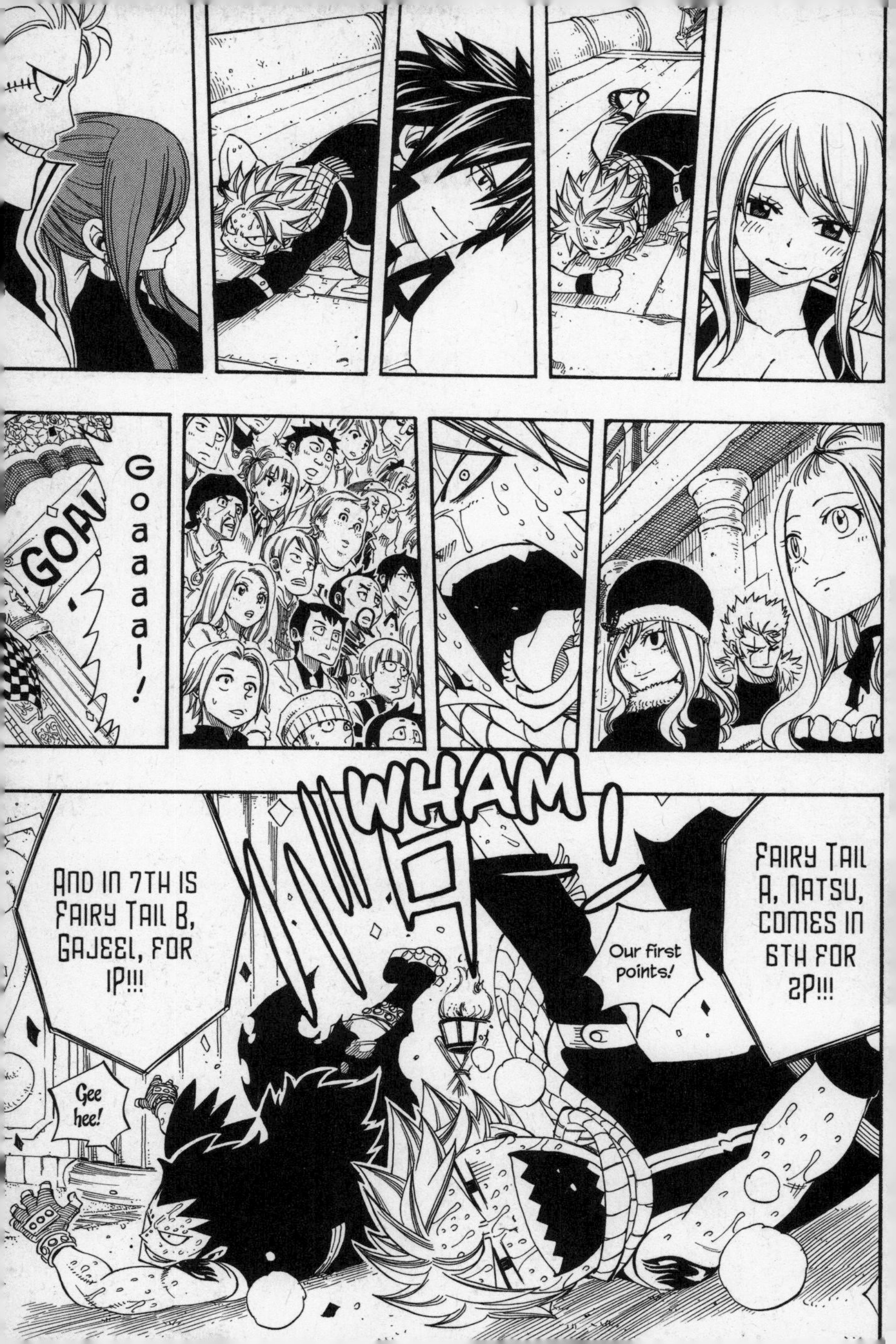
Goaaaal!
Fairy Tail A, Natsu, comes in 6th for 2P!!!
Our first points!
WHAM
And in 7th is Fairy Tail B, Gajeel, for 1P!!!
Gee hee!

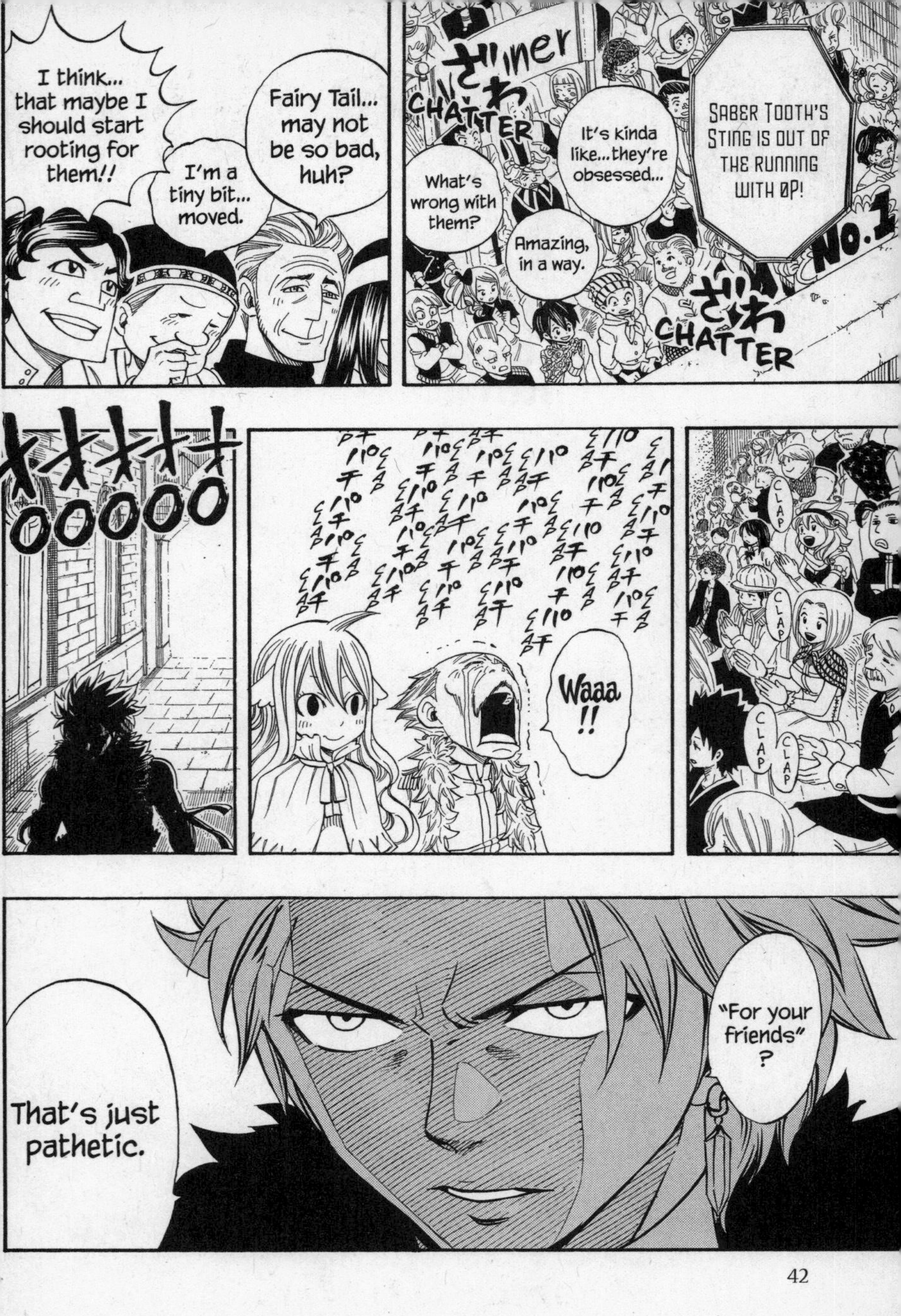

Saber Tooth's Sting is out of the running with 0P!
No.1
ざわ CHATTER
It's kinda like...they're obsessed...
ざわ CHATTER
What's wrong with them?
Amazing, in a way.
Fairy Tail... may not be so bad, huh?
I'm a tiny bit... moved.
I think... that maybe I should start rooting for them!!
CLAP CLAP CLAP CLAP
パチ CLAP パチ CLAP パチ CLAP
Waaa!!
オオオオオ OOOOO
"For your friends"?
That's just pathetic.

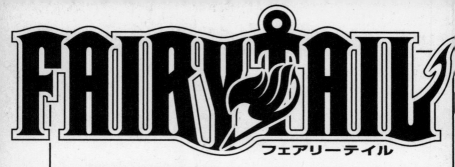

FAIRY TAIL

フェアリーテイル

Grand Magic Games: Second Day Results (still in progress)

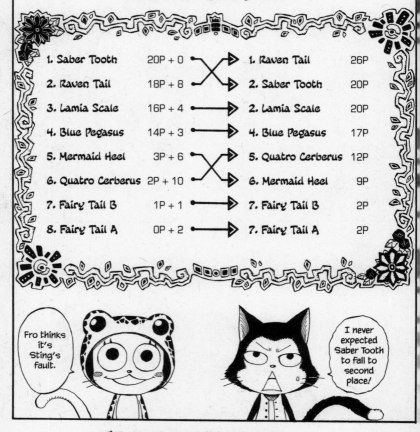

1. Saber Tooth	20P + 0	1. Raven Tail	26P
2. Raven Tail	18P + 8	2. Saber Tooth	20P
3. Lamia Scale	16P + 4	2. Lamia Scale	20P
4. Blue Pegasus	14P + 3	4. Blue Pegasus	17P
5. Mermaid Heel	3P + 6	5. Quatro Cerberus	12P
6. Quatro Cerberus	2P + 10	6. Mermaid Heel	9P
7. Fairy Tail B	1P + 1	7. Fairy Tail B	2P
8. Fairy Tail A	0P + 2	7. Fairy Tail A	2P

I never expected Saber Tooth to fall to second place!
Fro thinks it's Sting's fault.

Chapter 277: Socks

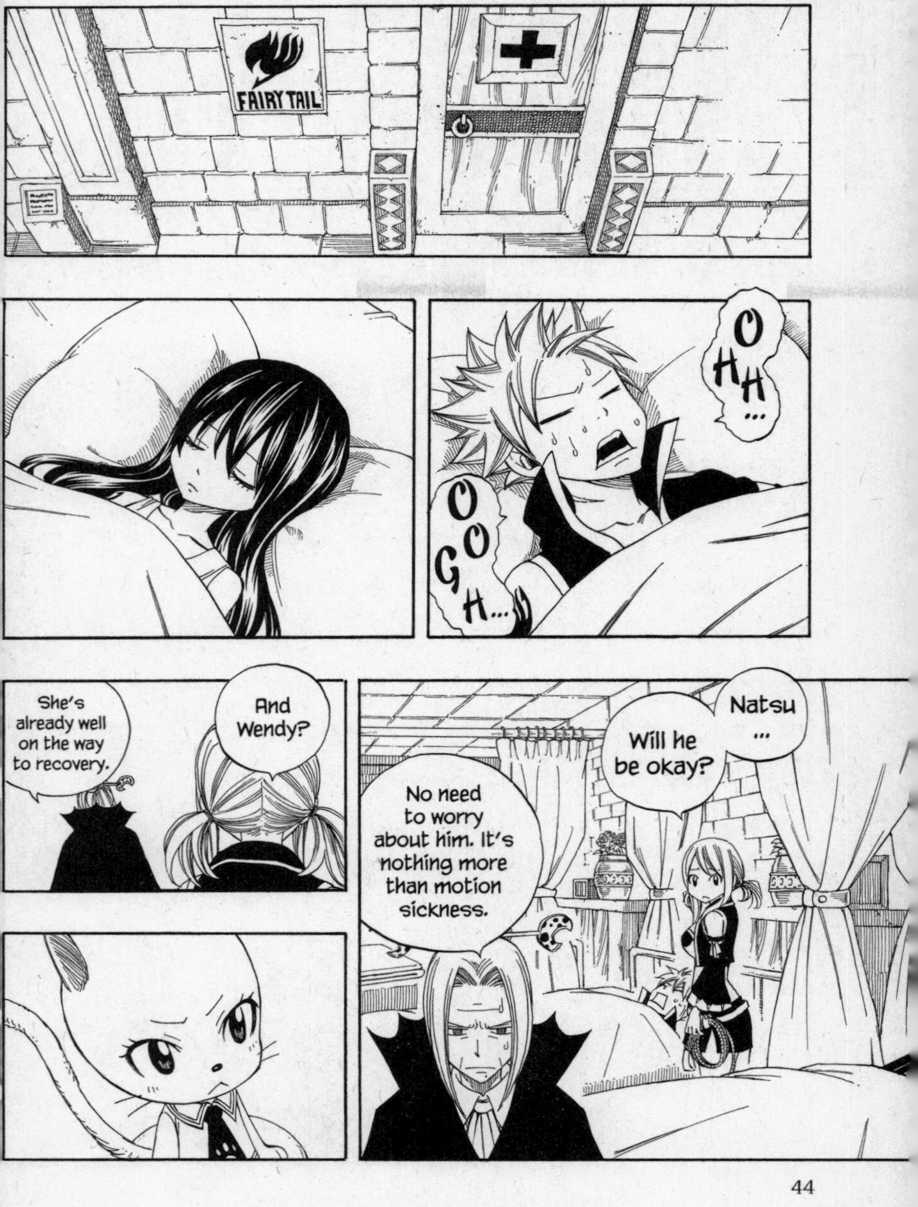
FAIRY TAIL
OHH...
OOGH...
Natsu ...
Will he be okay?
No need to worry about him. It's nothing more than motion sickness.
And Wendy?
She's already well on the way to recovery.

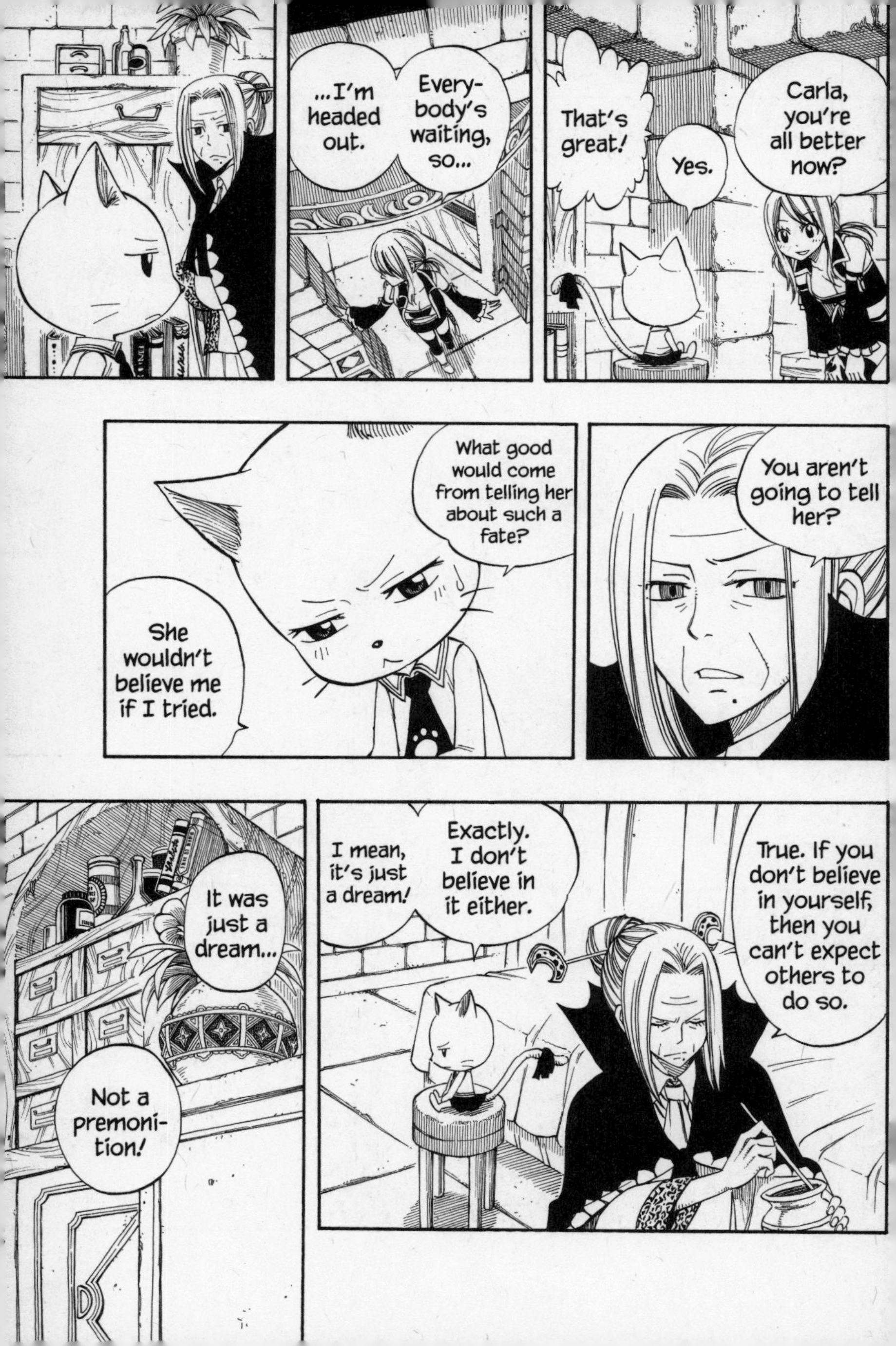

Carla, you're all better now?
Yes.
That's great!
Every-body's waiting, so...
...I'm headed out.
You aren't going to tell her?
What good would come from telling her about such a fate?
She wouldn't believe me if I tried.
True. If you don't believe in yourself, then you can't expect others to do so.
Exactly. I don't believe in it either.
I mean, it's just a dream!
It was just a dream...
Not a premoni-tion!

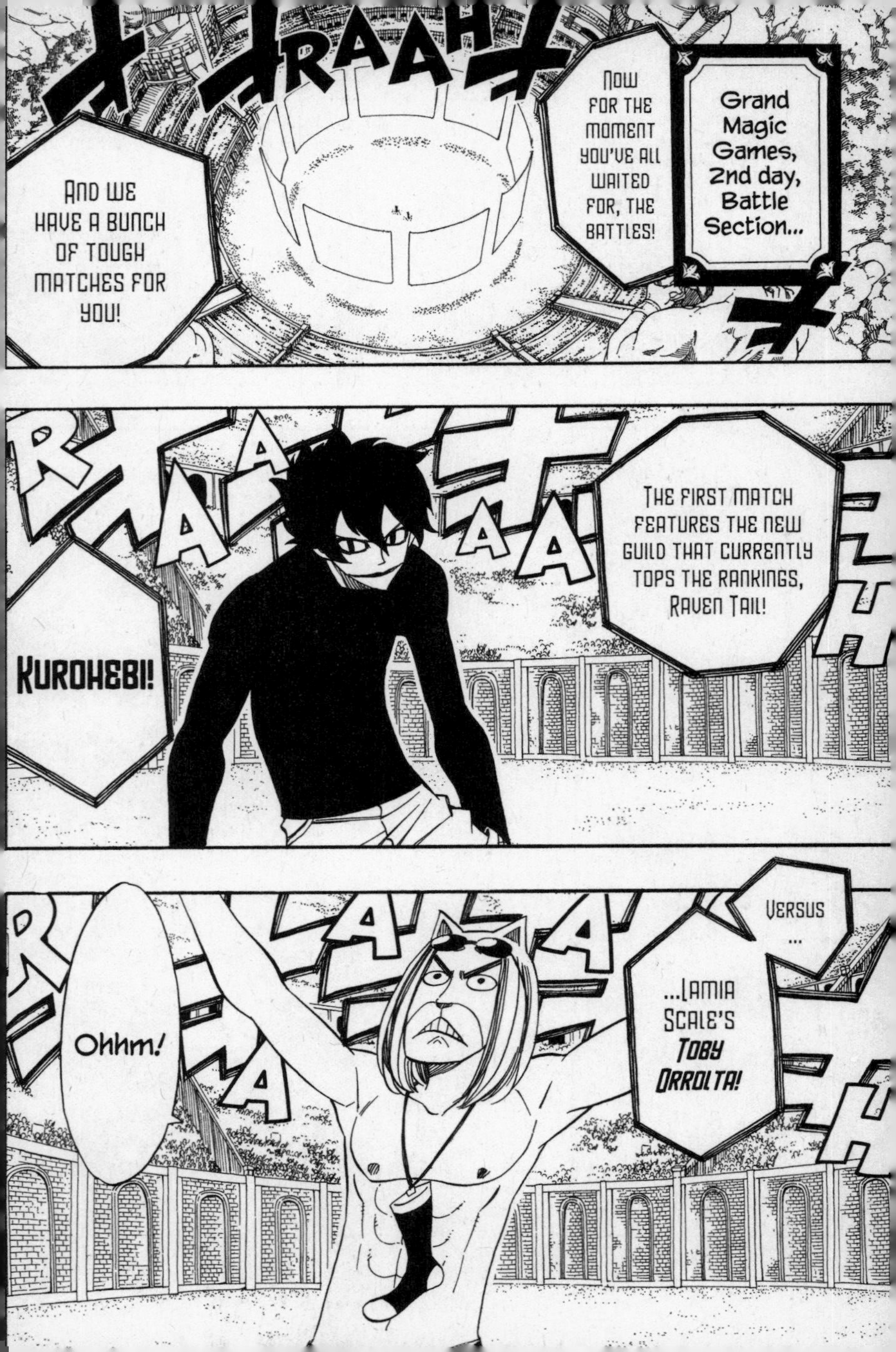
Grand Magic Games, 2nd day, Battle Section...
Now for the moment you've all waited for, the battles!
And we have a bunch of tough matches for you!
RAAH
The first match features the new guild that currently tops the rankings, Raven Tail!
Kurohebi!
Versus...
...Lamia Scale's Toby Orrolta!
Ohhm!

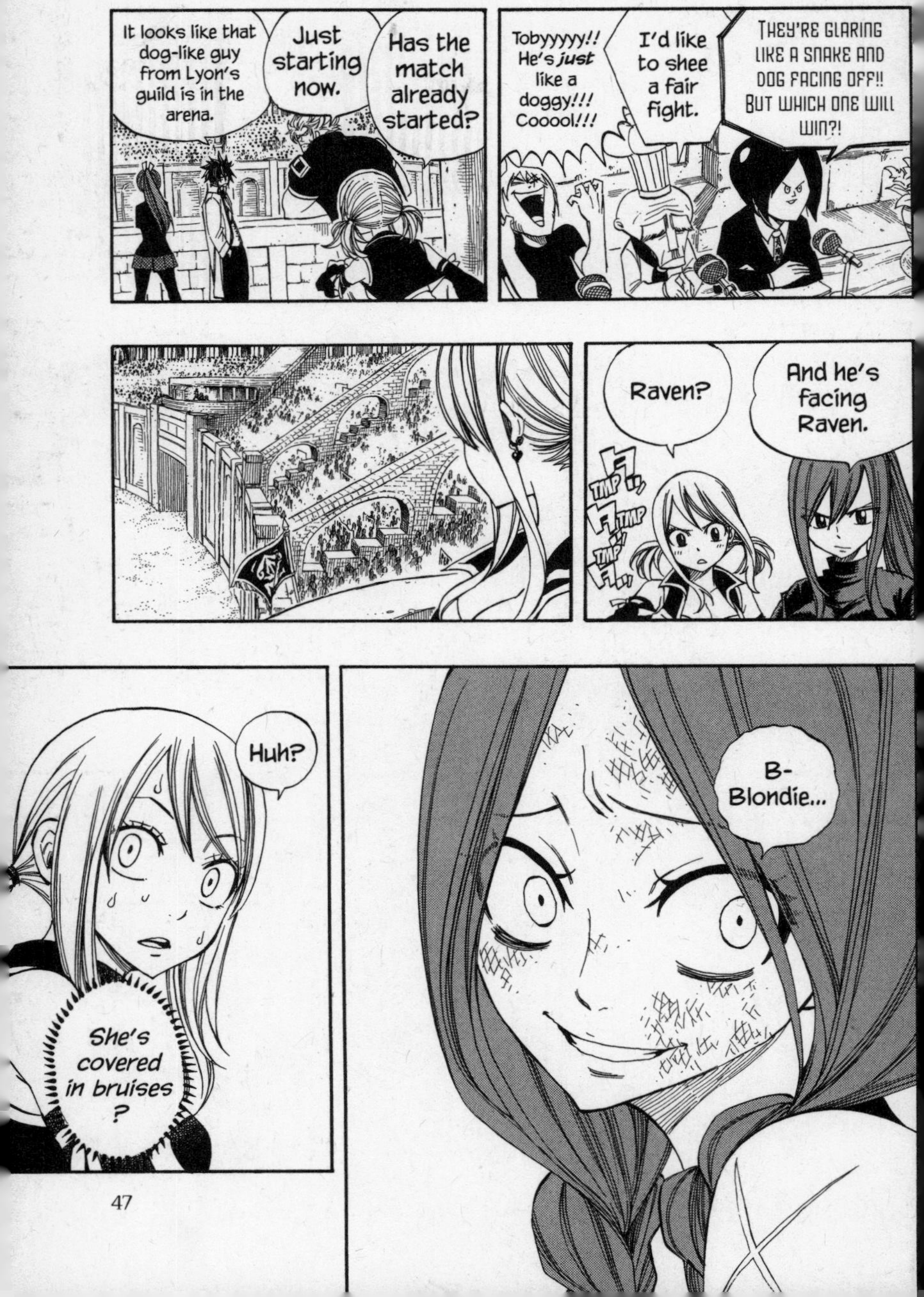
THEY'RE GLARING LIKE A SNAKE AND DOG FACING OFF!! BUT WHICH ONE WILL WIN?!
I'd like to shee a fair fight.
Tobyyyyy!! He's *just* like a doggy!!! Cooool!!!
Has the match already started?
Just starting now.
It looks like that dog-like guy from Lyon's guild is in the arena.
And he's facing Raven.
Raven?
TMP
TMP
TMP
B- Blondie...
Huh?
She's covered in bruises?

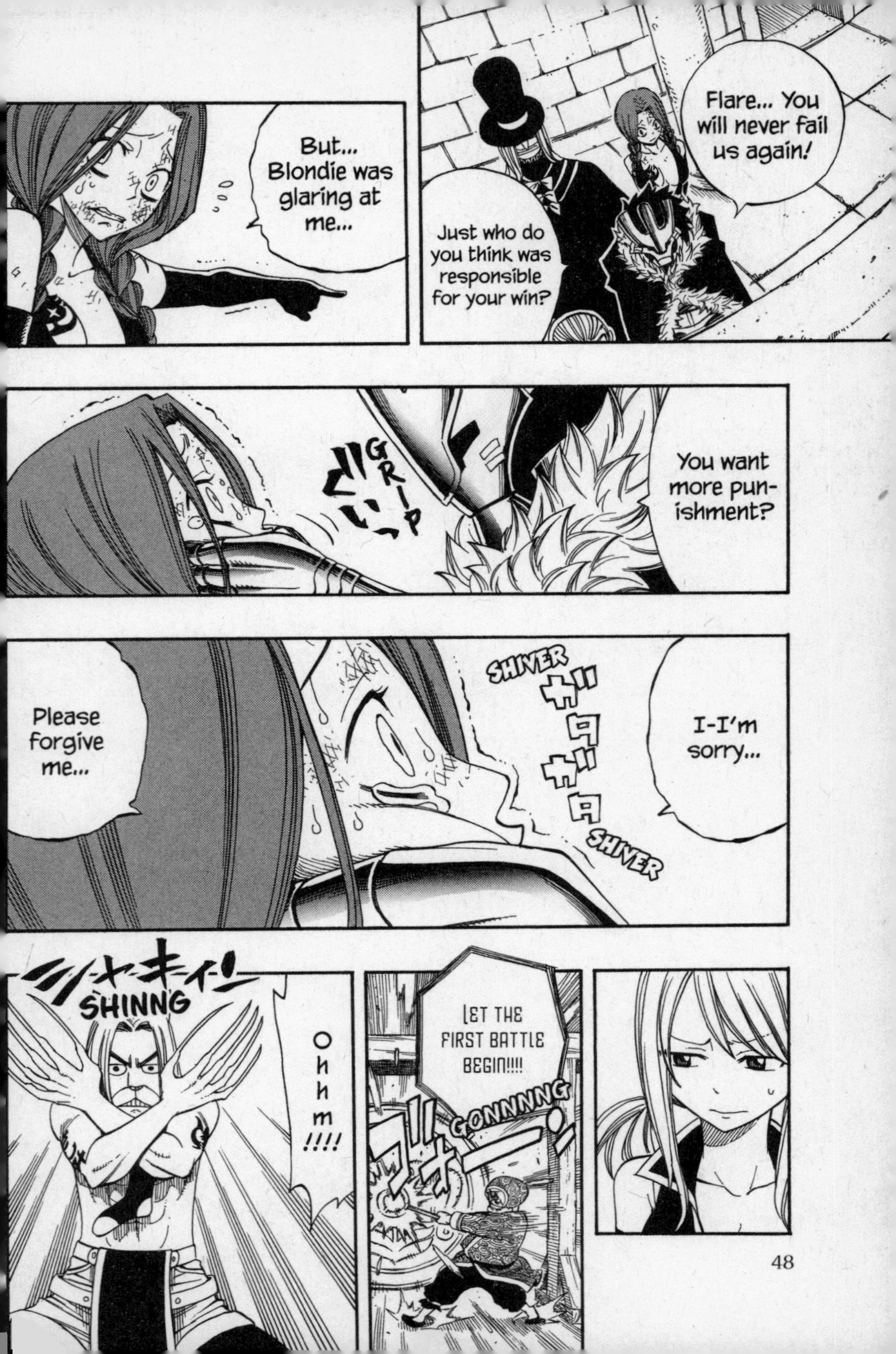

Flare... You will never fail us again!
Just who do you think was responsible for your win?
But... Blondie was glaring at me...
You want more punishment?
GRIP
ぐいっ
I-I'm sorry...
SHIVER
ガタガタ
SHIVER
Please forgive me...
LET THE FIRST BATTLE BEGIN!!!!
GONNNNG
Ohhm!!!!
SHINNG

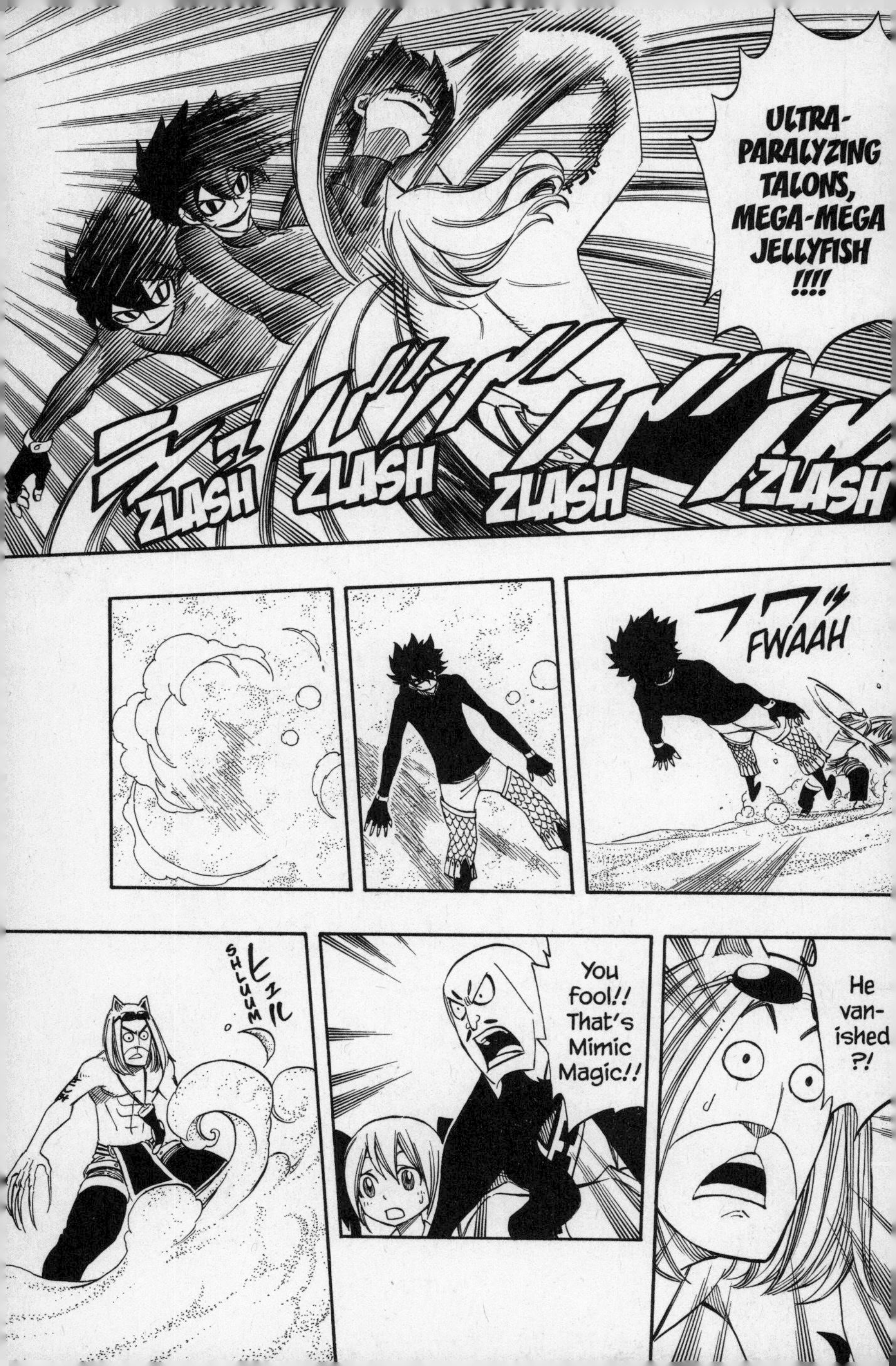
ULTRA-PARALYZING TALONS, MEGA-MEGA JELLYFISH!!!!
ZLASH
ZLASH
ZLASH
ZLASH
FWAAH
He vanished?!
You fool!! That's Mimic Magic!!
SHLUUM

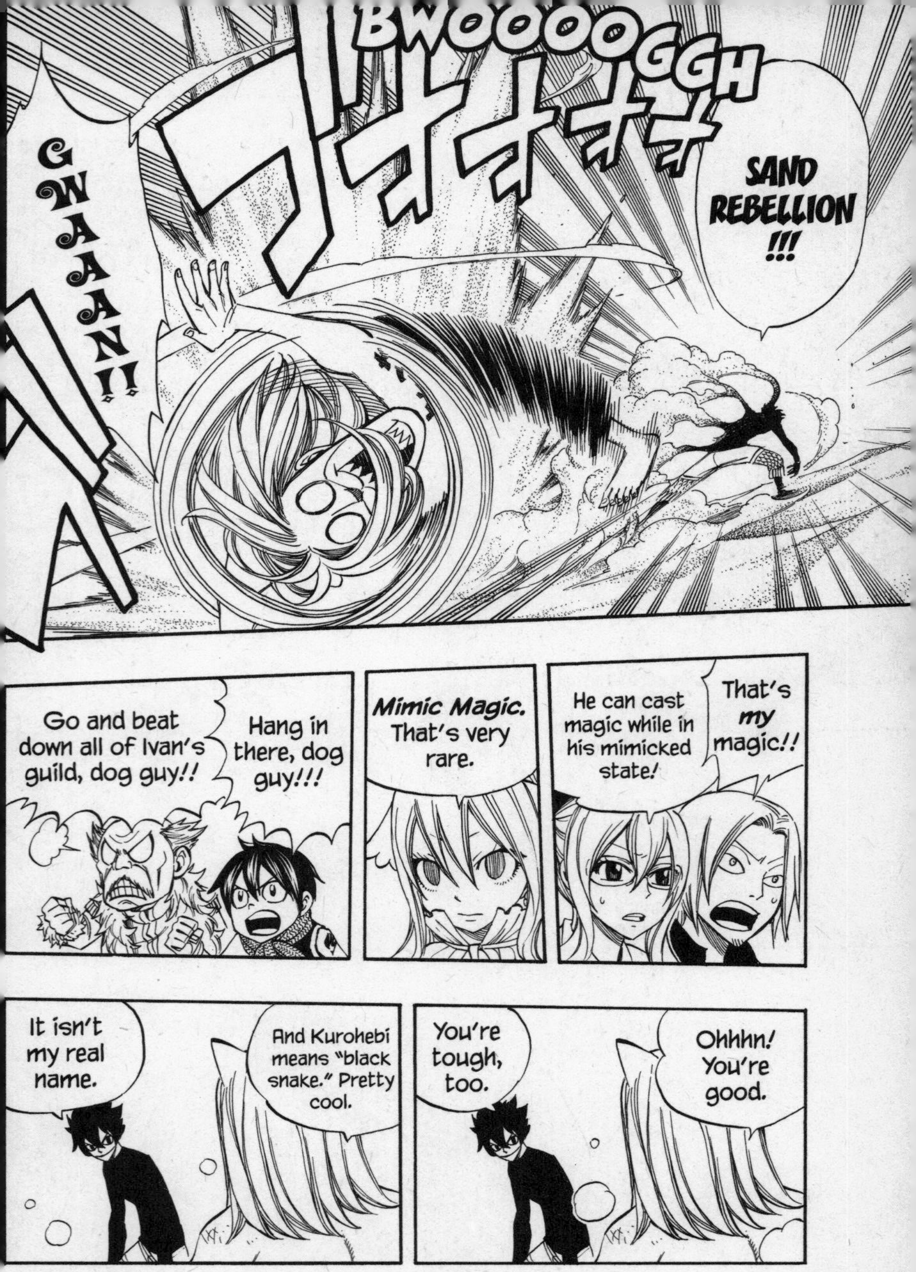
SAND REBELLION!!!
BWOOOOGGH
ゴオオオ
GWAAAAN!!
That's *my* magic!!
He can cast magic while in his mimicked state!
Mimic Magic. That's very rare.
Hang in there, dog guy!!!
Go and beat down all of Ivan's guild, dog guy!!
Ohhhn! You're good.
You're tough, too.
And Kurohebi means "black snake." Pretty cool.
It isn't my real name.

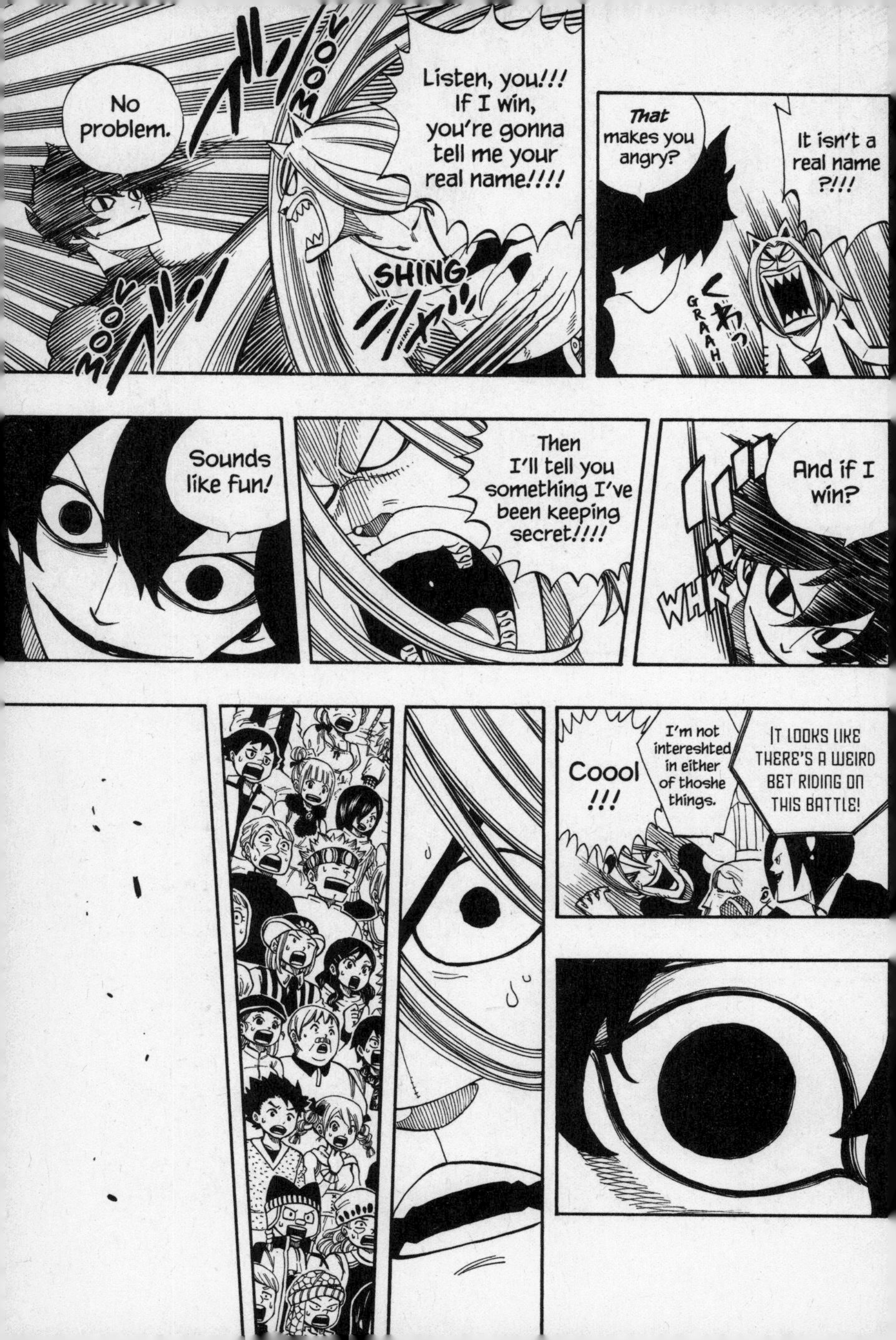
It isn't a real name ?!!!
That makes you angry?
GRAAH
Listen, you!!! If I win, you're gonna tell me your real name!!!!
VOOOM
SHING
No problem.
VOOOM
And if I win?
WHK
Then I'll tell you something I've been keeping secret!!!!
Sounds like fun!
IT LOOKS LIKE THERE'S A WEIRD BET RIDING ON THIS BATTLE!
I'm not intereshted in either of thoshe things.
Coool !!!

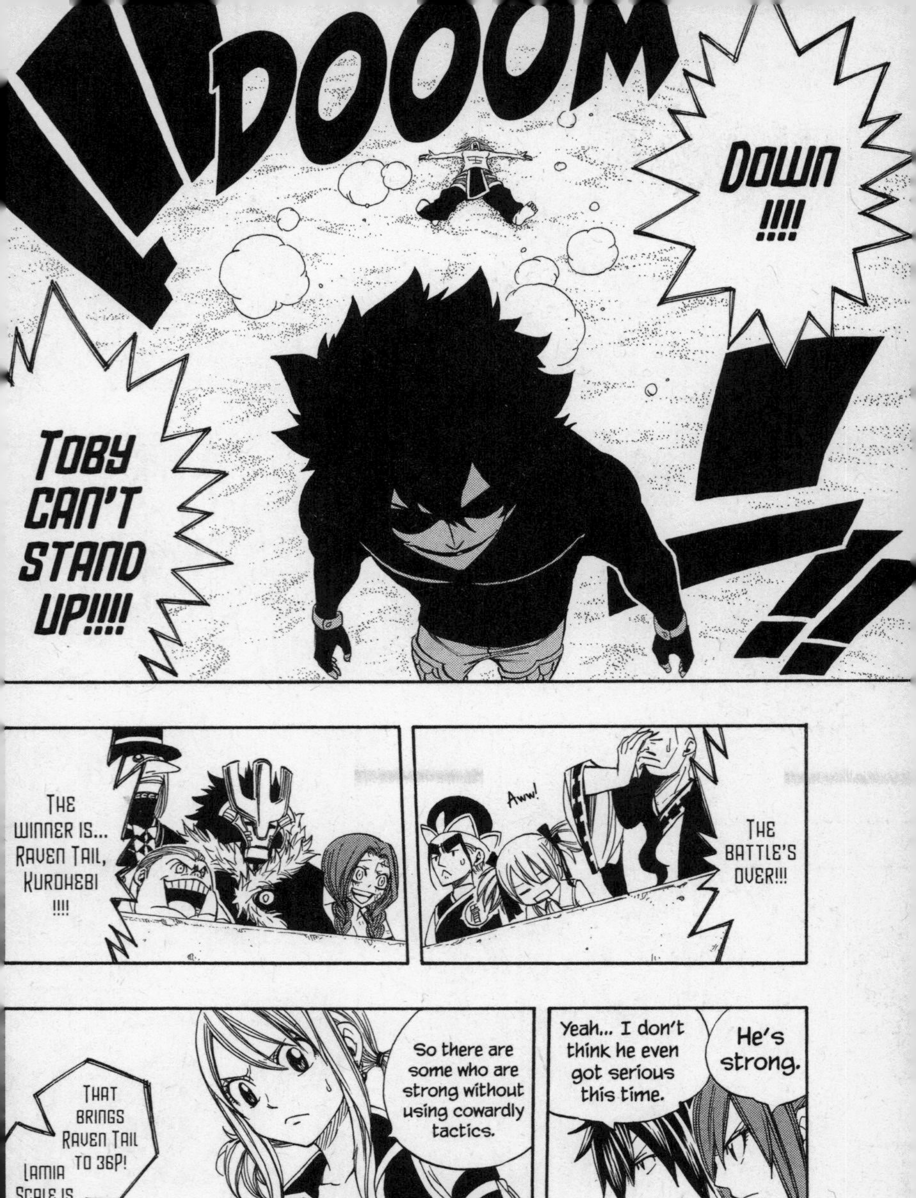
DOOOM
DOWN!!!!
TOBY CAN'T STAND UP!!!!
Aww!
THE BATTLE'S OVER!!!
THE WINNER IS... RAVEN TAIL, KUROHEBI!!!!
He's strong.
Yeah... I don't think he even got serious this time.
So there are some who are strong without using cowardly tactics.
THAT BRINGS RAVEN TAIL TO 36P!
LAMIA SCALE IS AT 20P.

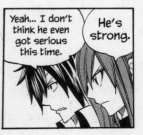

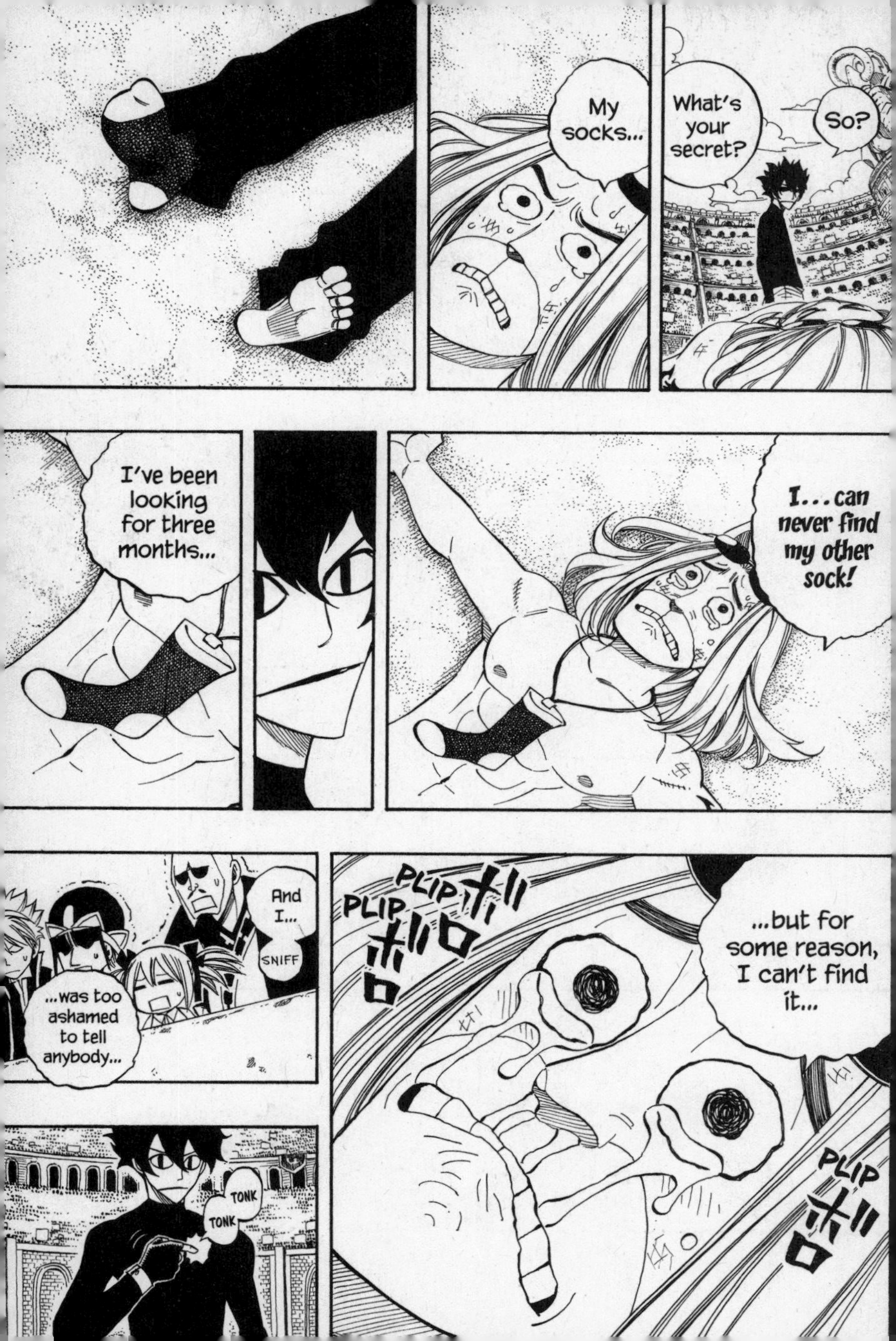
So?
What's your secret?
My socks...
I...can never find my other sock!
I've been looking for three months...
...but for some reason, I can't find it...
PLIP
PLIP
PLIP
And I...
SNIFF
...was too ashamed to tell anybody...
TONK
TONK

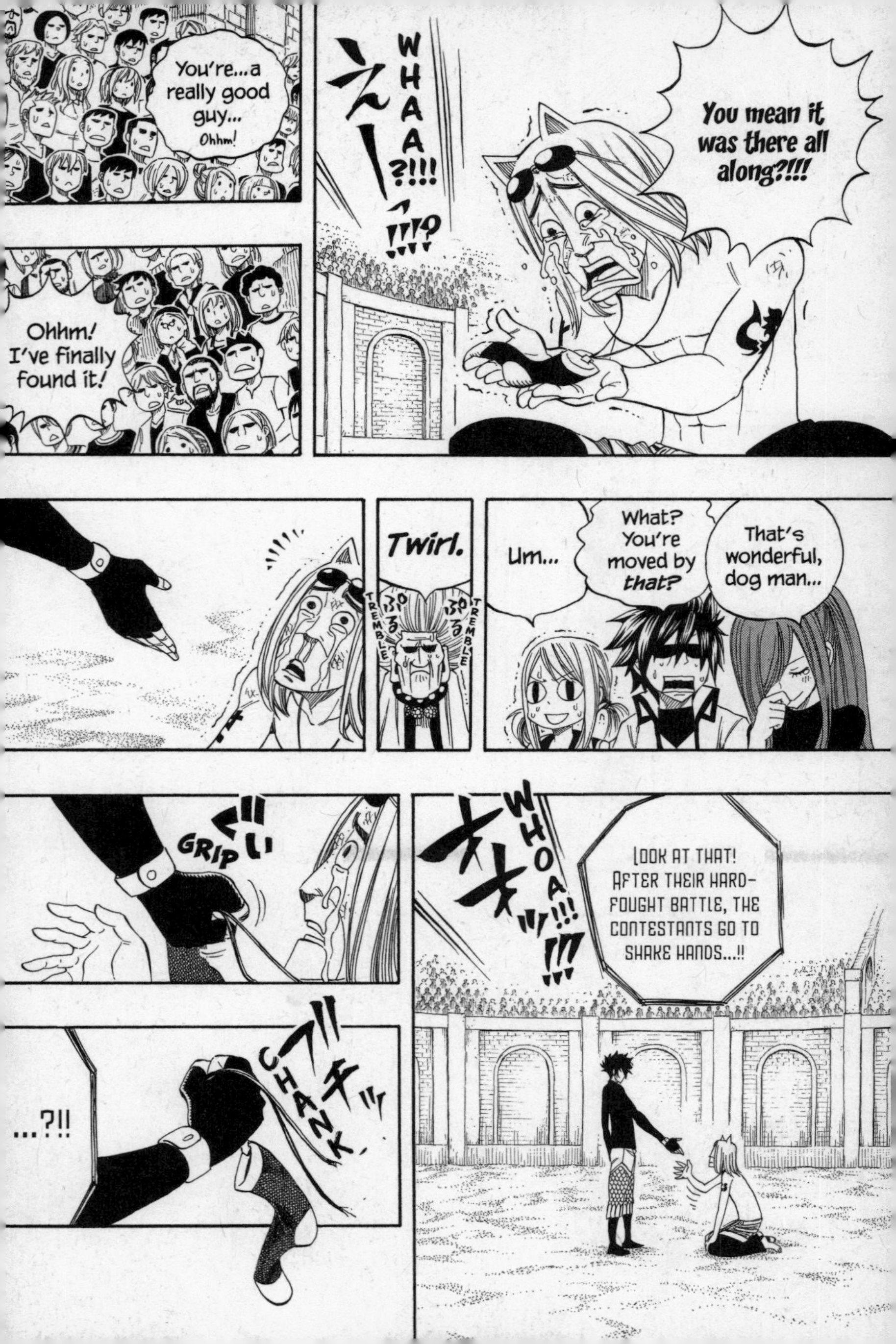
WHAA?!!!
You mean it was there all along?!!!
You're...a really good guy...
Ohhm!
Ohhm! I've finally found it!
That's wonderful, dog man...
What? You're moved by *that?*
Um...
Twirl.
TREMBLE
TREMBLE
WHOA!!!
LOOK AT THAT! AFTER THEIR HARD-FOUGHT BATTLE, THE CONTESTANTS GO TO SHAKE HANDS...!!
GRIP
CHANK
...?!!

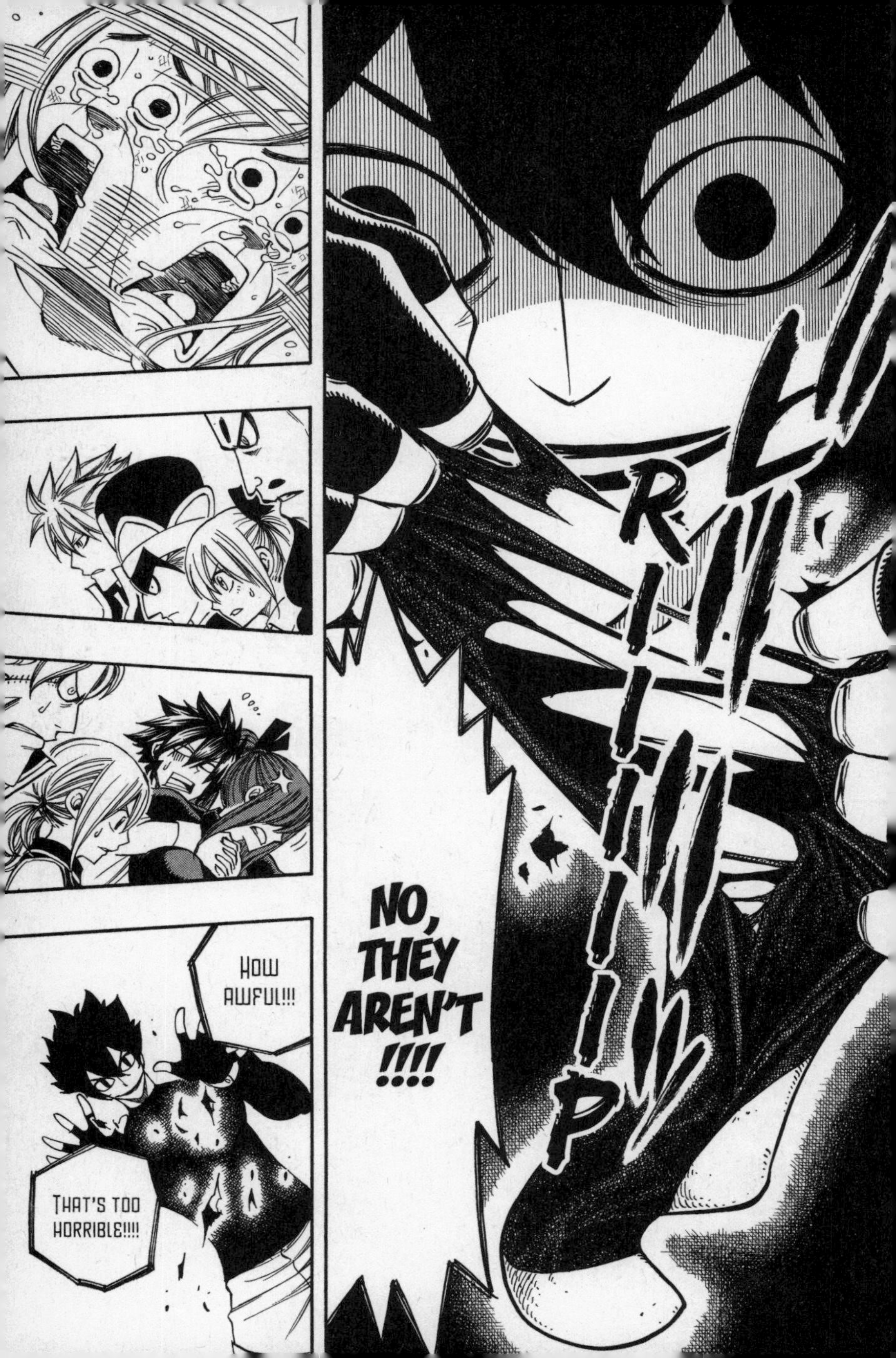
RIIIIP
NO, THEY AREN'T!!!!
How AWFUL!!!
THAT'S TOO HORRIBLE!!!!

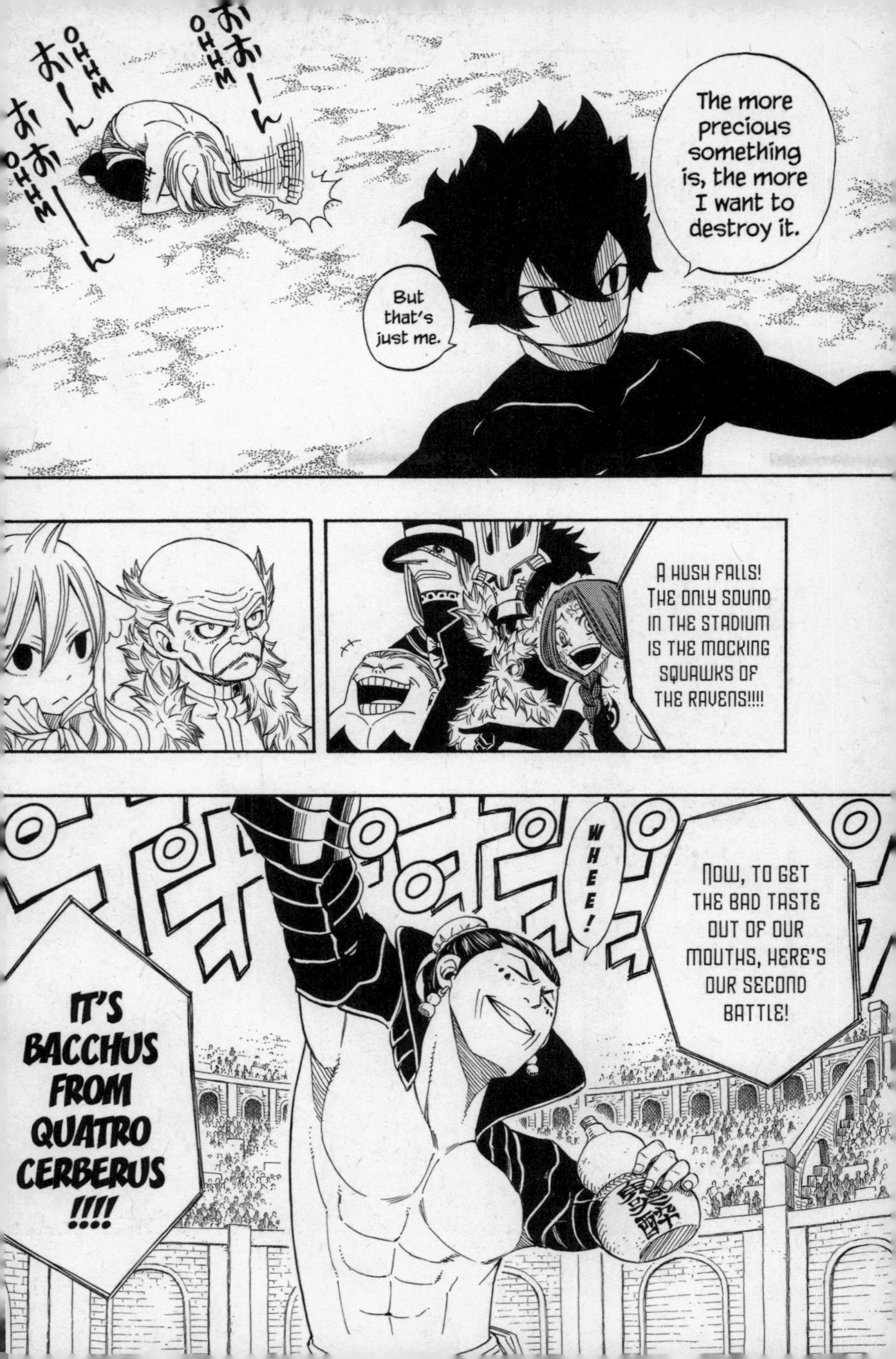

The more precious something is, the more I want to destroy it.
But that's just me.
おおーん OHHM
おーん OHHM
おおーーん OHHM
A HUSH FALLS! THE ONLY SOUND IN THE STADIUM IS THE MOCKING SQUAWKS OF THE RAVENS!!!!
NOW, TO GET THE BAD TASTE OUT OF OUR MOUTHS, HERE'S OUR SECOND BATTLE!
WHEE!
IT'S BACCHUS FROM QUATRO CERBERUS!!!!

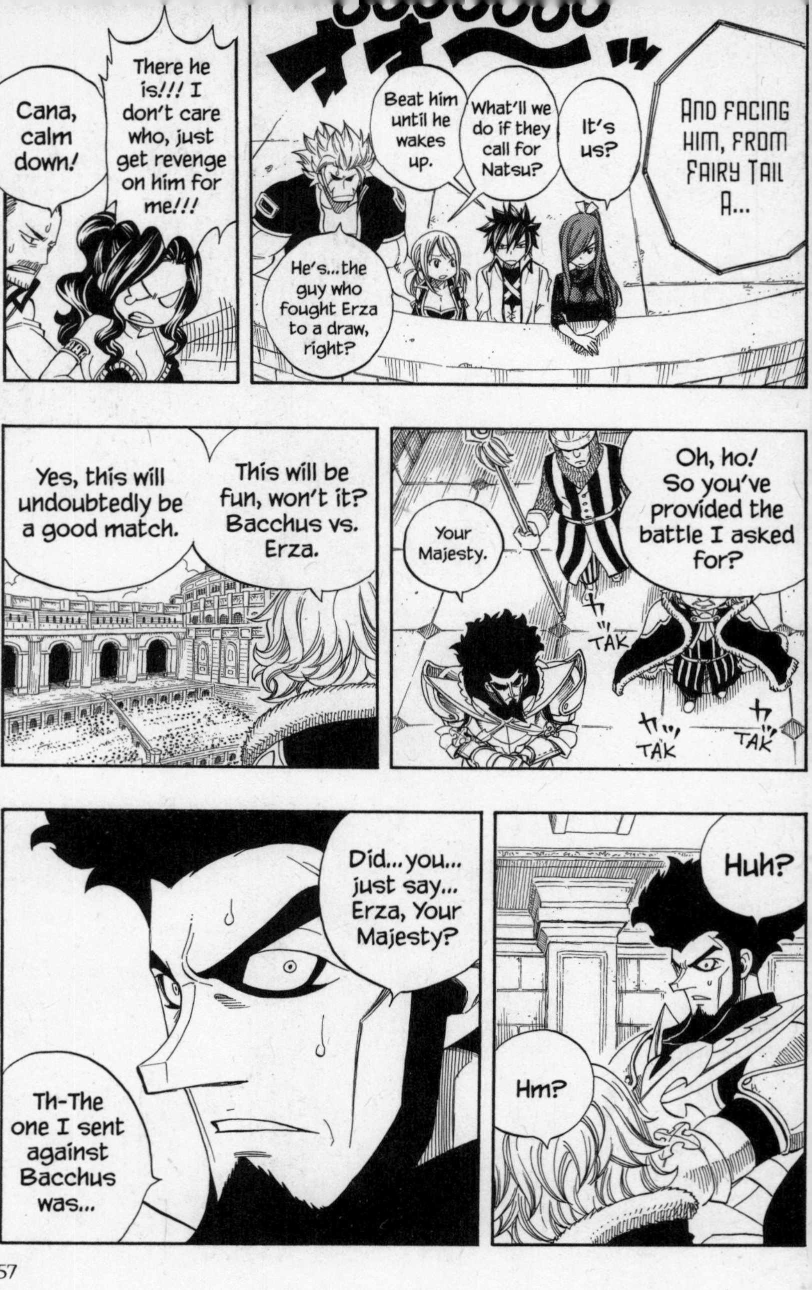
AND FACING HIM, FROM FAIRY TAIL A...
It's us?
What'll we do if they call for Natsu?
Beat him until he wakes up.
He's...the guy who fought Erza to a draw, right?
There he is!!! I don't care who, just get revenge on him for me!!!
Cana, calm down!
Oh, ho! So you've provided the battle I asked for?
Your Majesty.
カッ TAK
カッ TAK
カッ TAK
This will be fun, won't it? Bacchus vs. Erza.
Yes, this will undoubtedly be a good match.
Huh?
Hm?
Did...you... just say... Erza, Your Majesty?
Th-The one I sent against Bacchus was...

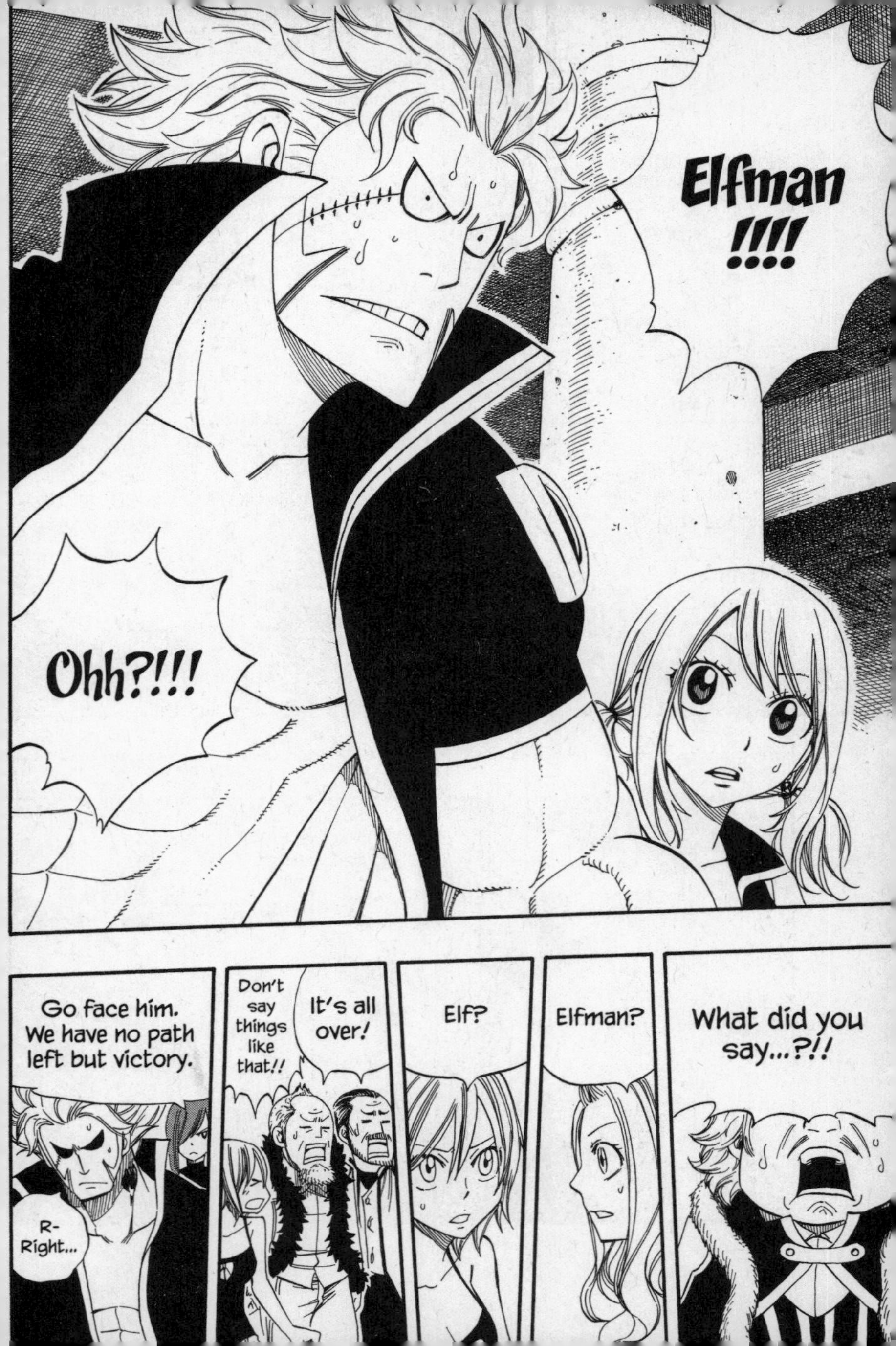
Elfman!!!!
Ohh?!!!
What did you say...?!!
Elfman?
Elf?
It's all over!
Don't say things like that!!
Go face him. We have no path left but victory.
R-Right...

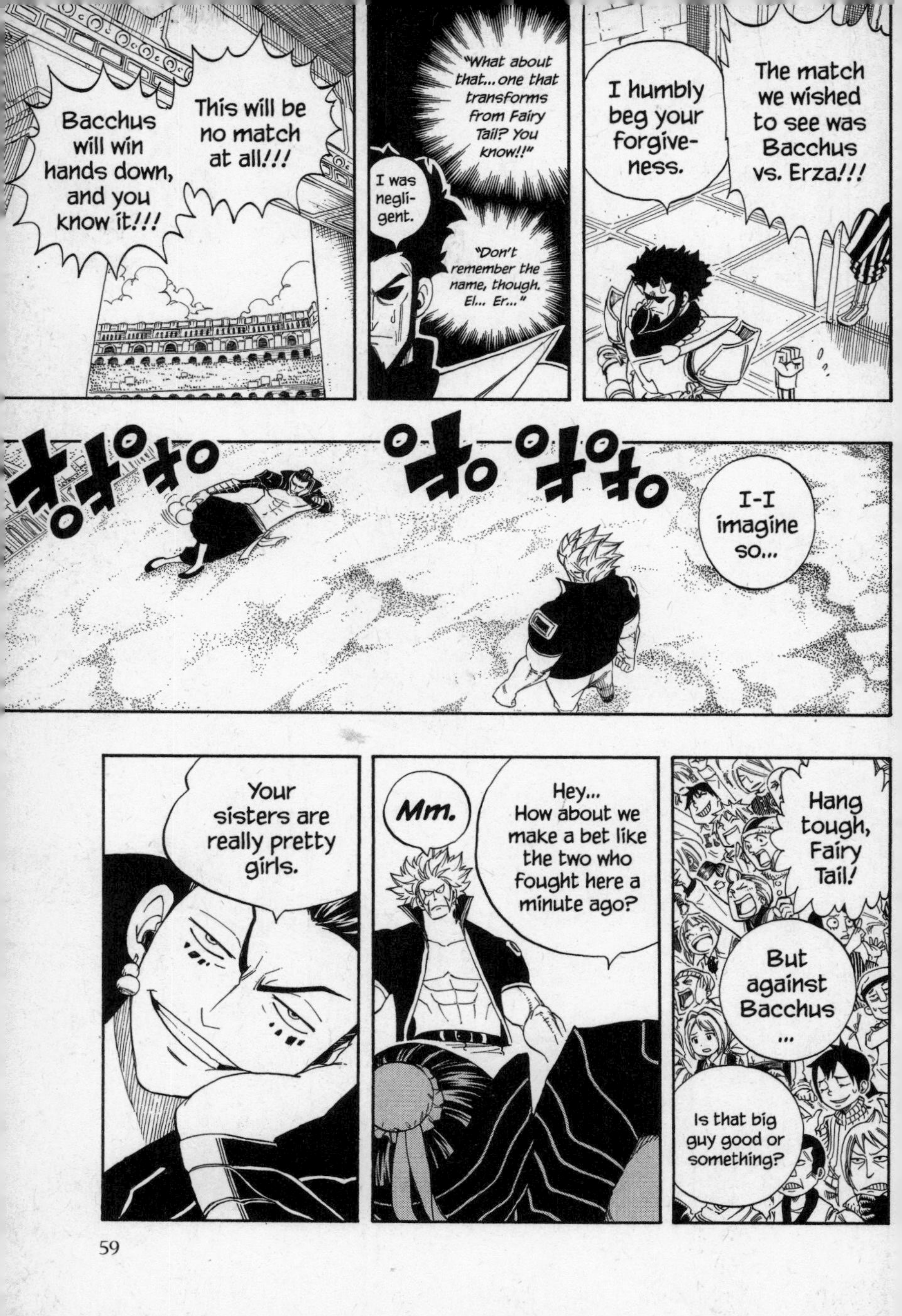
The match we wished to see was Bacchus vs. Erza!!!
I humbly beg your forgive-ness.
"What about that...one that transforms from Fairy Tail? You know!!"
I was negli-gent.
"Don't remember the name, though. El... Er..."
This will be no match at all!!!
Bacchus will win hands down, and you know it!!!
I-I imagine so...
Hang tough, Fairy Tail!
But against Bacchus ...
Is that big guy good or something?
Hey... How about we make a bet like the two who fought here a minute ago?
Mm.
Your sisters are really pretty girls.

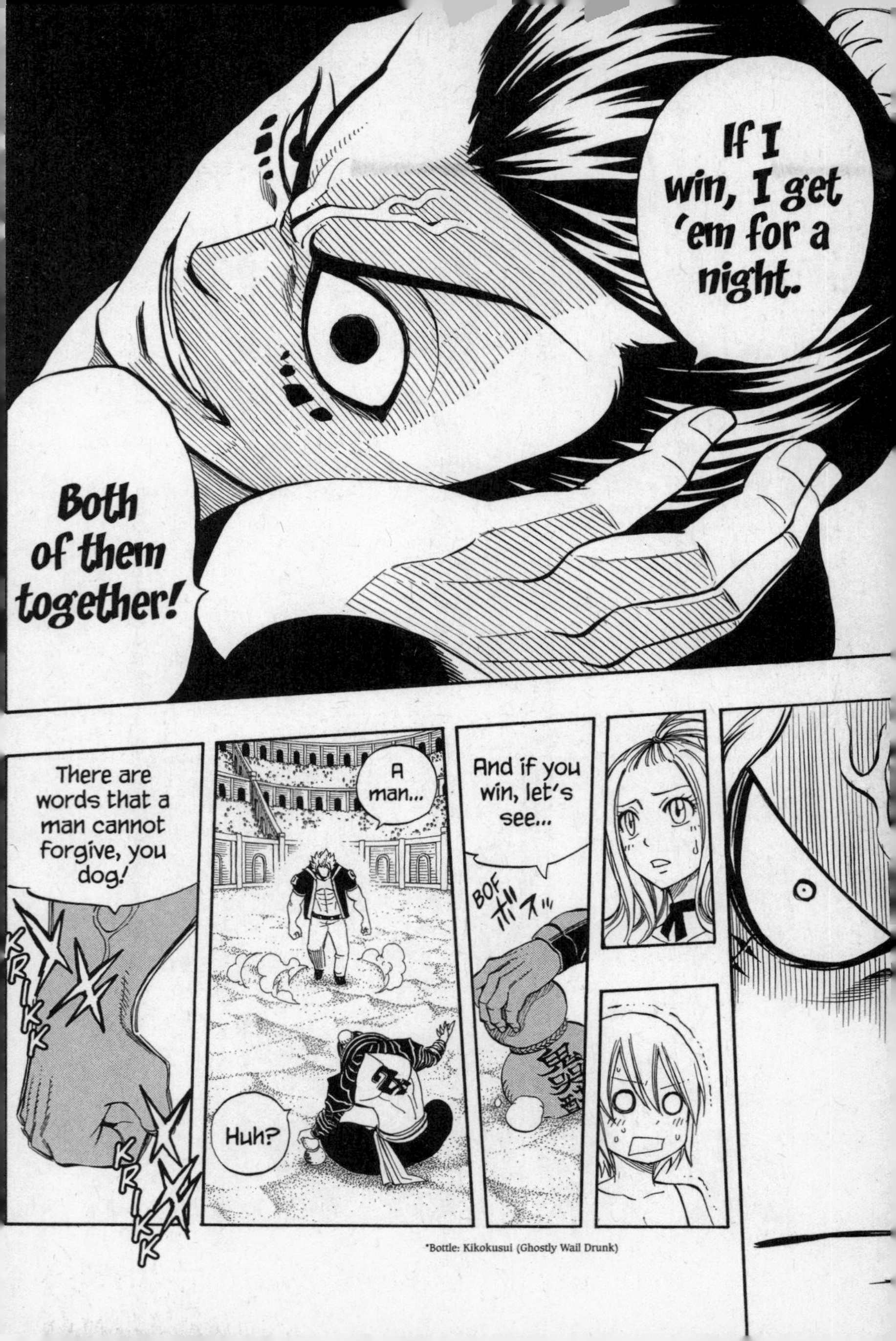
If I win, I get 'em for a night.
Both of them together!
And if you win, let's see...
BOF
A man...
Huh?
There are words that a man cannot forgive, you dog!
KRIKK
KRIKK
*Bottle: Kikokusui (Ghostly Wail Drunk)

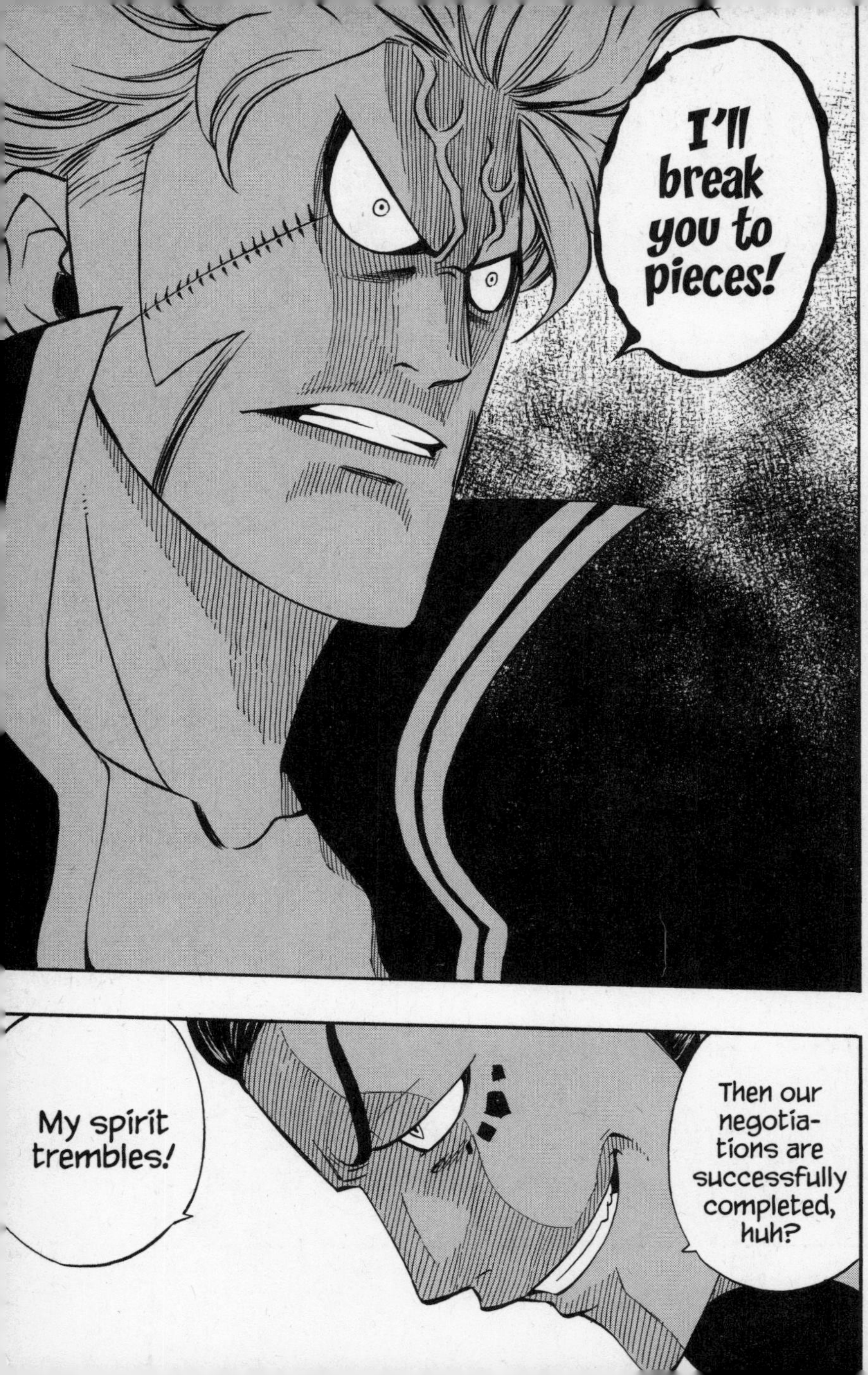
I'll break you to pieces!
Then our negotiations are successfully completed, huh?
My spirit trembles!

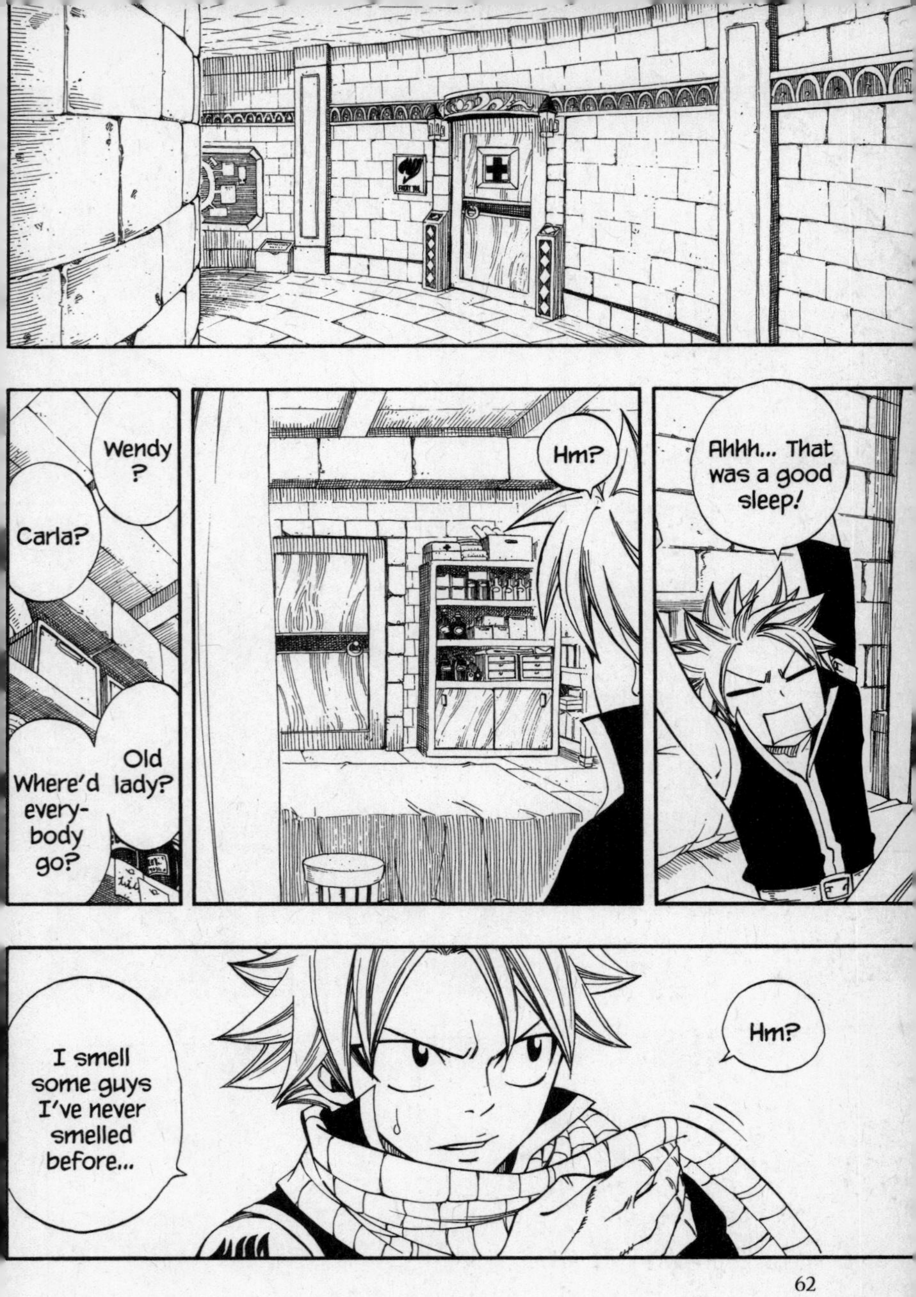
Ahhh... That was a good sleep!
Hm?
Wendy?
Carla?
Old lady?
Where'd everybody go?
Hm?
I smell some guys I've never smelled before...

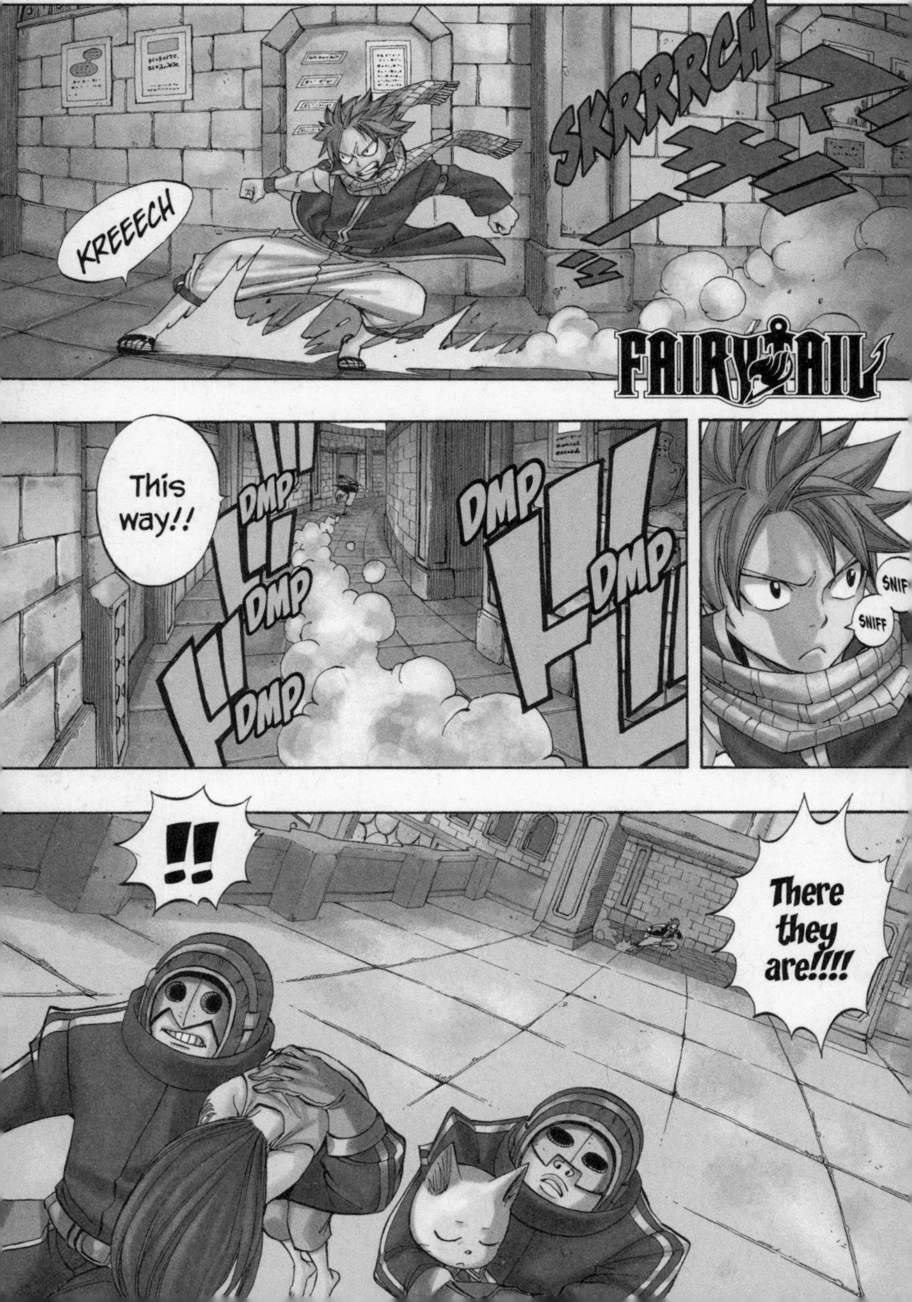
SKRRRCH
KREEECH
FAIRY TAIL
SNIF
SNIFF
DMP
DMP
This way!!
DMP
DMP
DMP
There they are!!!!
!!

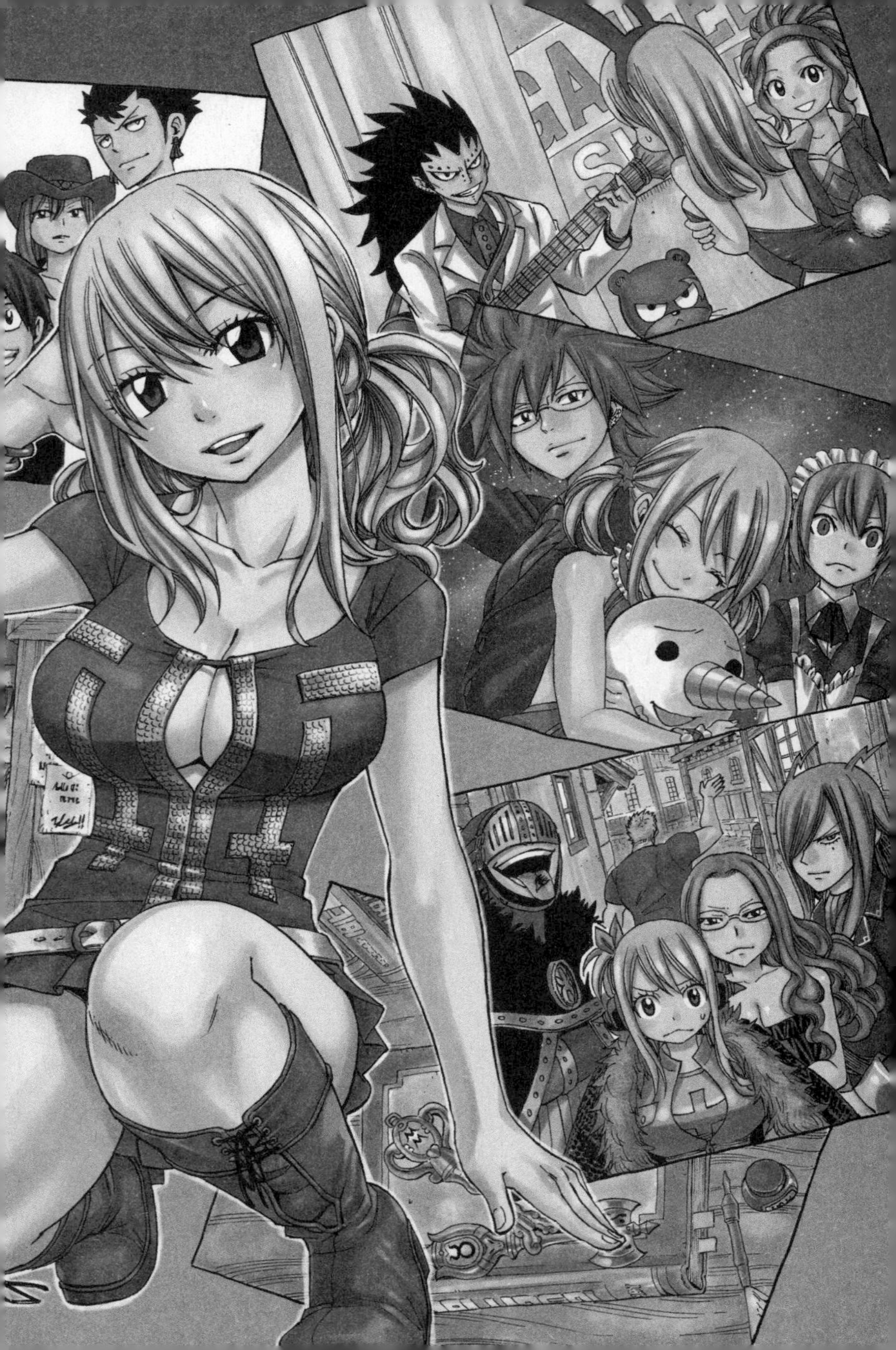

Chapter 278: Elfman vs. Bacchus

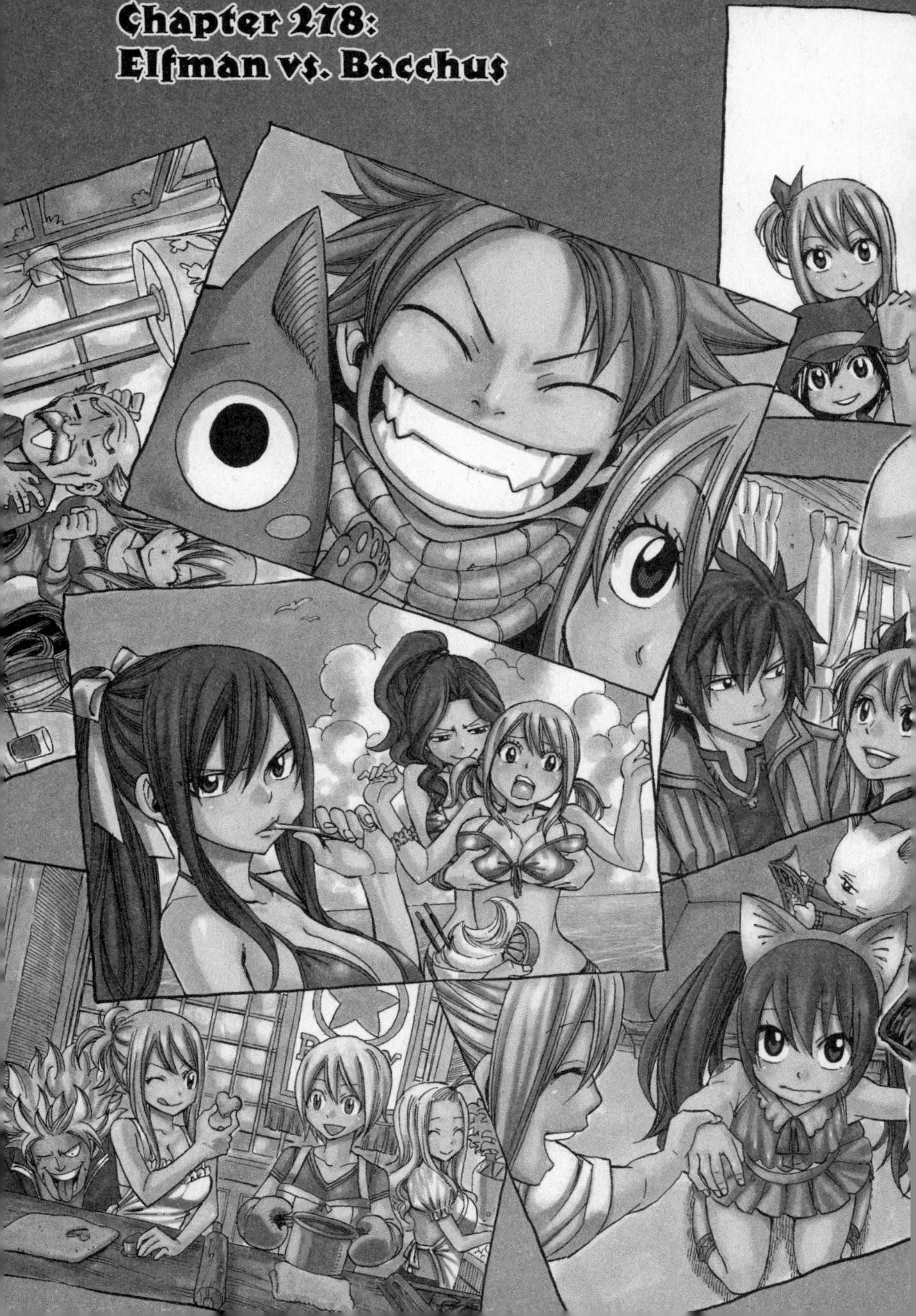

FAIRYTAIL

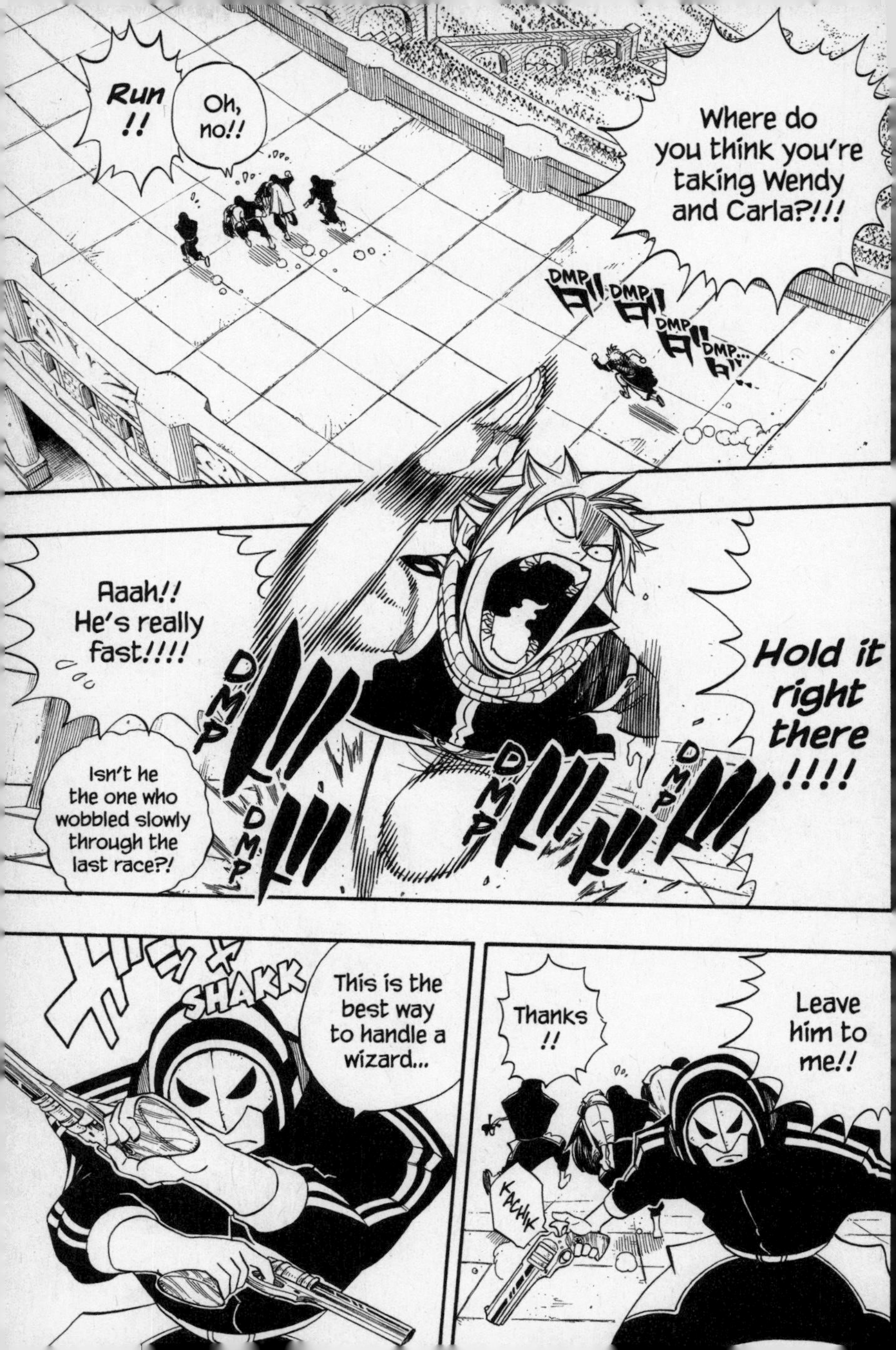
Where do you think you're taking Wendy and Carla?!!!
DMP DMP DMP DMP...
Oh, no!!
Run!!
Hold it right there!!!!
DMP DMP DMP DMP
Aaah!! He's really fast!!!!
Isn't he the one who wobbled slowly through the last race?!
Leave him to me!!
Thanks!!
KACHIK
This is the best way to handle a wizard...
SHAKK

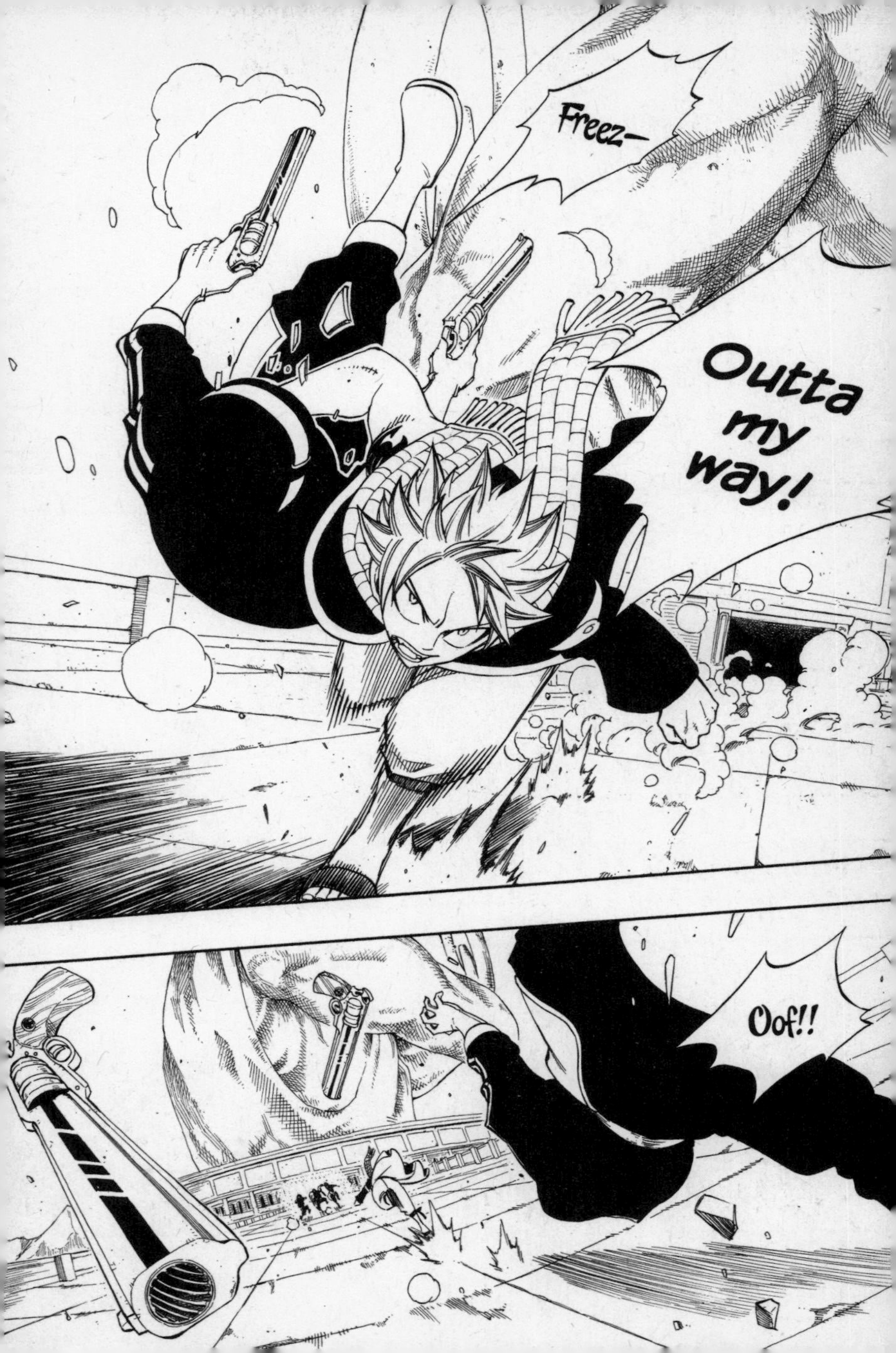
Freez—
Outta my way!
Oof!!

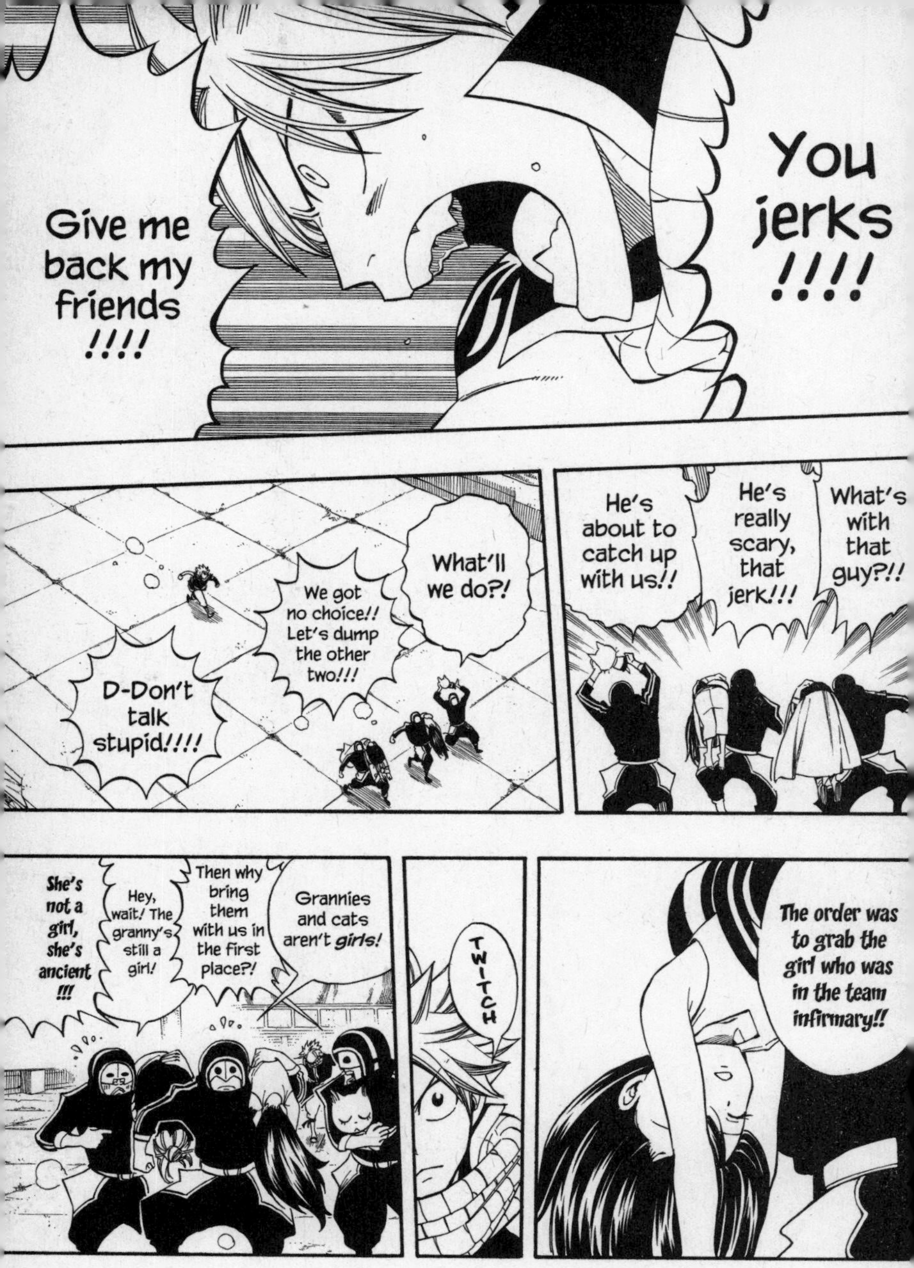
You jerks!!!!
Give me back my friends!!!!
What's with that guy?!!
He's really scary, that jerk!!!
He's about to catch up with us!!
What'll we do?!
We got no choice!! Let's dump the other two!!!
D-Don't talk stupid!!!!
The order was to grab the girl who was in the team infirmary!!
TWITCH
Grannies and cats aren't *girls!*
Then why bring them with us in the first place?!
Hey, wait! The granny's still a girl!
She's not a girl, she's ancient!!!

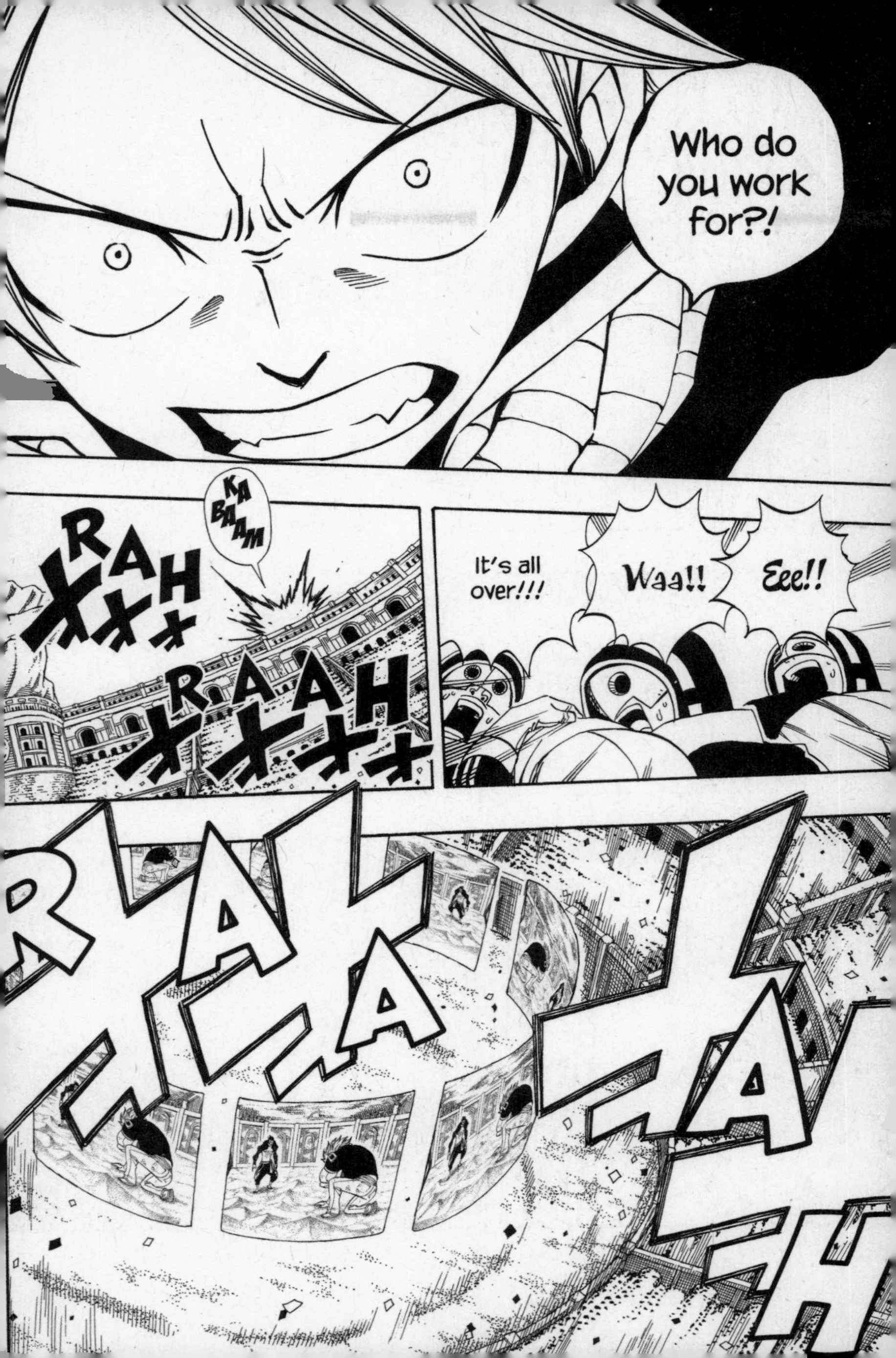
Who do you work for?!
Eee!!
Waa!!
It's all over!!!
KABAAM
RAH
RAAH
RAAAH

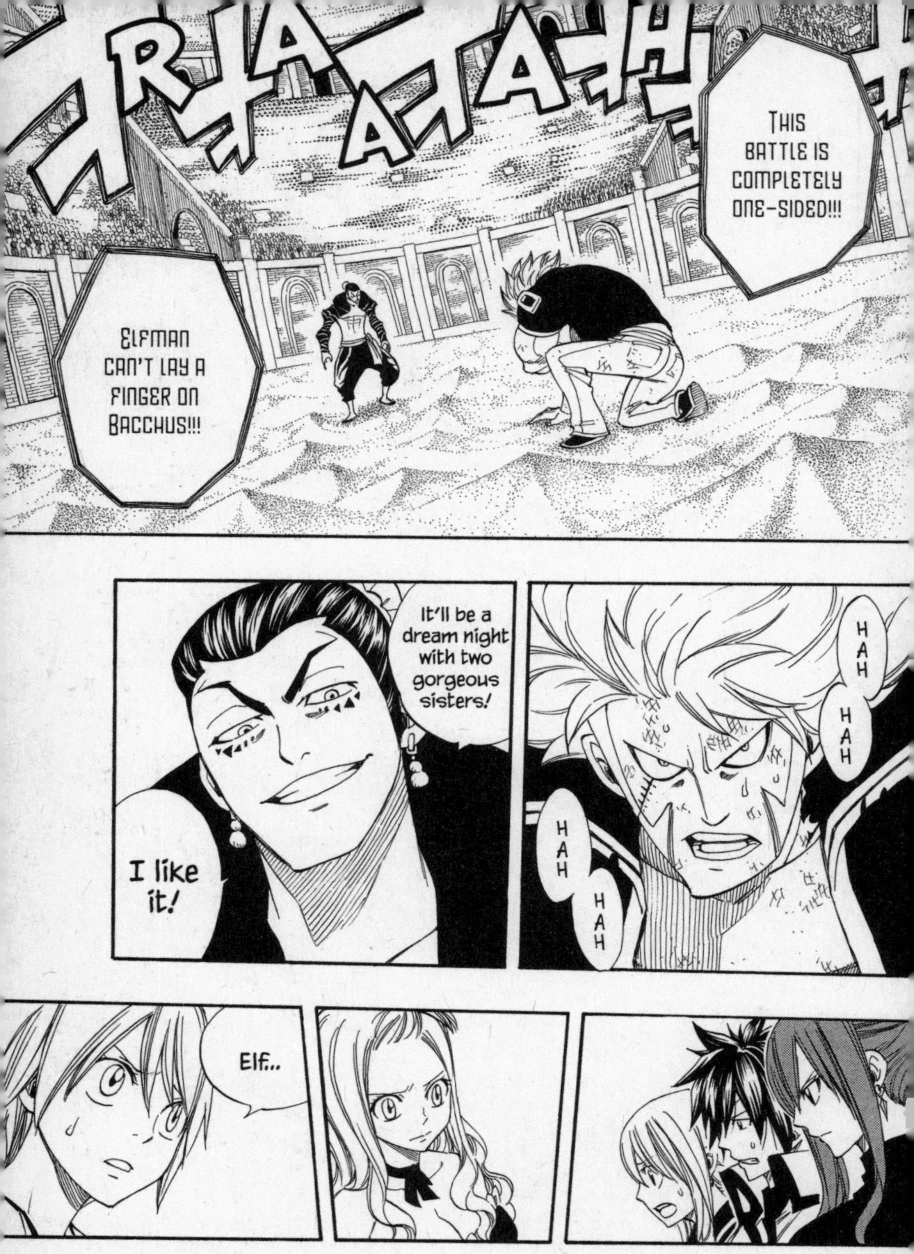
THIS BATTLE IS COMPLETELY ONE-SIDED!!!
ELFMAN CAN'T LAY A FINGER ON BACCHUS!!!
HAH HAH
HAH HAH
It'll be a dream night with two gorgeous sisters!
I like it!
Elf...

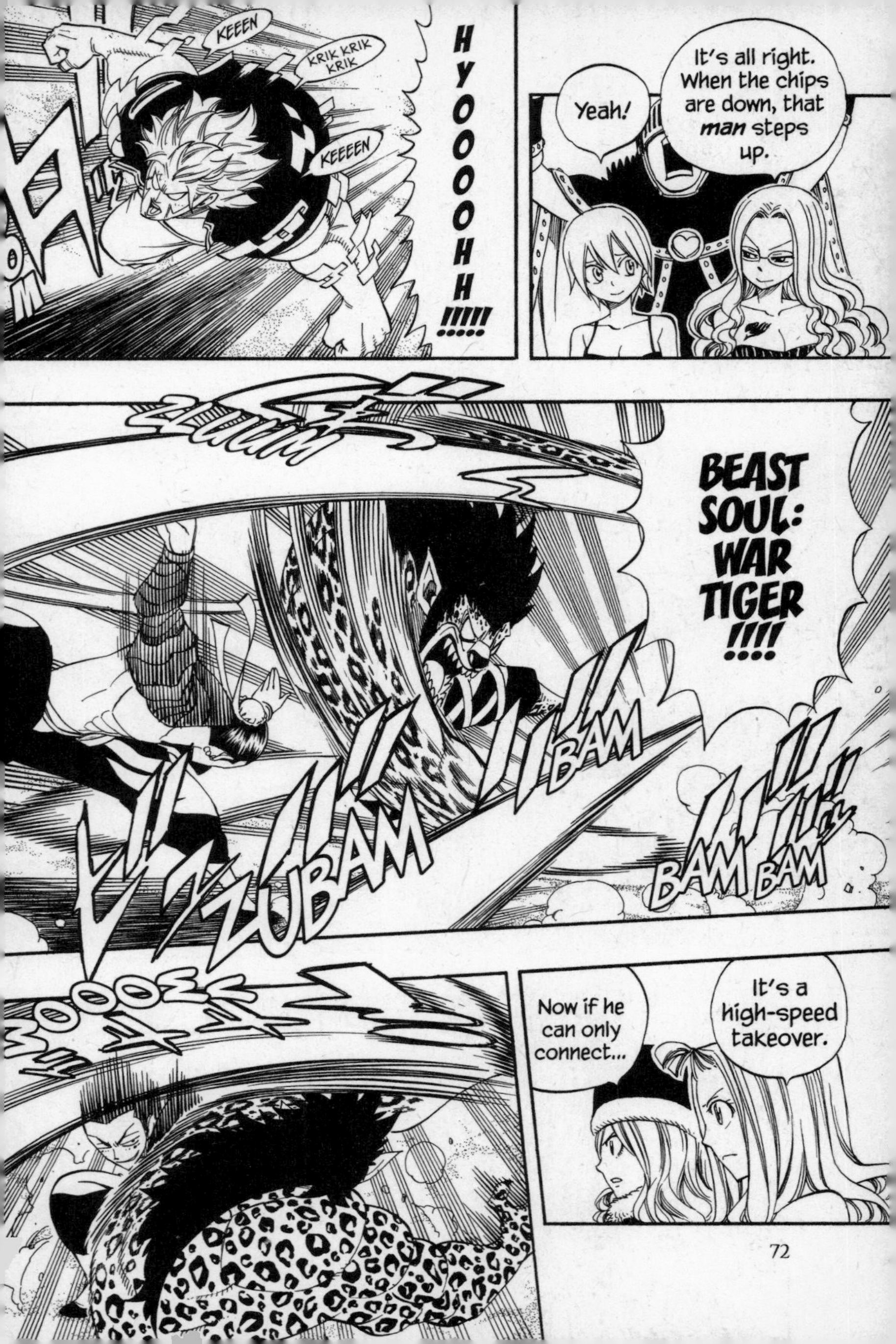
It's all right. When the chips are down, that *man* steps up.
Yeah!
HYOOOOOHH!!!!!
KEEEN
KRIK KRIK KRIK
KEEEEN
BEAST SOUL: WAR TIGER!!!!
BAM
BAM BAM
ZUBAM
It's a high-speed takeover.
Now if he can only connect...

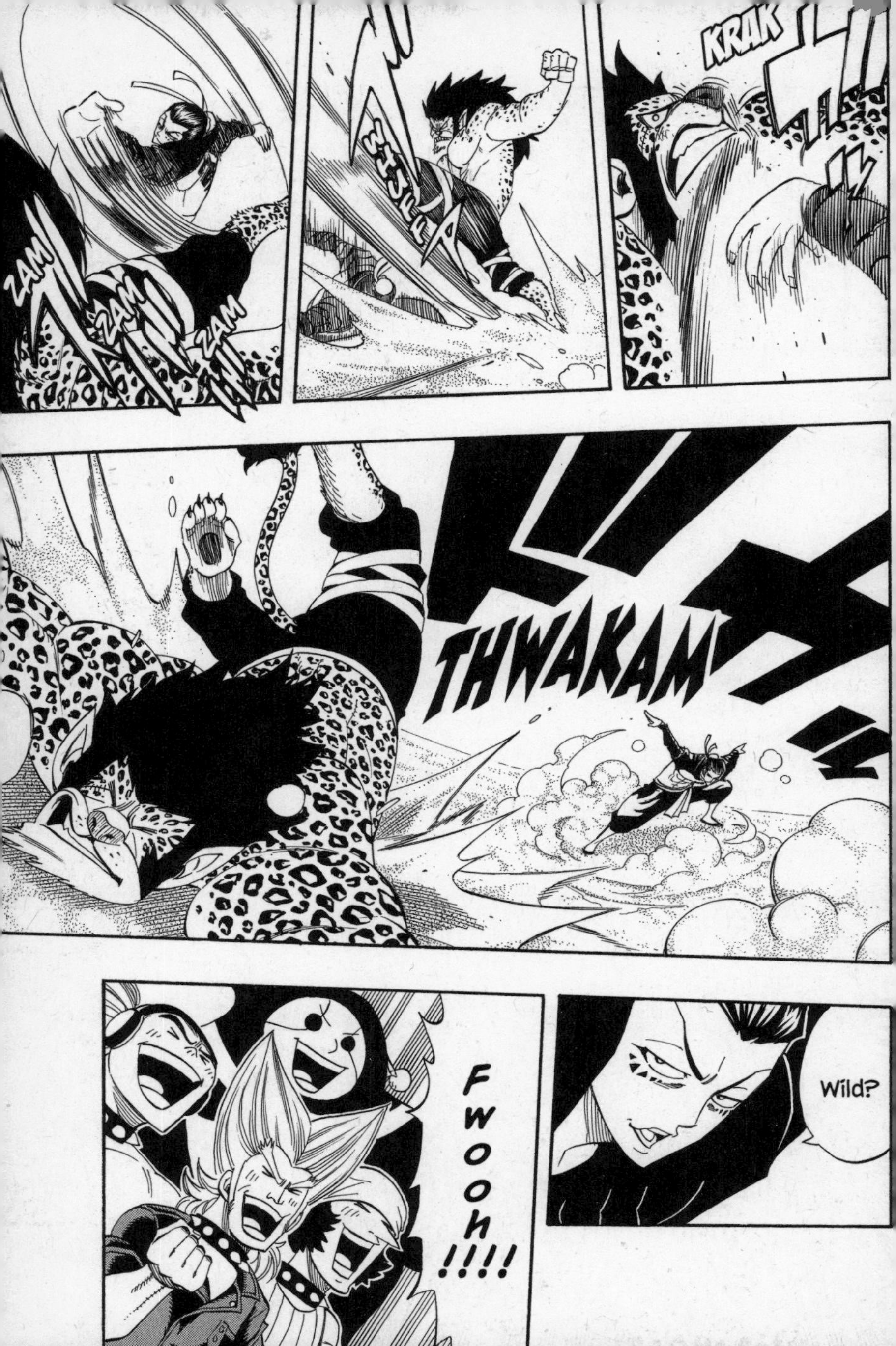
KRAK
ZAM
ZAM
ZAM
THWAKAM
Wild?
Fwooh!!!!

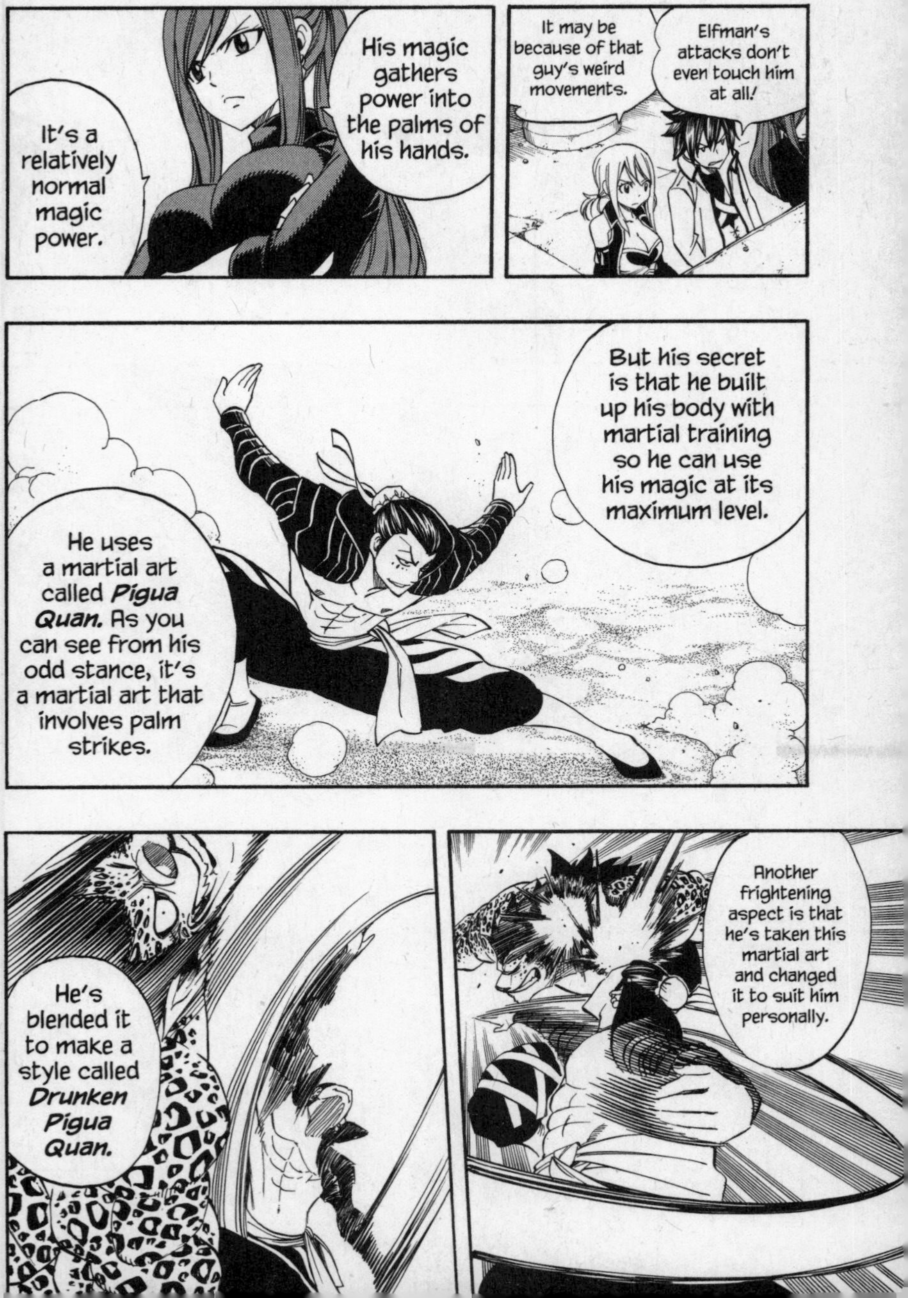

Elfman's attacks don't even touch him at all!
It may be because of that guy's weird movements.
His magic gathers power into the palms of his hands.
It's a relatively normal magic power.
But his secret is that he built up his body with martial training so he can use his magic at its maximum level.
He uses a martial art called *Pigua Quan.* As you can see from his odd stance, it's a martial art that involves palm strikes.
Another frightening aspect is that he's taken this martial art and changed it to suit him personally.
He's blended it to make a style called *Drunken Pigua Quan.*

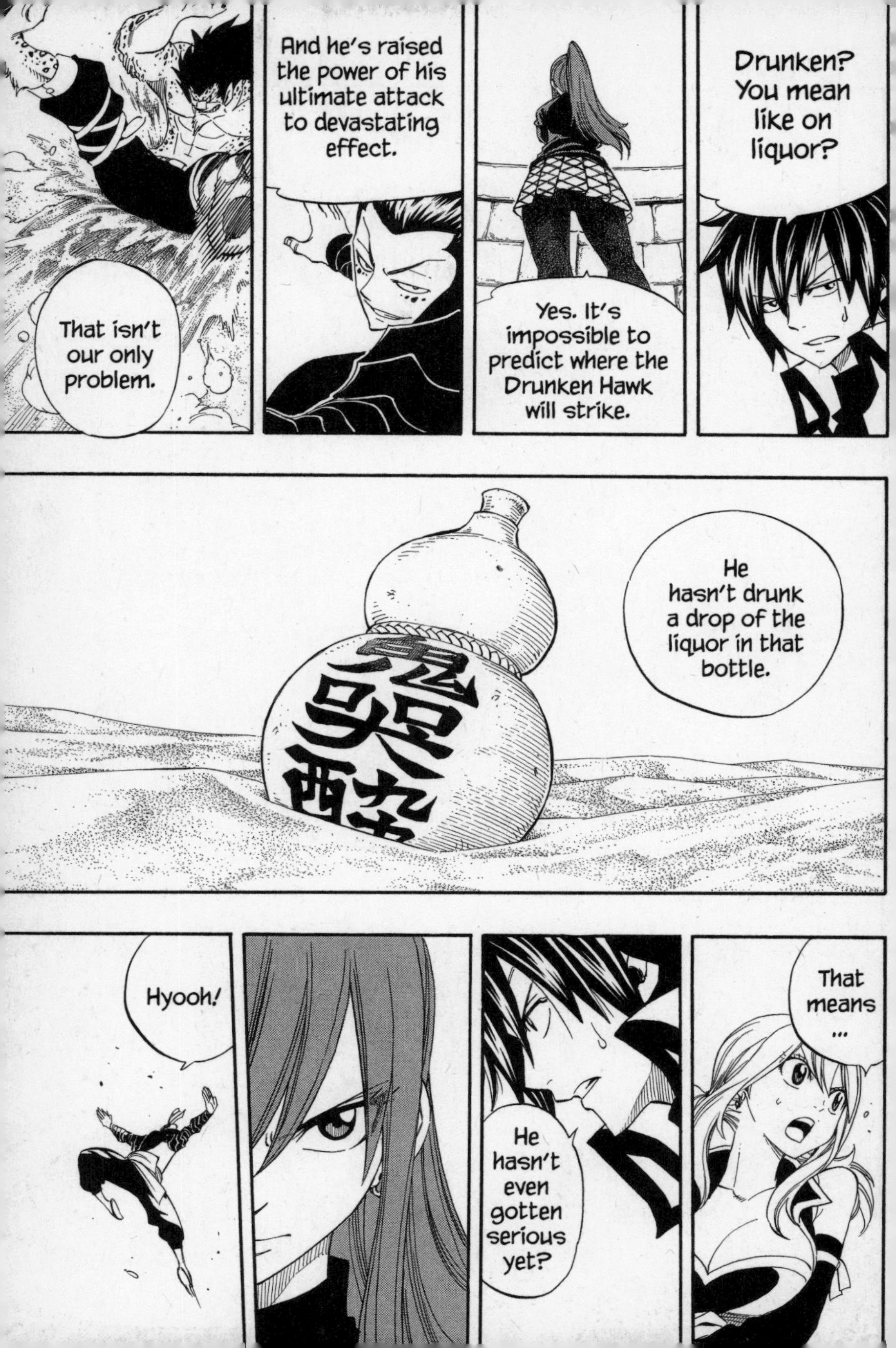
Drunken? You mean like on liquor?
Yes. It's impossible to predict where the Drunken Hawk will strike.
And he's raised the power of his ultimate attack to devastating effect.
That isn't our only problem.
He hasn't drunk a drop of the liquor in that bottle.
That means ...
He hasn't even gotten serious yet?
Hyooh!

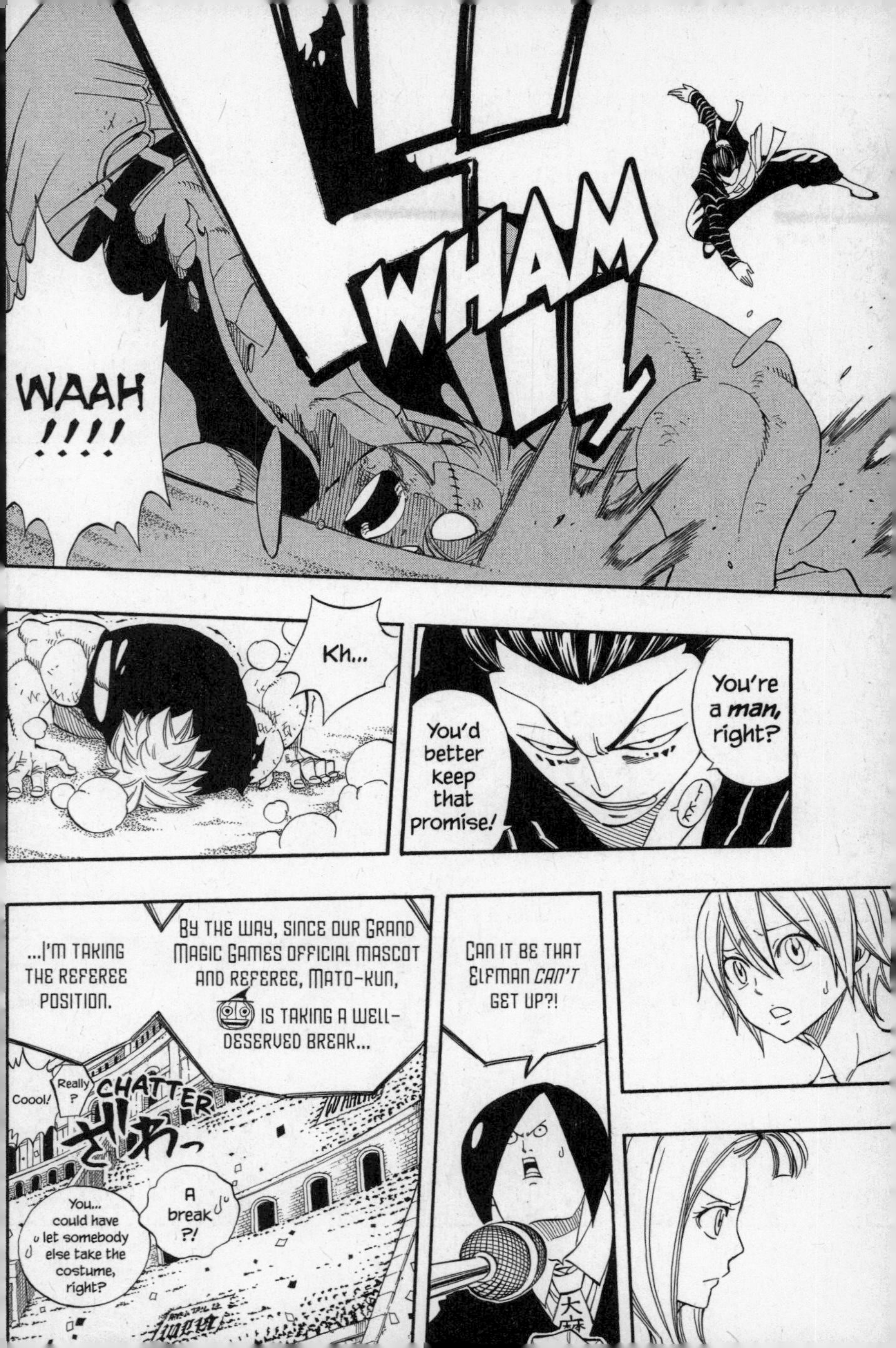
WHAM
WAAH!!!!
You're a *man,* right?
You'd better keep that promise!
Kh...
Can it be that Elfman *can't* get up?!
By the way, since our Grand Magic Games official mascot and referee, Mato-kun, is taking a well-deserved break...
...I'm taking the referee position.
Really?
Coool!
CHATTER
A break?!
You... could have let somebody else take the costume, right?

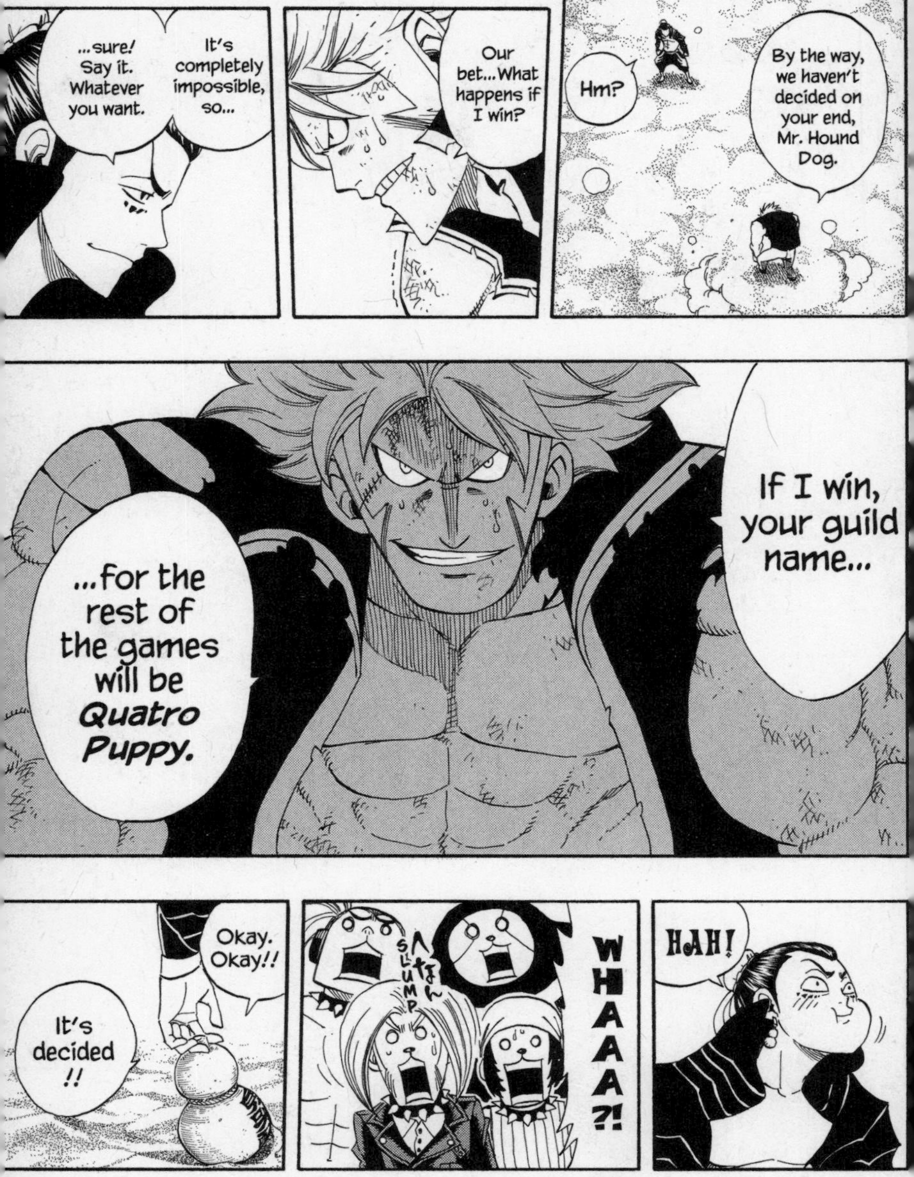
By the way, we haven't decided on your end, Mr. Hound Dog.
Hm?
Our bet...What happens if I win?
It's completely impossible, so...
...sure! Say it. Whatever you want.
If I win, your guild name...
...for the rest of the games will be *Quatro Puppy.*
HAH!
WHAAAA?!
SLUMP
Okay. Okay!!
It's decided!!

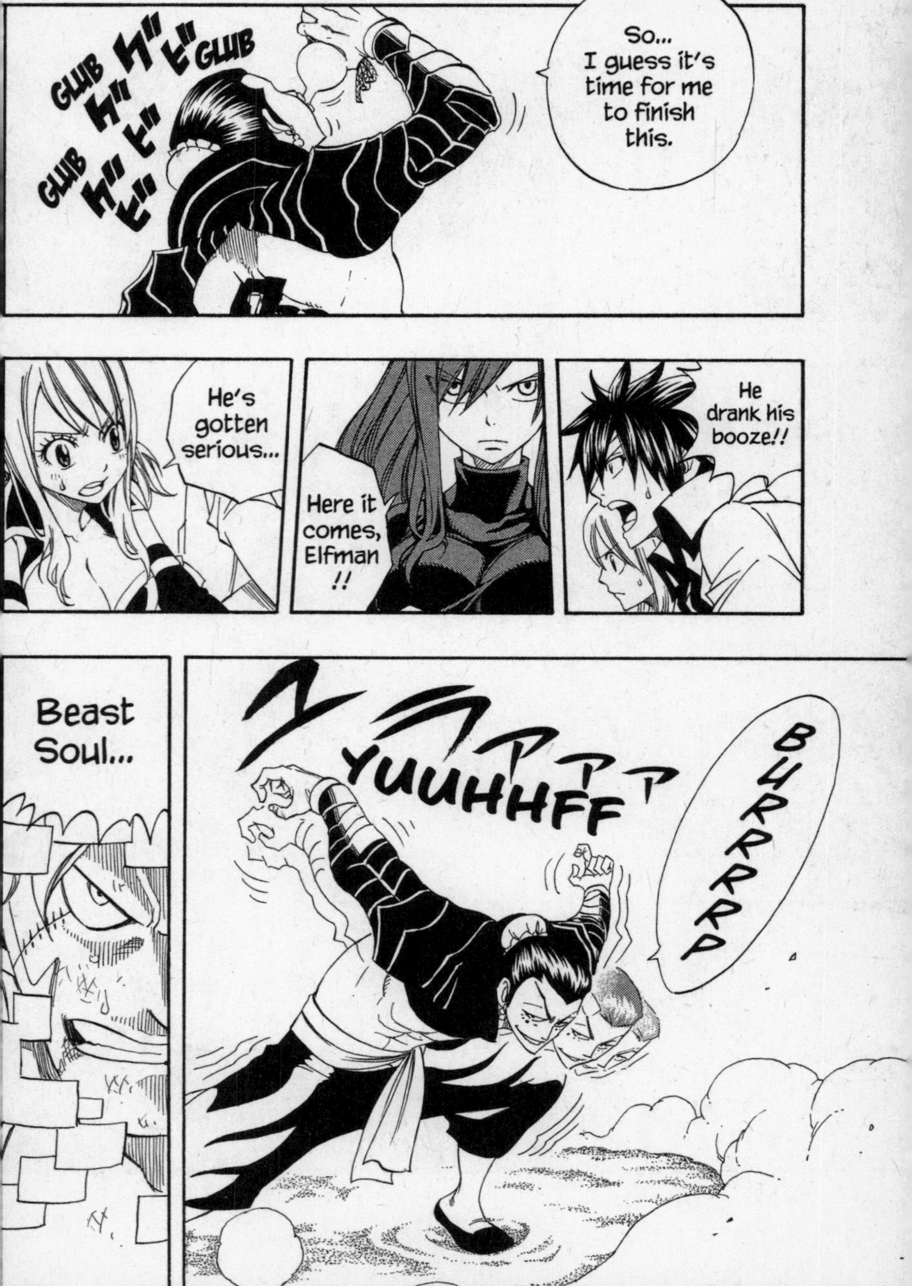
So... I guess it's time for me to finish this.
GLUB
GLUB
He drank his booze!!
Here it comes, Elfman!!
He's gotten serious...
BURRRRP
YUUHHFF
Beast Soul...

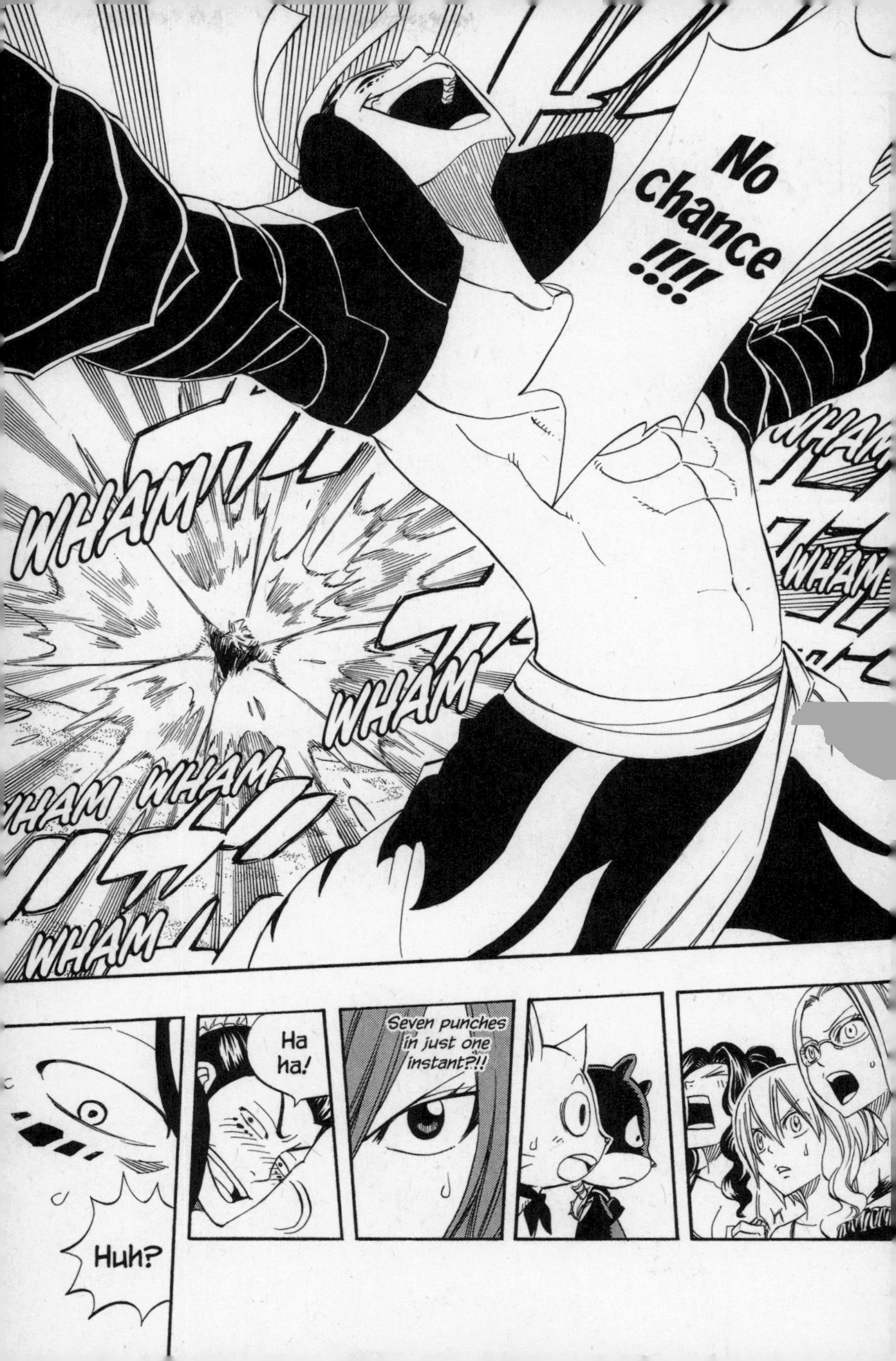

No chance!!!!
WHAM
WHAM
WHAM
WHAM
WHAM
WHAM
Seven punches in just one instant?!!
Ha ha!
Huh?

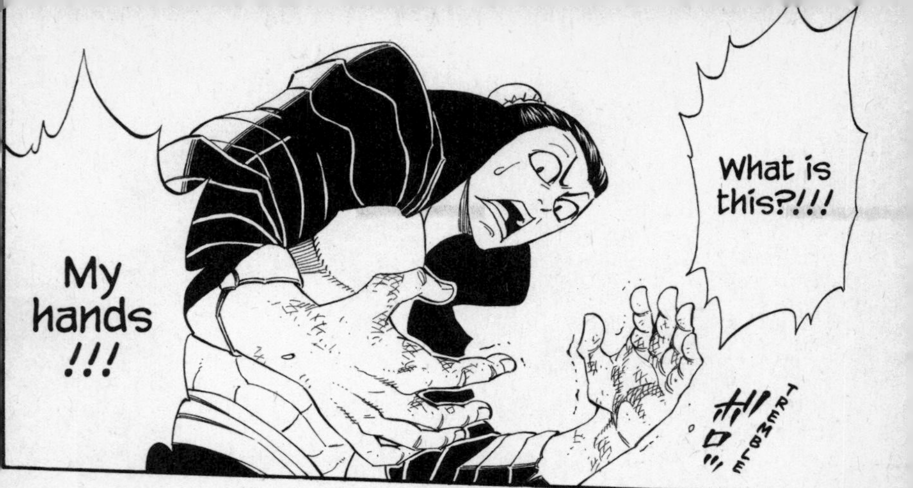
What is this?!!!
TREMBLE
My hands !!!
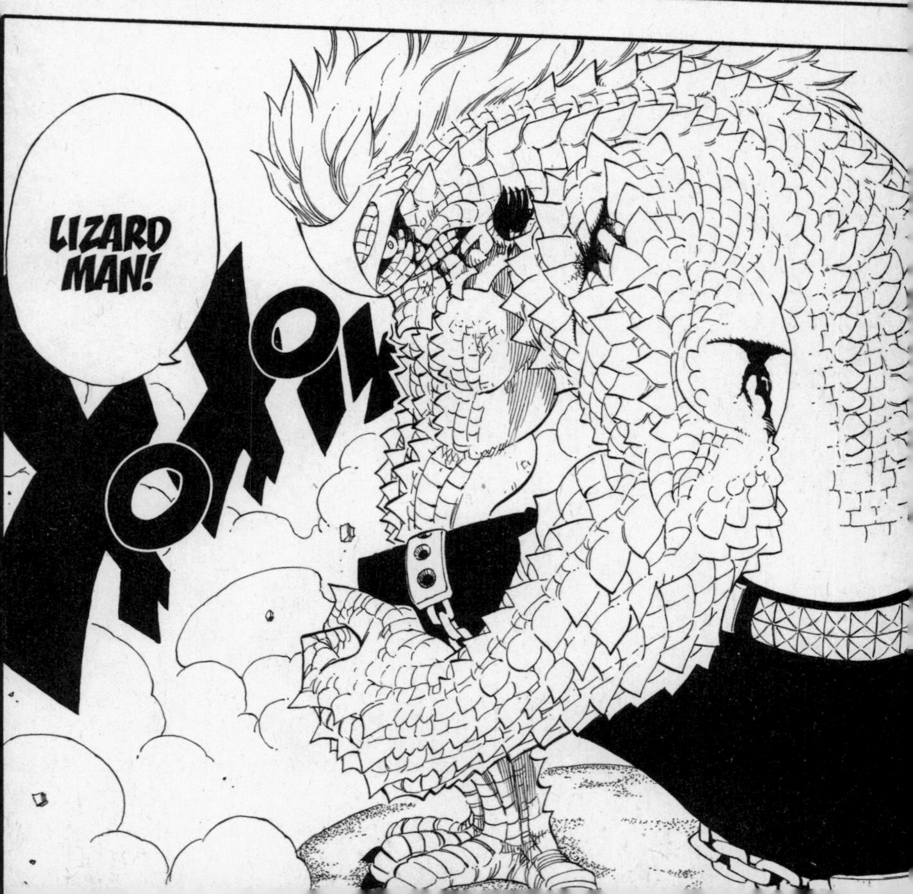
LIZARD MAN!

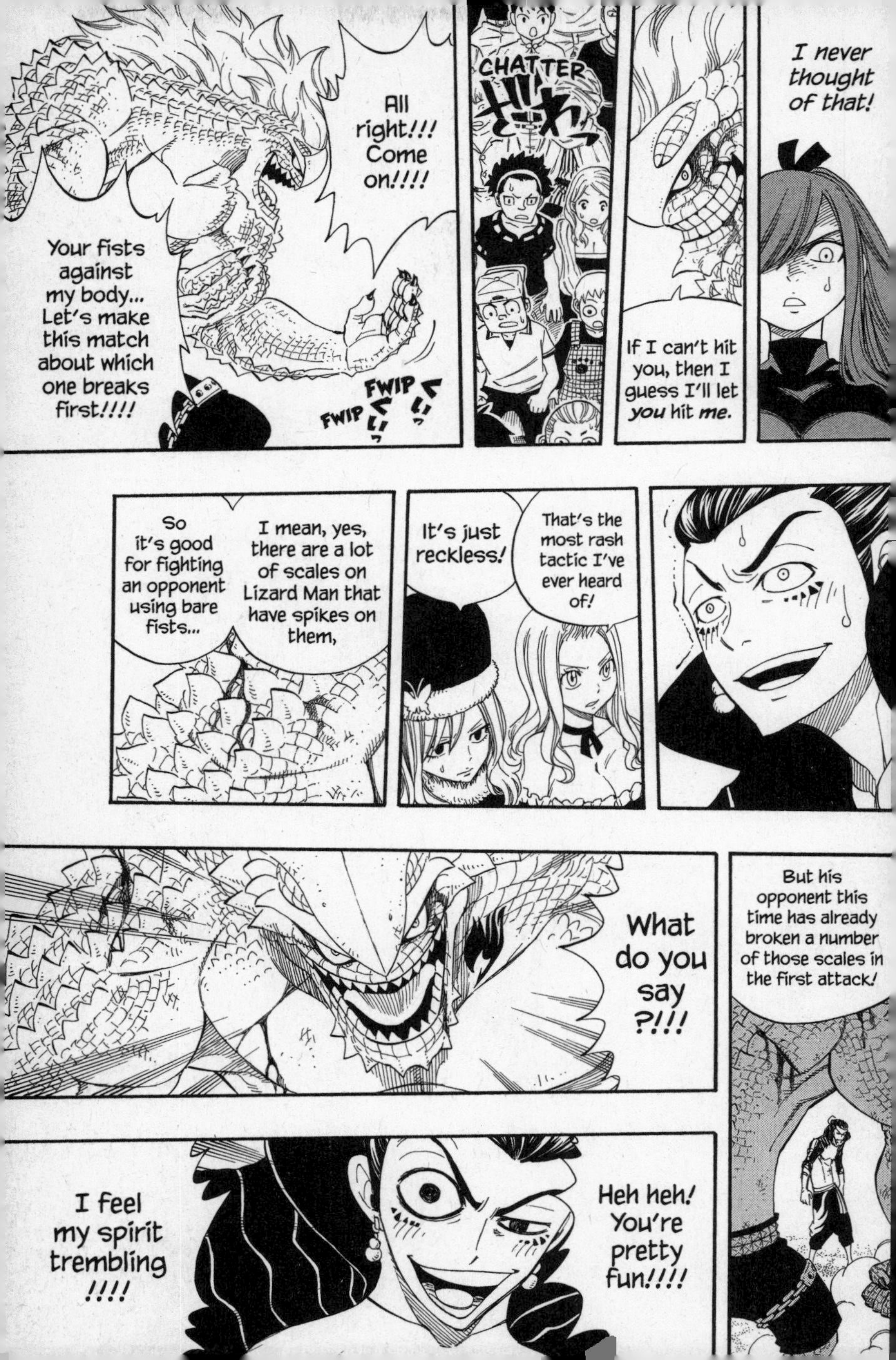
I never thought of that!
If I can't hit you, then I guess I'll let *you* hit *me*.
CHATTER
All right!!! Come on!!!!
Your fists against my body... Let's make this match about which one breaks first!!!!
FWIP
FWIP
That's the most rash tactic I've ever heard of!
It's just reckless!
I mean, yes, there are a lot of scales on Lizard Man that have spikes on them,
So it's good for fighting an opponent using bare fists...
But his opponent this time has already broken a number of those scales in the first attack!
What do you say?!!!
Heh heh! You're pretty fun!!!!
I feel my spirit trembling!!!!

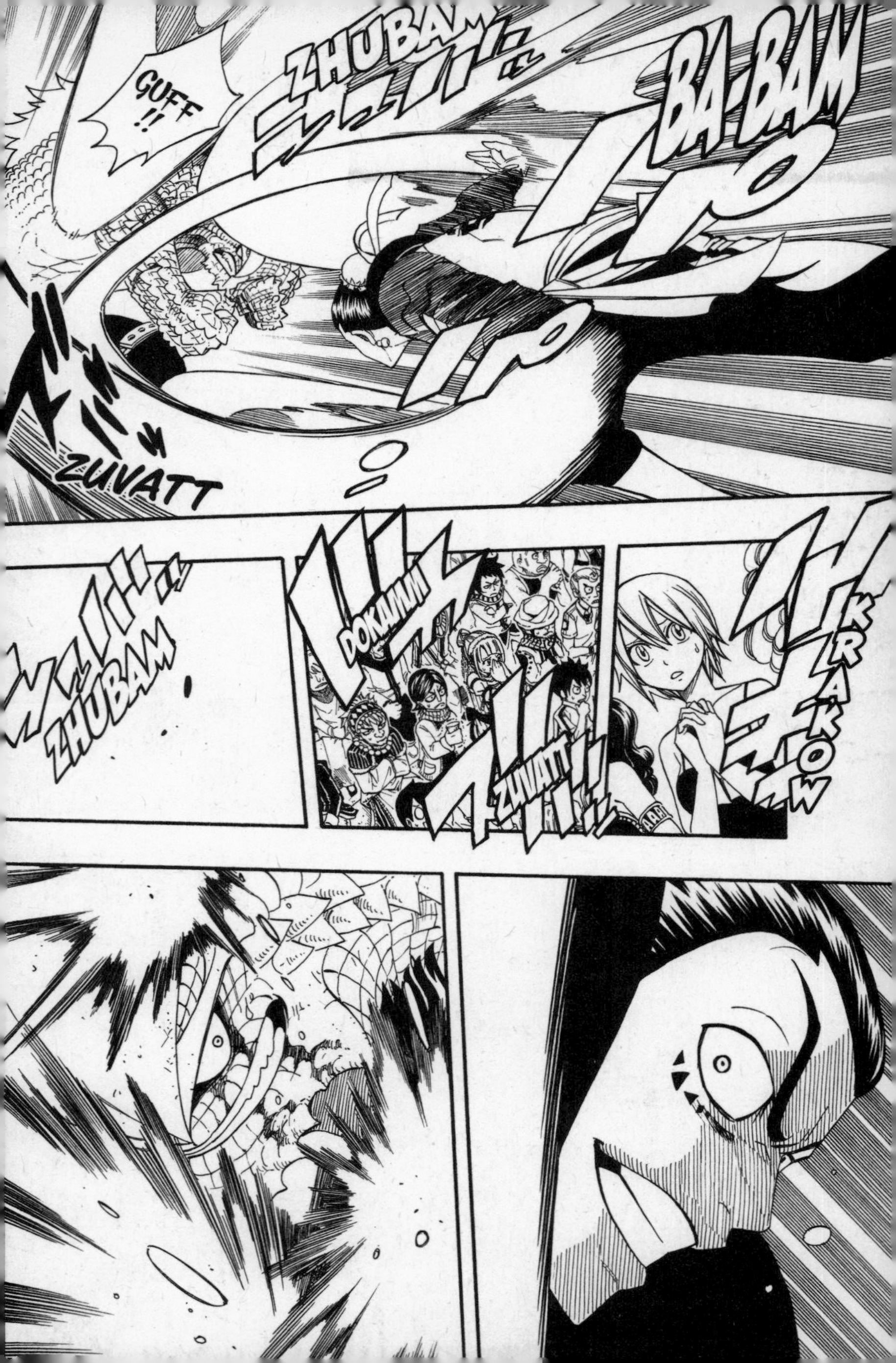
BA-BAM
ZHUBAM
GUFF!!
ZUVATT
KRAKOW
DOKAMM
ZUVATT!!
ZHUBAM

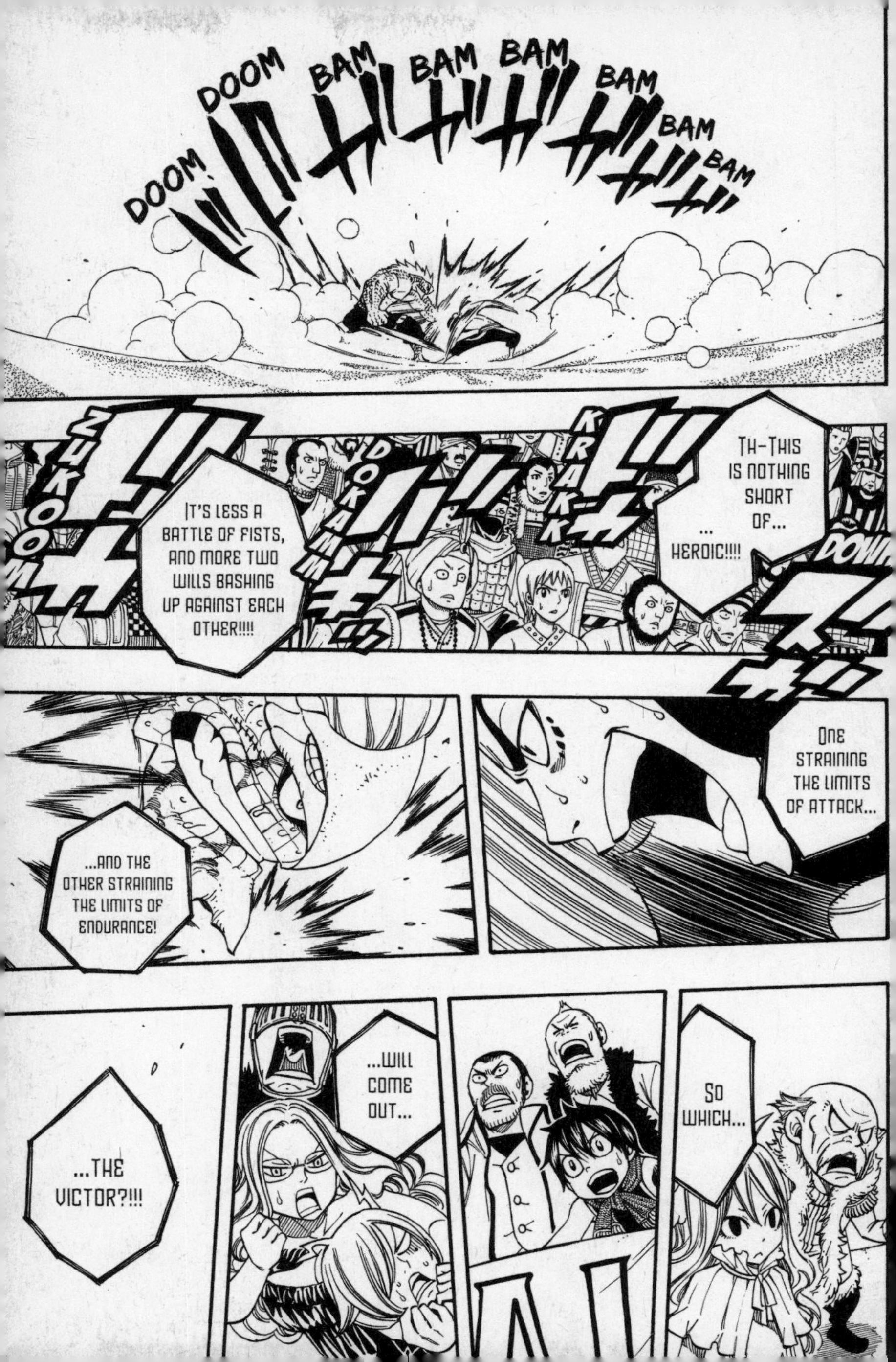
DOOM
DOOM
BAM
BAM
BAM
BAM
BAM
BAM
TH-THIS IS NOTHING SHORT OF...
...HEROIC!!!!
DOWN
KRAK-K
DOKAM
IT'S LESS A BATTLE OF FISTS, AND MORE TWO WILLS BASHING UP AGAINST EACH OTHER!!!!
ZUKOOM
ONE STRAINING THE LIMITS OF ATTACK...
...AND THE OTHER STRAINING THE LIMITS OF ENDURANCE!
SO WHICH...
...WILL COME OUT...
...THE VICTOR?!!!

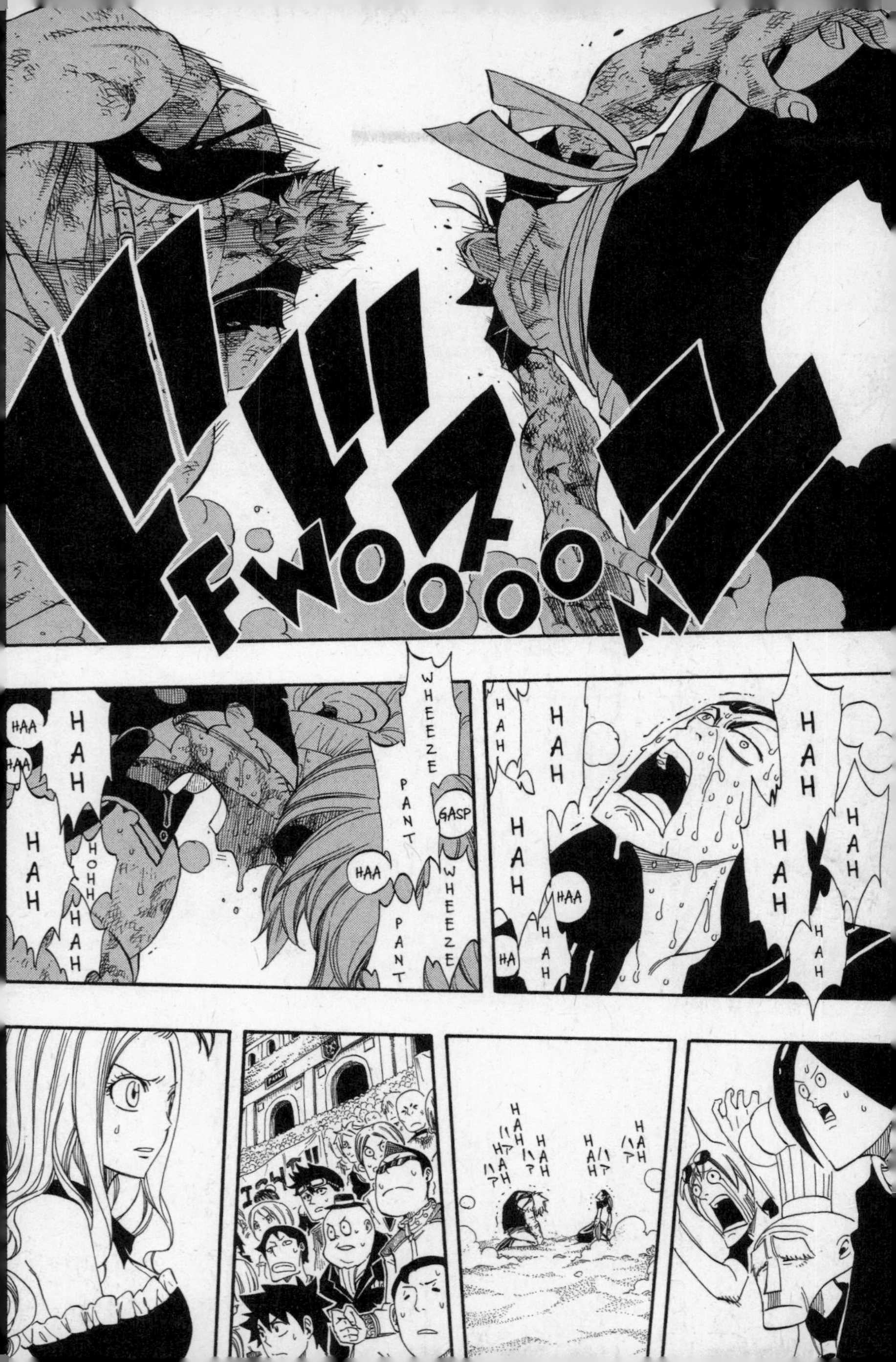
FWOOOOM
HAH HAH HAH
HAH HAH
HAH
HAH HAH
HAH
HAA
HAH
HA
WHEEZE
PANT
GASP
HAA
WHEEZE
PANT
HAH
HAA
HAA
HAH
HOHH
HAH
HAH HAH
HAH HAH
HAH
HAH

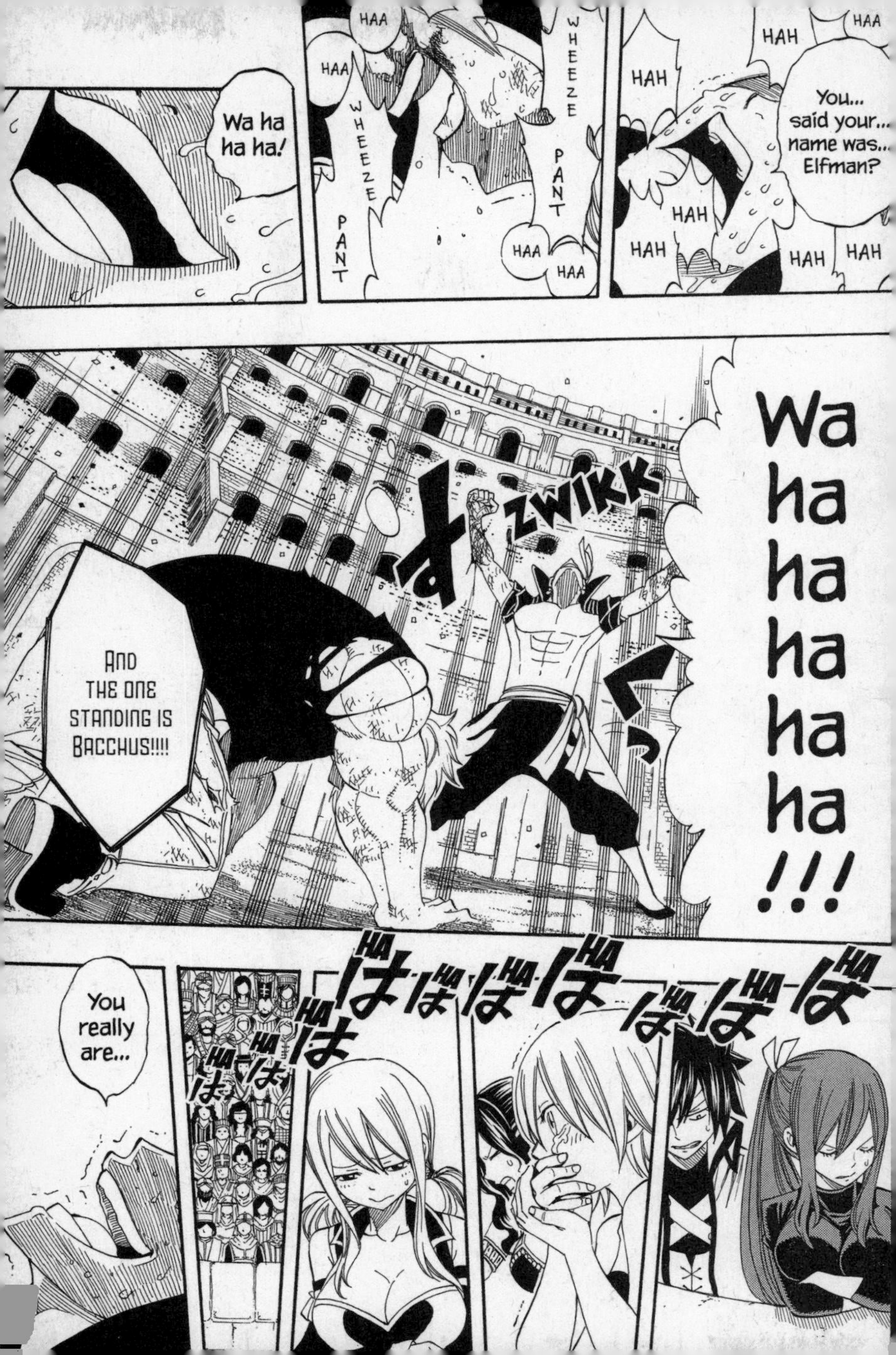
HAA
HAH
You... said your... name was... Elfman?
HAH
HAH
HAH
HAH
HAH
WHEEZE
HAA
HAA
WHEEZE
PANT
WHEEZE
PANT
HAA
HAA
Wa ha ha ha!
Wa ha ha ha ha ha ha!!!
ZWIKK
And the one standing is Bacchus!!!!
HA HA HA HA HA HA HA HA HA HA HA
You really are...

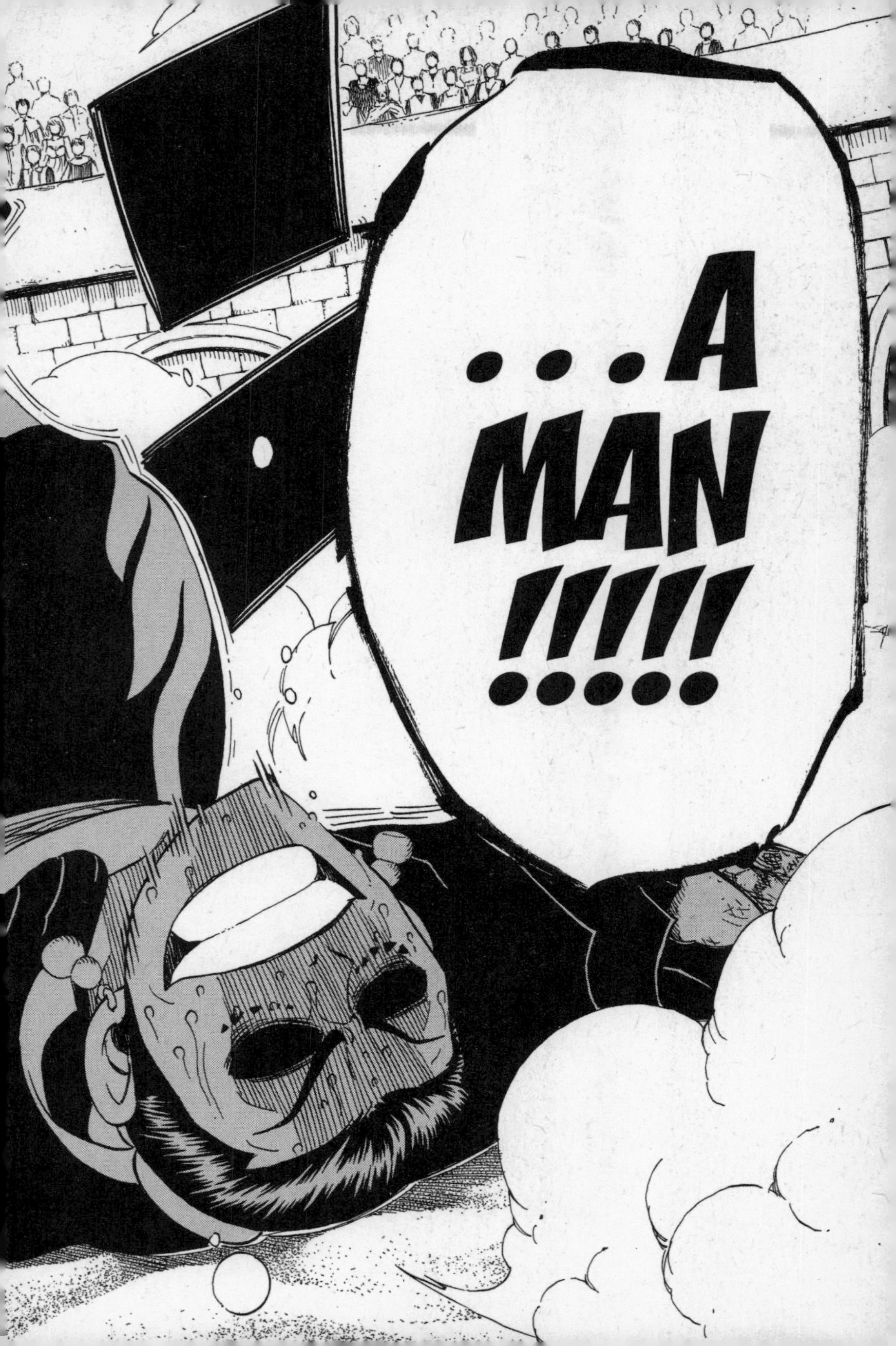
...A MAN!!!!!.....

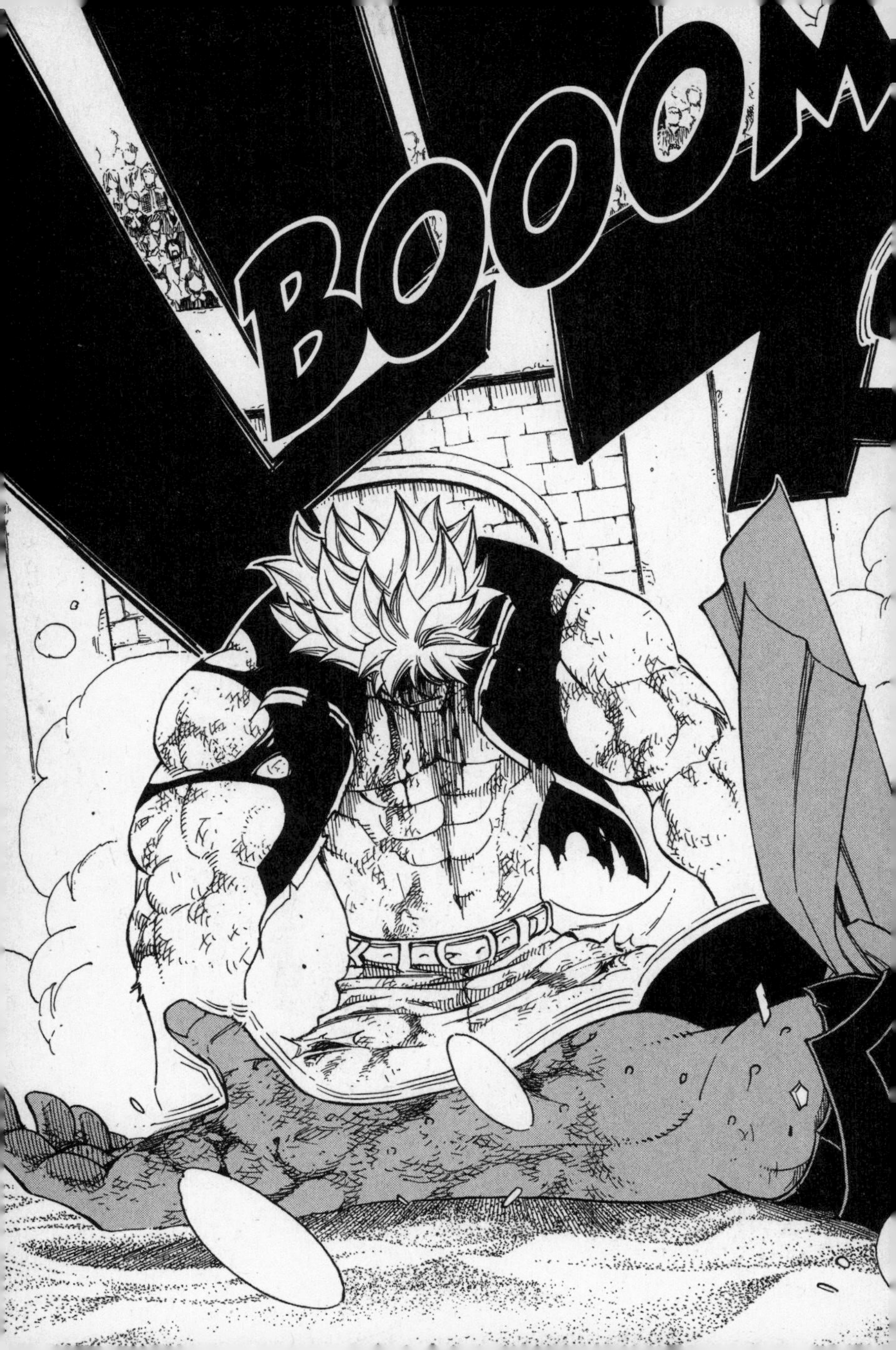
BOOOM

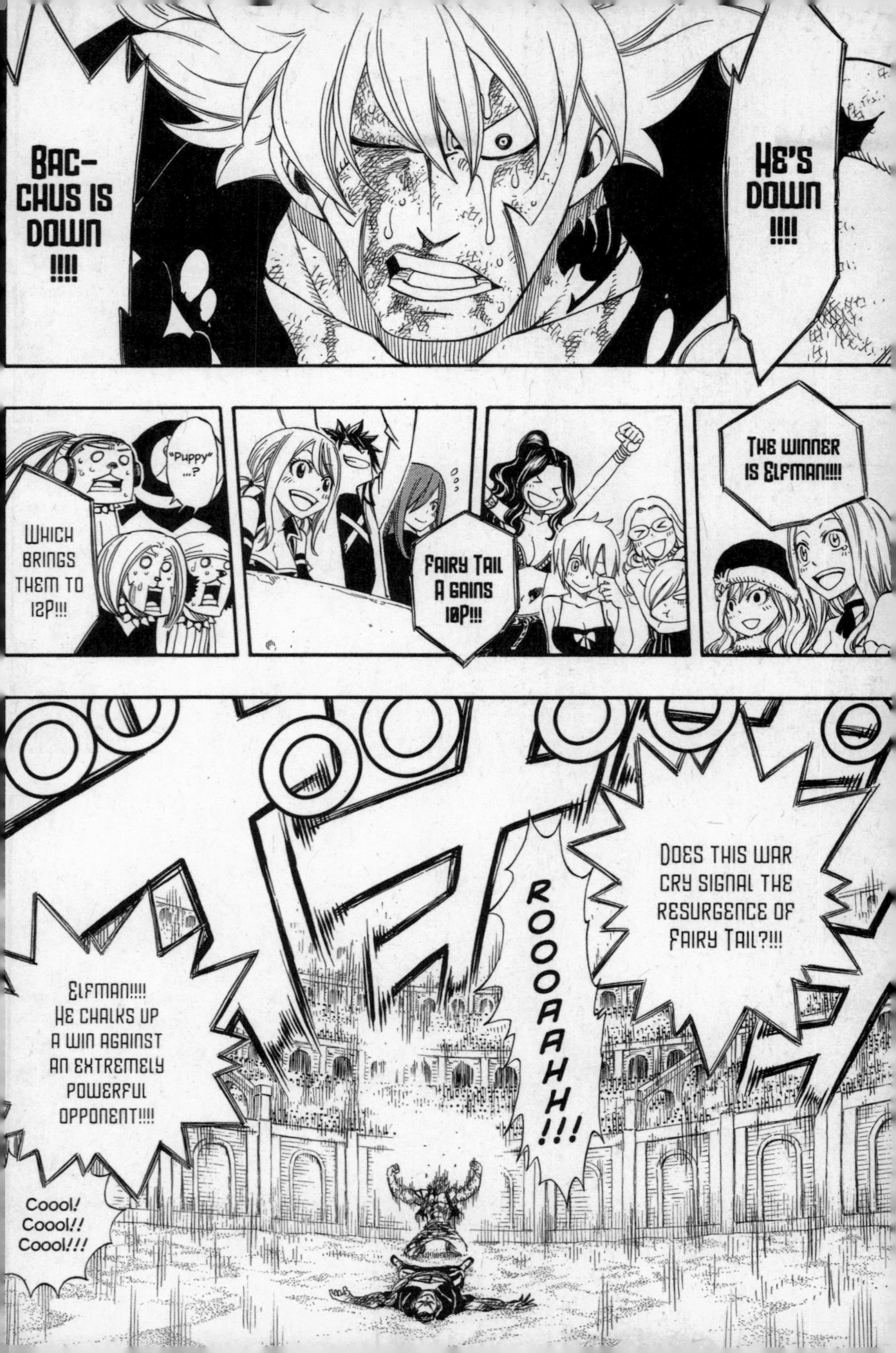
He's down!!!!
Bacchus is down!!!!
The winner is Elfman!!!!
Fairy Tail A gains 10P!!!
"Puppy" ...?
Which brings them to 12P!!!
Does this war cry signal the resurgence of Fairy Tail?!!!
ROOOAAHH!!!
Elfman!!!! He chalks up a win against an extremely powerful opponent!!!!
Coool! Coool!! Coool!!!

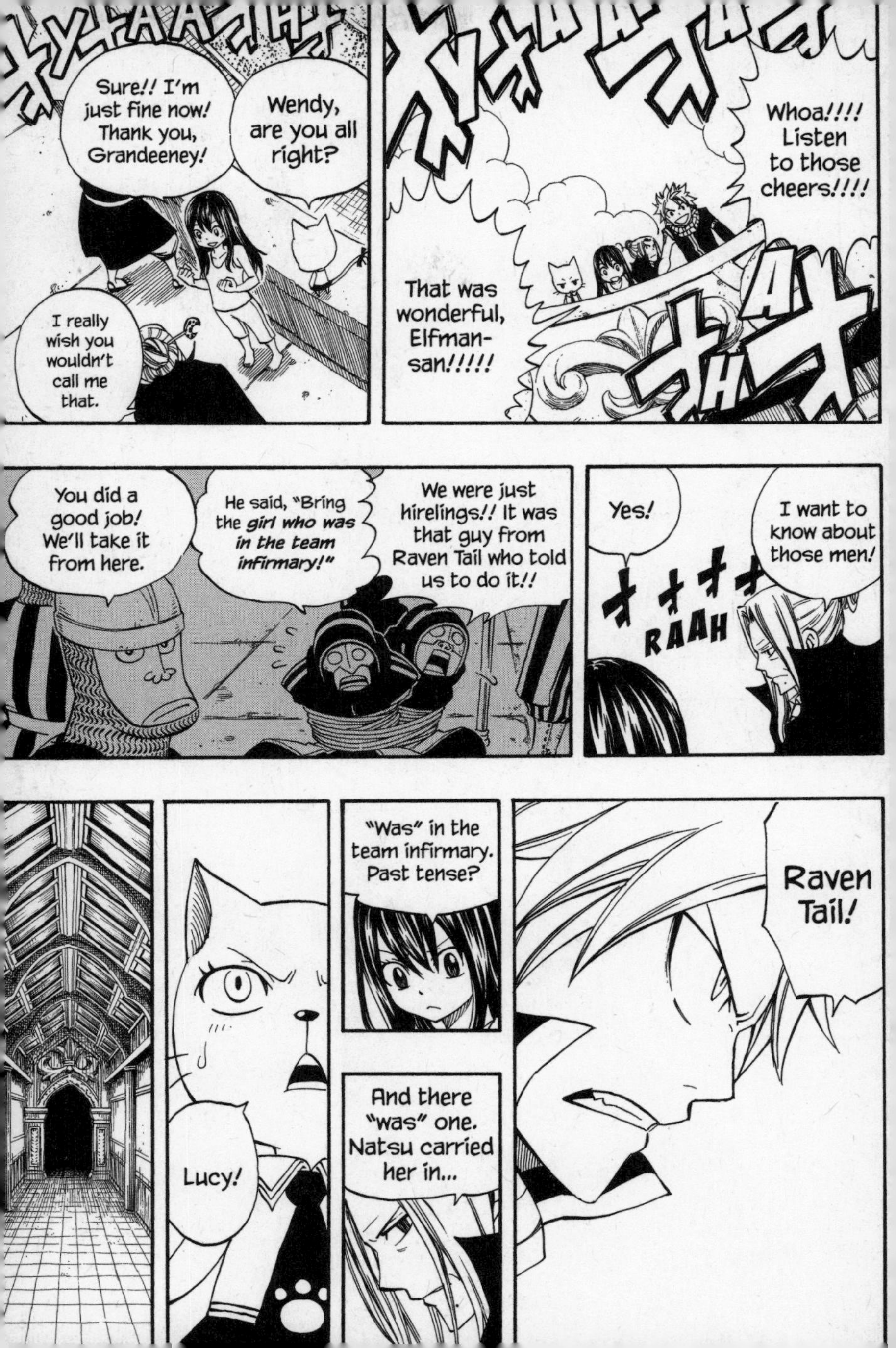
Whoa!!!! Listen to those cheers!!!!
That was wonderful, Elfman-san!!!!!
Wendy, are you all right?
Sure!! I'm just fine now! Thank you, Grandeeney!
I really wish you wouldn't call me that.
I want to know about those men!
Yes!
RAAH
We were just hirelings!! It was that guy from Raven Tail who told us to do it!!
He said, "Bring the *girl who was in the team infirmary!*"
You did a good job! We'll take it from here.
Raven Tail!
"Was" in the team infirmary. Past tense?
And there "was" one. Natsu carried her in...
Lucy!

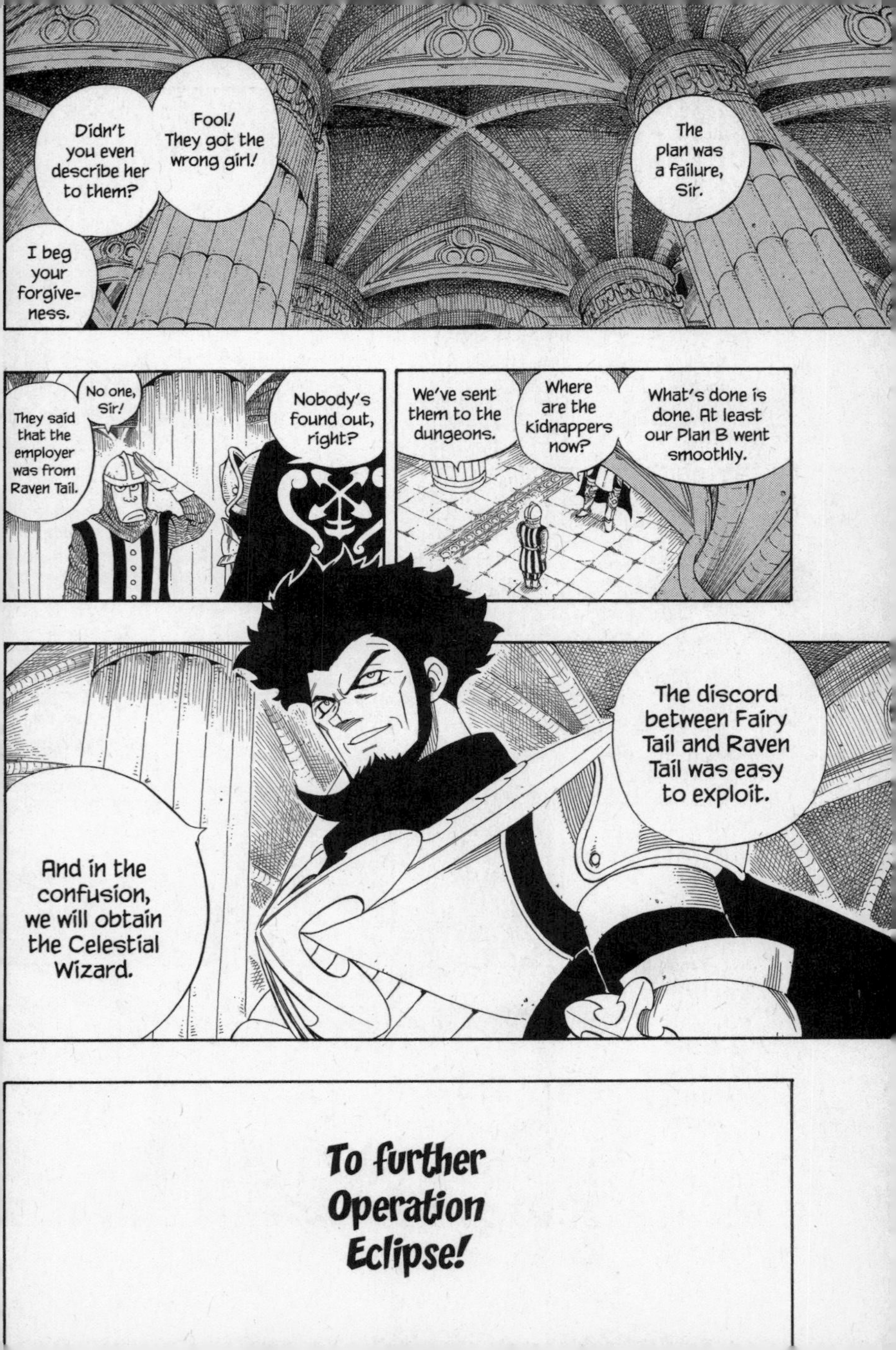
The plan was a failure, Sir.
Fool! They got the wrong girl!
Didn't you even describe her to them?
I beg your forgive-ness.
What's done is done. At least our Plan B went smoothly.
Where are the kidnappers now?
We've sent them to the dungeons.
Nobody's found out, right?
No one, Sir!
They said that the employer was from Raven Tail.
The discord between Fairy Tail and Raven Tail was easy to exploit.
And in the confusion, we will obtain the Celestial Wizard.
To further Operation Eclipse!

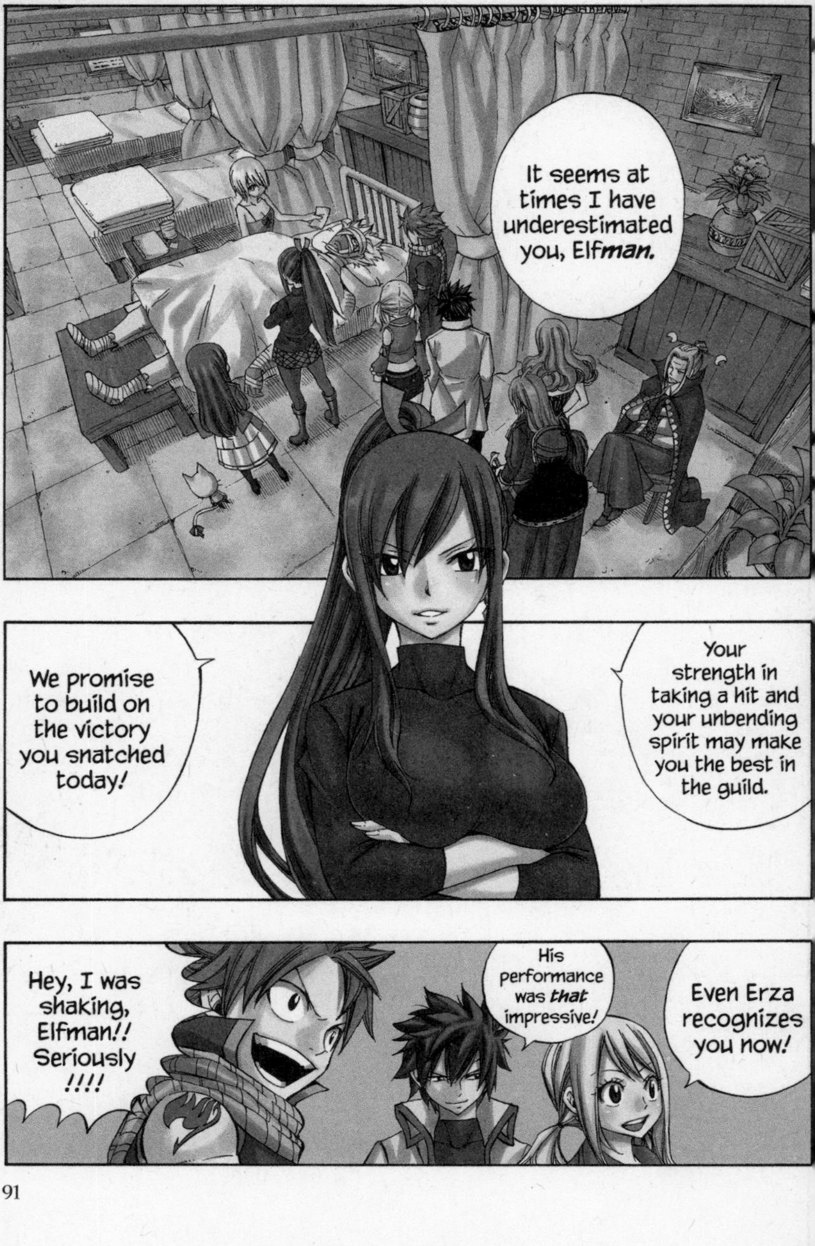
It seems at times I have underestimated you, Elf*man.*
Your strength in taking a hit and your unbending spirit may make you the best in the guild.
We promise to build on the victory you snatched today!
Even Erza recognizes you now!
His performance was *that* impressive!
Hey, I was shaking, Elfman!! Seriously!!!!

Chapter 279: A Door Sunken into Darkness

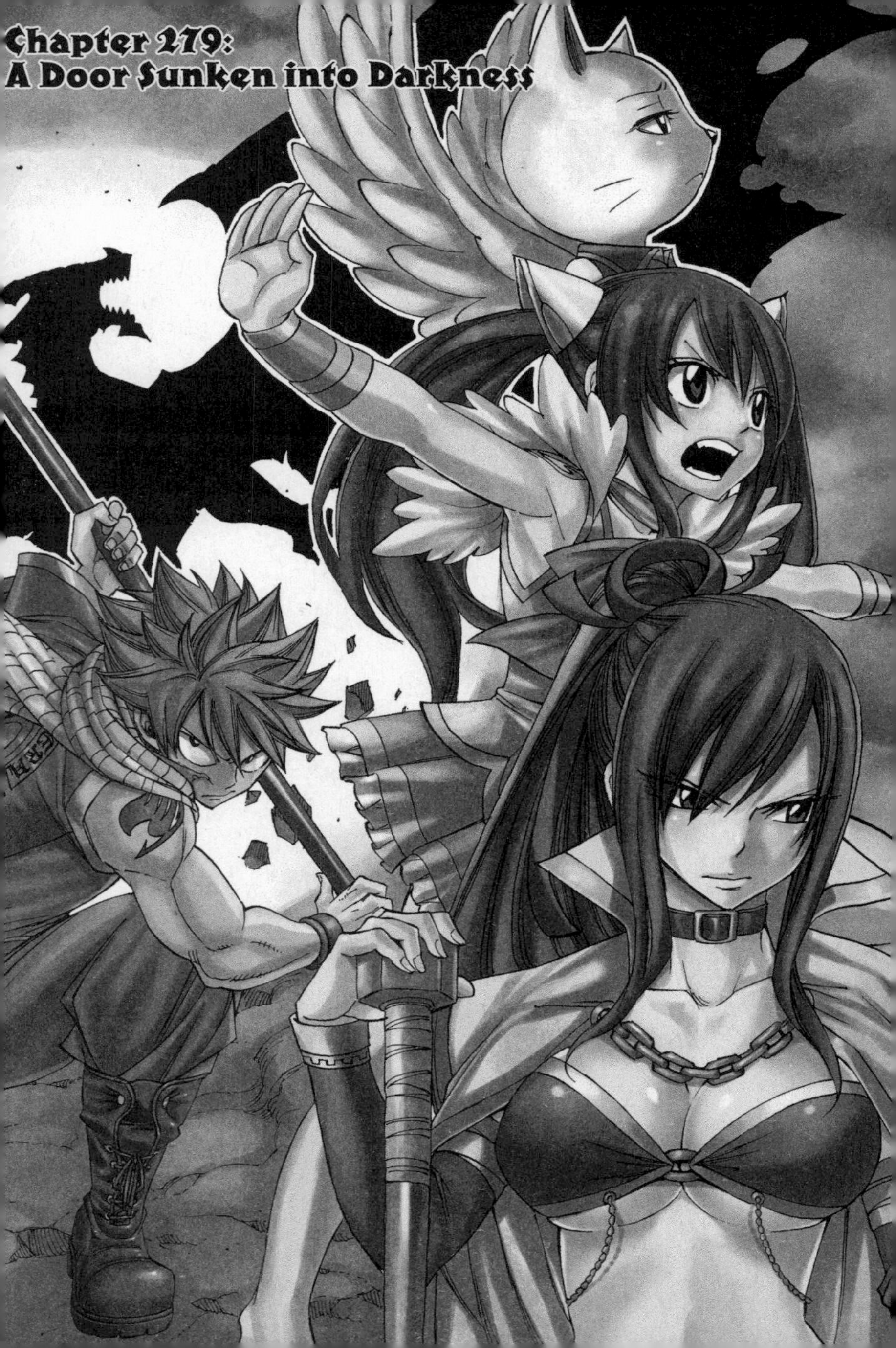

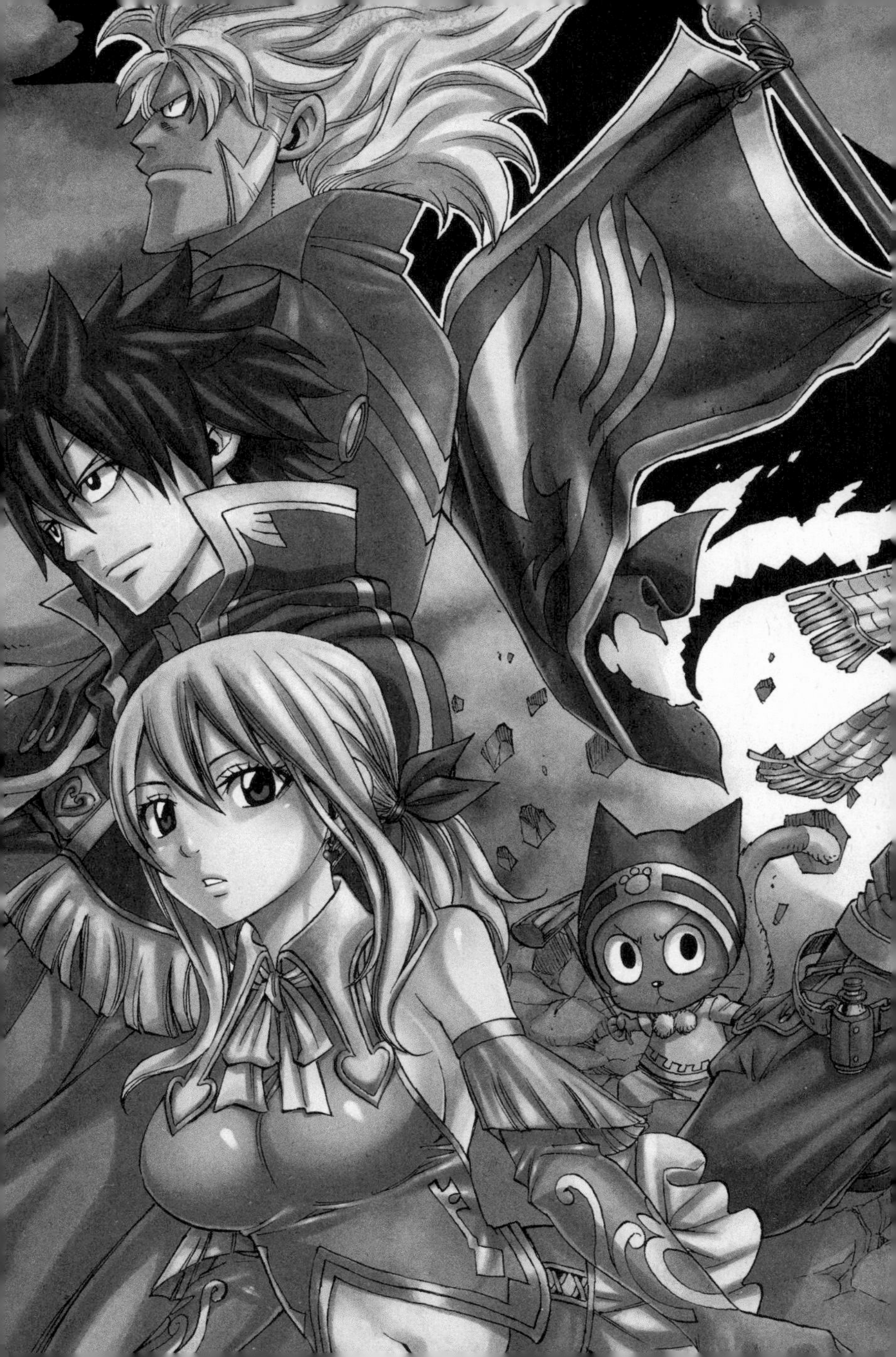

FAIRY TAIL

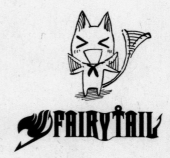

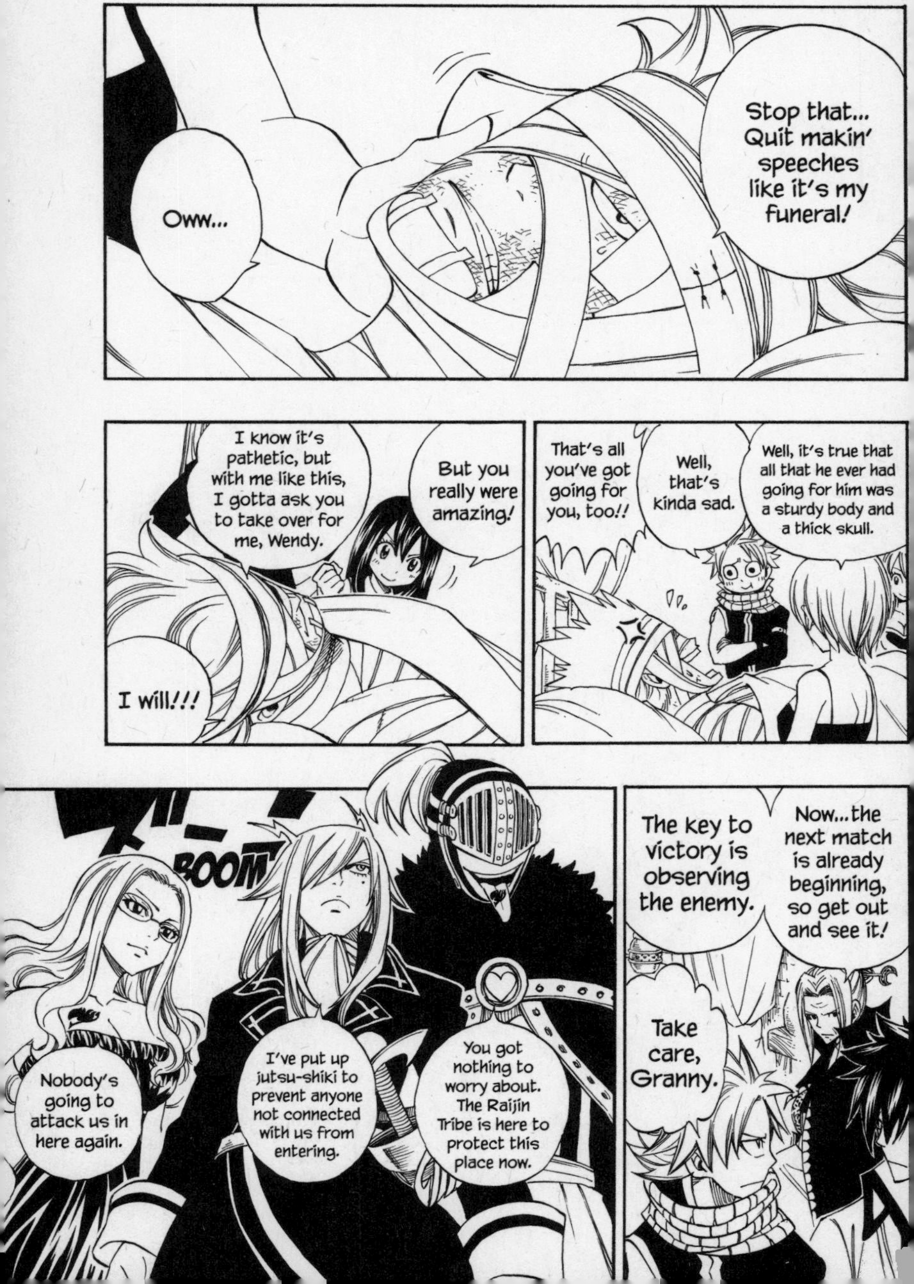
Stop that... Quit makin' speeches like it's my funeral!
Oww...
Well, it's true that all that he ever had going for him was a sturdy body and a thick skull.
Well, that's kinda sad.
That's all you've got going for you, too!!
But you really were amazing!
I know it's pathetic, but with me like this, I gotta ask you to take over for me, Wendy.
I will!!!
Now...the next match is already beginning, so get out and see it!
The key to victory is observing the enemy.
Take care, Granny.
BOOM
You got nothing to worry about. The Raijin Tribe is here to protect this place now.
I've put up jutsu-shiki to prevent anyone not connected with us from entering.
Nobody's going to attack us in here again.

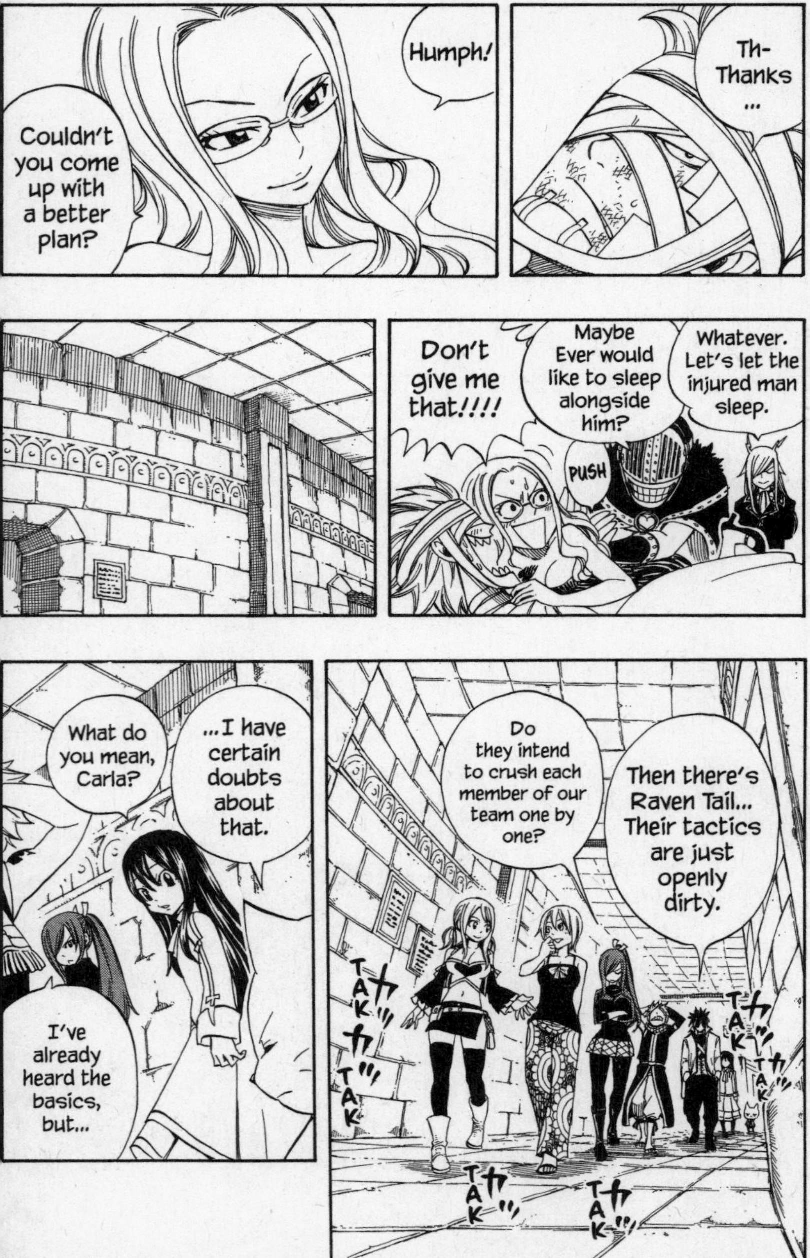
Th-
Thanks
...
Humph!
Couldn't you come up with a better plan?
Whatever. Let's let the injured man sleep.
Maybe Ever would like to sleep alongside him?
Don't give me that!!!!
PUSH
Then there's Raven Tail... Their tactics are just openly dirty.
Do they intend to crush each member of our team one by one?
TAK TAK
TAK TAK
TAK
TAK
...I have certain doubts about that.
What do you mean, Carla?
I've already heard the basics, but...

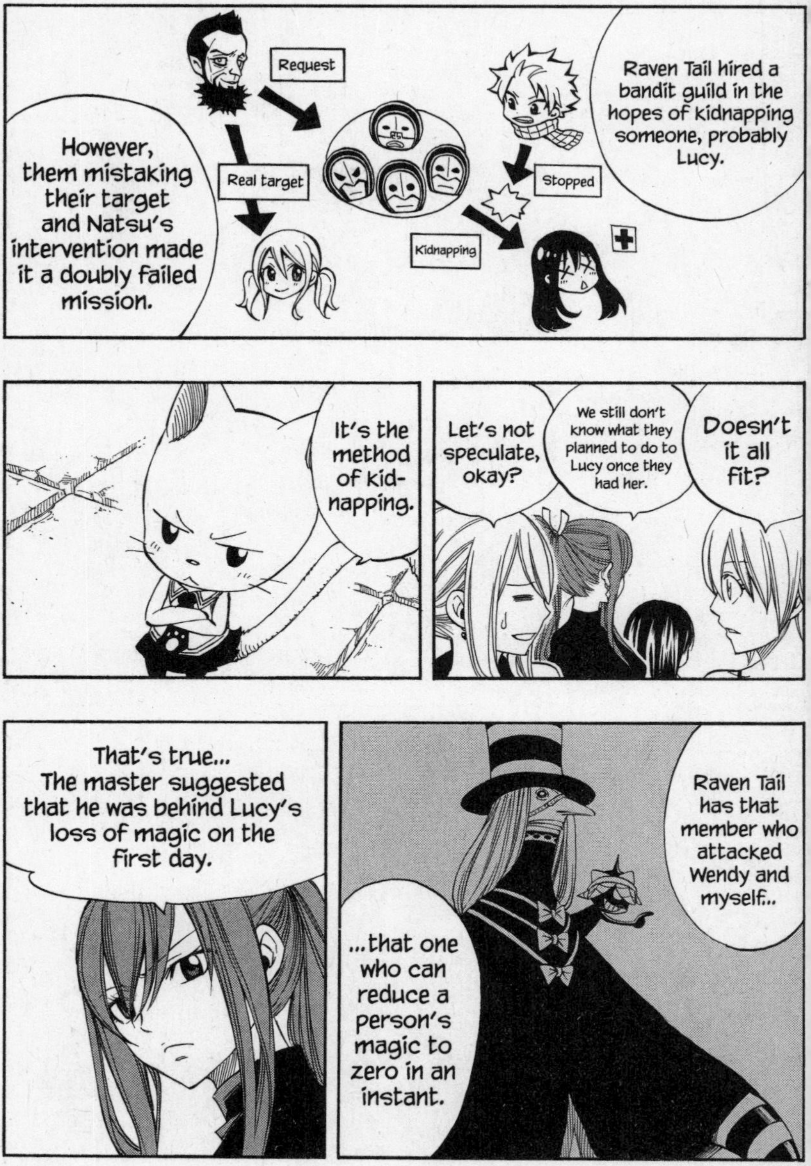

Raven Tail hired a bandit guild in the hopes of kidnapping someone, probably Lucy.
Request
Stopped
However, them mistaking their target and Natsu's intervention made it a doubly failed mission.
Real target
Kidnapping
Doesn't it all fit?
We still don't know what they planned to do to Lucy once they had her.
Let's not speculate, okay?
It's the method of kid-napping.
Raven Tail has that member who attacked Wendy and myself...
...that one who can reduce a person's magic to zero in an instant.
That's true... The master suggested that he was behind Lucy's loss of magic on the first day.

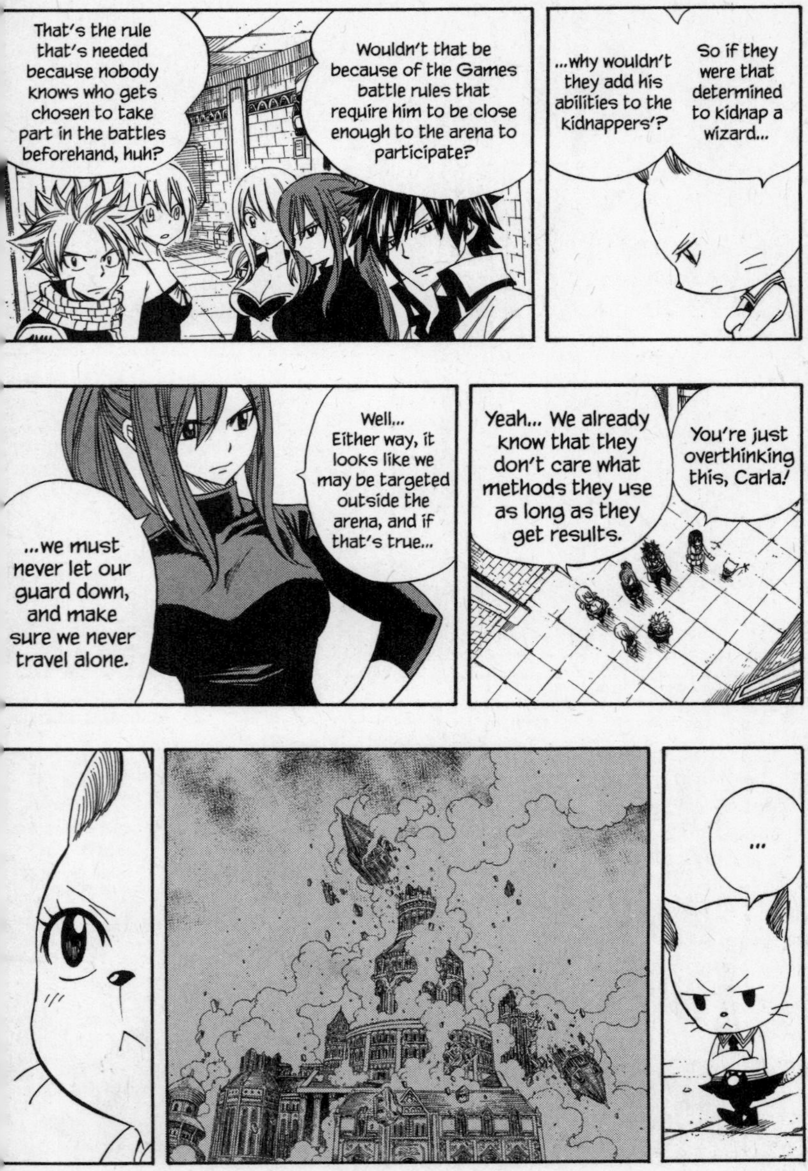
So if they were that determined to kidnap a wizard...
...why wouldn't they add his abilities to the kidnappers'?
Wouldn't that be because of the Games battle rules that require him to be close enough to the arena to participate?
That's the rule that's needed because nobody knows who gets chosen to take part in the battles beforehand, huh?
You're just overthinking this, Carla!
Yeah... We already know that they don't care what methods they use as long as they get results.
Well... Either way, it looks like we may be targeted outside the arena, and if that's true...
...we must never let our guard down, and make sure we never travel alone.
...

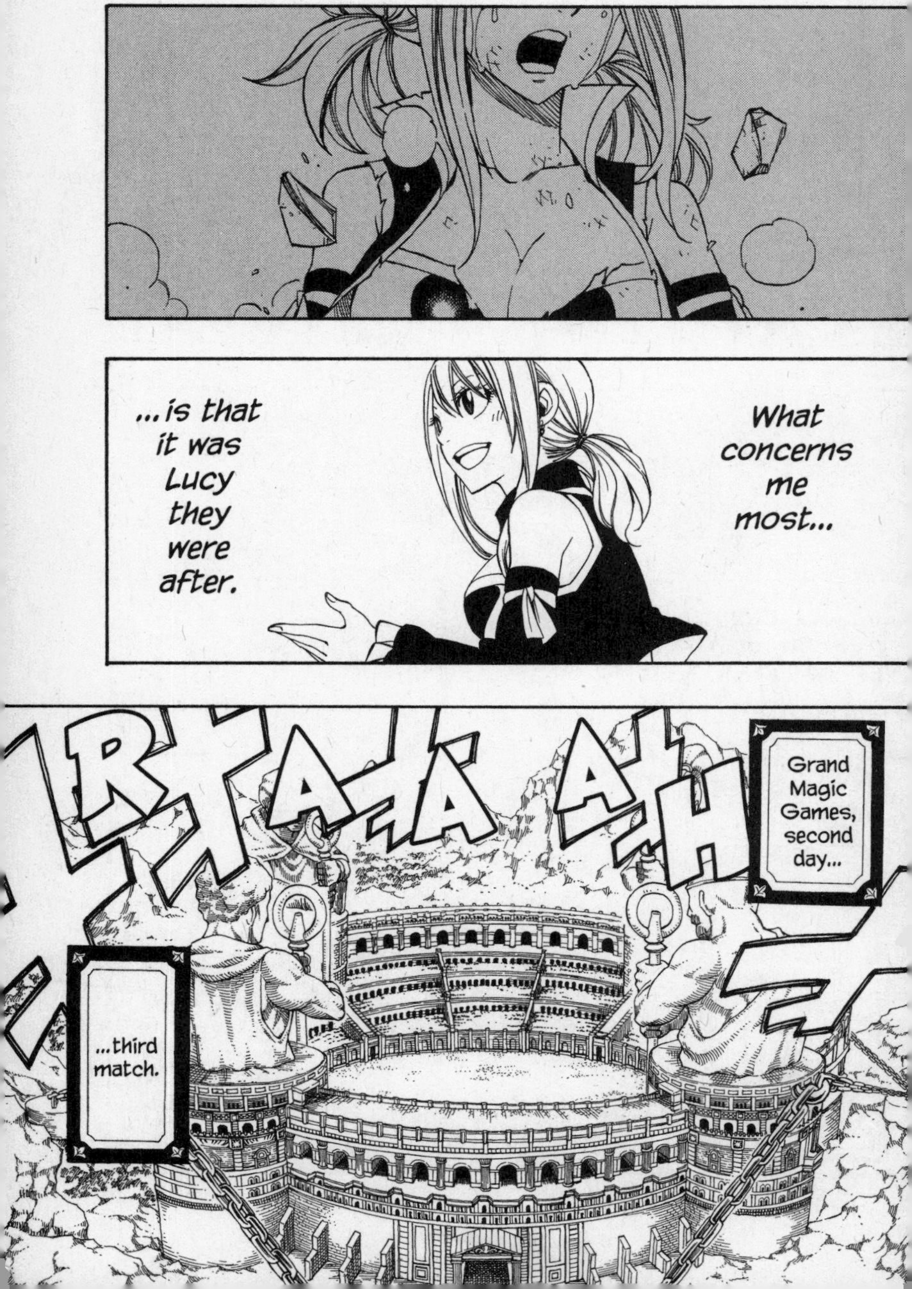
What concerns me most...
...is that it was Lucy they were after.
RAAAH
Grand Magic Games, second day...
...third match.

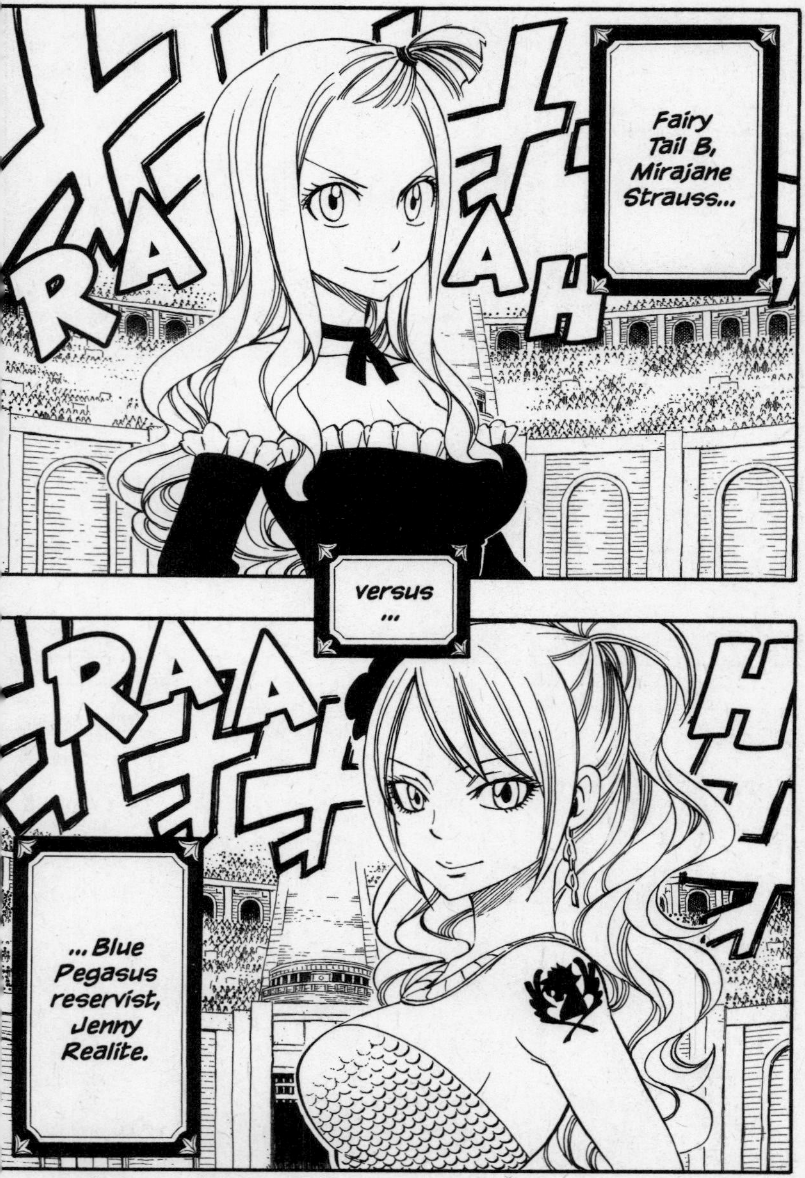
Fairy Tail B, Mirajane Strauss...
versus ...
... Blue Pegasus reservist, Jenny Realite.

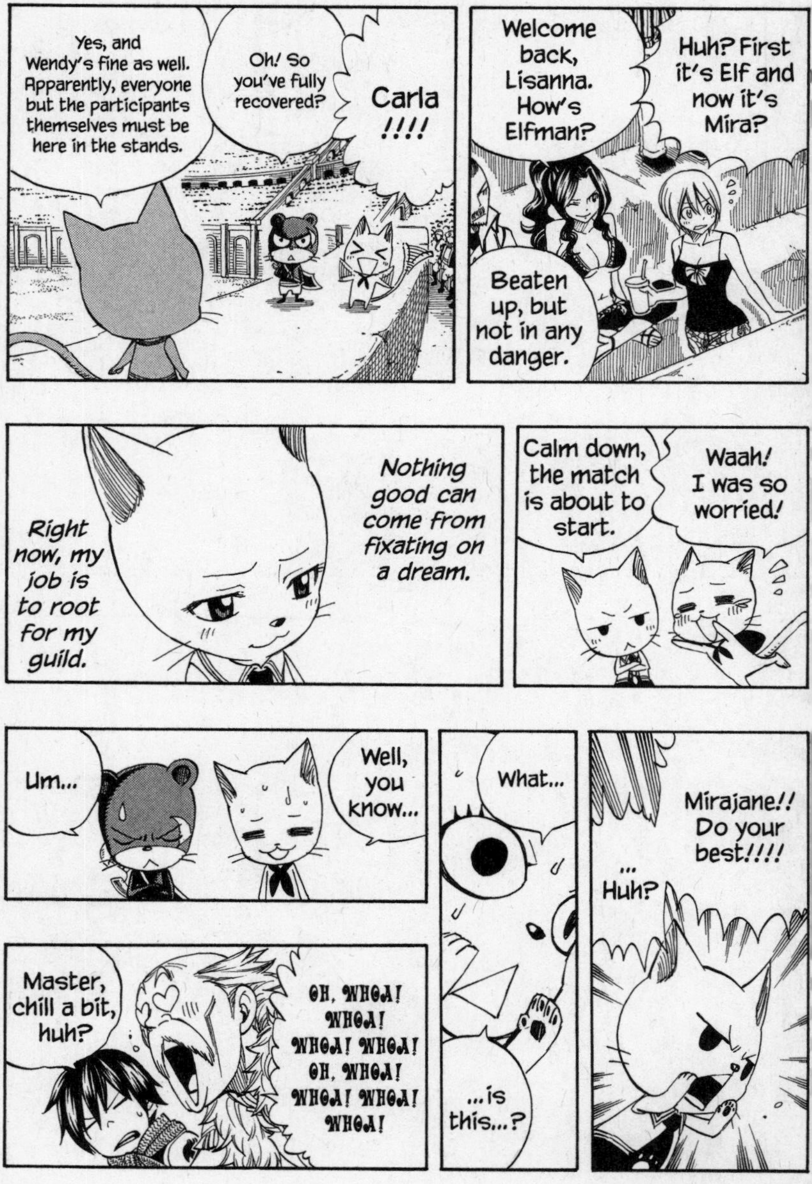

Huh? First it's Elf and now it's Mira?
Welcome back, Lisanna. How's Elfman?
Beaten up, but not in any danger.
Carla!!!!
Oh! So you've fully recovered?
Yes, and Wendy's fine as well. Apparently, everyone but the participants themselves must be here in the stands.
Waah! I was so worried!
Calm down, the match is about to start.
Nothing good can come from fixating on a dream.
Right now, my job is to root for my guild.
Mirajane!! Do your best!!!!
... Huh?
What...
...is this...?
Well, you know...
Um...
OH, WHOA! WHOA! WHOA! WHOA! OH, WHOA! WHOA! WHOA! WHOA!
Master, chill a bit, huh?

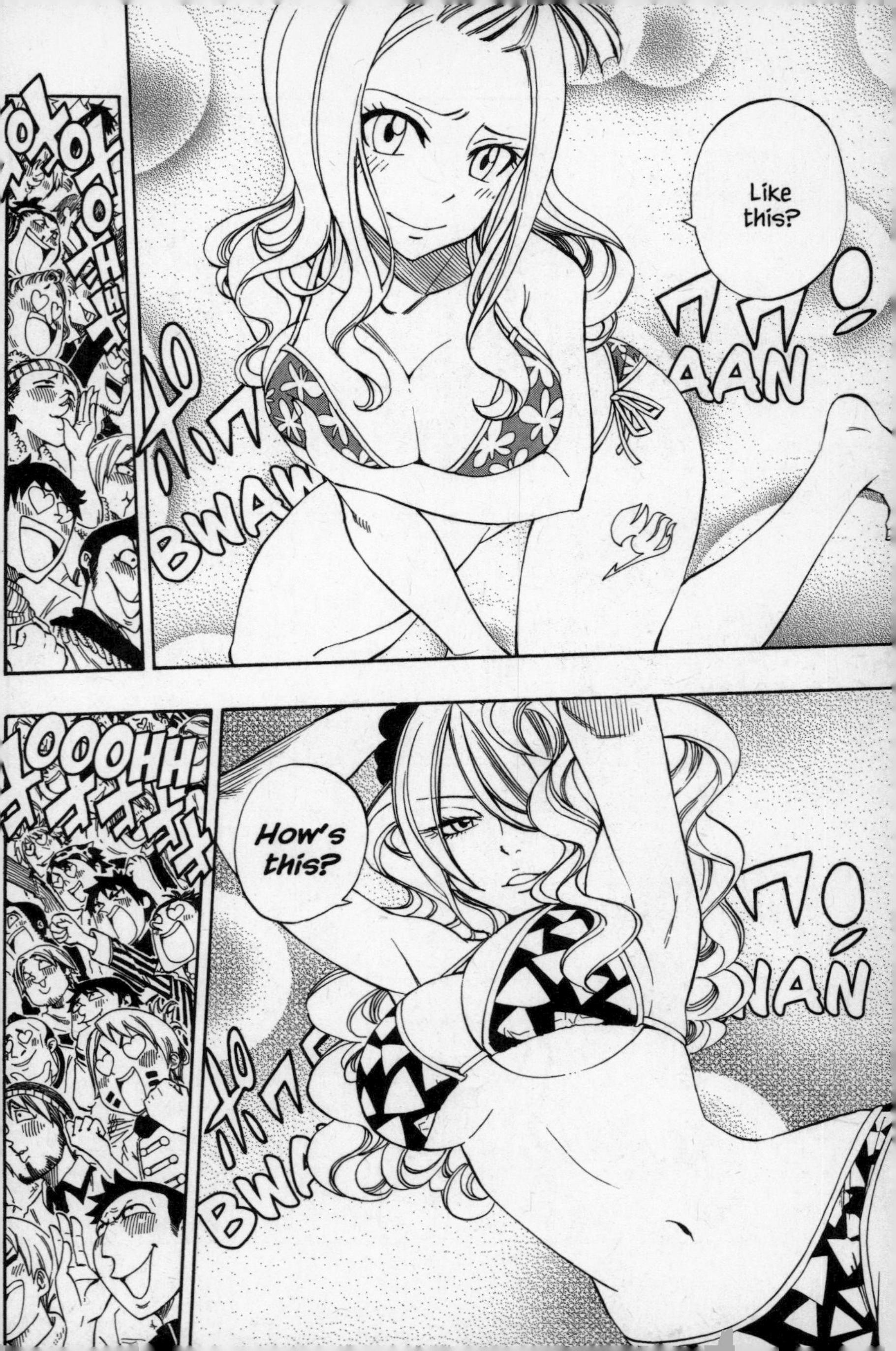
Like this?
AAN
BWAW
How's this?
IAN
BWA
OOOHH

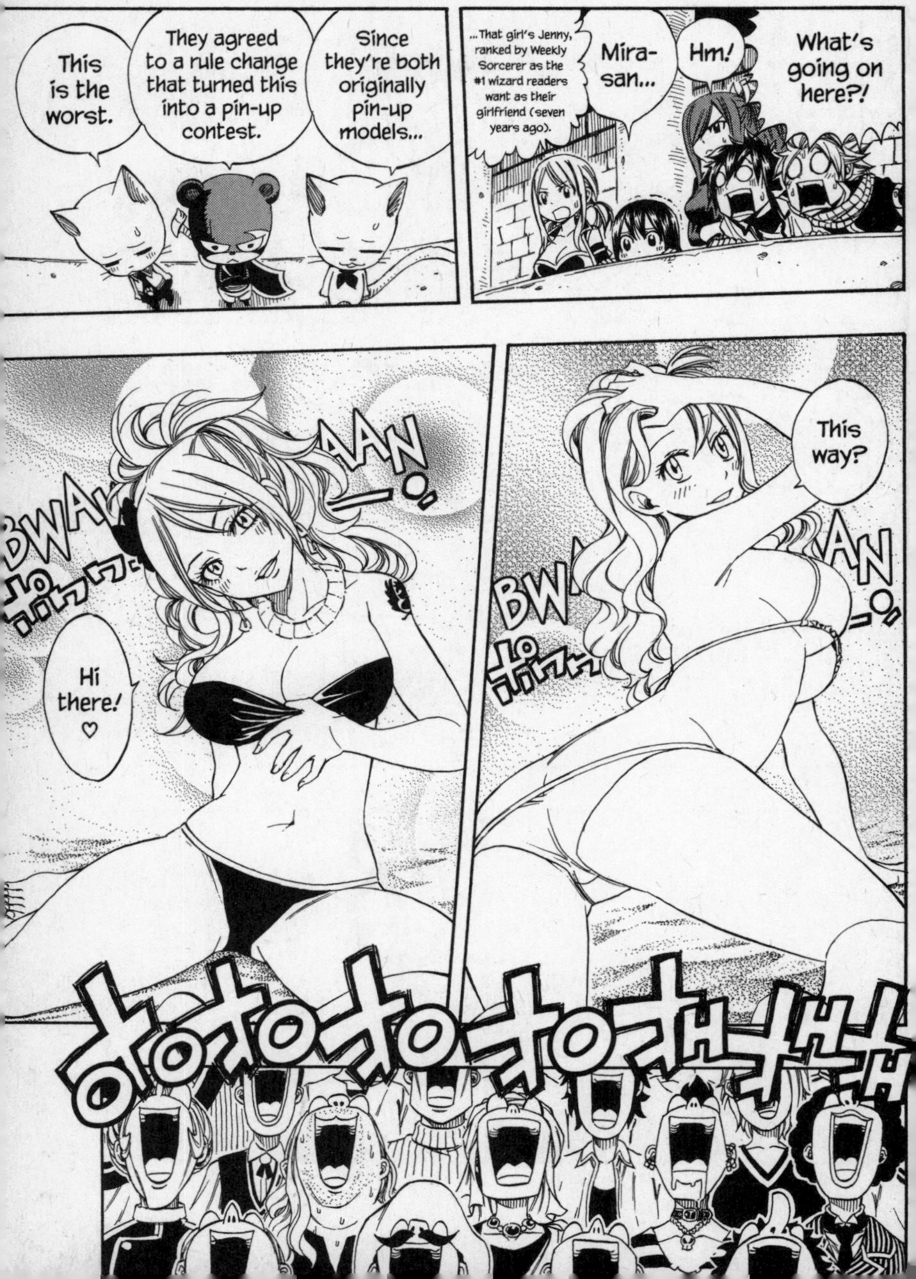
What's going on here?!
Hm!
Mira-san...
...That girl's Jenny, ranked by Weekly Sorcerer as the #1 wizard readers want as their girlfriend (seven years ago).
Since they're both originally pin-up models...
They agreed to a rule change that turned this into a pin-up contest.
This is the worst.
This way?
Hi there! ♡

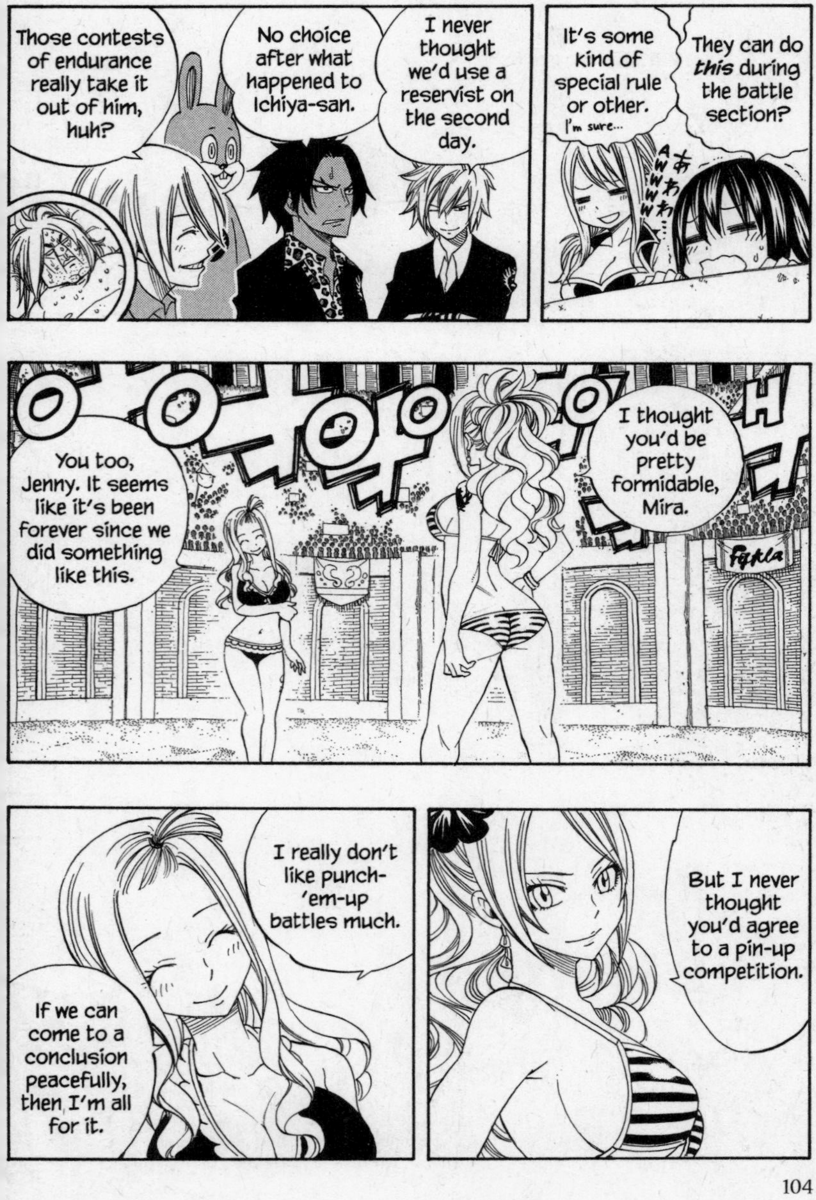
They can do *this* during the battle section?
It's some kind of special rule or other.
I'm sure...
AWWWW
I never thought we'd use a reservist on the second day.
No choice after what happened to Ichiya-san.
Those contests of endurance really take it out of him, huh?
I thought you'd be pretty formidable, Mira.
You too, Jenny. It seems like it's been forever since we did something like this.
But I never thought you'd agree to a pin-up competition.
I really don't like punch-'em-up battles much.
If we can come to a conclusion peacefully, then I'm all for it.

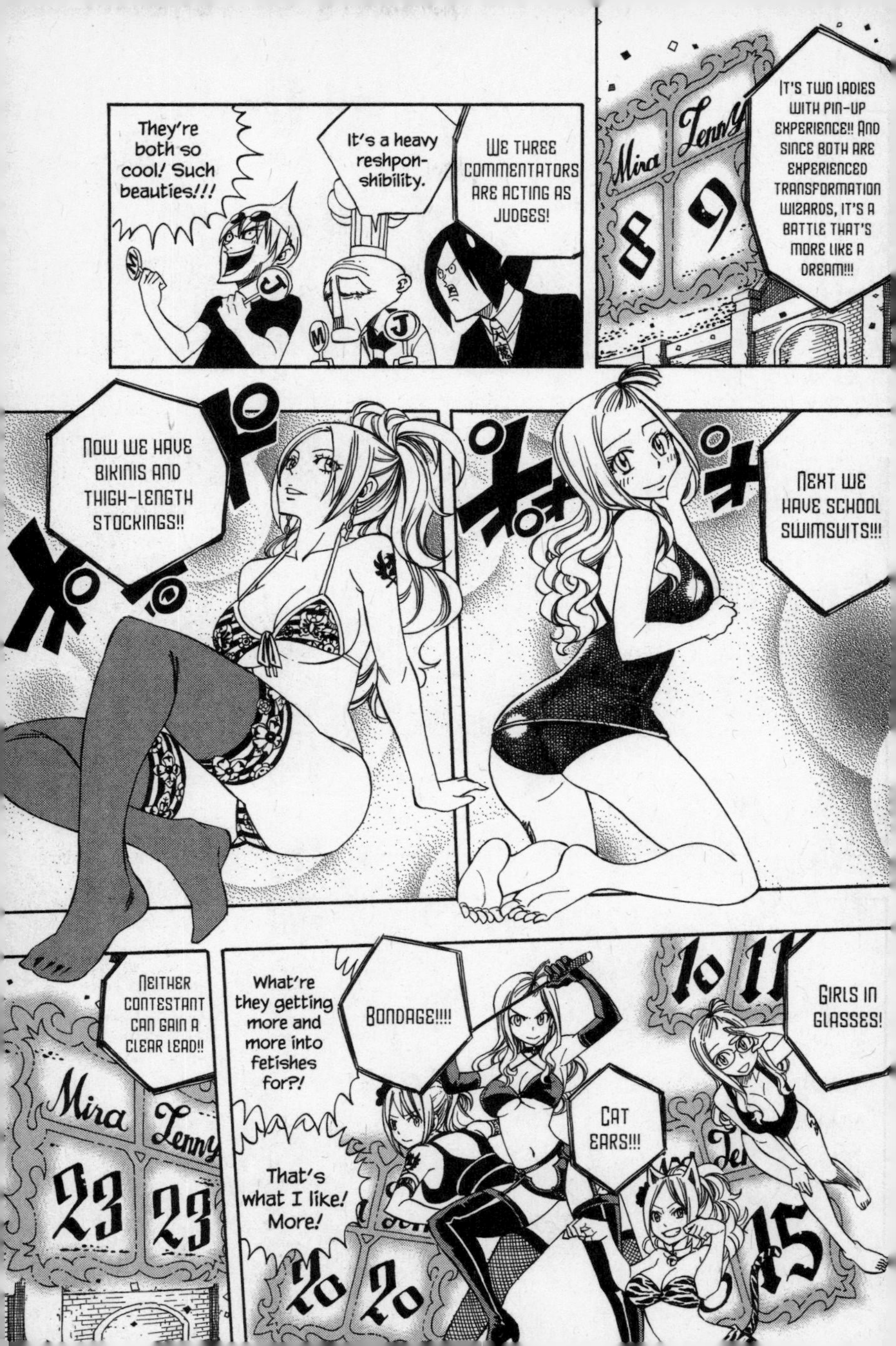
It's two ladies with pin-up experience!! And since both are experienced transformation wizards, it's a battle that's more like a dream!!!
Mira
Jenny
8
9
We three commentators are acting as judges!
It's a heavy reshpon-shibility.
They're both so cool! Such beauties!!!
Next we have school swimsuits!!!
Now we have bikinis and thigh-length stockings!!
Girls in glasses!
10
11
Cat ears!!!
15
Bondage!!!!
What're they getting more and more into fetishes for?!
That's what I like! More!
20
20
Neither contestant can gain a clear lead!!
Mira
Jenny
23
23

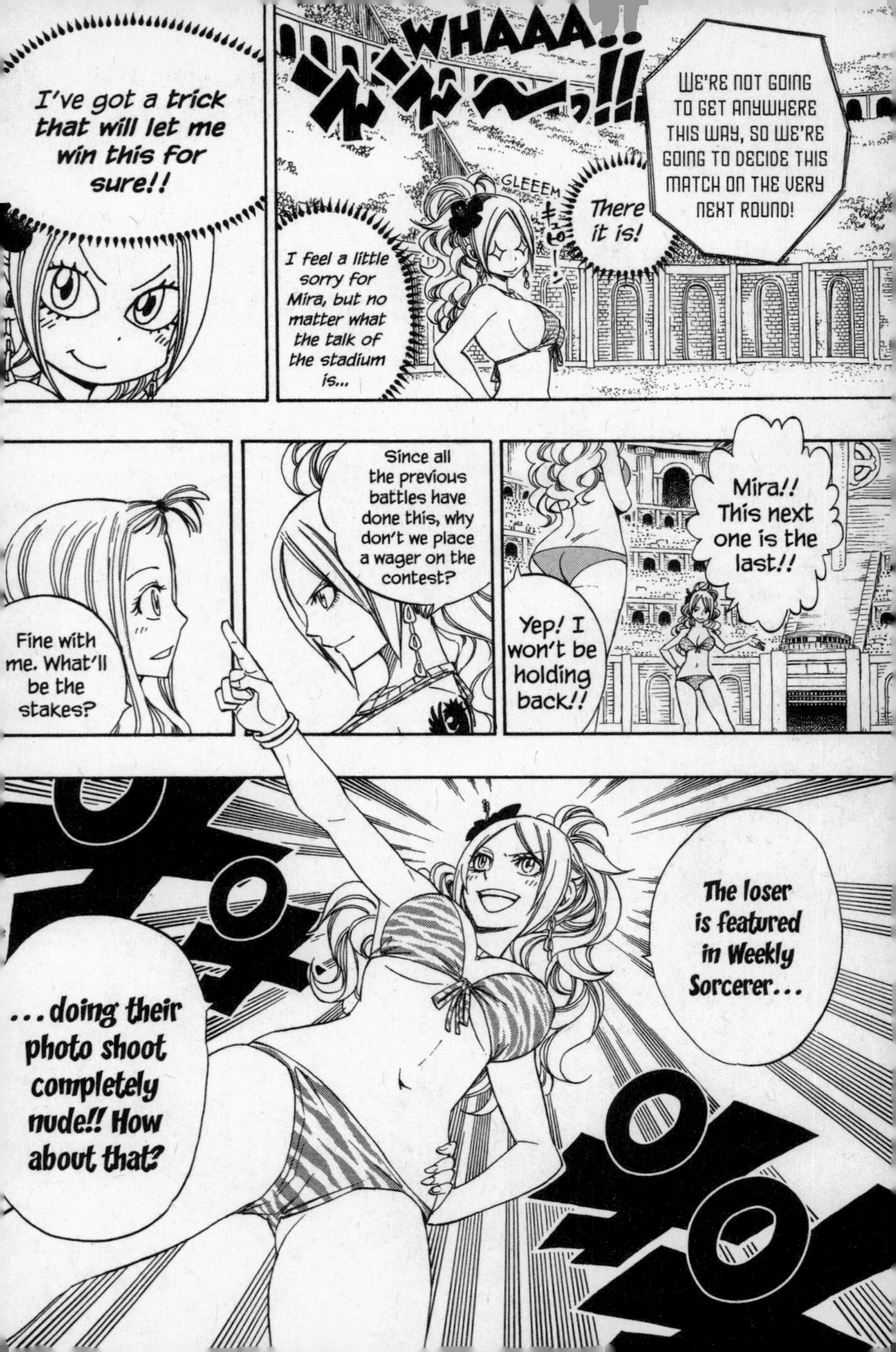
WHAAA..!!
WE'RE NOT GOING TO GET ANYWHERE THIS WAY, SO WE'RE GOING TO DECIDE THIS MATCH ON THE VERY NEXT ROUND!
There it is!
GLEEEM
I feel a little sorry for Mira, but no matter what the talk of the stadium is...
I've got a trick that will let me win this for sure!!
Mira!! This next one is the last!!
Yep! I won't be holding back!!
Since all the previous battles have done this, why don't we place a wager on the contest?
Fine with me. What'll be the stakes?
The loser is featured in Weekly Sorcerer...
...doing their photo shoot completely nude!! How about that?

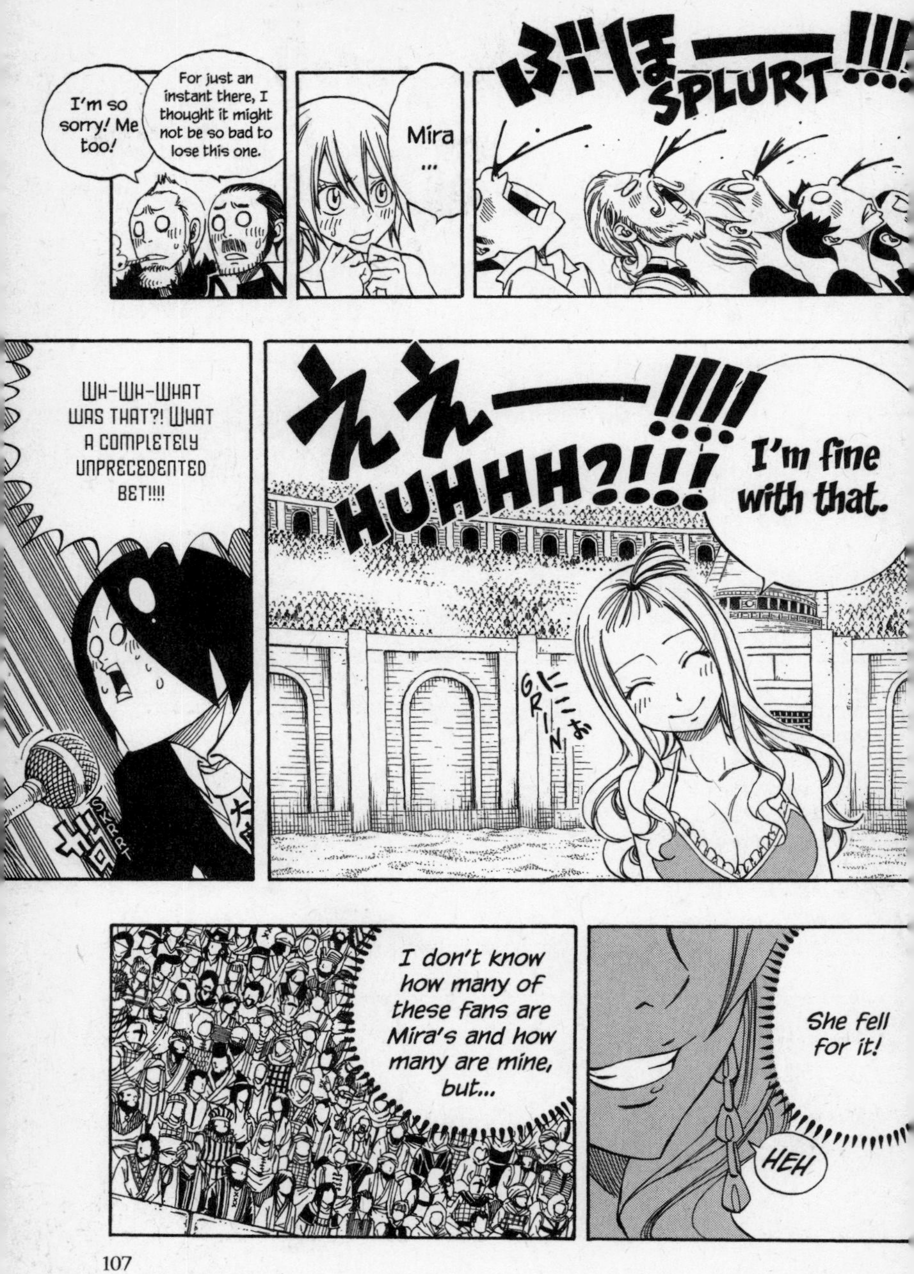

ぶほー!!!!
SPLURT!!!!
Mira ...
For just an instant there, I thought it might not be so bad to lose this one.
I'm so sorry! Me too!
ええー!!!!
HUHHH?!!!!
I'm fine with that.
GRIN
にこぉ
Wh-Wh-What was that?! What a completely unprecedented bet!!!!
SKRRT
She fell for it!
HEH
I don't know how many of these fans are Mira's and how many are mine, but...

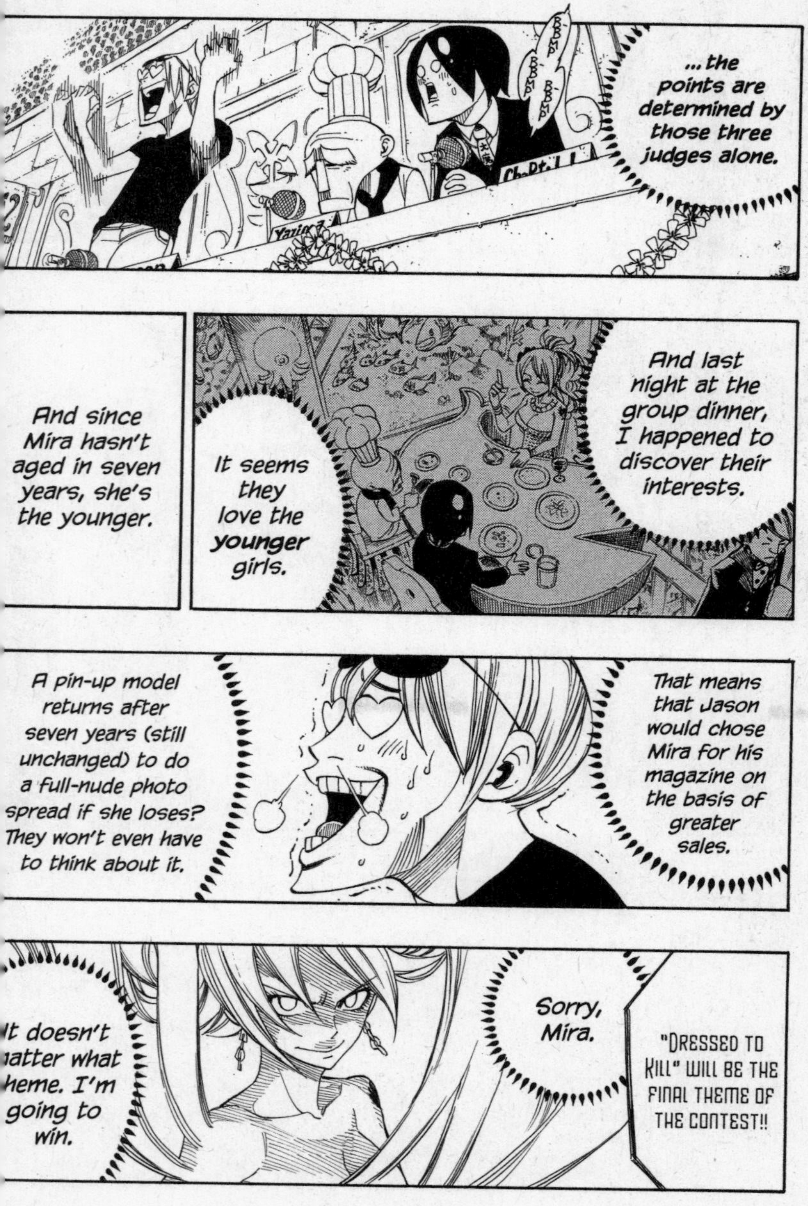
BBMP-BBMP-BBMP
...the points are determined by those three judges alone.
And last night at the group dinner, I happened to discover their interests.
It seems they love the **younger** girls.
And since Mira hasn't aged in seven years, she's the younger.
That means that Jason would chose Mira for his magazine on the basis of greater sales.
A pin-up model returns after seven years (still unchanged) to do a full-nude photo spread if she loses? They won't even have to think about it.
"DRESSED TO KILL" WILL BE THE FINAL THEME OF THE CONTEST!!
Sorry, Mira.
It doesn't atter what heme. I'm going to win.

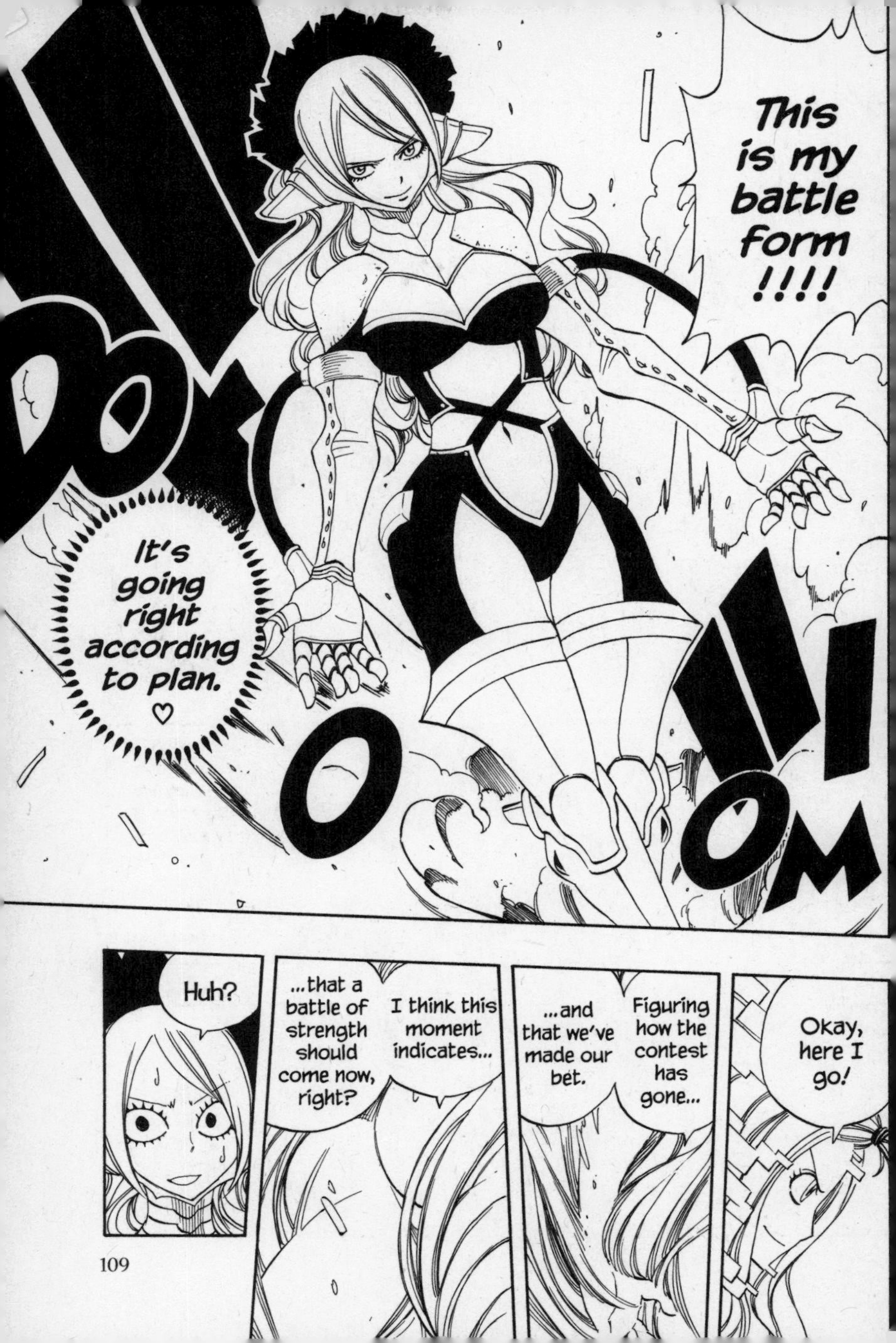
This is my battle form!!!!
DOOOM
It's going right according to plan. ♡
Okay, here I go!
Figuring how the contest has gone...
...and that we've made our bet.
I think this moment indicates...
...that a battle of strength should come now, right?
Huh?

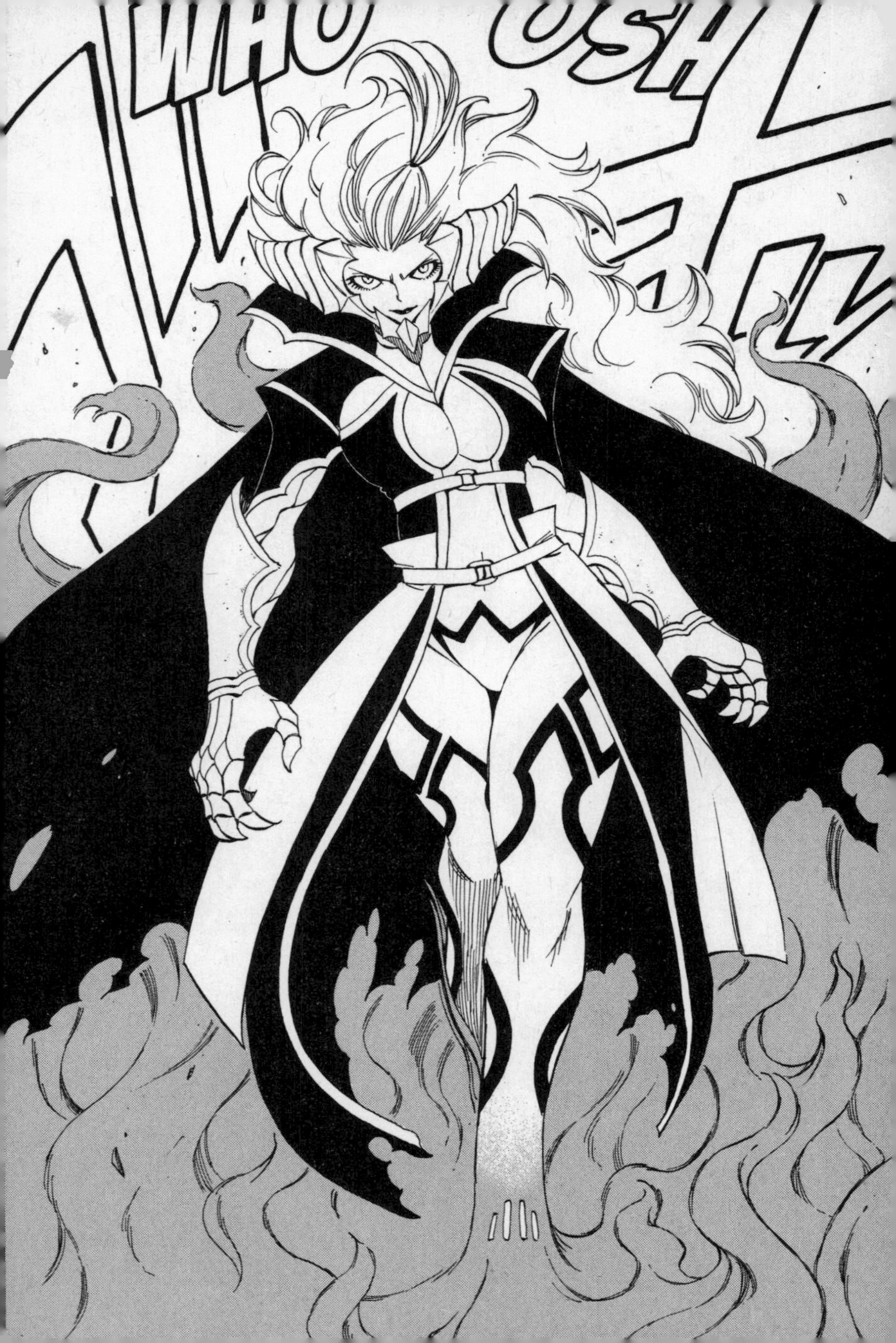
WHO OSH

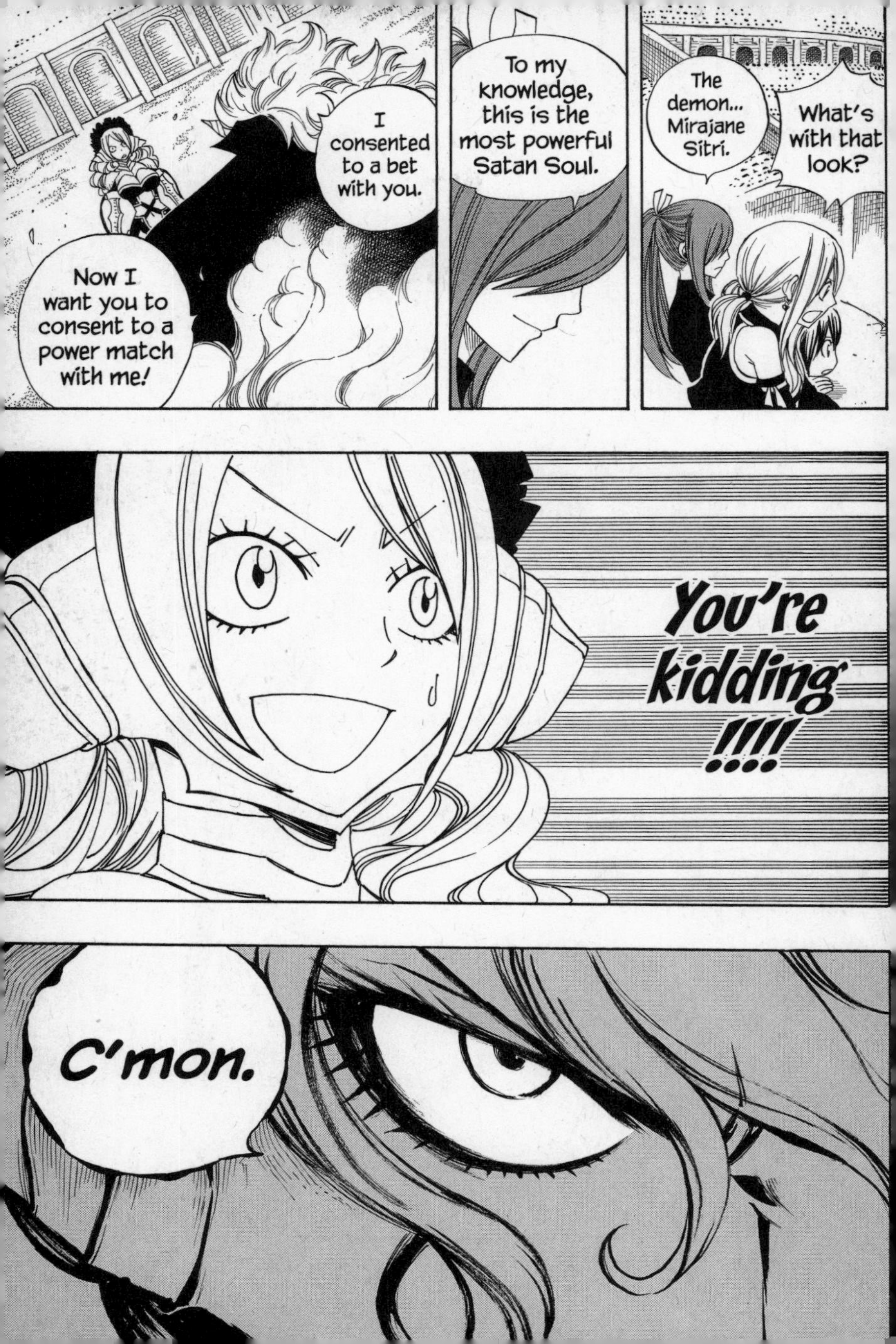

What's with that look?
The demon... Mirajane Sitri.
To my knowledge, this is the most powerful Satan Soul.
I consented to a bet with you.
Now I want you to consent to a power match with me!
You're kidding!!!!
C'mon.

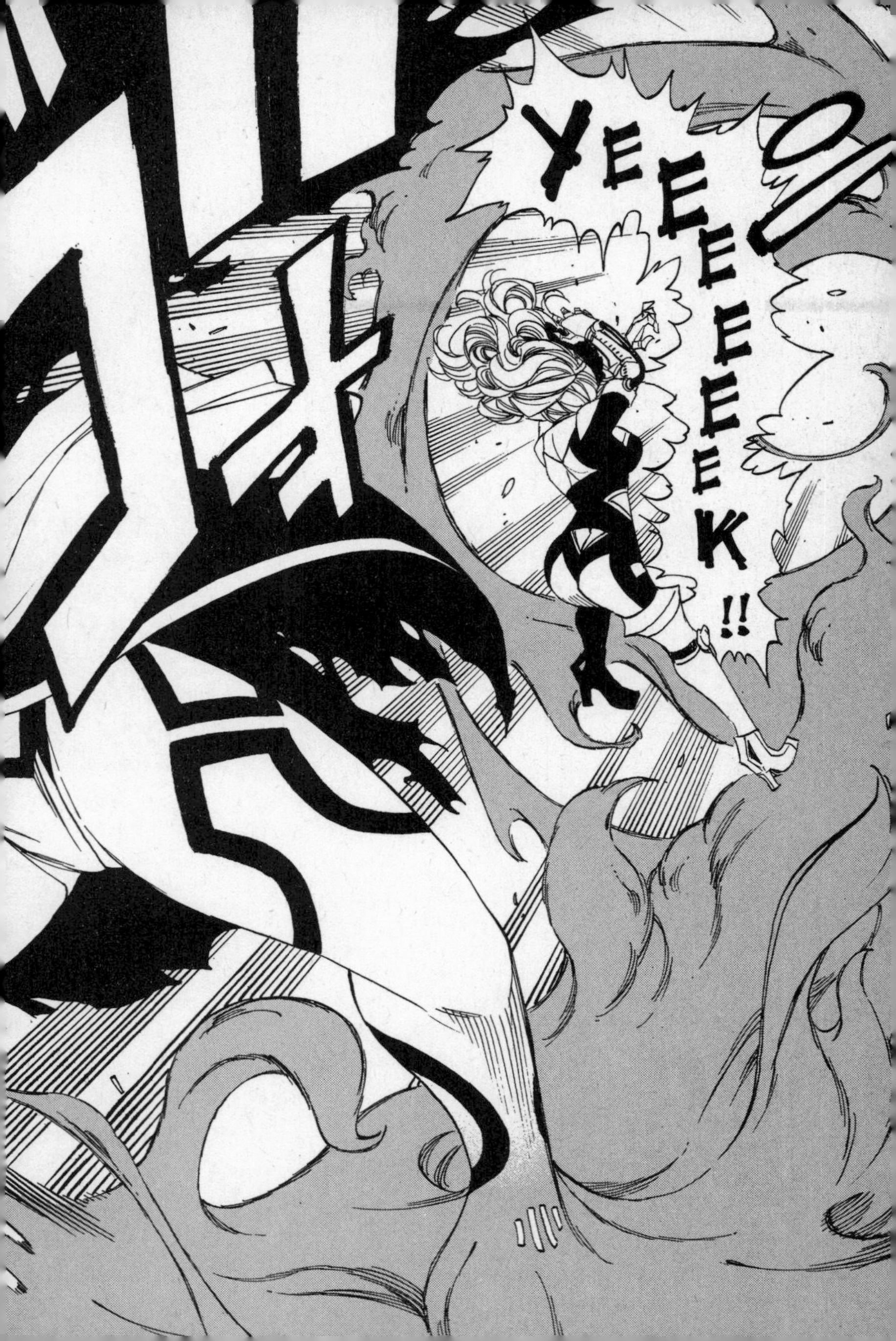
YEEEEEEK!!

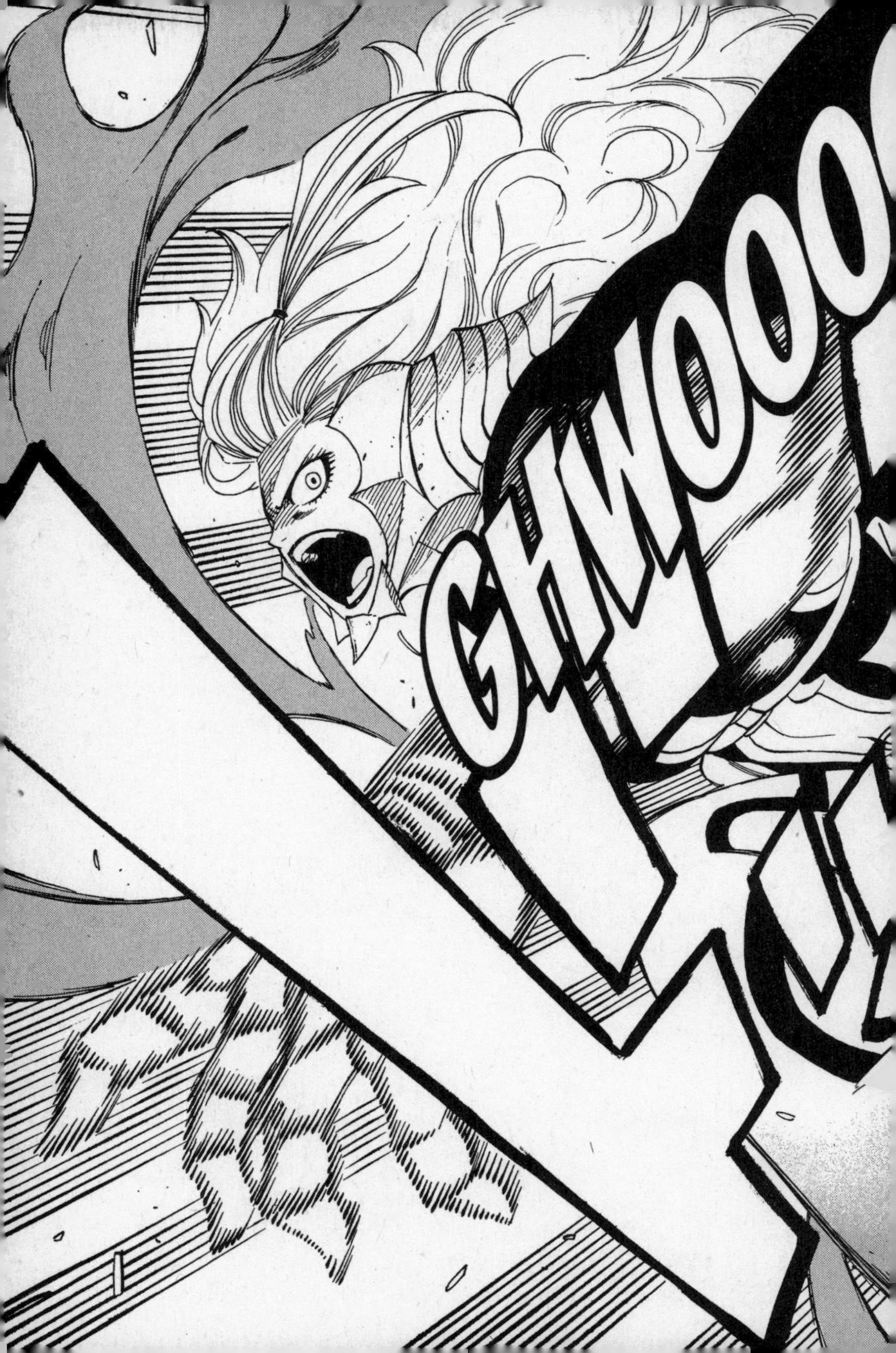
GHWOOO

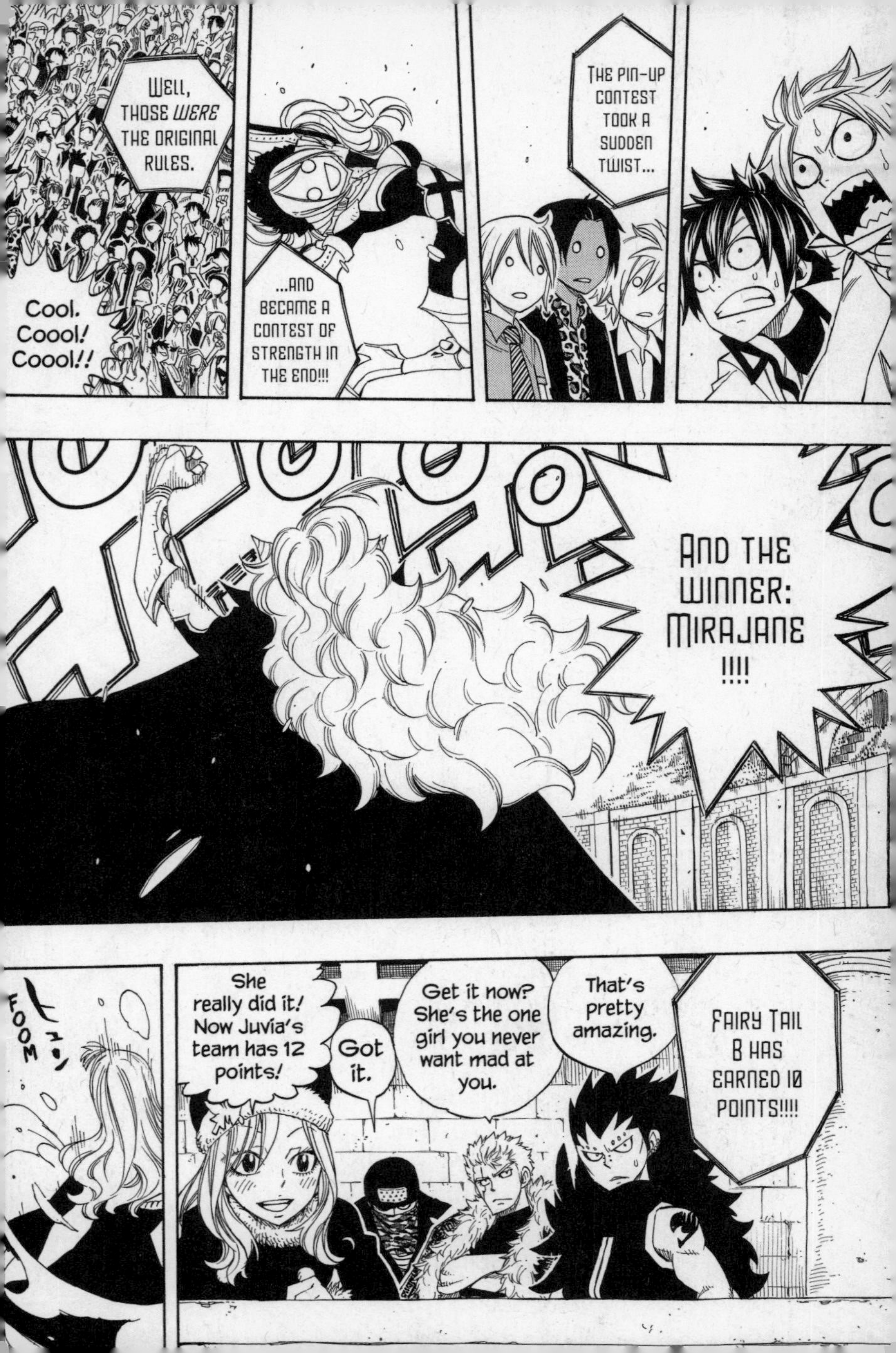
The pin-up contest took a sudden twist...
...and became a contest of strength in the end!!!
Well, those *were* the original rules.
Cool. Coool! Coool!!
And the winner: Mirajane !!!!
Fairy Tail B has earned 10 points!!!!
That's pretty amazing.
Get it now? She's the one girl you never want mad at you.
Got it.
She really did it! Now Juvia's team has 12 points!
FOOM

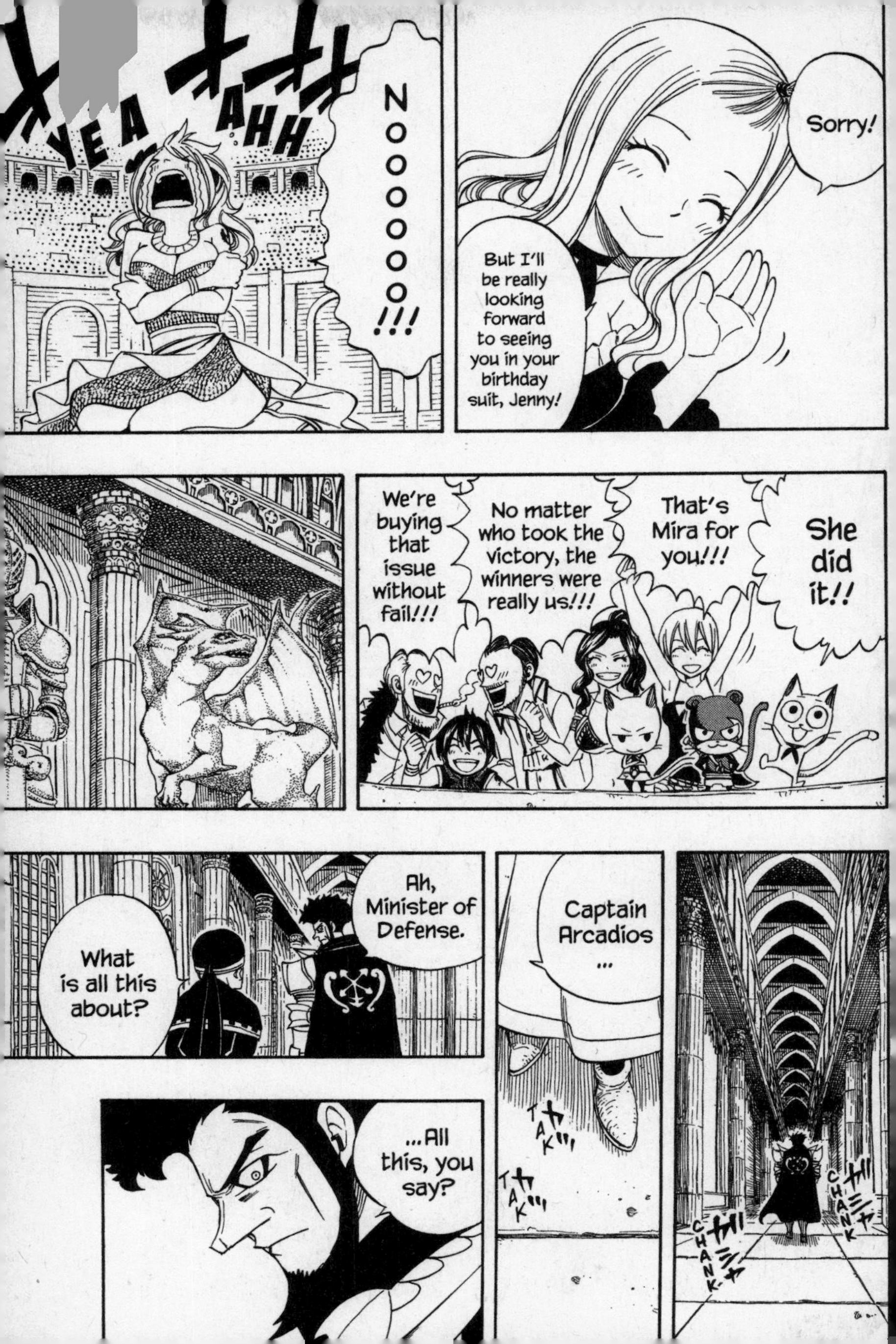
Sorry!
But I'll be really looking forward to seeing you in your birthday suit, Jenny!
NOOOOOOO!!!
YEA AHH
She did it!!
That's Mira for you!!!
No matter who took the victory, the winners were really us!!!
We're buying that issue without fail!!!
CHANK
CHANK
Captain Arcadios ...
TAK
TAK
Ah, Minister of Defense.
What is all this about?
...All this, you say?

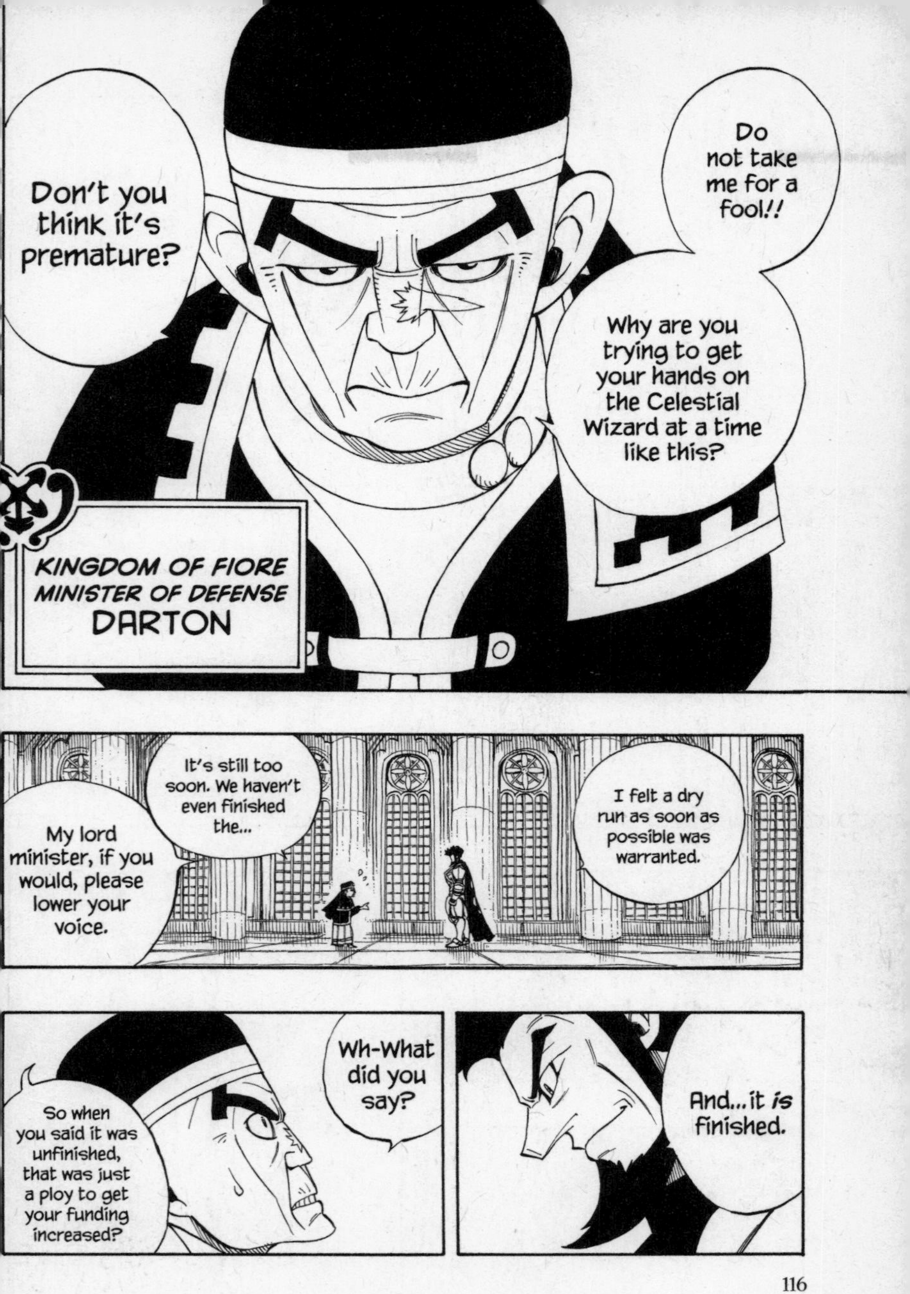
Do not take me for a fool!!
Why are you trying to get your hands on the Celestial Wizard at a time like this?
Don't you think it's premature?
KINGDOM OF FIORE MINISTER OF DEFENSE DARTON
I felt a dry run as soon as possible was warranted.
It's still too soon. We haven't even finished the...
My lord minister, if you would, please lower your voice.
And...it *is* finished.
Wh-What did you say?
So when you said it was unfinished, that was just a ploy to get your funding increased?

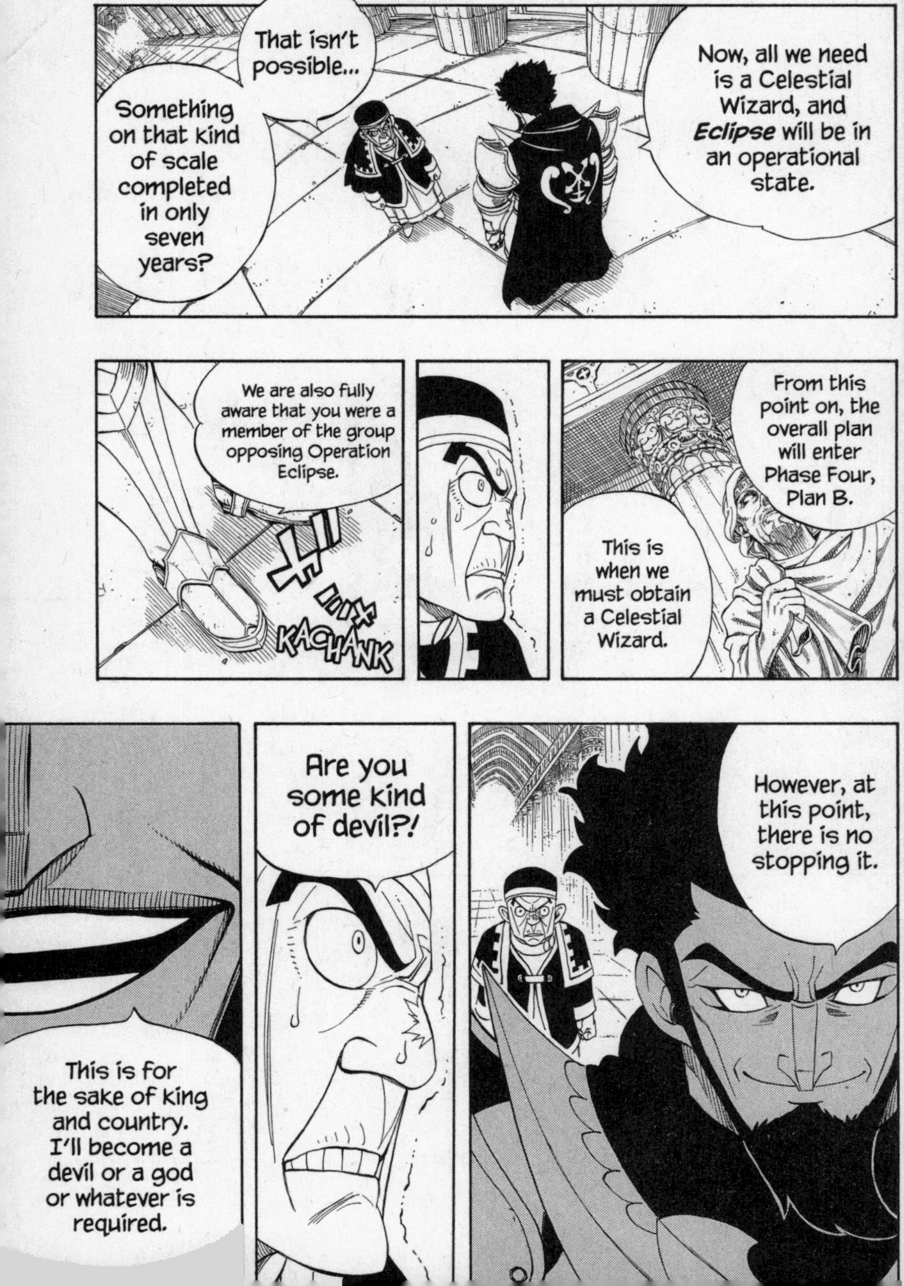
Now, all we need is a Celestial Wizard, and *Eclipse* will be in an operational state.
That isn't possible...
Something on that kind of scale completed in only seven years?
From this point on, the overall plan will enter Phase Four, Plan B.
This is when we must obtain a Celestial Wizard.
We are also fully aware that you were a member of the group opposing Operation Eclipse.
KACHANK
However, at this point, there is no stopping it.
Are you some kind of devil?!
This is for the sake of king and country. I'll become a devil or a god or whatever is required.

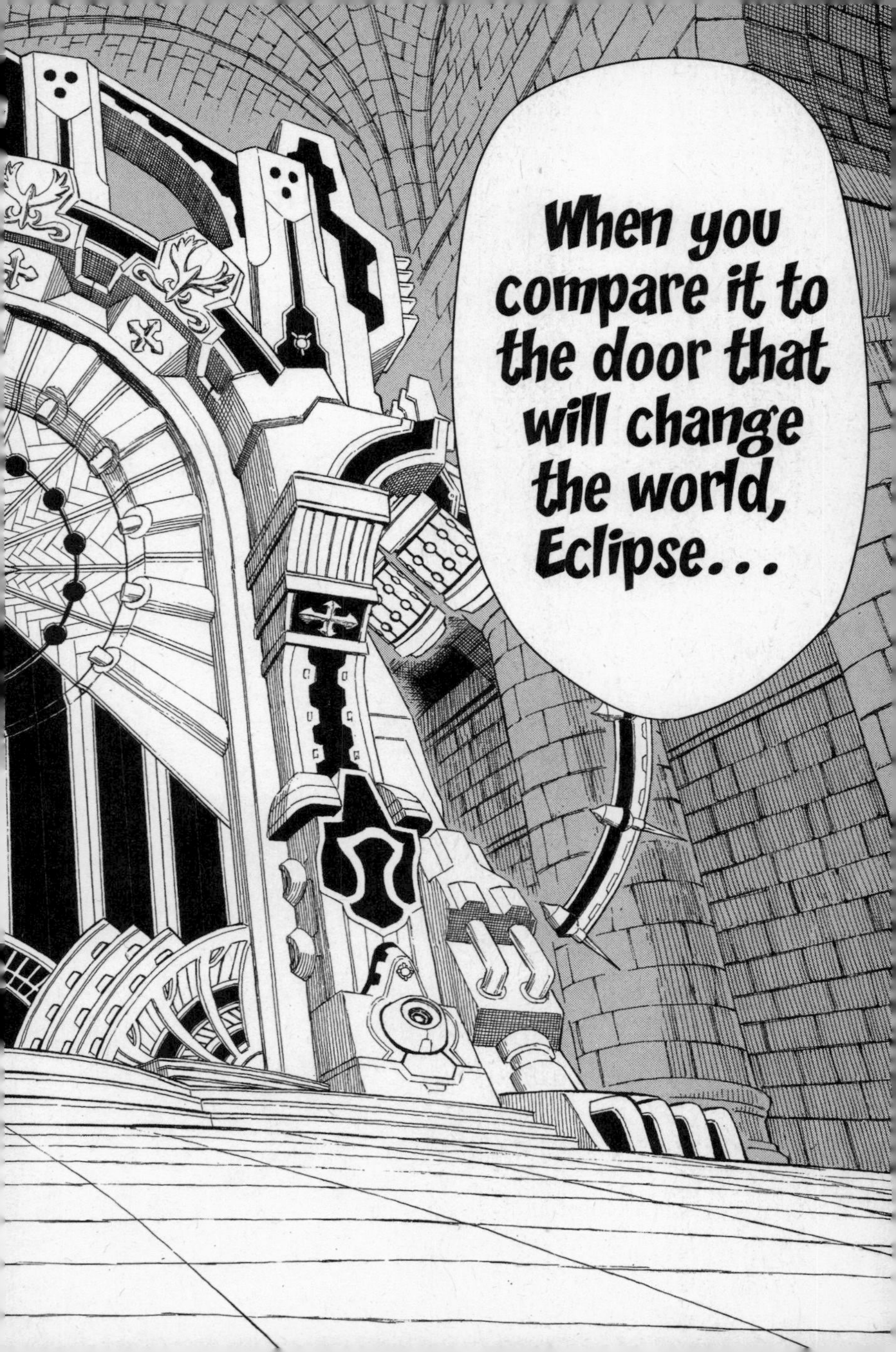
When you compare it to the door that will change the world, Eclipse...

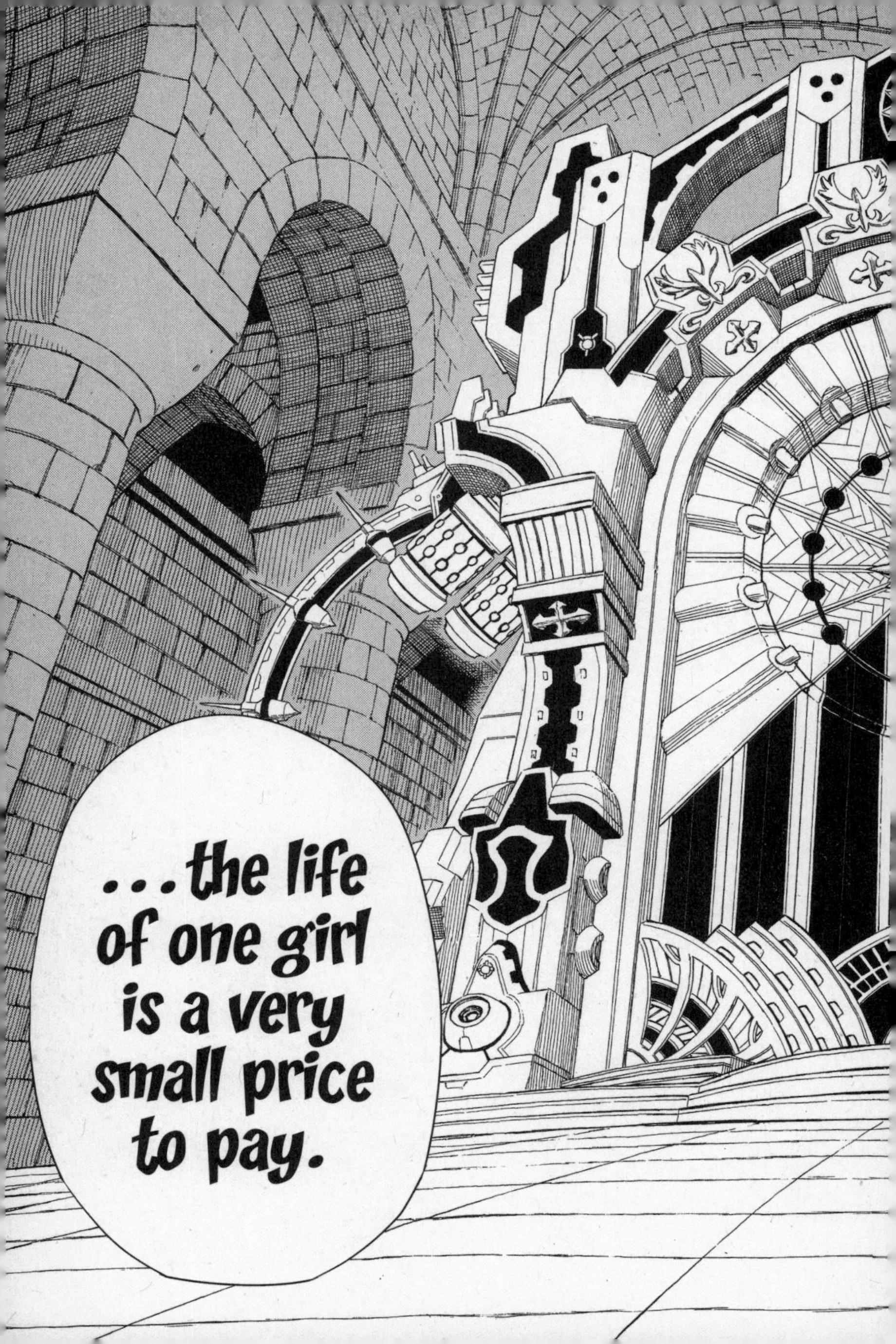
...the life of one girl is a very small price to pay.

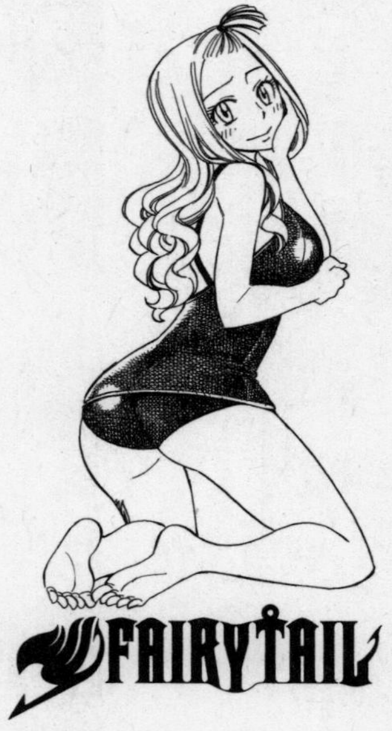

FAIRY TAIL

FAIRY TAIL

フェアリーテイル

Chapter 280: Kagura vs. Yukino

Mushroom

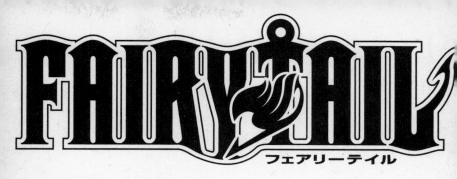

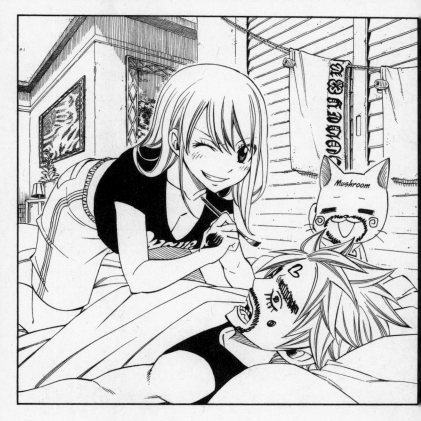

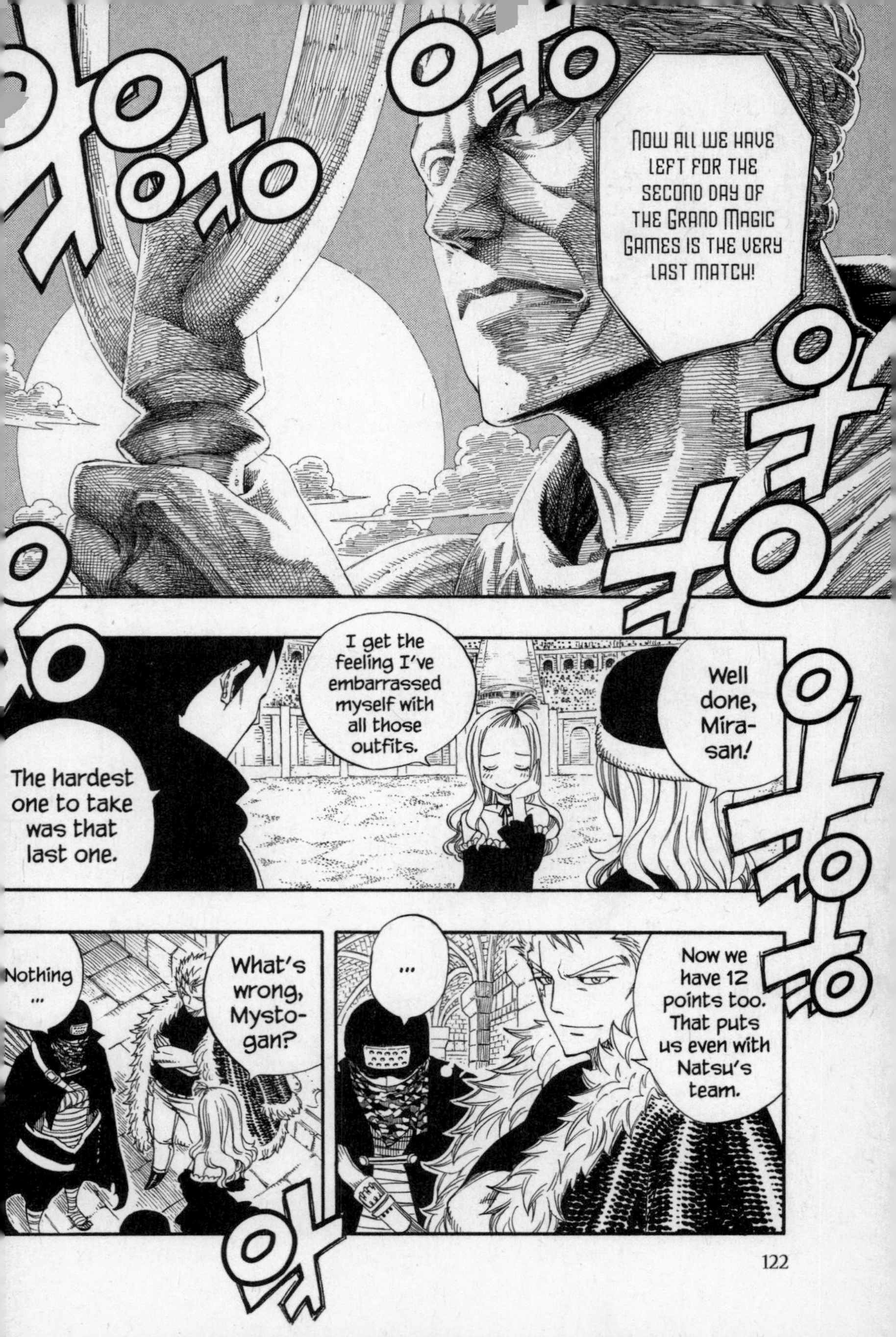
NOW ALL WE HAVE LEFT FOR THE SECOND DAY OF THE GRAND MAGIC GAMES IS THE VERY LAST MATCH!
Well done, Mira-san!
I get the feeling I've embarrassed myself with all those outfits.
The hardest one to take was that last one.
Now we have 12 points too. That puts us even with Natsu's team.
...
What's wrong, Mystogan?
Nothing ...

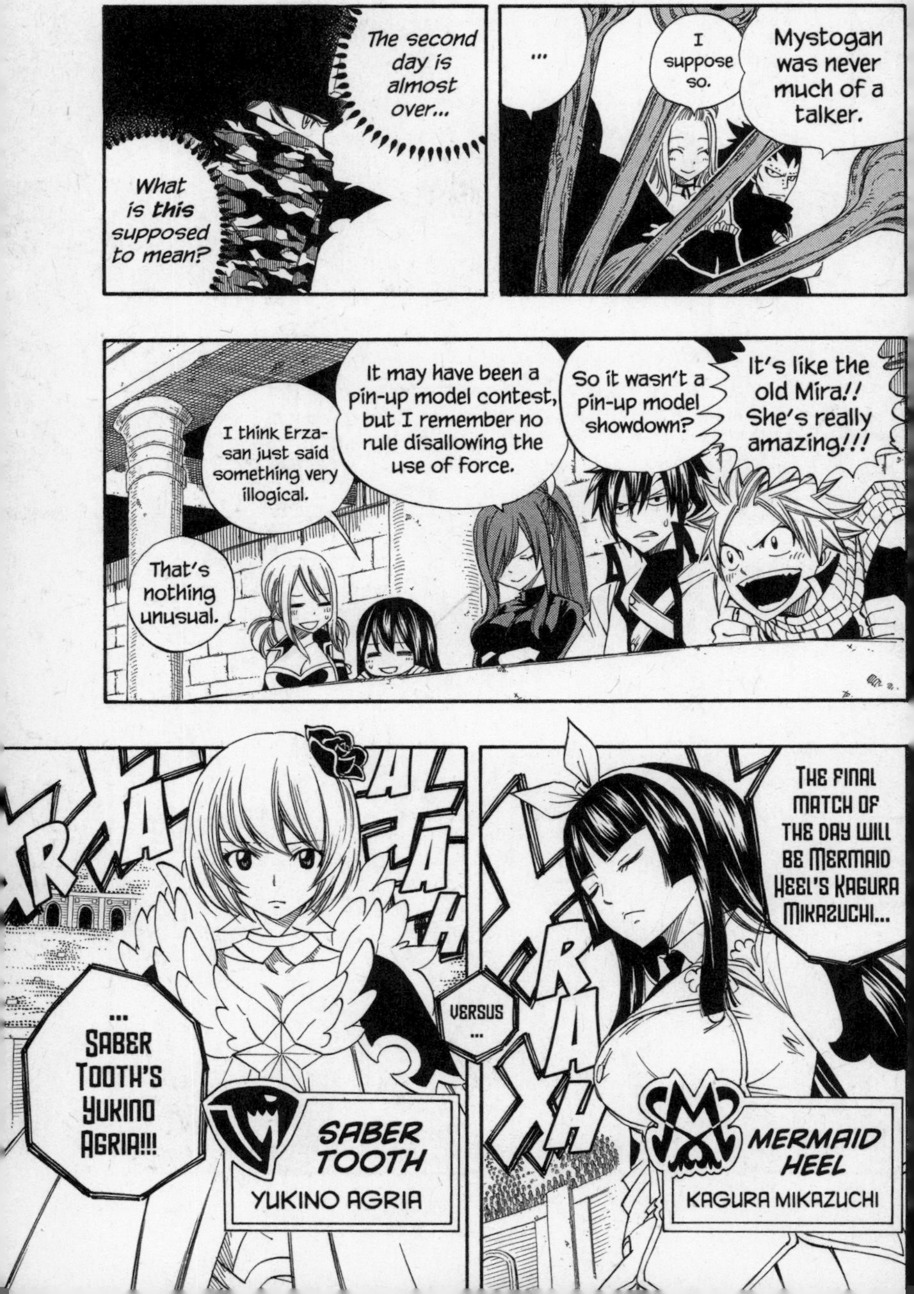
Mystogan was never much of a talker.
I suppose so.
...
The second day is almost over...
What is this supposed to mean?
It's like the old Mira!! She's really amazing!!!
So it wasn't a pin-up model showdown?
It may have been a pin-up model contest, but I remember no rule disallowing the use of force.
I think Erza-san just said something very illogical.
That's nothing unusual.
The final match of the day will be Mermaid Heel's Kagura Mikazuchi...
Versus ...
MERMAID HEEL
KAGURA MIKAZUCHI
... Saber Tooth's Yukino Agria!!!
SABER TOOTH
YUKINO AGRIA

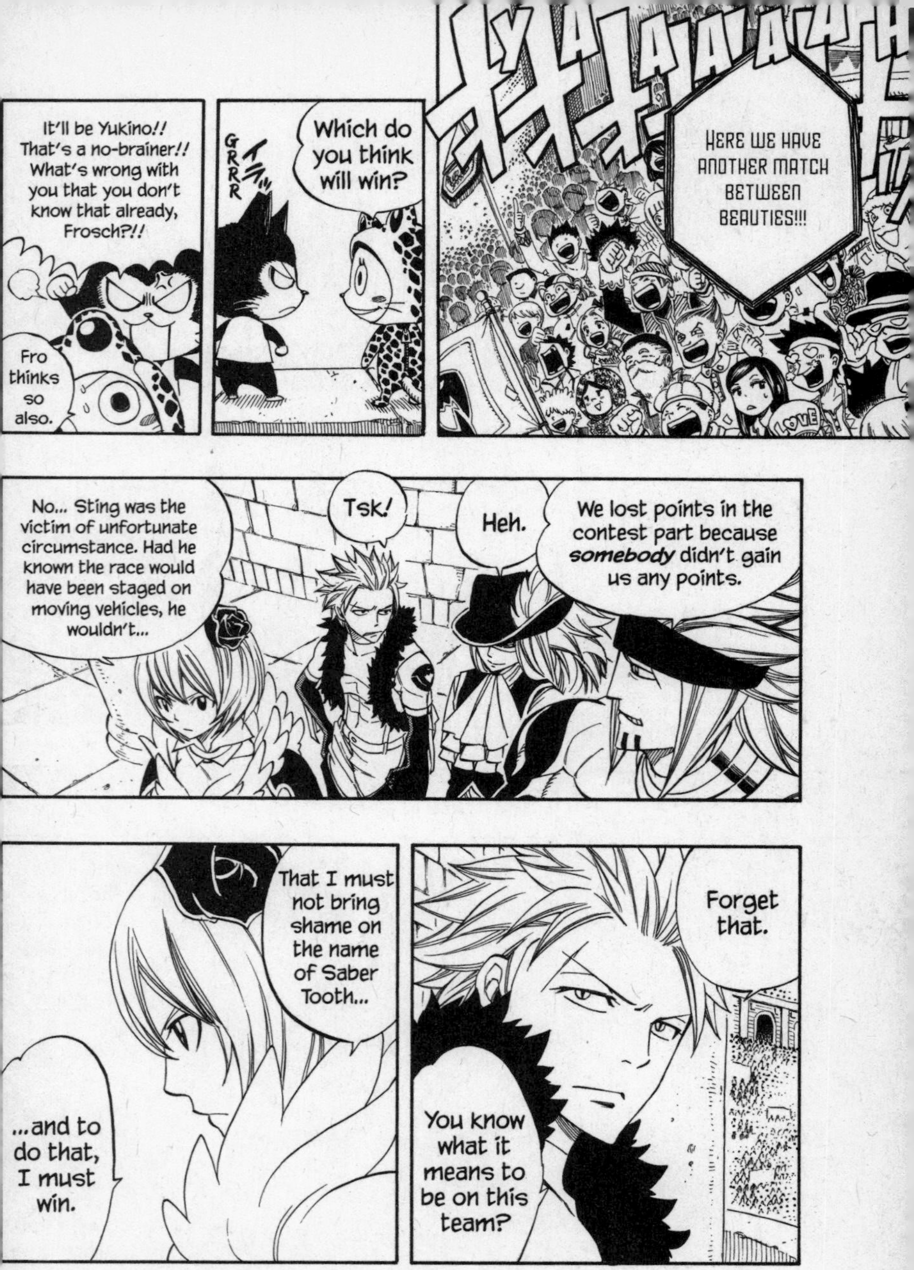

YAAAAAAH
HERE WE HAVE ANOTHER MATCH BETWEEN BEAUTIES!!!
Which do you think will win?
GRRR
It'll be Yukino!! That's a no-brainer!! What's wrong with you that you don't know that already, Frosch?!!
Fro thinks so also.
We lost points in the contest part because *somebody* didn't gain us any points.
Heh.
Tsk!
No... Sting was the victim of unfortunate circumstance. Had he known the race would have been staged on moving vehicles, he wouldn't...
Forget that.
You know what it means to be on this team?
That I must not bring shame on the name of Saber Tooth...
...and to do that, I must win.

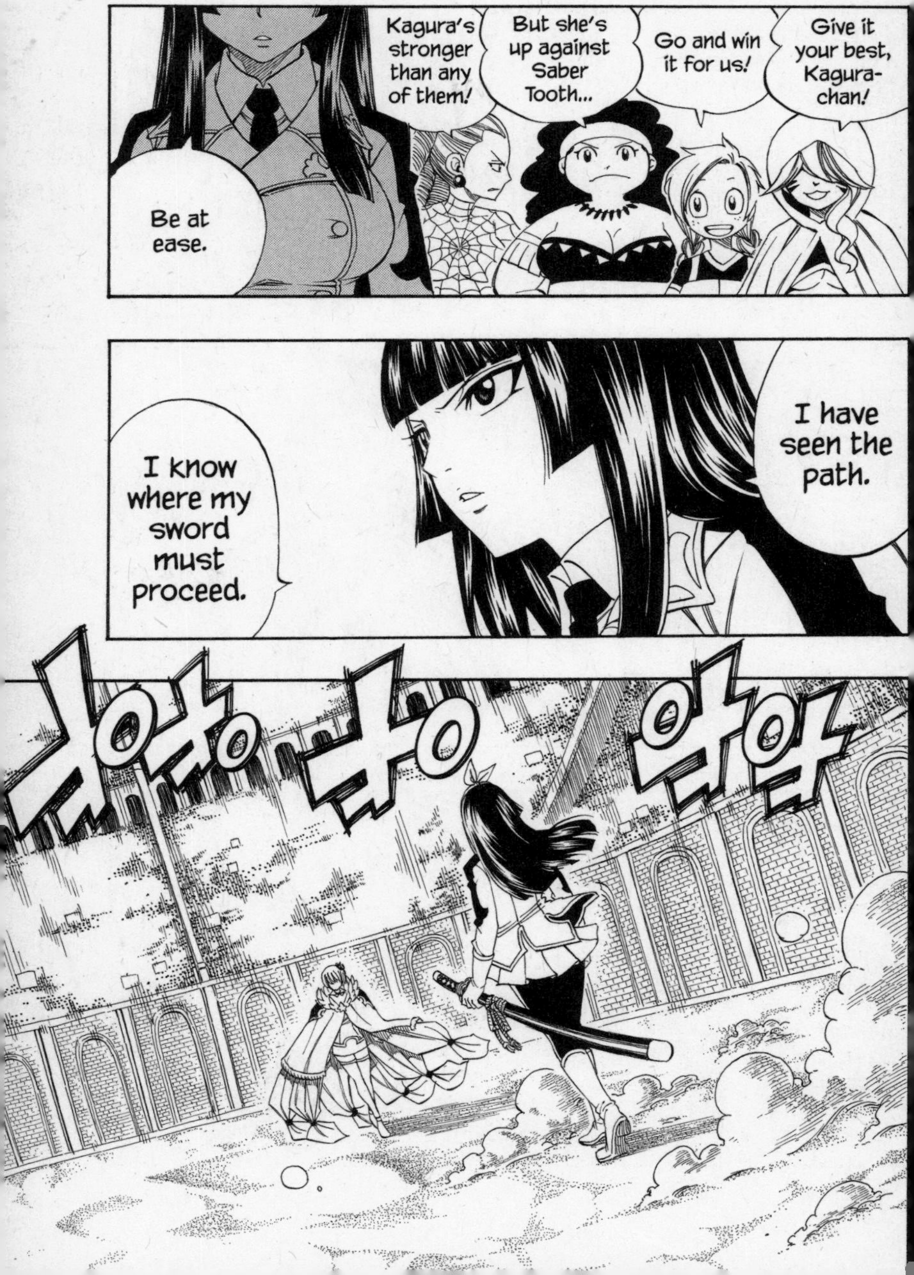
Give it your best, Kagura-chan!
Go and win it for us!
But she's up against Saber Tooth...
Kagura's stronger than any of them!
Be at ease.
I have seen the path.
I know where my sword must proceed.

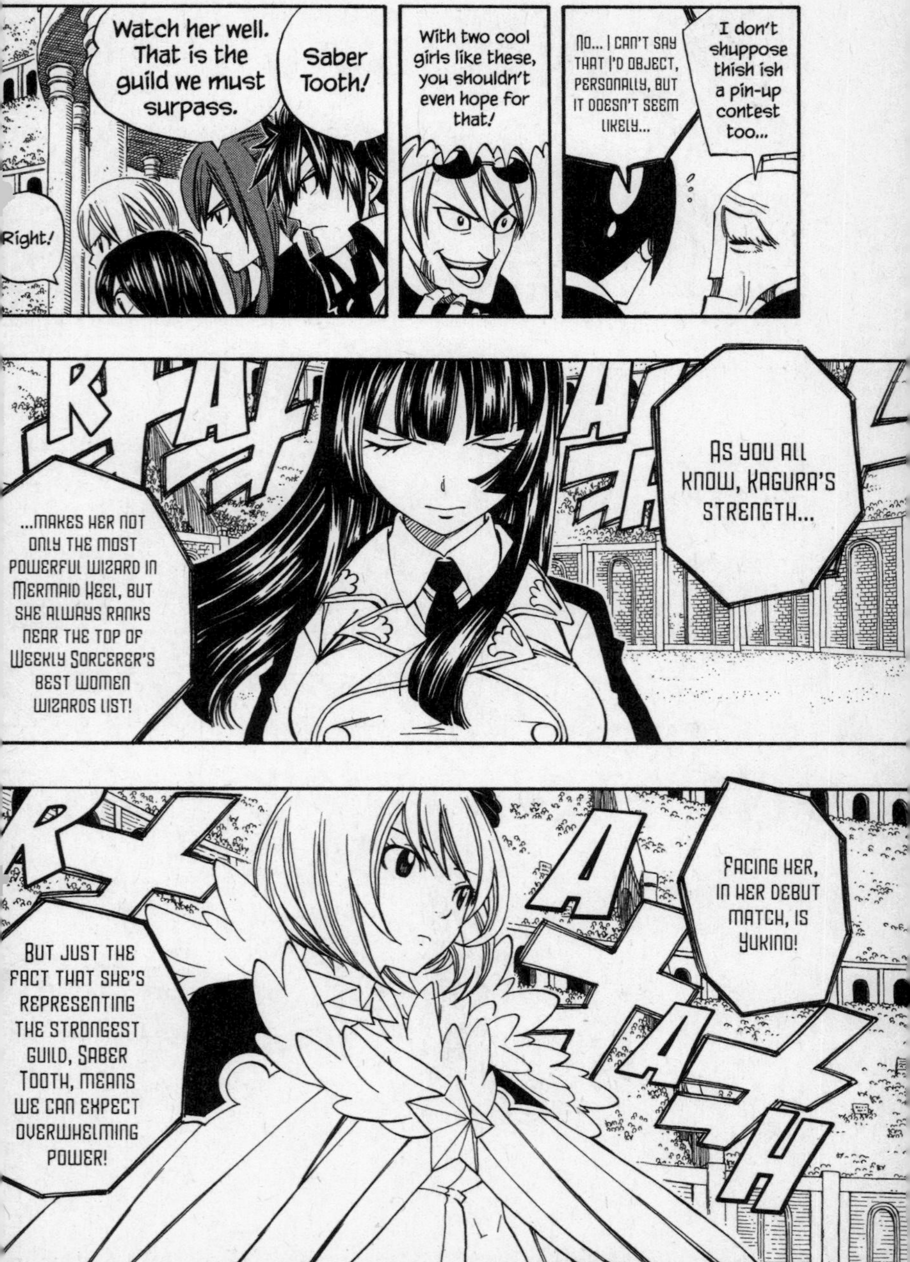
I don't shuppose thish ish a pin-up contest too...
No... I can't say that I'd object, personally, but it doesn't seem likely...
With two cool girls like these, you shouldn't even hope for that!
Watch her well. That is the guild we must surpass.
Saber Tooth!
Right!
As you all know, Kagura's strength...
...makes her not only the most powerful wizard in Mermaid Heel, but she always ranks near the top of Weekly Sorcerer's best women wizards list!
Facing her, in her debut match, is Yukino!
But just the fact that she's representing the strongest guild, Saber Tooth, means we can expect overwhelming power!
RAAAAH

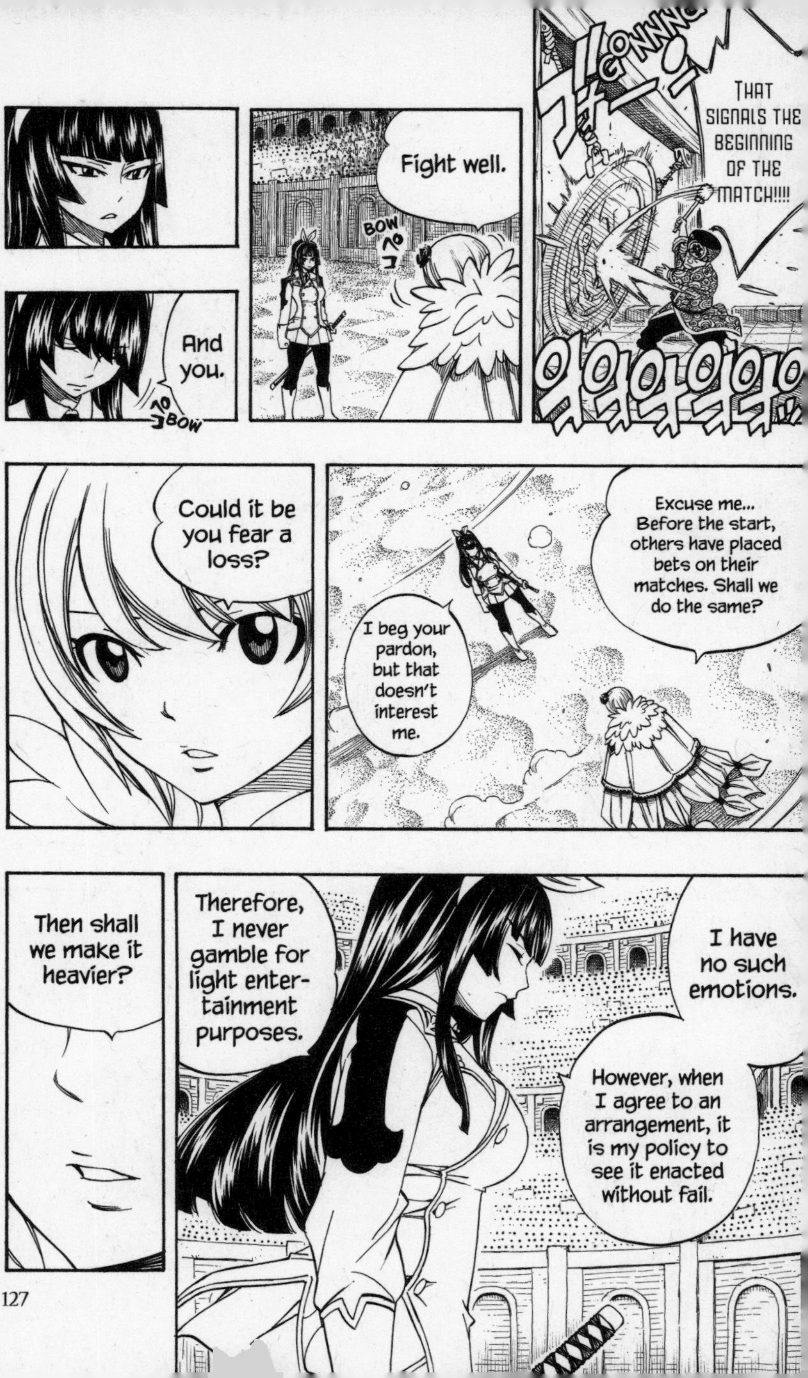

THAT SIGNALS THE BEGINNING OF THE MATCH!!!!
Fight well.
BOW
And you.
BOW
Excuse me... Before the start, others have placed bets on their matches. Shall we do the same?
I beg your pardon, but that doesn't interest me.
Could it be you fear a loss?
I have no such emotions.
Therefore, I never gamble for light entertainment purposes.
However, when I agree to an arrangement, it is my policy to see it enacted without fail.
Then shall we make it heavier?

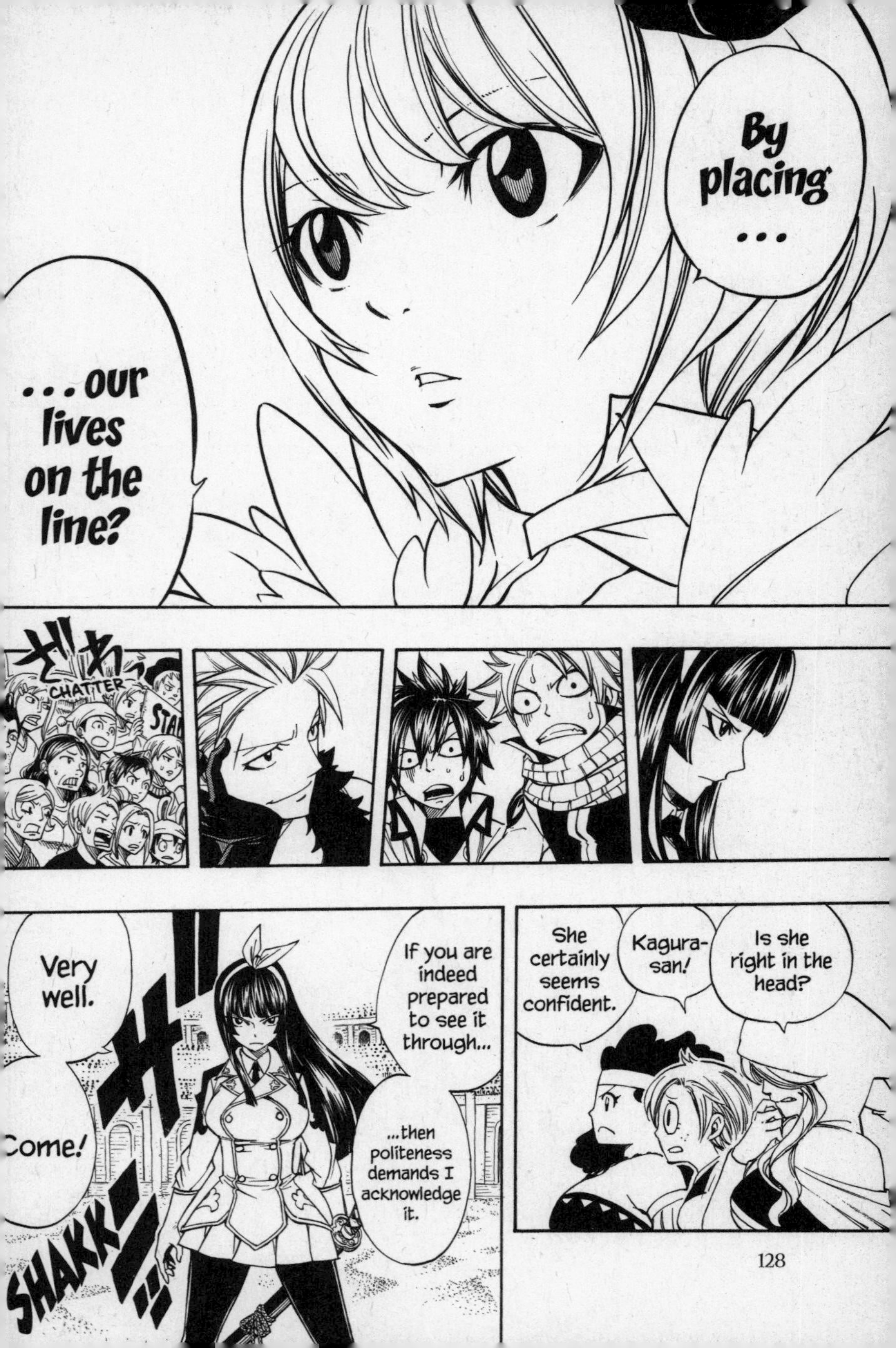
By placing...
...our lives on the line?
CHATTER
Is she right in the head?
Kagura-san!
She certainly seems confident.
If you are indeed prepared to see it through...
...then politeness demands I acknowledge it.
Very well.
Come!
SHAKK!!

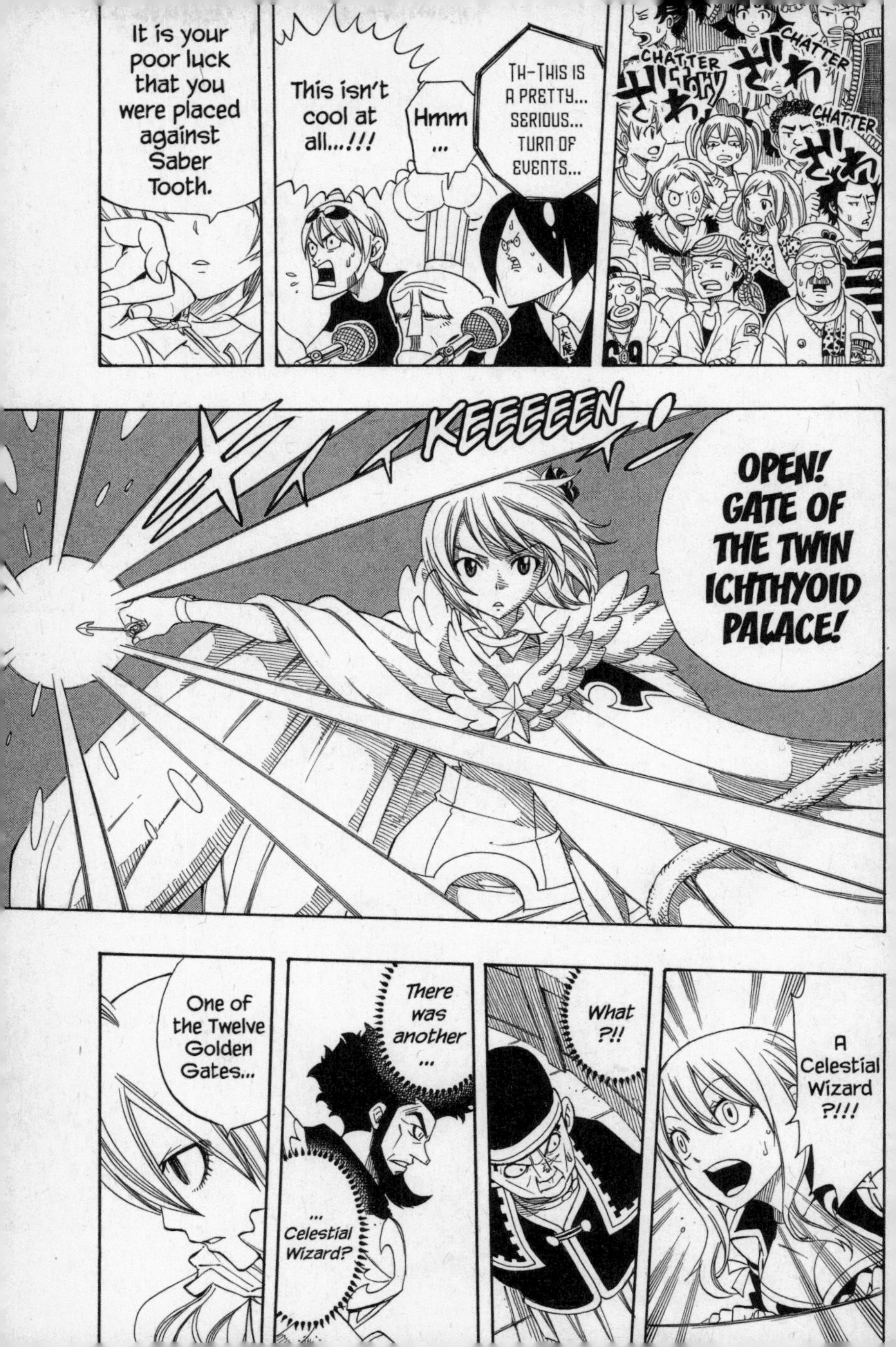
CHATTER
CHATTER
CHATTER
TH-THIS IS A PRETTY... SERIOUS... TURN OF EVENTS...
Hmm ...
This isn't cool at all...!!!
It is your poor luck that you were placed against Saber Tooth.
OPEN! GATE OF THE TWIN ICHTHYOID PALACE!
KEEEEEN
A Celestial Wizard ?!!!
What ?!!
There was another ...
... Celestial Wizard?
One of the Twelve Golden Gates...

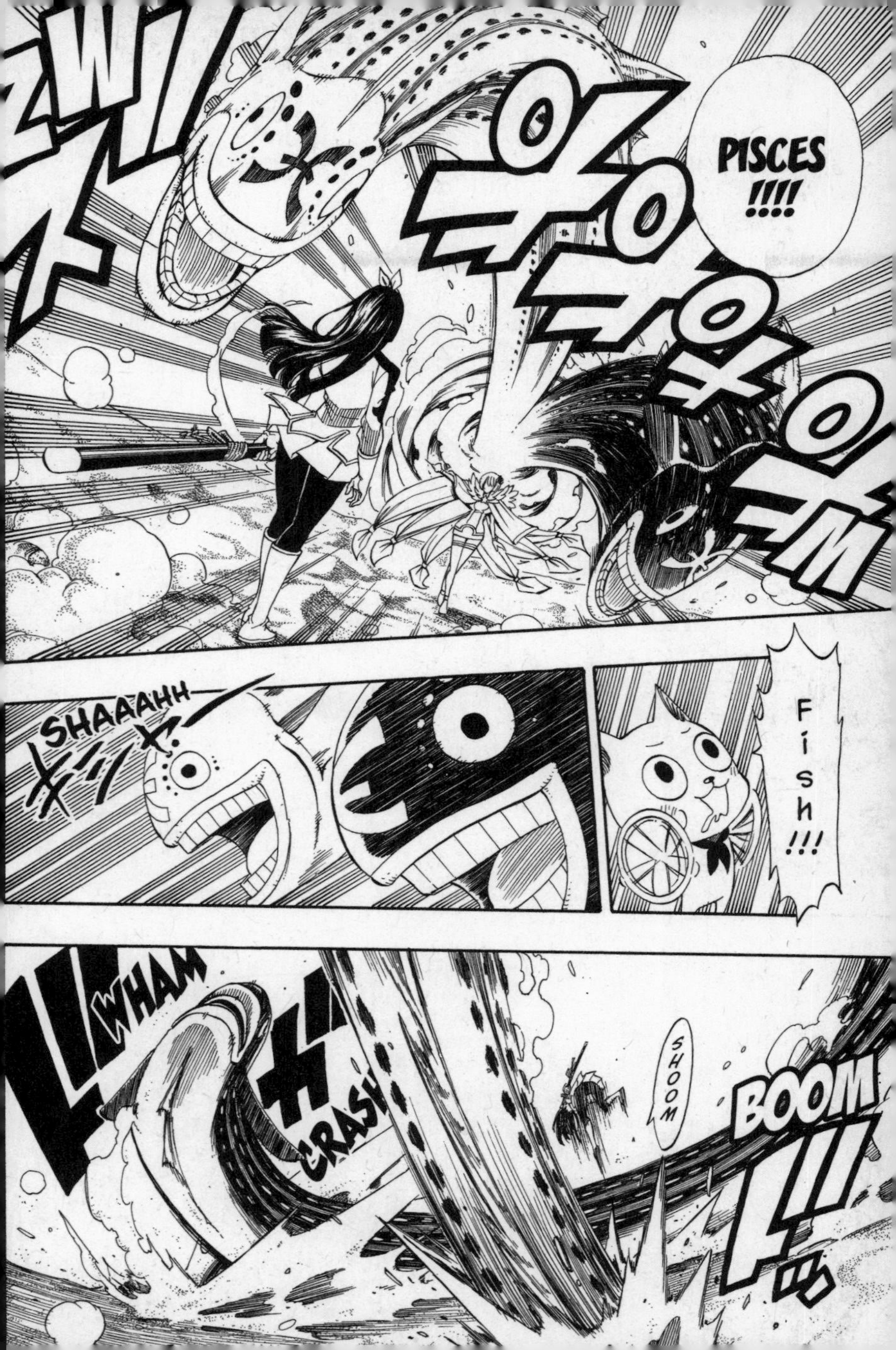
PISCES !!!!
Fish!!!
SHAAAHH
BOOM!!
SHOOM
CRASH
WHAM

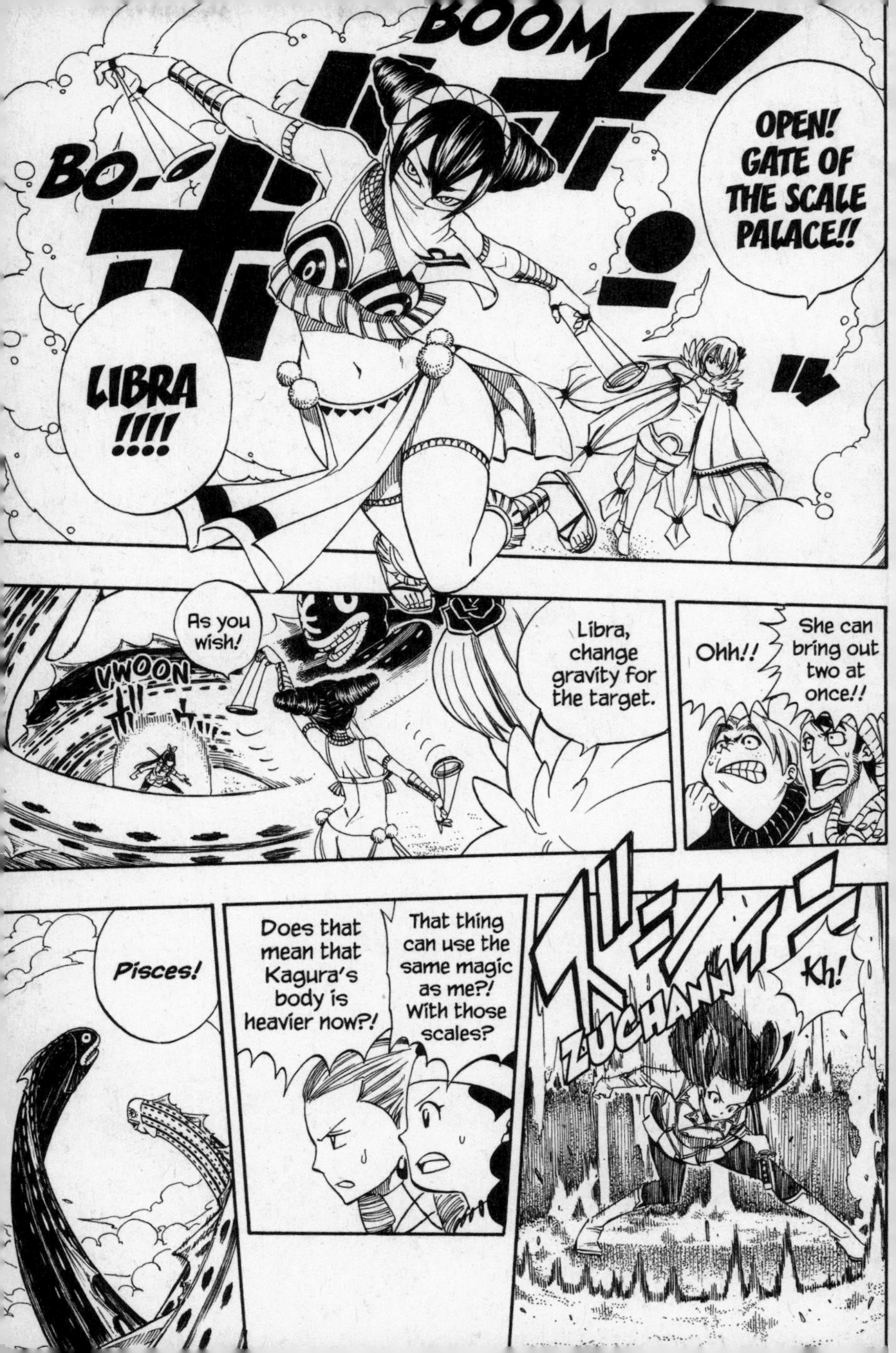
OPEN! GATE OF THE SCALE PALACE!!
BOOM
BO-
LIBRA!!!!
She can bring out two at once!!
Ohh!!
Libra, change gravity for the target.
As you wish!
VWOON
Kh!
ZUCHANN
That thing can use the same magic as me?! With those scales?
Does that mean that Kagura's body is heavier now?!
Pisces!

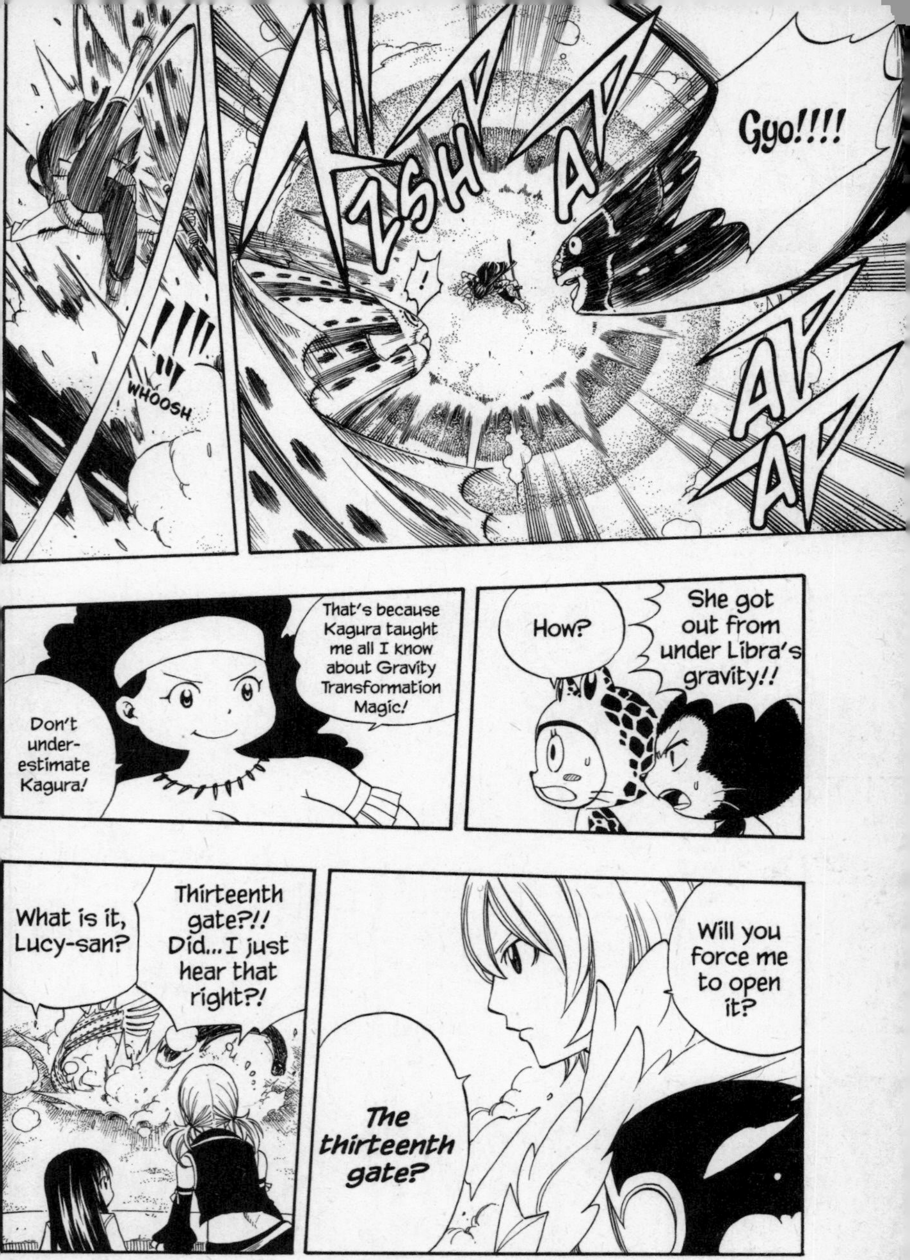

Gyo!!!!
ZSH
A
A
A
A
!
WHOOSH
She got out from under Libra's gravity!!
How?
That's because Kagura taught me all I know about Gravity Transformation Magic!
Don't under-estimate Kagura!
Will you force me to open it?
The thirteenth gate?
Thirteenth gate?!! Did...I just hear that right?!
What is it, Lucy-san?

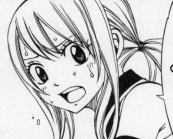

Just as the name implies, the Twelve Golden Gate Keys are twelve keys for twelve gates.
But there are rumors out there that I've heard.
Rumors of some unknown thirteenth spirit that outshines the Twelve Golden Gates!
This is an omen of very bad luck.
KEEEN
From the moment I was born, I never trusted in luck.
All is the result of one's own decisions!
Open! Gate of the Serpent Bearer Palace!
I guide myself toward my own fate!!

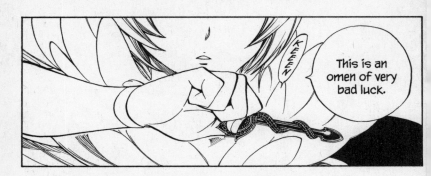

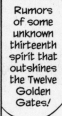

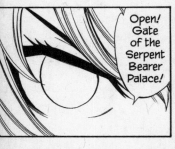

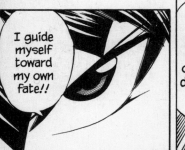

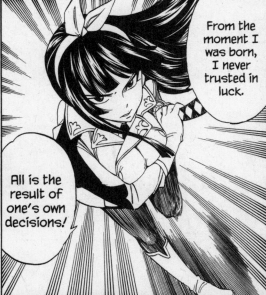

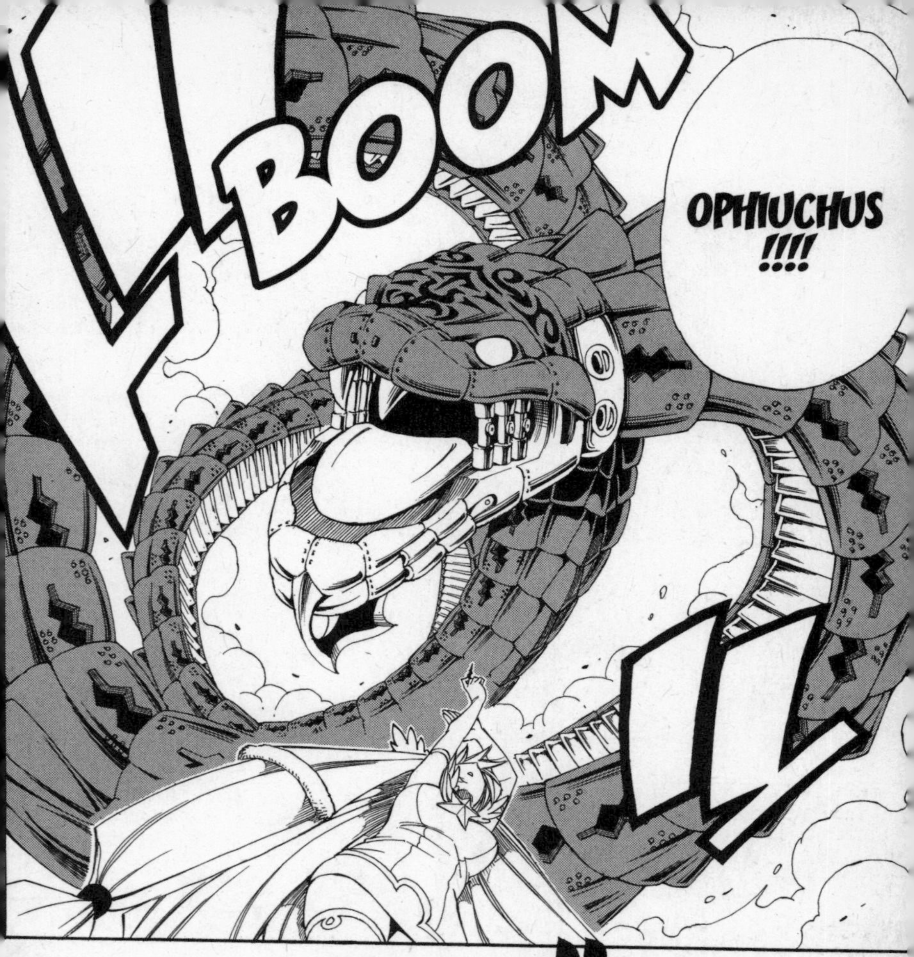
L-BOOM
OPHIUCHUS !!!!
!!

*Vengeance Sword: Archenemy

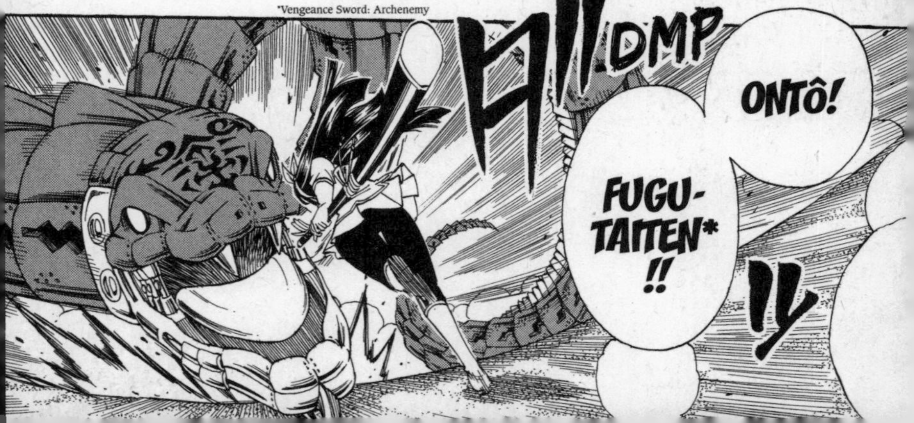
ONTÔ!
FUGU-TAITEN* !!
!!

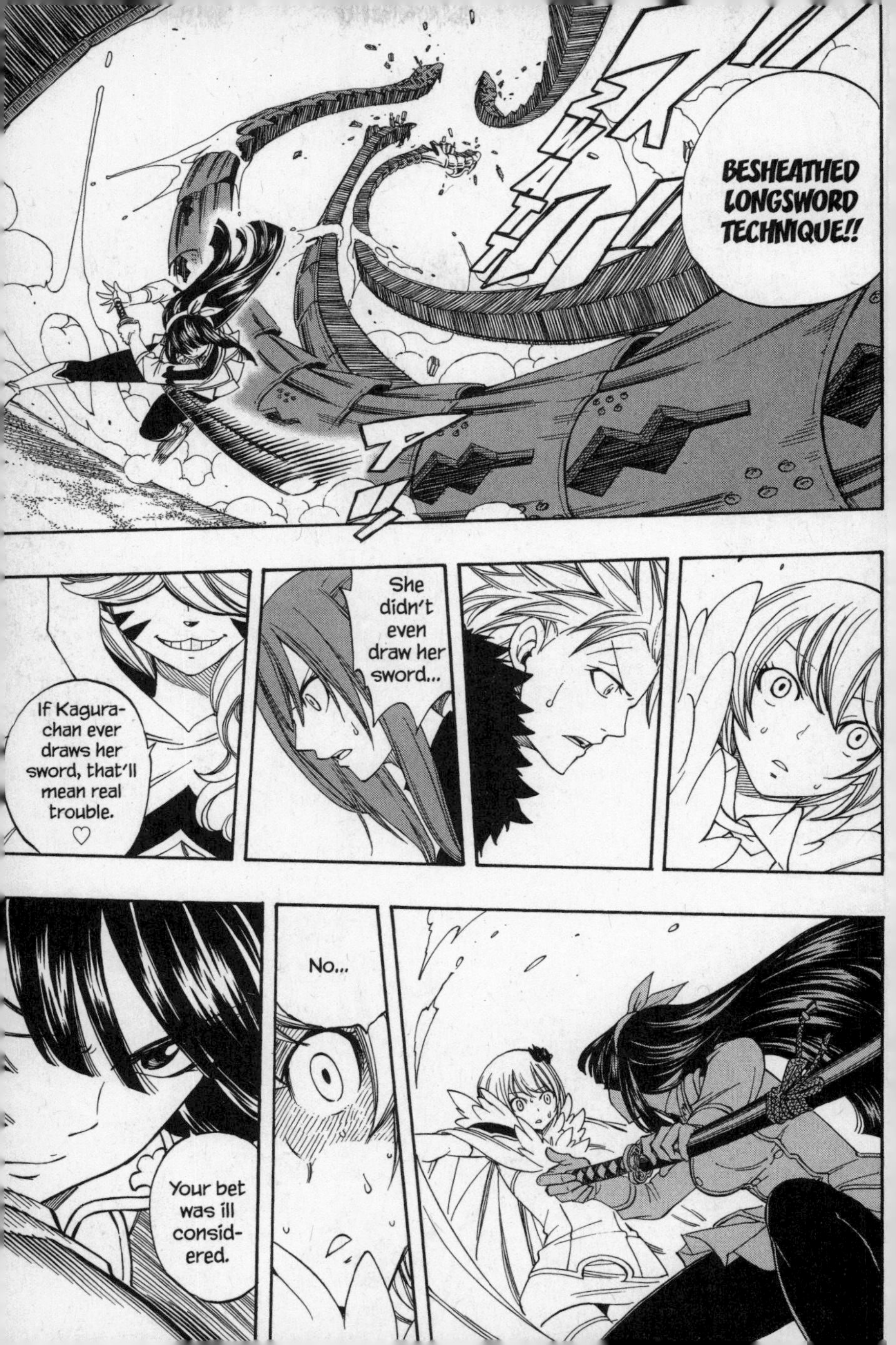
BESHEATHED LONGSWORD TECHNIQUE!!
She didn't even draw her sword...
If Kagura-chan ever draws her sword, that'll mean real trouble. ♡
No...
Your bet was ill consid-ered.

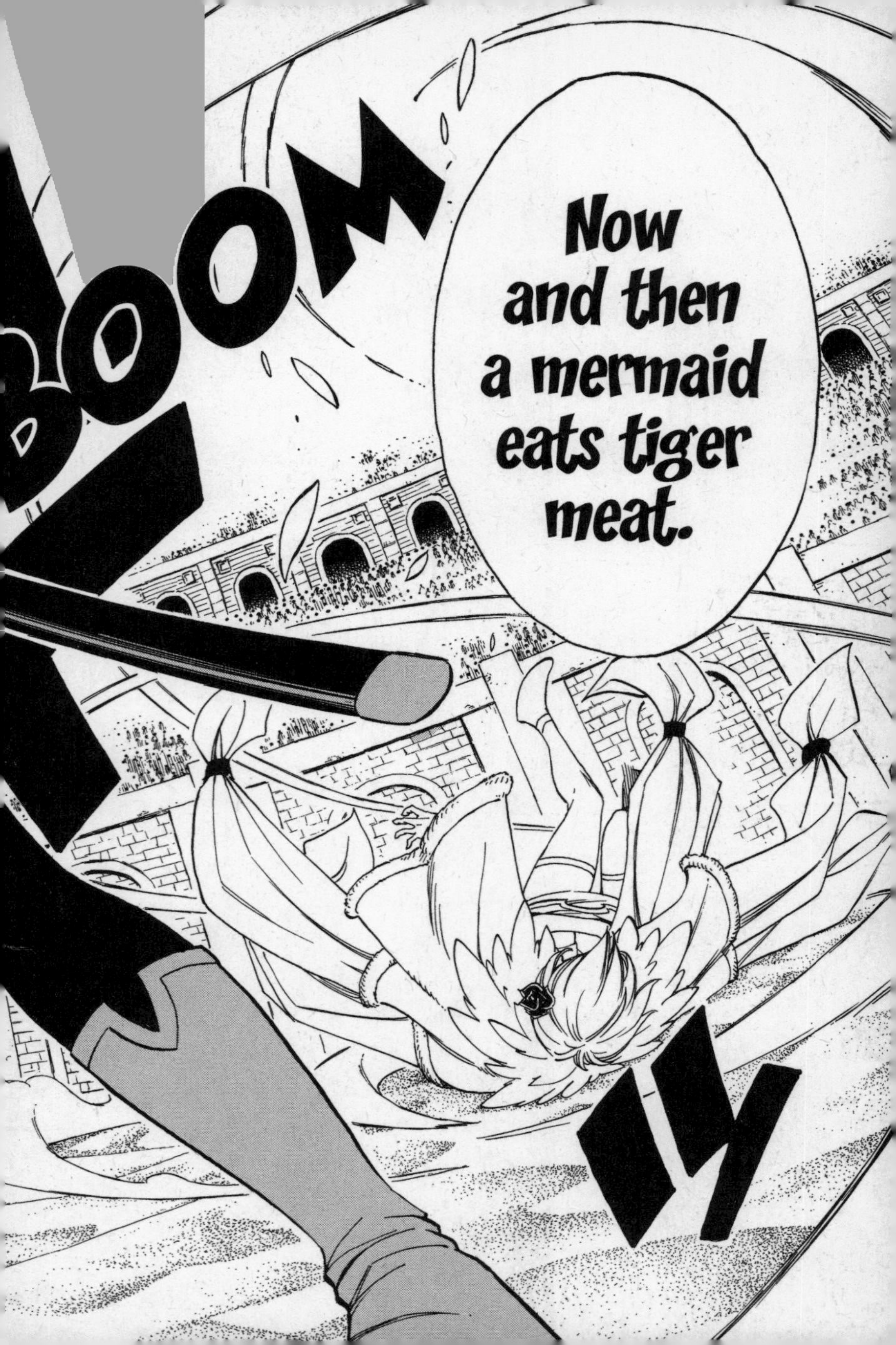
Now and then a mermaid eats tiger meat.
BOOM

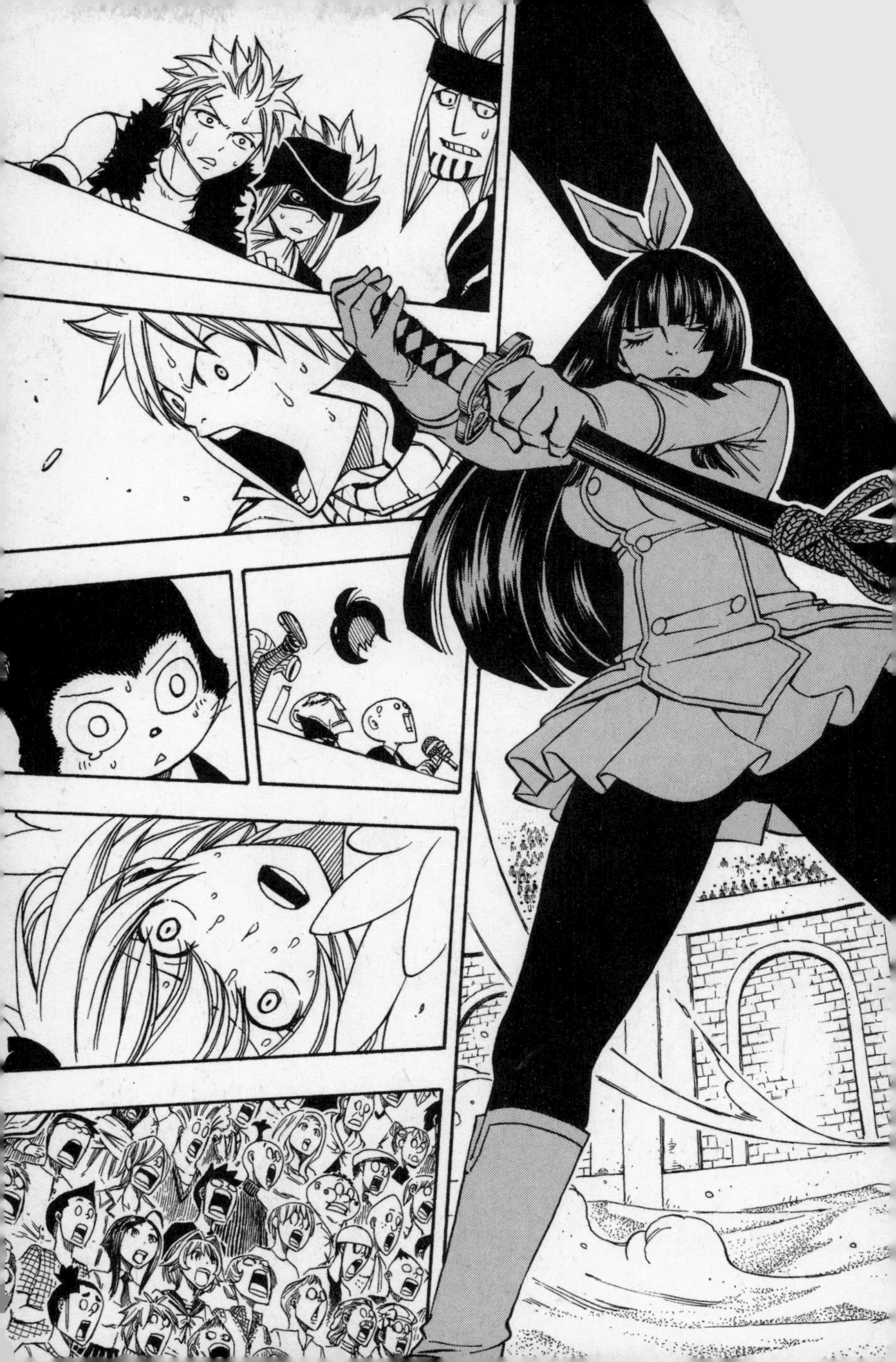

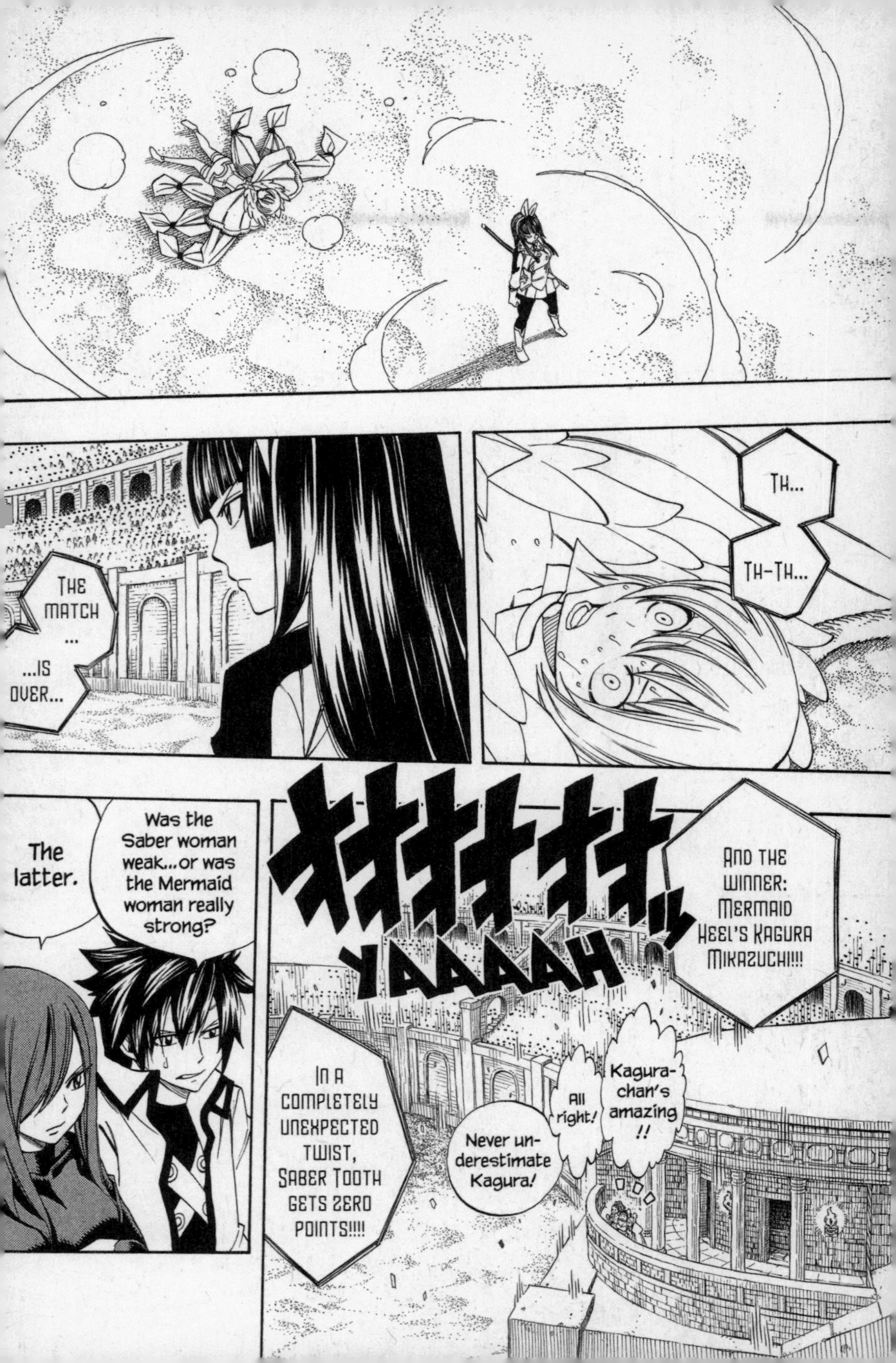
Th...
Th-th...
The match... ...is over...
KYAAAAH!!
And the winner: Mermaid Heel's Kagura Mikazuchi!!!
Kagura-chan's amazing!!
All right!
Never underestimate Kagura!
In a completely unexpected twist, Saber Tooth gets zero points!!!!
Was the Saber woman weak...or was the Mermaid woman really strong?
The latter.

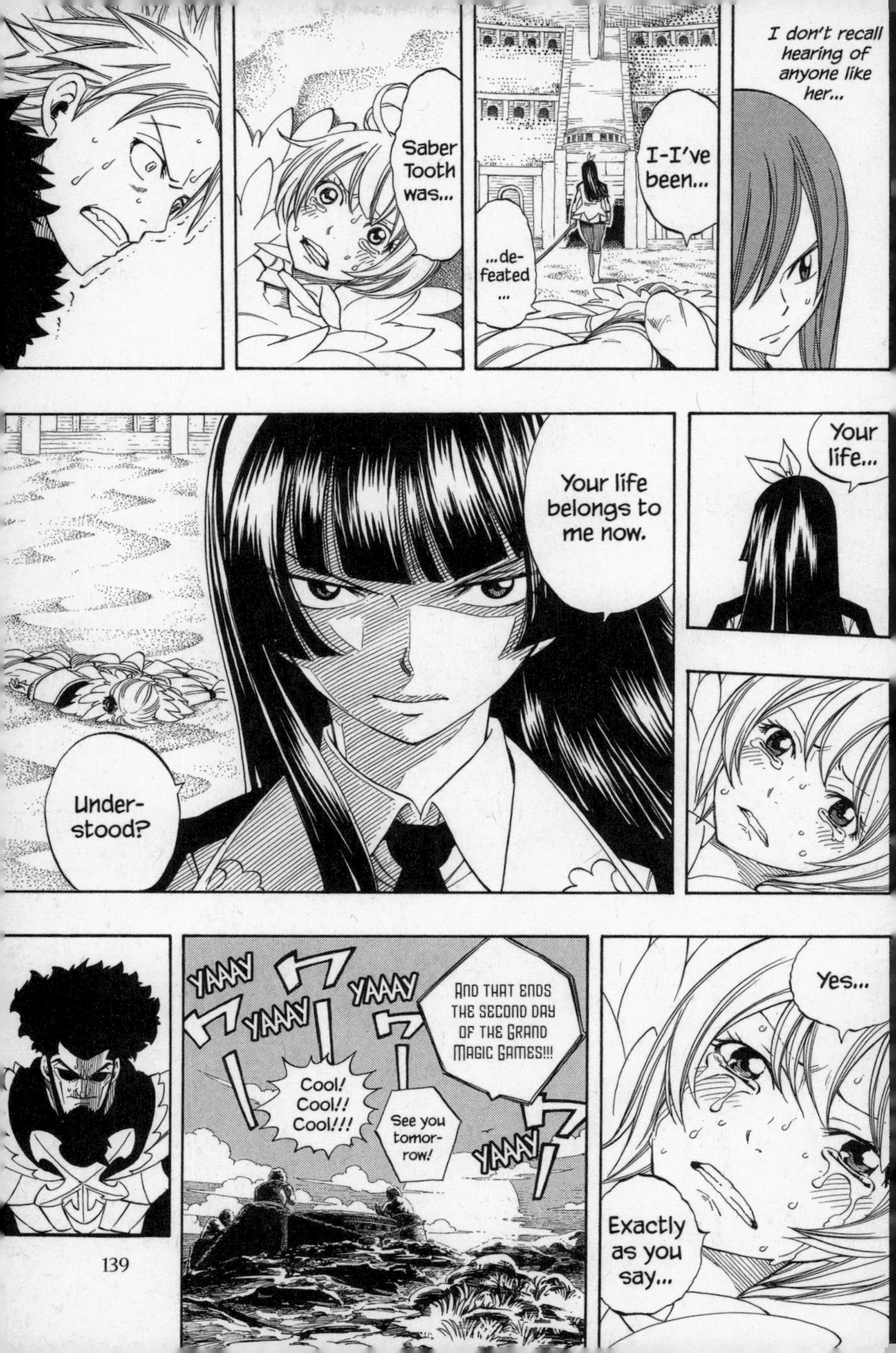
I don't recall hearing of anyone like her...
I-I've been...
...de-feated...
Saber Tooth was...
Your life...
Your life belongs to me now.
Under-stood?
Yes...
Exactly as you say...
AND THAT ENDS THE SECOND DAY OF THE GRAND MAGIC GAMES!!!
YAAAY
YAAAY
YAAAY
YAAAY
Cool! Cool!! Cool!!!
See you tomor-row!

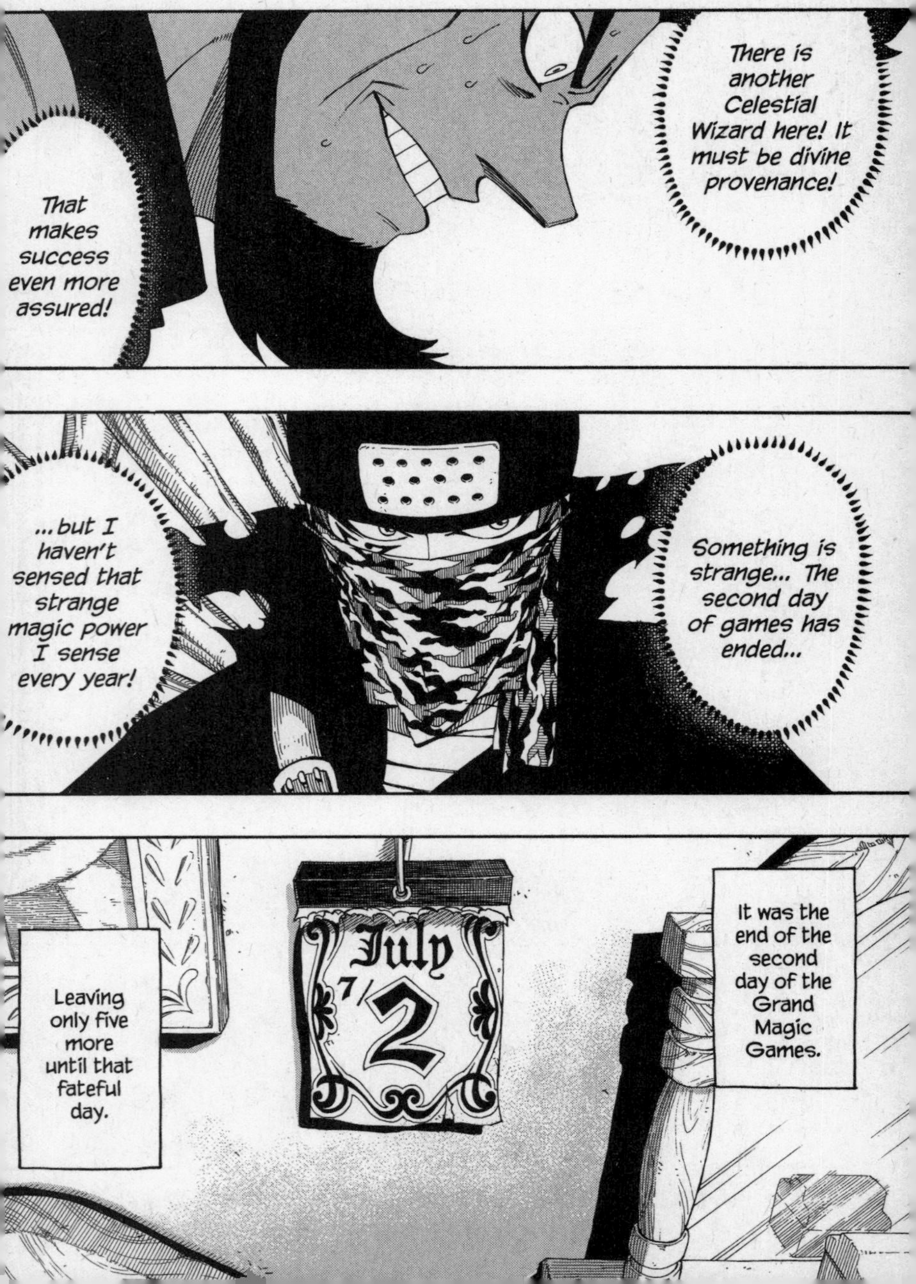
There is another Celestial Wizard here! It must be divine provenance!
That makes success even more assured!
Something is strange... The second day of games has ended...
...but I haven't sensed that strange magic power I sense every year!
It was the end of the second day of the Grand Magic Games.
July
7/2
Leaving only five more until that fateful day.

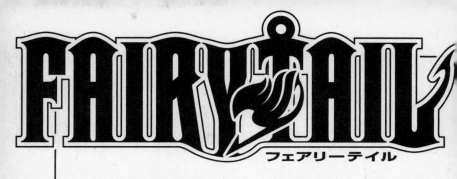

FAIRY TAIL

フェアリーテイル

Grand Magic Games Results of the 2nd Day

1. Raven Tail	26P + 10	1. Raven Tail	36P
2. Saber Tooth	20P + 0	2. Saber Tooth	20P
2. Lamia Scale	20P + 0	2. Lamia Scale	20P
4. Blue Pegasus	17P + 0	4. Mermaid Heel	19P
5. Quatro Puppy	12P + 0	5. Blue Pegasus	17P
6. Mermaid Heel	9P + 10	6. Quatro Puppy	12P
7. Fairy Tail B	2P + 10	6. Fairy Tail B	12P
7. Fairy Tail A	2P + 10	6. Fairy Tail A	12P

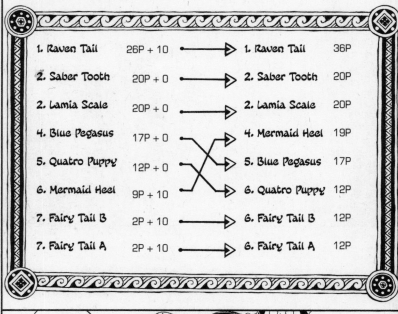

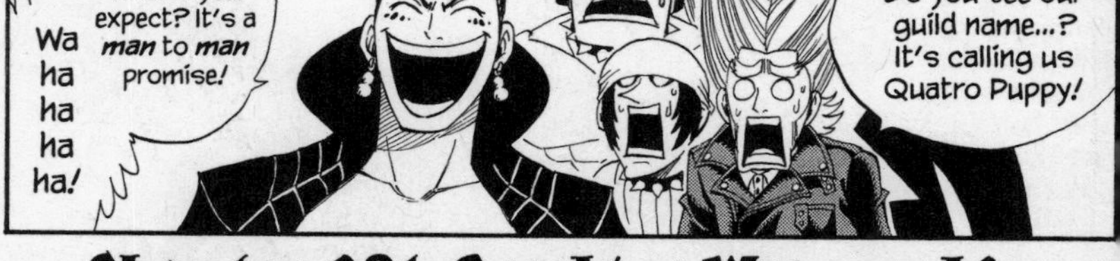

Um... Do you see our guild name...? It's calling us Quatro Puppy!
What'd you expect? It's a *man* to *man* promise!
Wa ha ha ha ha!

Chapter 281: Grudges Wrapped in the Curtain of Night

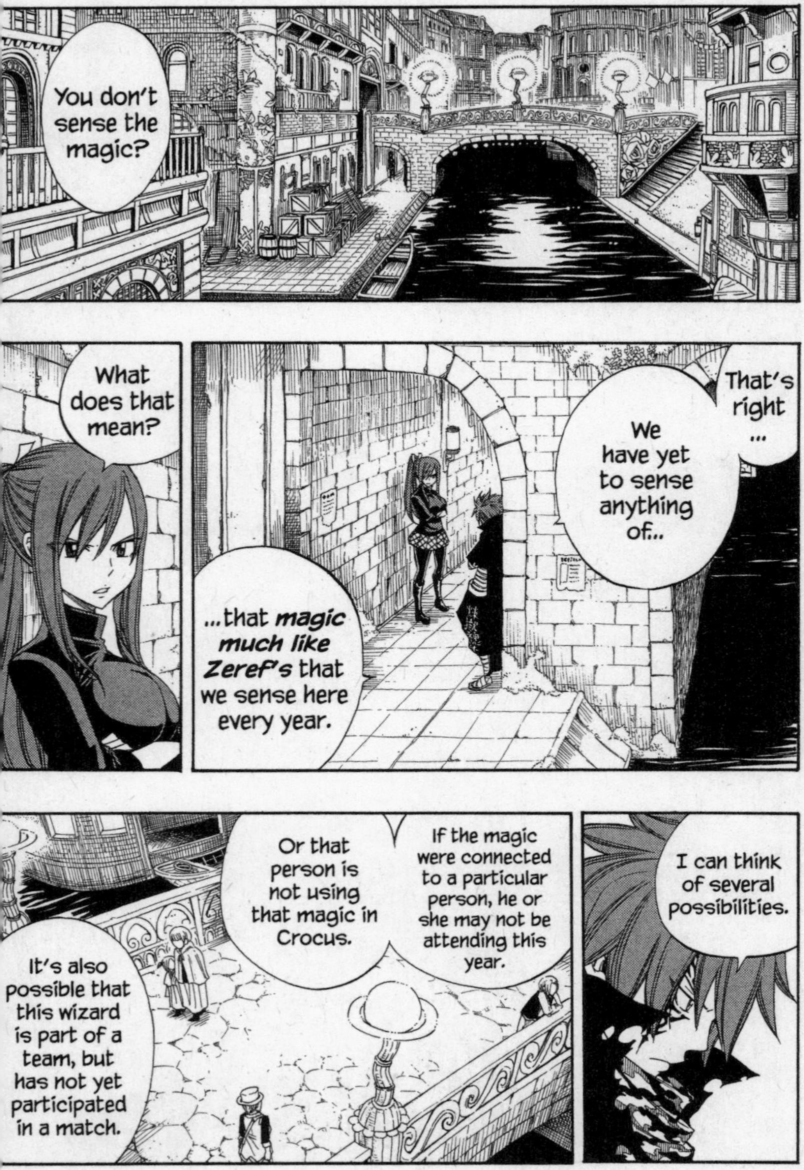
You don't sense the magic?
That's right...
We have yet to sense anything of...
...that *magic much like Zeref's* that we sense here every year.
What does that mean?
I can think of several possibilities.
If the magic were connected to a particular person, he or she may not be attending this year.
Or that person is not using that magic in Crocus.
It's also possible that this wizard is part of a team, but has not yet participated in a match.

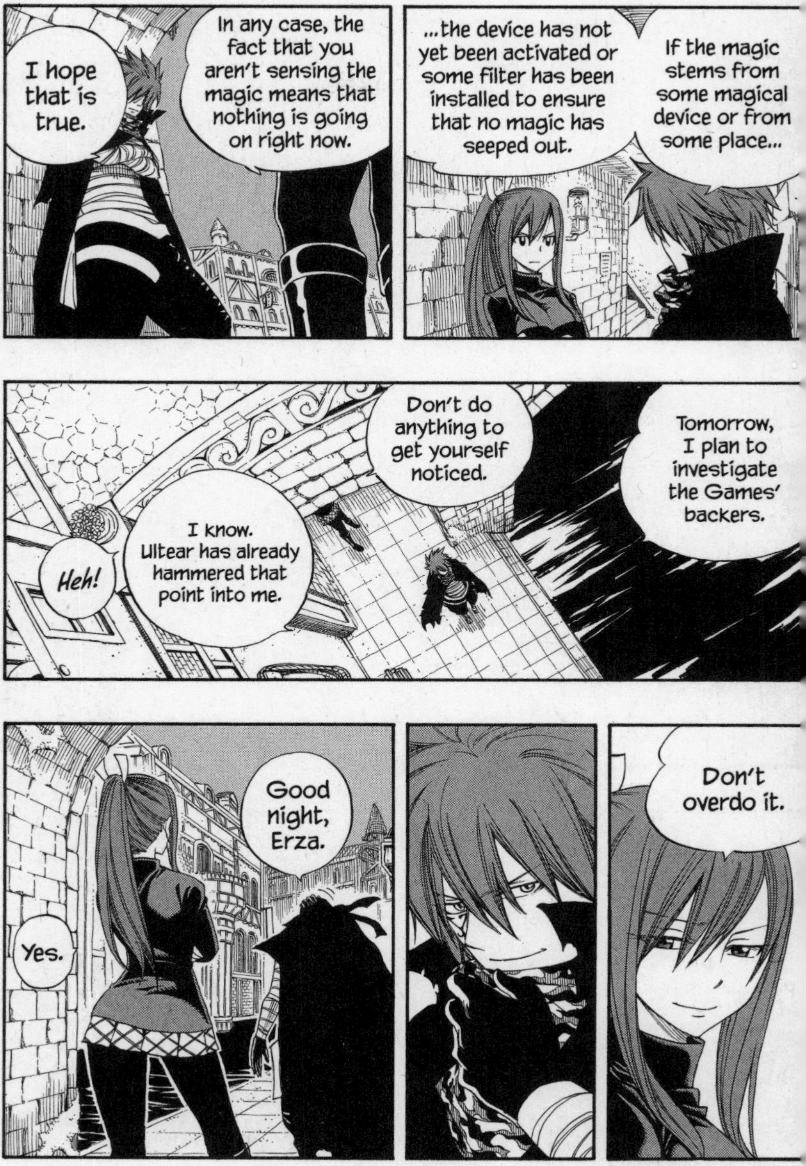
If the magic stems from some magical device or from some place...
...the device has not yet been activated or some filter has been installed to ensure that no magic has seeped out.
In any case, the fact that you aren't sensing the magic means that nothing is going on right now.
I hope that is true.
Tomorrow, I plan to investigate the Games' backers.
Don't do anything to get yourself noticed.
I know. Ultear has already hammered that point into me.
Heh!
Don't overdo it.
Good night, Erza.
Yes.

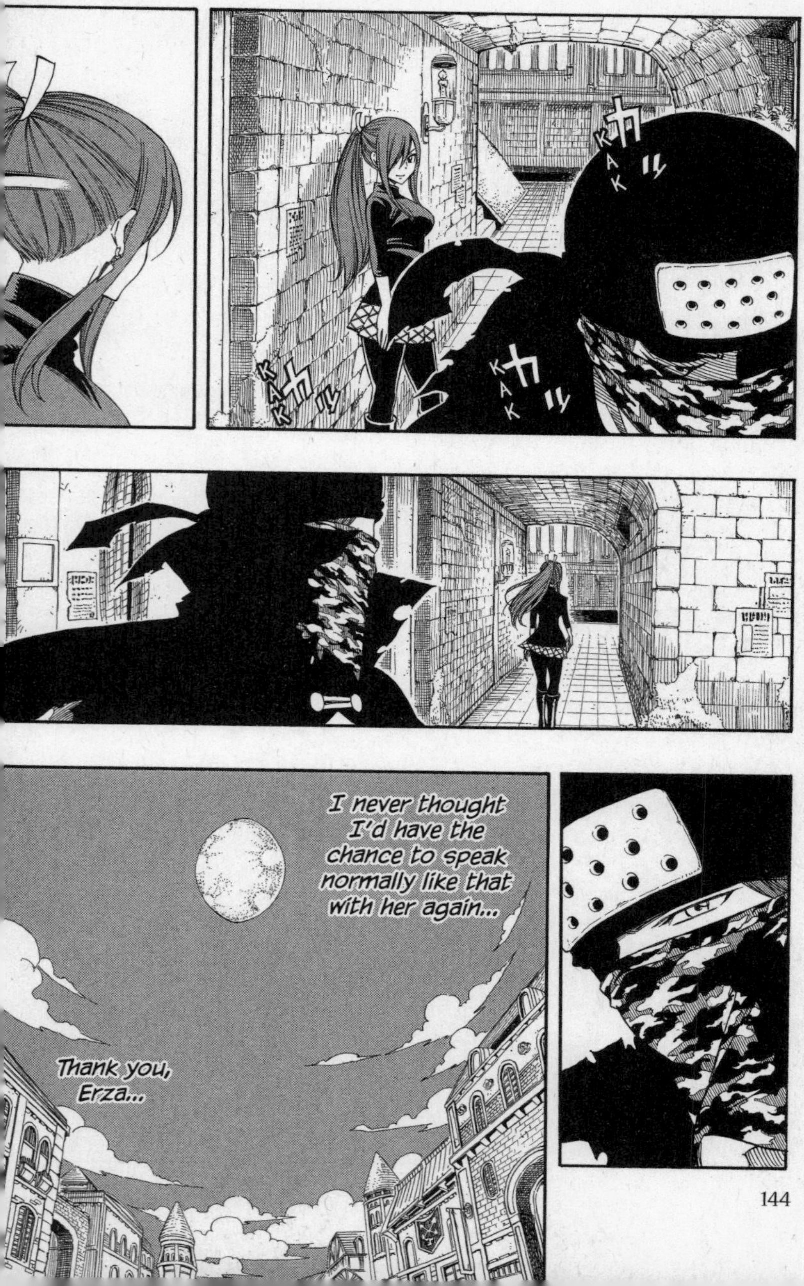

KAK カッ
KAK カッ
KAK カッ
I never thought I'd have the chance to speak normally like that with her again...
Thank you, Erza...

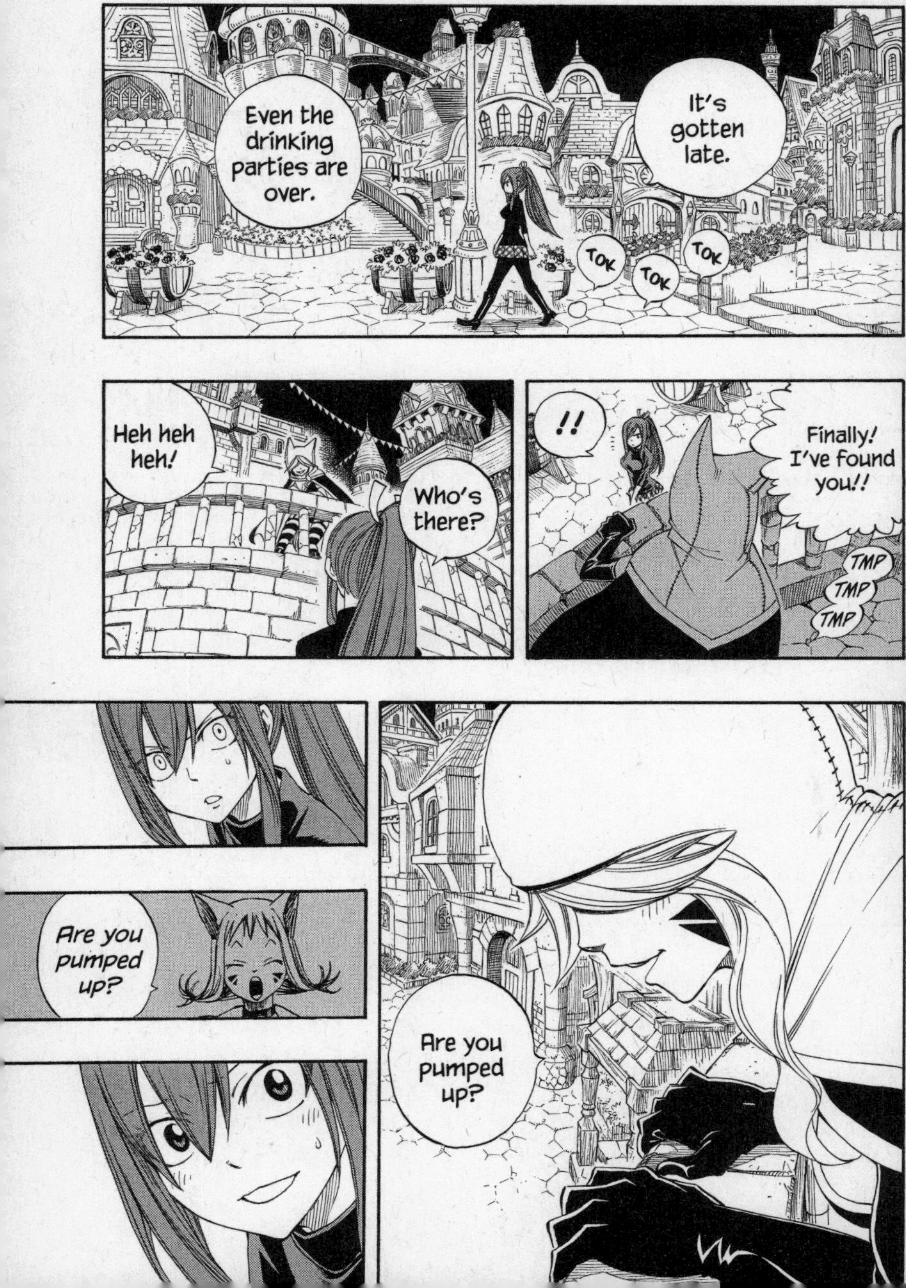
It's gotten late.
Even the drinking parties are over.
TOK
TOK
TOK
Finally! I've found you!!
TMP
TMP
TMP
!!
Who's there?
Heh heh heh!
Are you pumped up?
Are you pumped up?

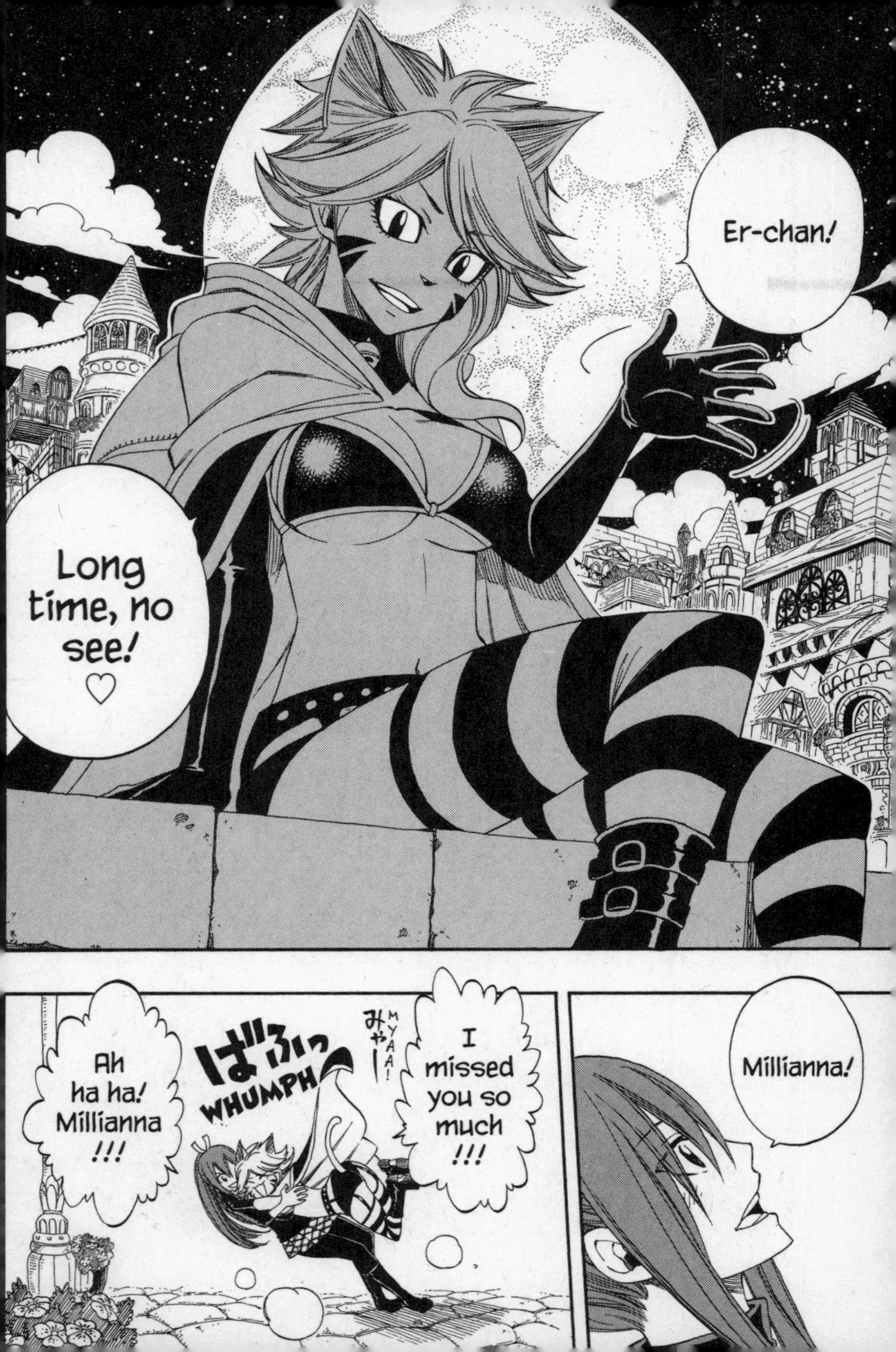
Er-chan!
Long time, no see! ♡
Millianna!
I missed you so much!!!
みゃー MYAA!
ばふっ WHUMPH
Ah ha ha! Millianna!!!

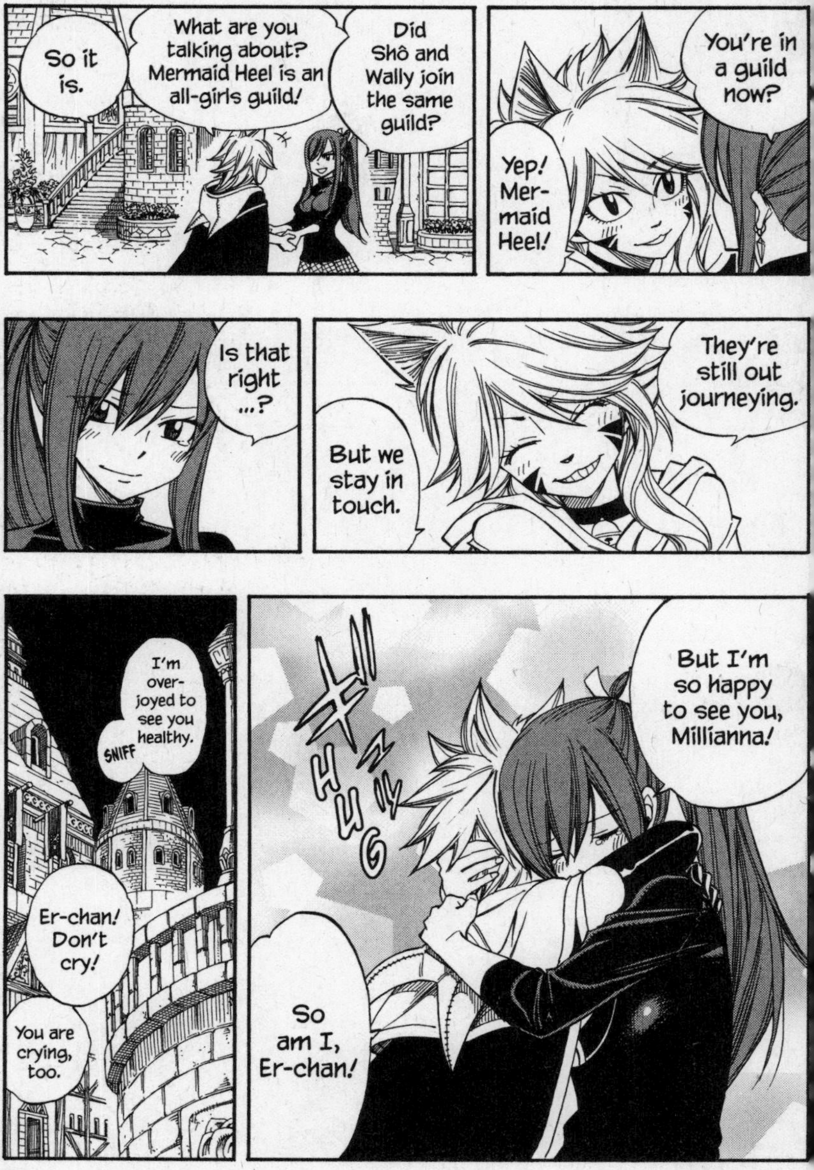
You're in a guild now?
Yep! Mermaid Heel!
Did Shô and Wally join the same guild?
What are you talking about? Mermaid Heel is an all-girls guild!
So it is.
They're still out journeying.
But we stay in touch.
Is that right ...?
But I'm so happy to see you, Millianna!
HUG
So am I, Er-chan!
I'm over-joyed to see you healthy.
SNIFF
Er-chan! Don't cry!
You are crying, too.

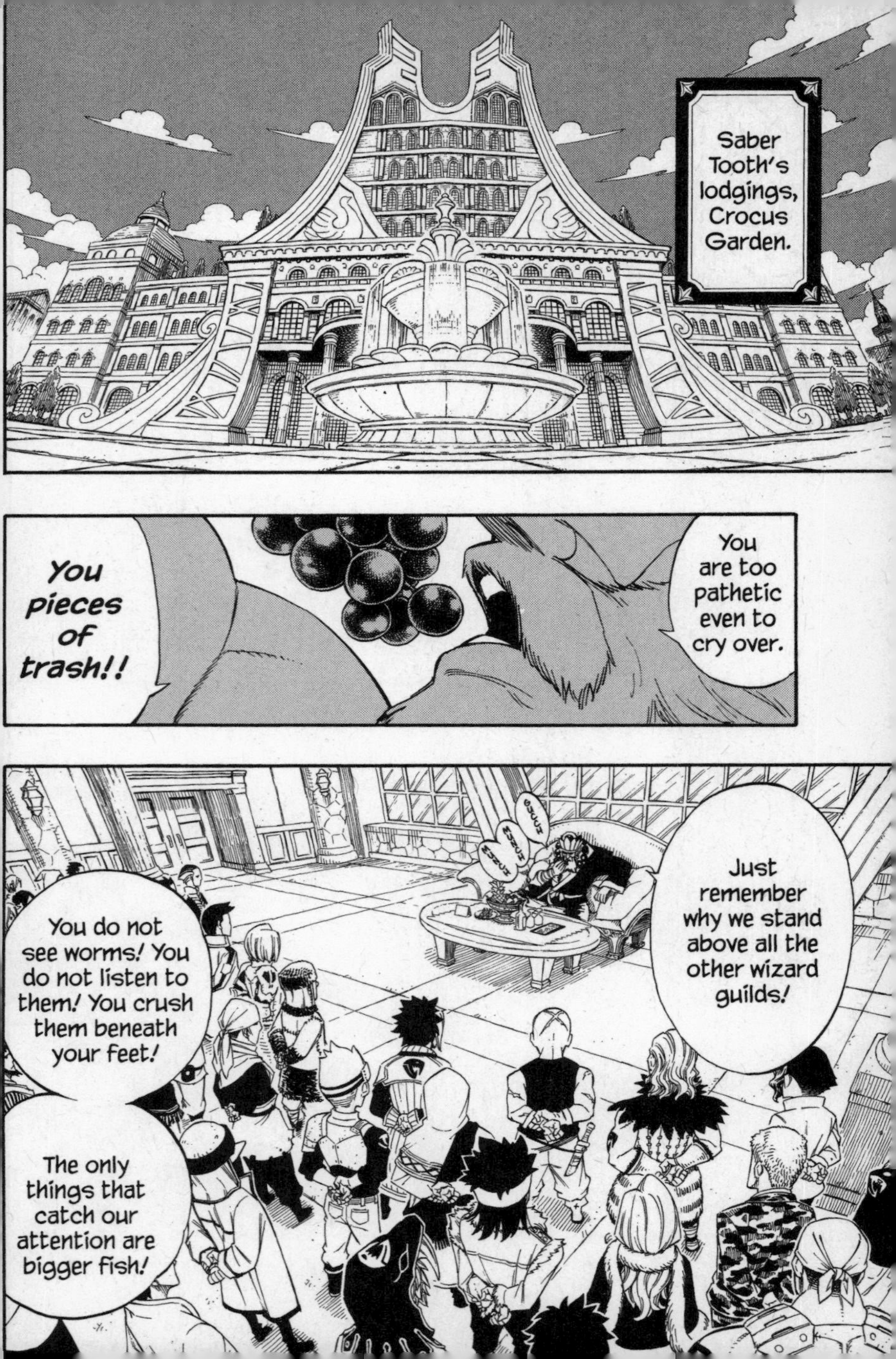
Saber Tooth's lodgings, Crocus Garden.
You are too pathetic even to cry over.
You pieces of trash!!
GUCCH
MUNCH
MUNCH
Just remember why we stand above all the other wizard guilds!
You do not see worms! You do not listen to them! You crush them beneath your feet!
The only things that catch our attention are bigger fish!

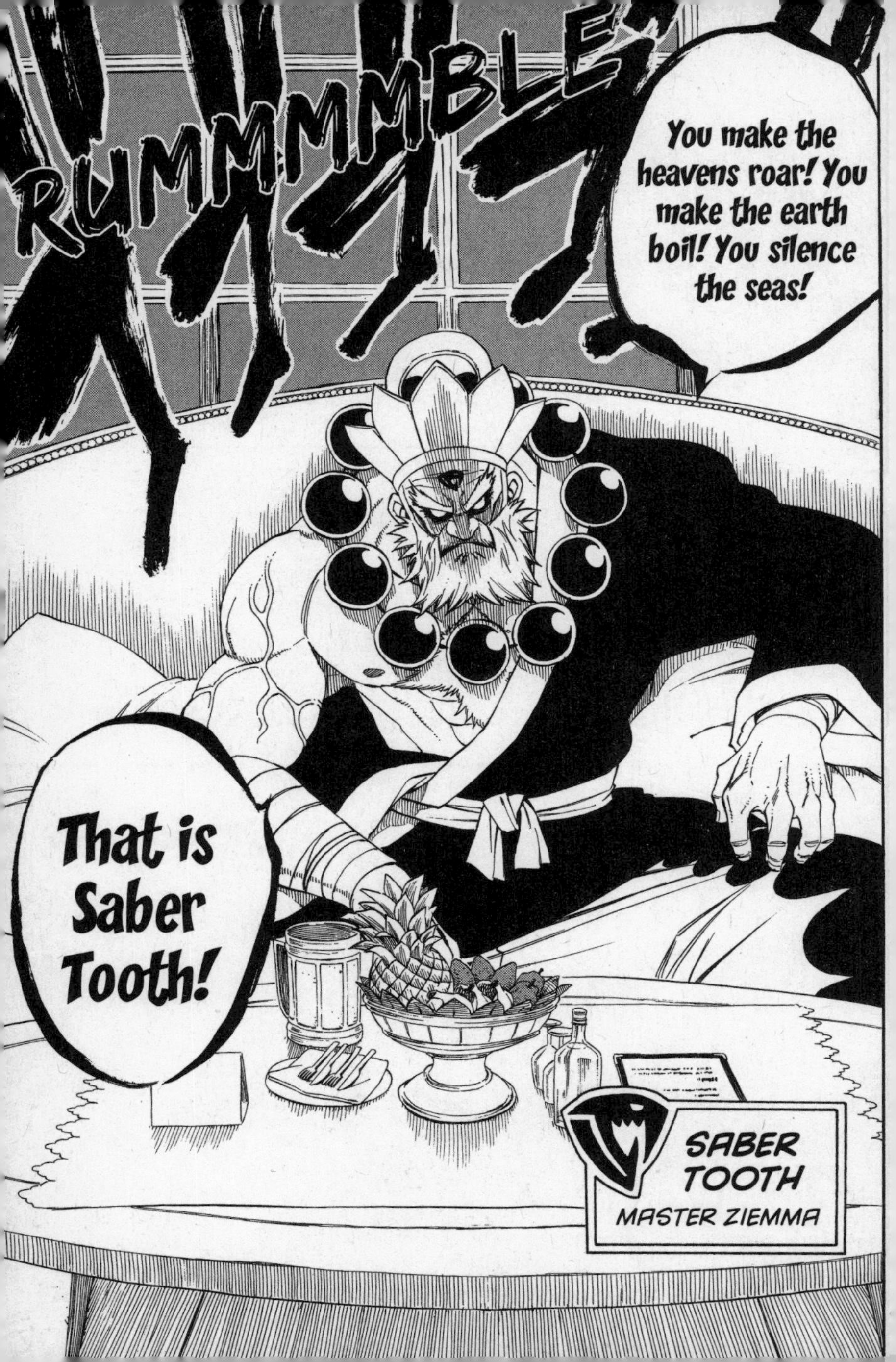
RUMMMMBLE
You make the heavens roar! You make the earth boil! You silence the seas!
That is Saber Tooth!
SABER TOOTH
MASTER ZIEMMA

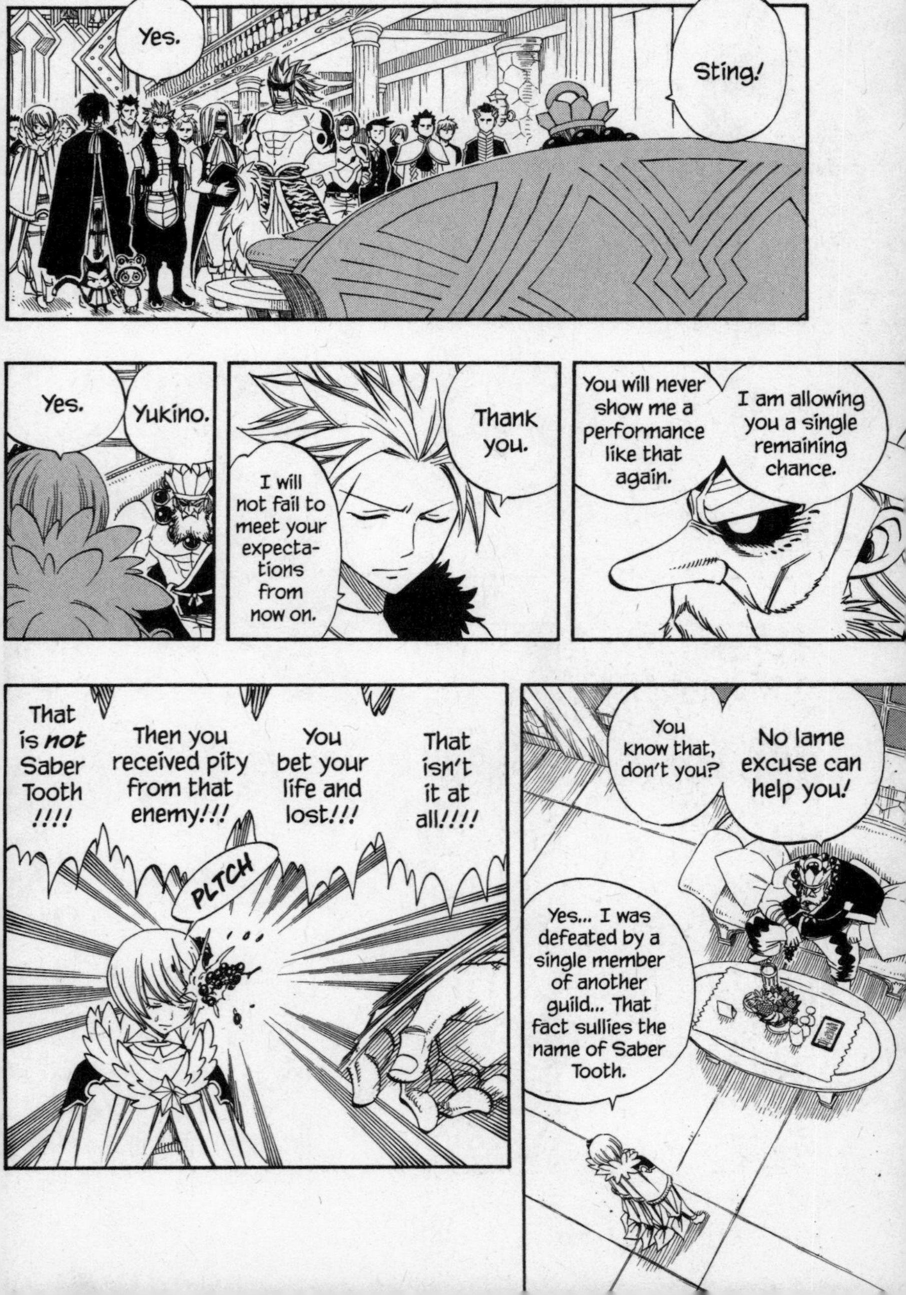
Sting!
Yes.
I am allowing you a single remaining chance.
You will never show me a performance like that again.
Thank you.
I will not fail to meet your expectations from now on.
Yukino.
Yes.
No lame excuse can help you!
You know that, don't you?
Yes... I was defeated by a single member of another guild... That fact sullies the name of Saber Tooth.
That isn't it at all!!!!
You bet your life and lost!!!
Then you received pity from that enemy!!!
That is *not* Saber Tooth!!!!
PLTCH
...

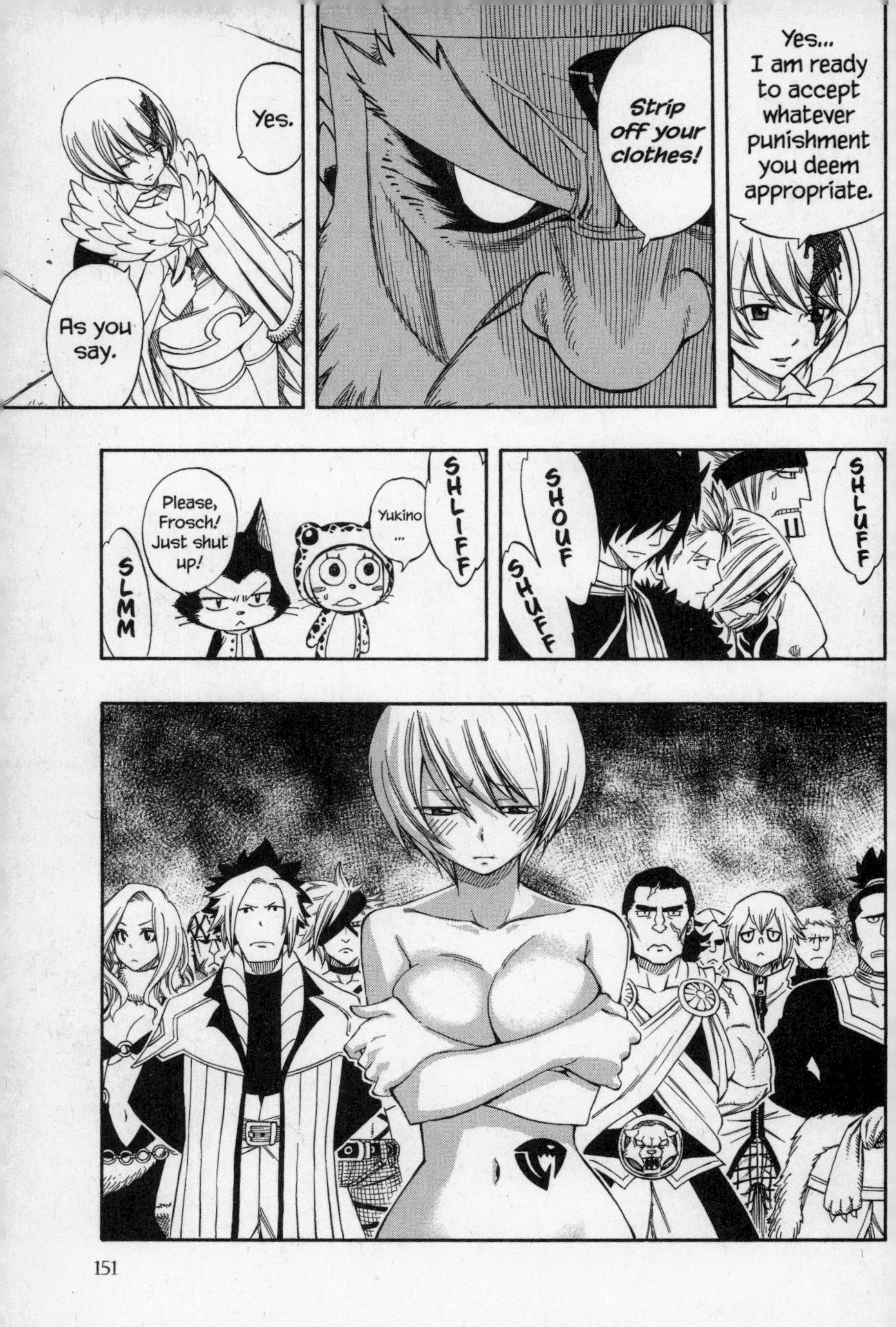
Yes... I am ready to accept whatever punishment you deem appropriate.
Strip off your clothes!
Yes.
As you say.
SHLUFF
SHOUF
SHUFF
SHLIFF
Yukino ...
Please, Frosch! Just shut up!
SLMM

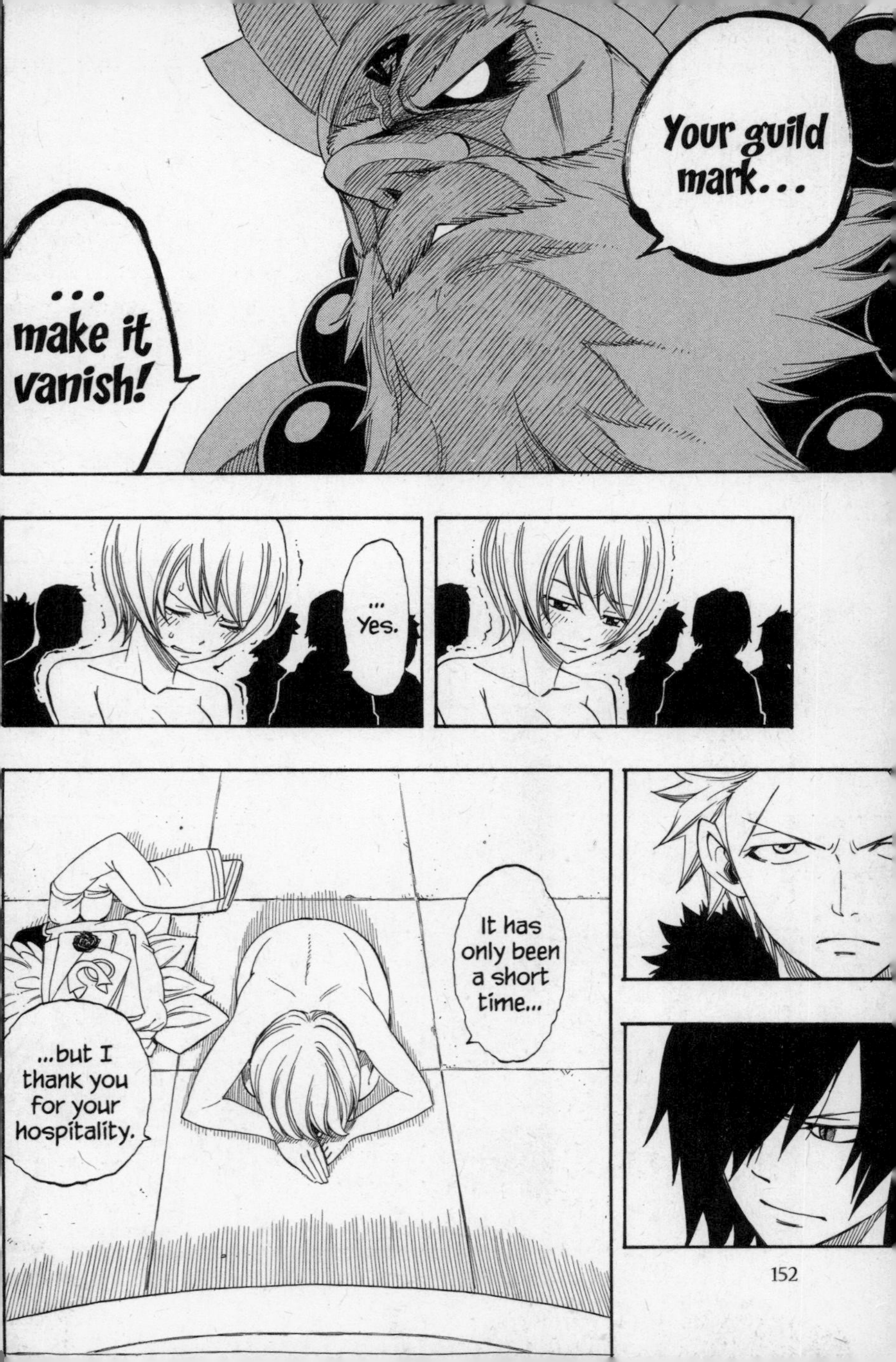

Your guild mark...
... make it vanish!
... Yes.
It has only been a short time...
...but I thank you for your hospitality.

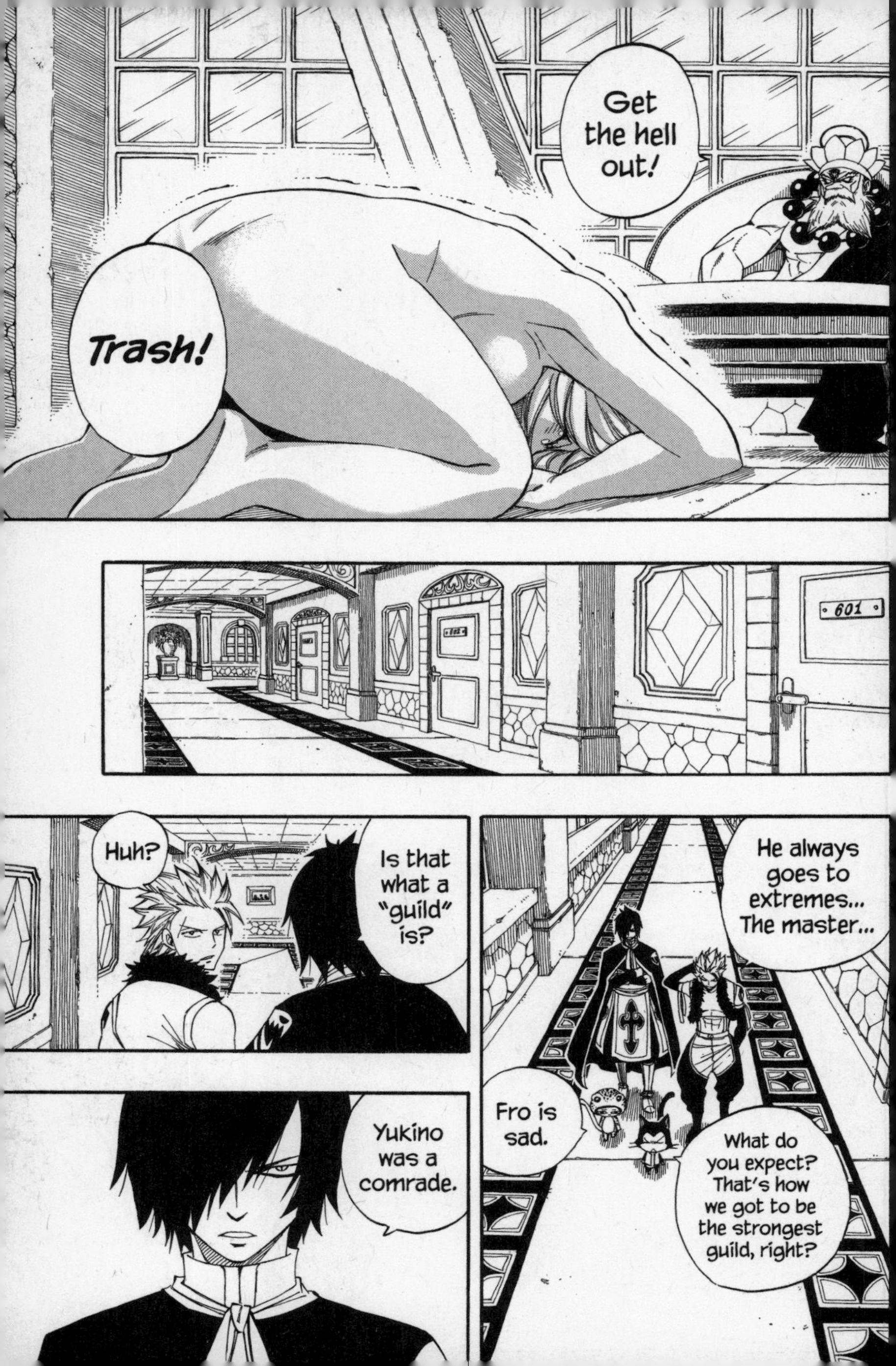
Get the hell out!
Trash!
601
He always goes to extremes... The master...
Fro is sad.
What do you expect? That's how we got to be the strongest guild, right?
Is that what a "guild" is?
Huh?
Yukino was a comrade.

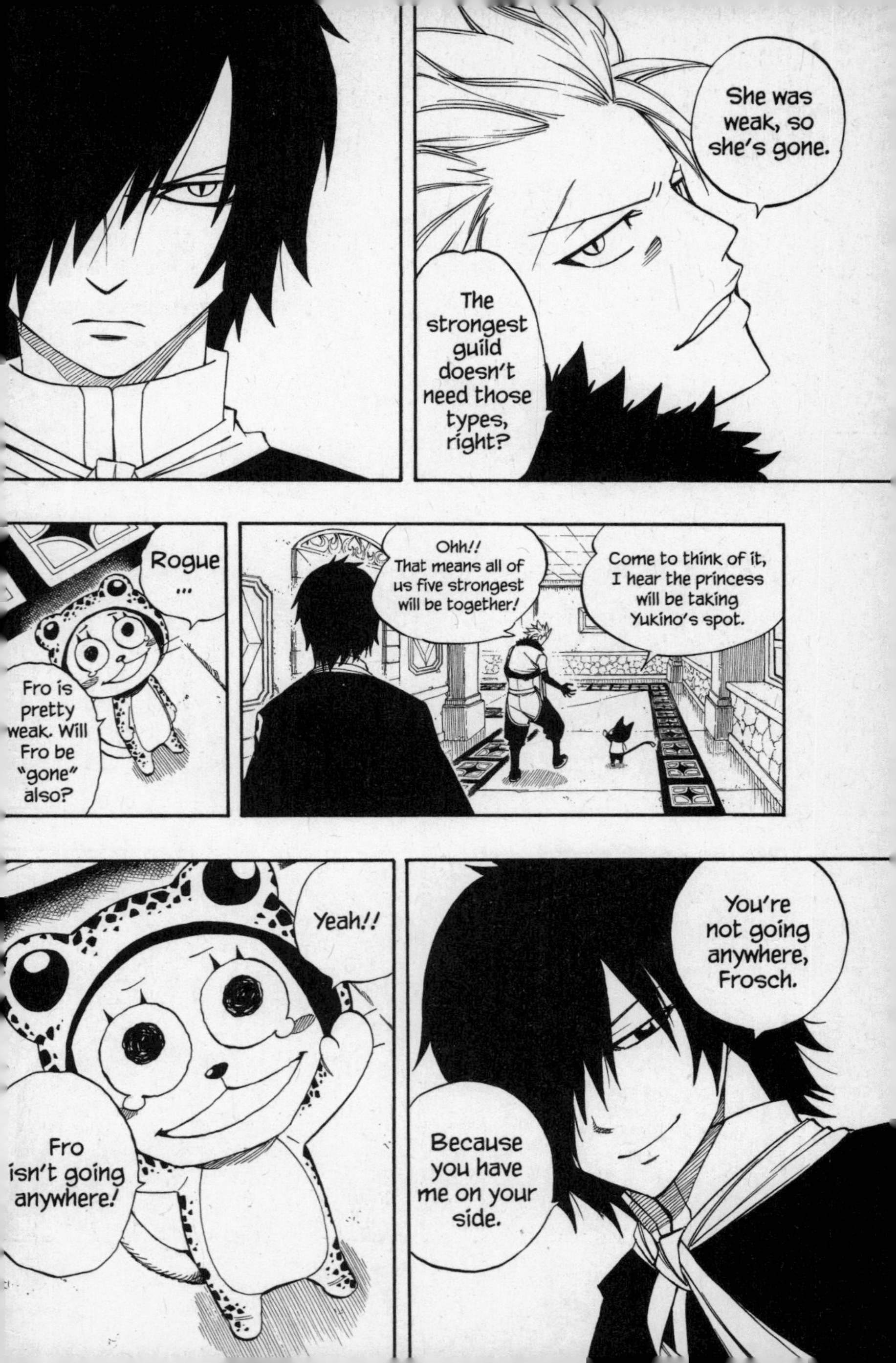
She was weak, so she's gone.
The strongest guild doesn't need those types, right?
Come to think of it, I hear the princess will be taking Yukino's spot.
Ohh!! That means all of us five strongest will be together!
Rogue ...
Fro is pretty weak. Will Fro be "gone" also?
You're not going anywhere, Frosch.
Because you have me on your side.
Yeah!!
Fro isn't going anywhere!

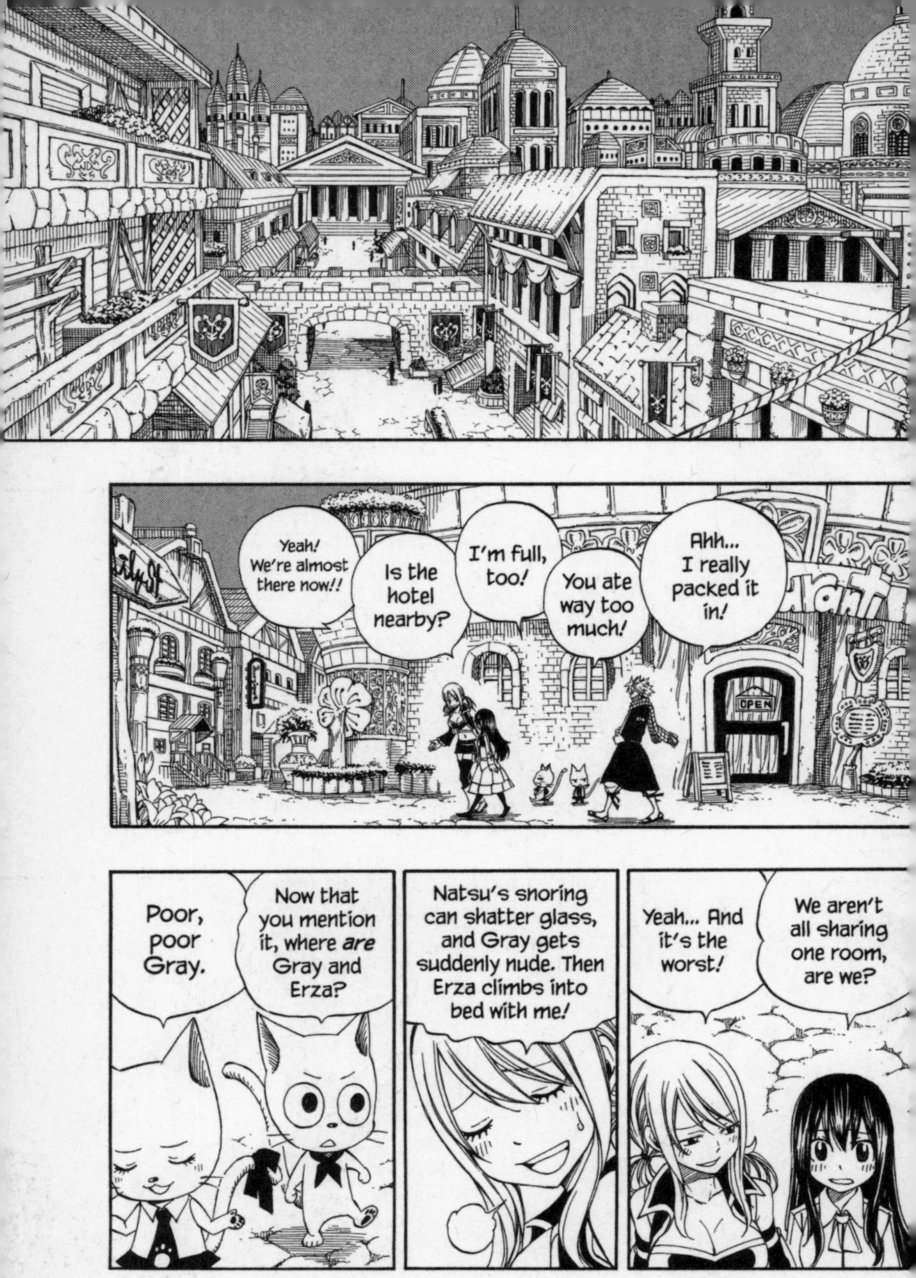
Ahh... I really packed it in!
You ate way too much!
I'm full, too!
Is the hotel nearby?
Yeah! We're almost there now!!
OPEN
We aren't all sharing one room, are we?
Yeah... And it's the worst!
Natsu's snoring can shatter glass, and Gray gets suddenly nude. Then Erza climbs into bed with me!
Now that you mention it, where *are* Gray and Erza?
Poor, poor Gray.

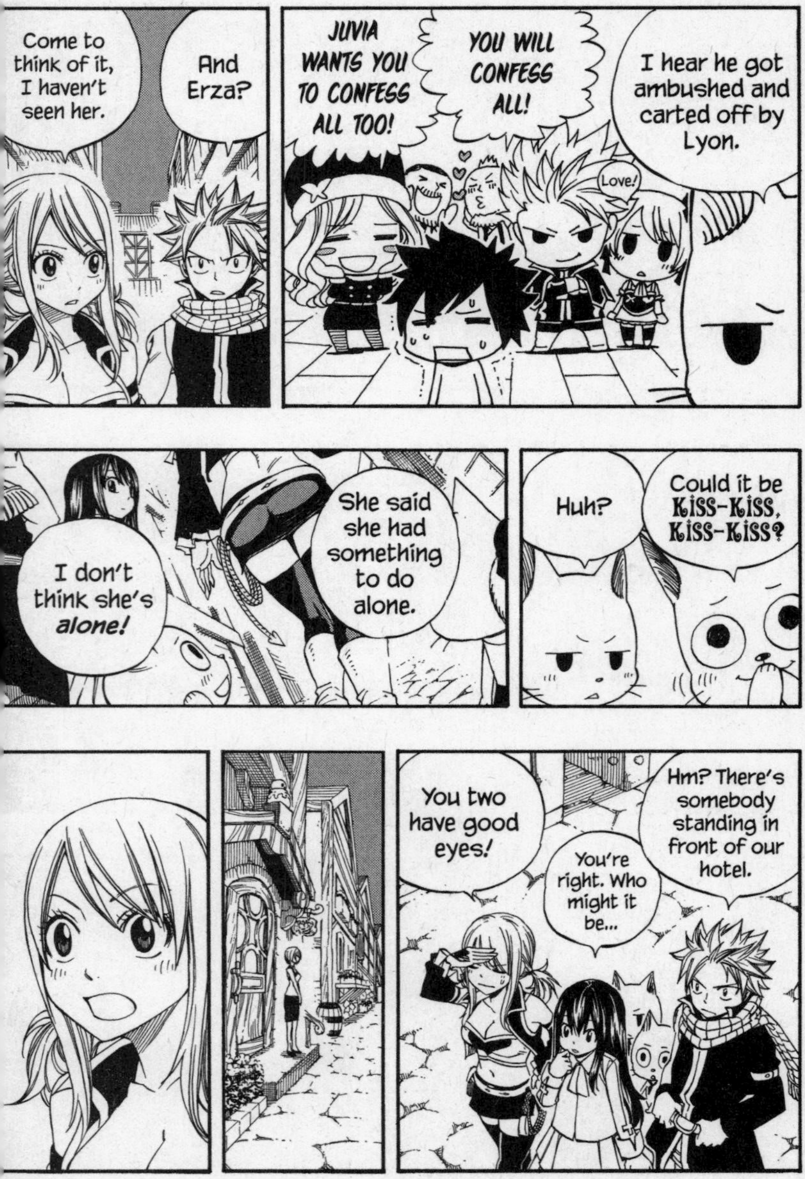
I hear he got ambushed and carted off by Lyon.
YOU WILL CONFESS ALL!
JUVIA WANTS YOU TO CONFESS ALL TOO!
Love!
And Erza?
Come to think of it, I haven't seen her.
Could it be KISS-KISS, KISS-KISS?
Huh?
She said she had something to do alone.
I don't think she's *alone!*
Hm? There's somebody standing in front of our hotel.
You're right. Who might it be...
You two have good eyes!

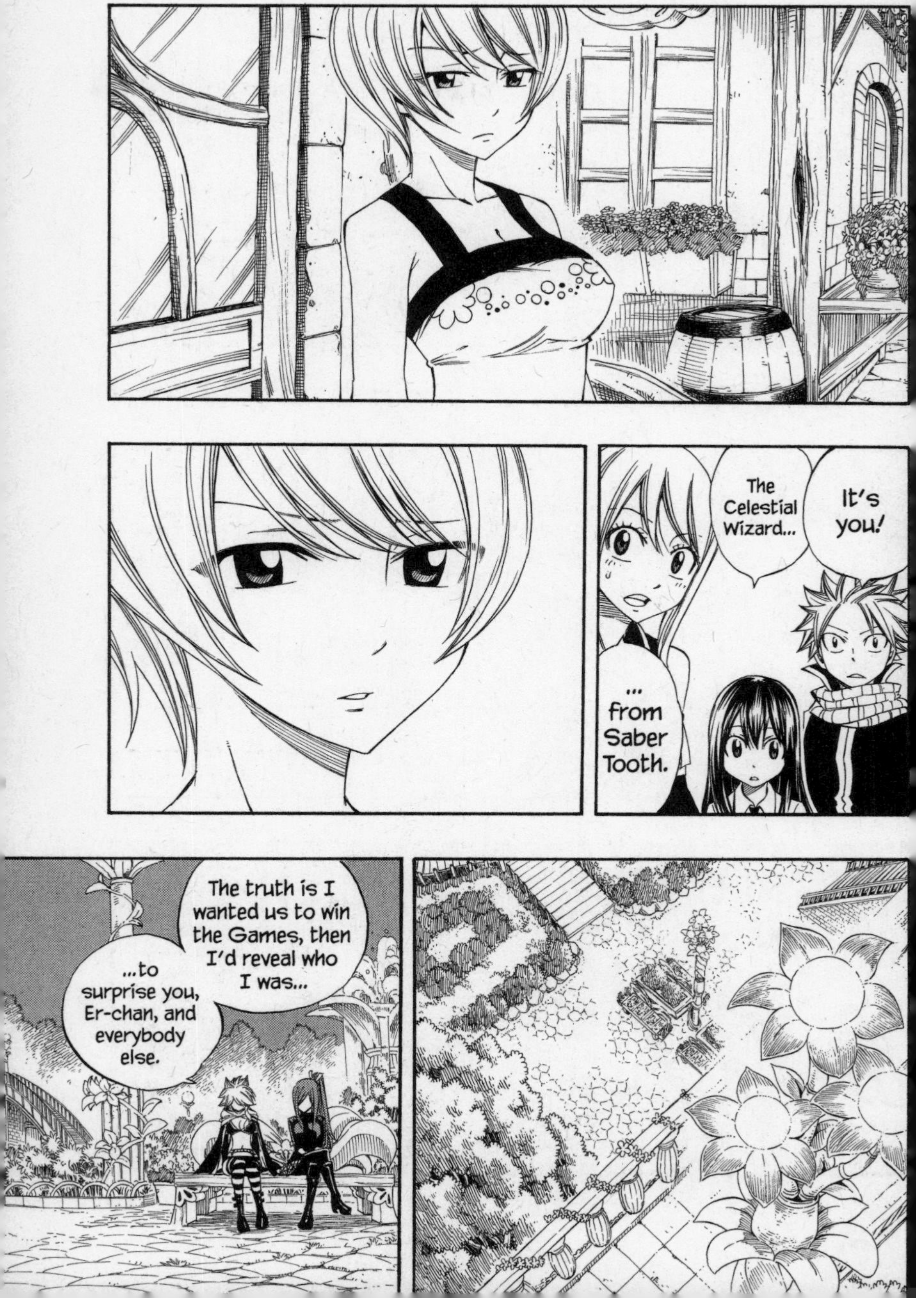
It's you!
The Celestial Wizard...
...from Saber Tooth.
The truth is I wanted us to win the Games, then I'd reveal who I was...
...to surprise you, Er-chan, and everybody else.

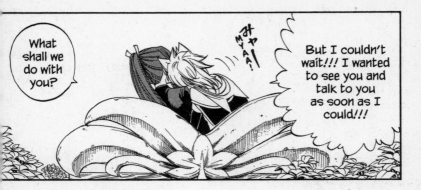

But I couldn't wait!!! I wanted to see you and talk to you as soon as I could!!!
みや MYAA!
What shall we do with you?
But I must say how impressed I was at the strength of Kagura from your guild.
She's great! If it came to blows, she might even be stronger than you, Er-chan!
I hope she and I can face off at some point.
You may even get the chance during these Games.
Oh... But Kagura-chan may never get really serious during the Games.
Is that right?
You saw her use that Fugutaiten sheathed sword, right?
Quite a violent name for a sword.

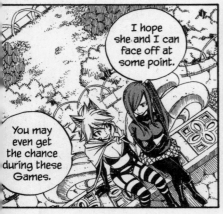

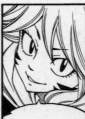

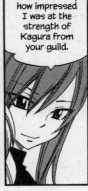

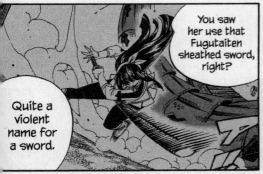

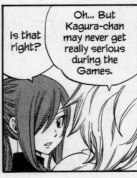

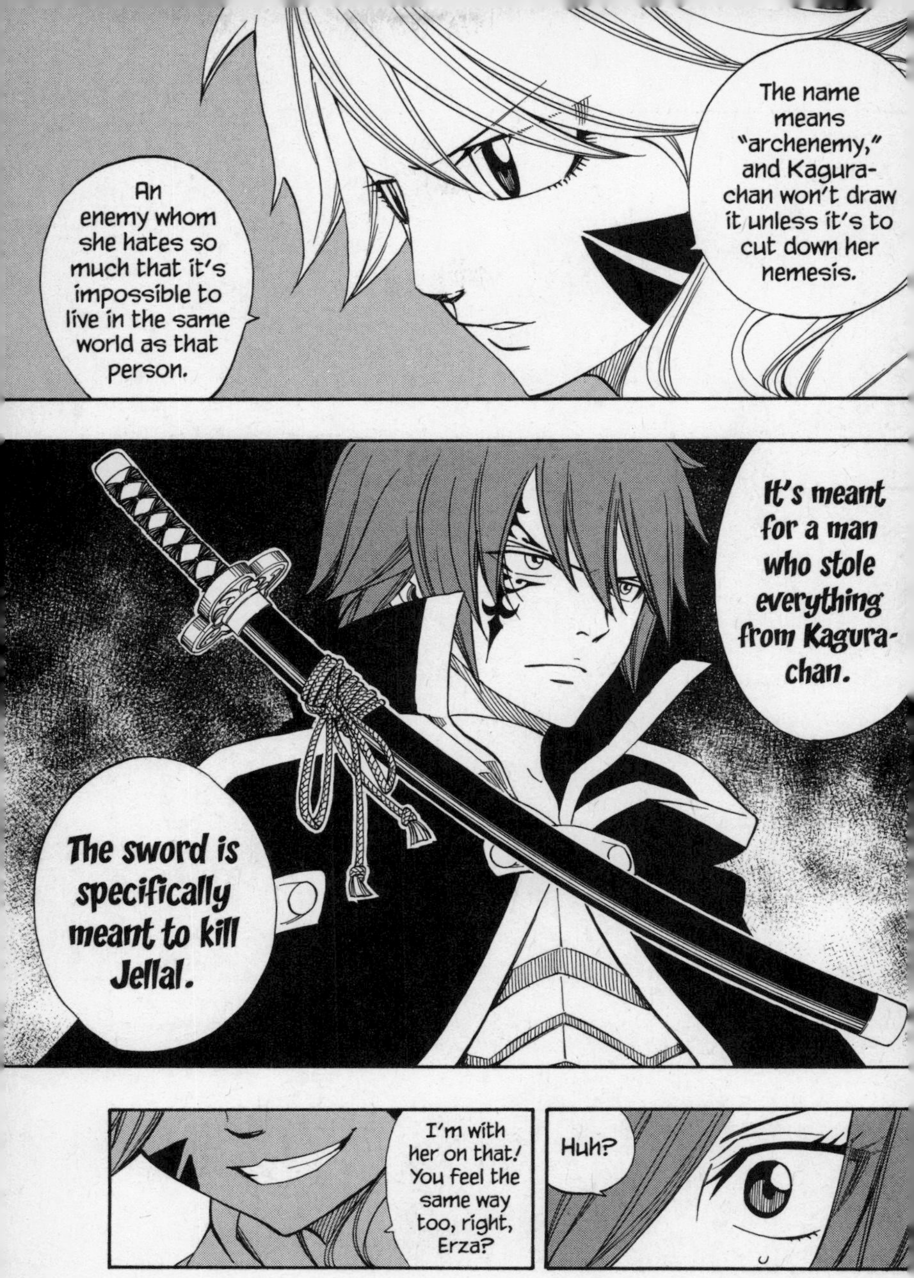
The name means "archenemy," and Kagura-chan won't draw it unless it's to cut down her nemesis.
An enemy whom she hates so much that it's impossible to live in the same world as that person.
It's meant for a man who stole everything from Kagura-chan.
The sword is specifically meant to kill Jellal.
Huh?
I'm with her on that! You feel the same way too, right, Erza?

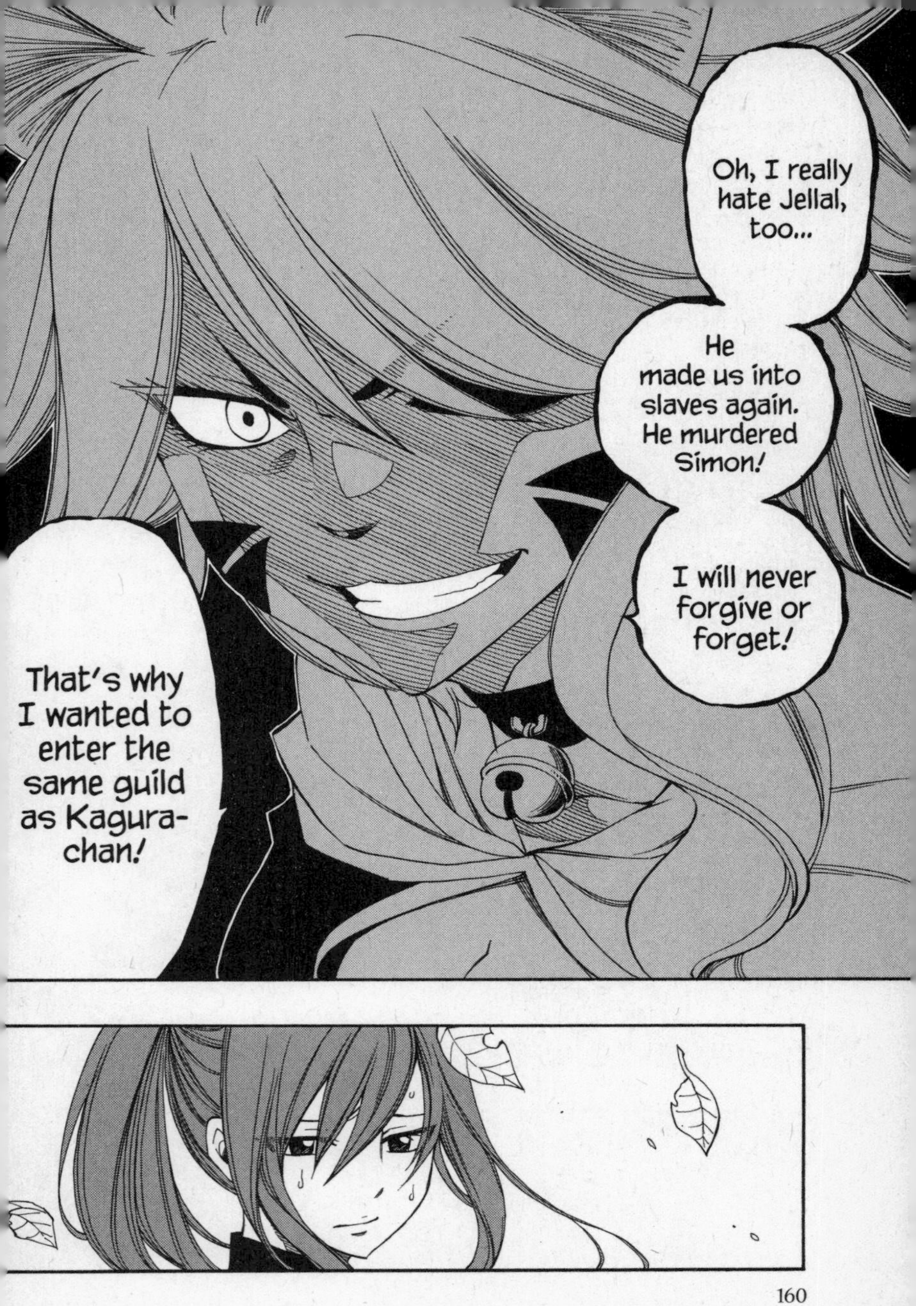
Oh, I really hate Jellal, too...
He made us into slaves again. He murdered Simon!
I will never forgive or forget!
That's why I wanted to enter the same guild as Kagura-chan!

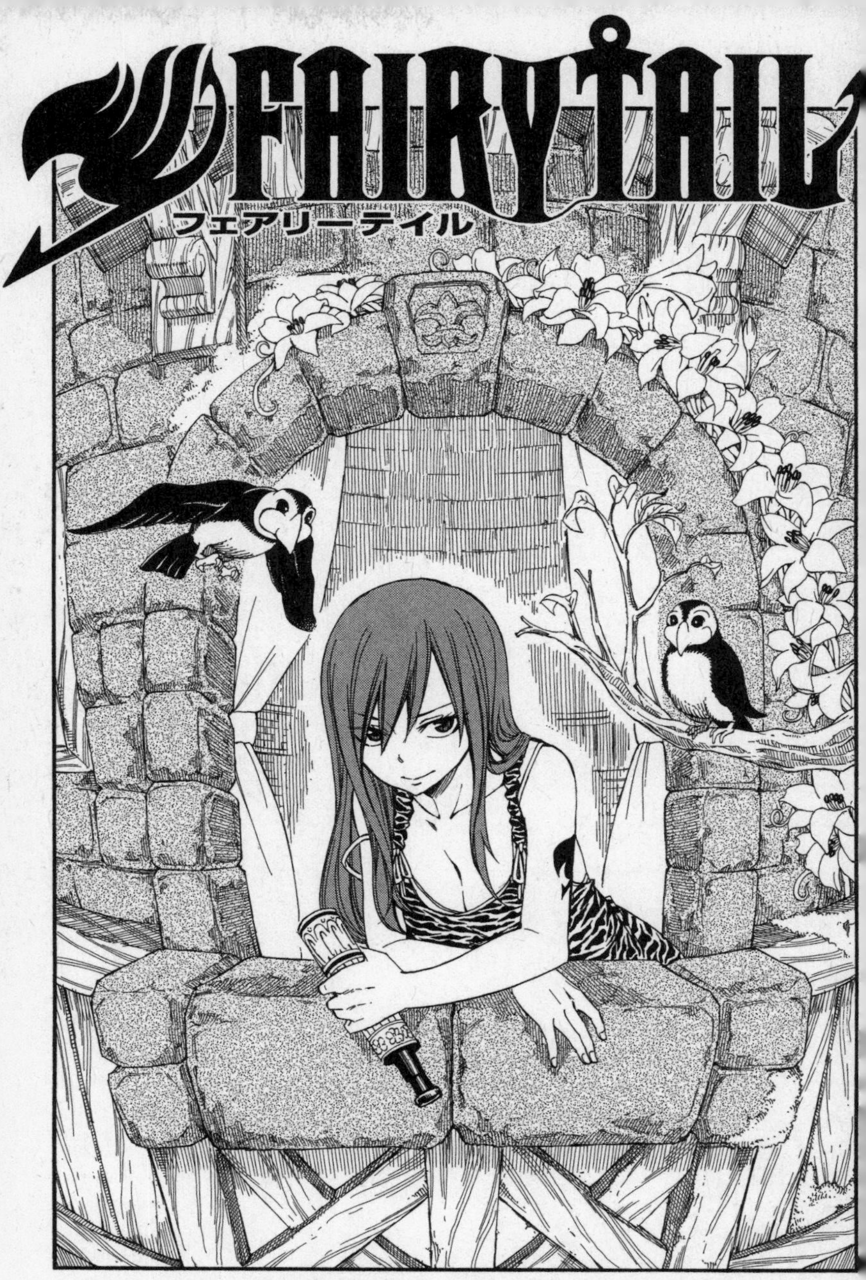
FAIRY TAIL
フェアリーテイル

Chapter 282: Ten Keys and Two Keys

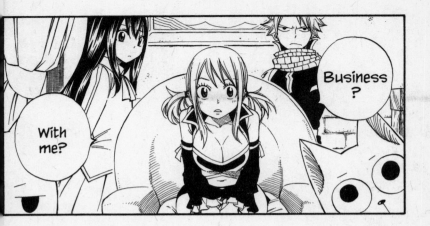

Business ?
With me?
Yes.
I have important business with you, Miss Lucy.
What business could Saber have?
Natsu-san. Let's at least hear what she has to say.
I am not here to fight.
These.
CHANK

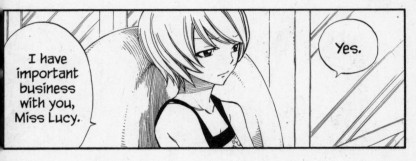

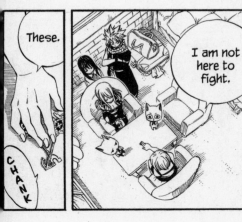

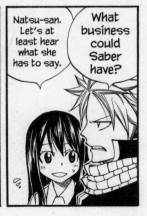

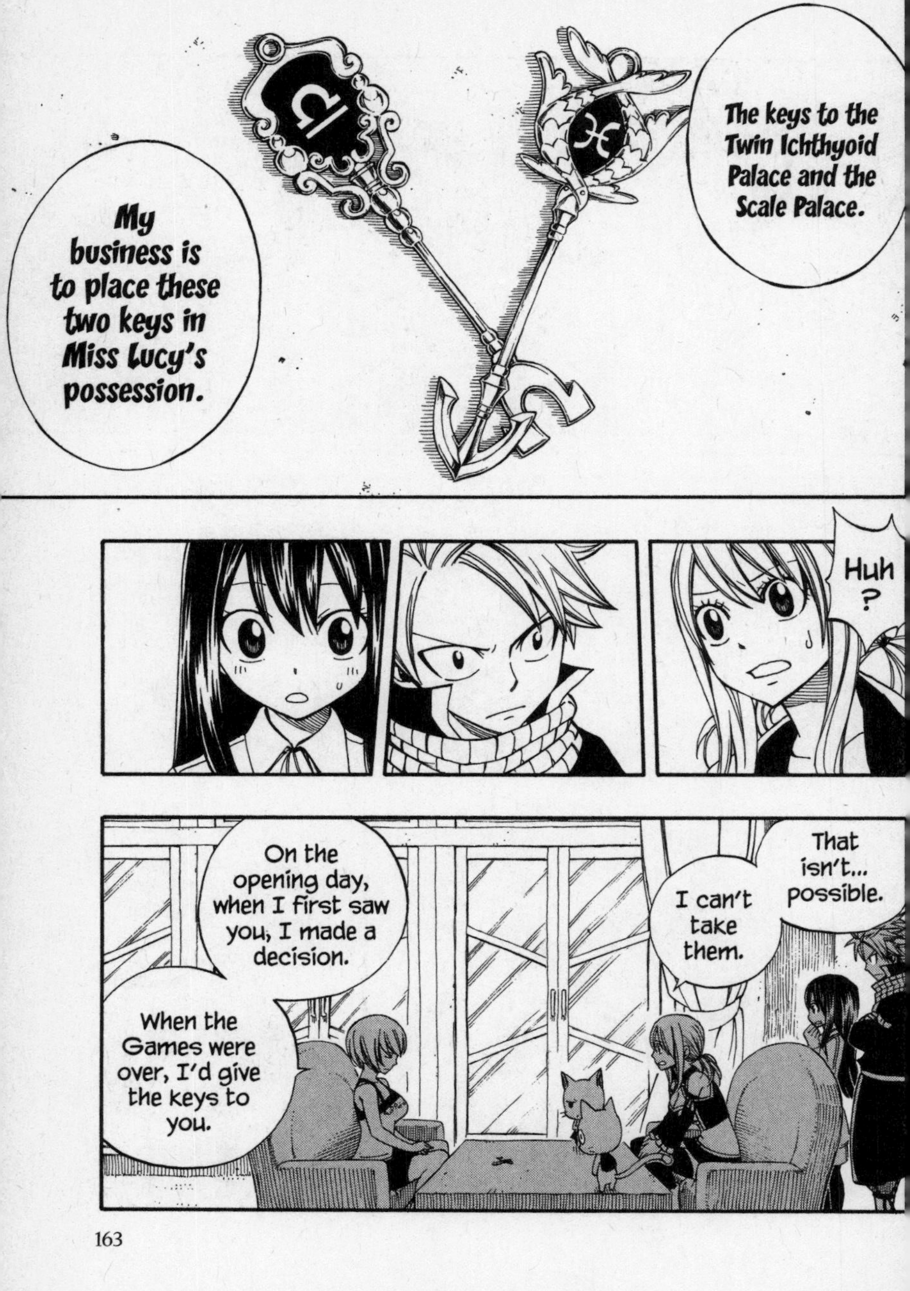
The keys to the Twin Ichthyoid Palace and the Scale Palace.
My business is to place these two keys in Miss Lucy's possession.
Huh?
That isn't... possible.
I can't take them.
On the opening day, when I first saw you, I made a decision.
When the Games were over, I'd give the keys to you.

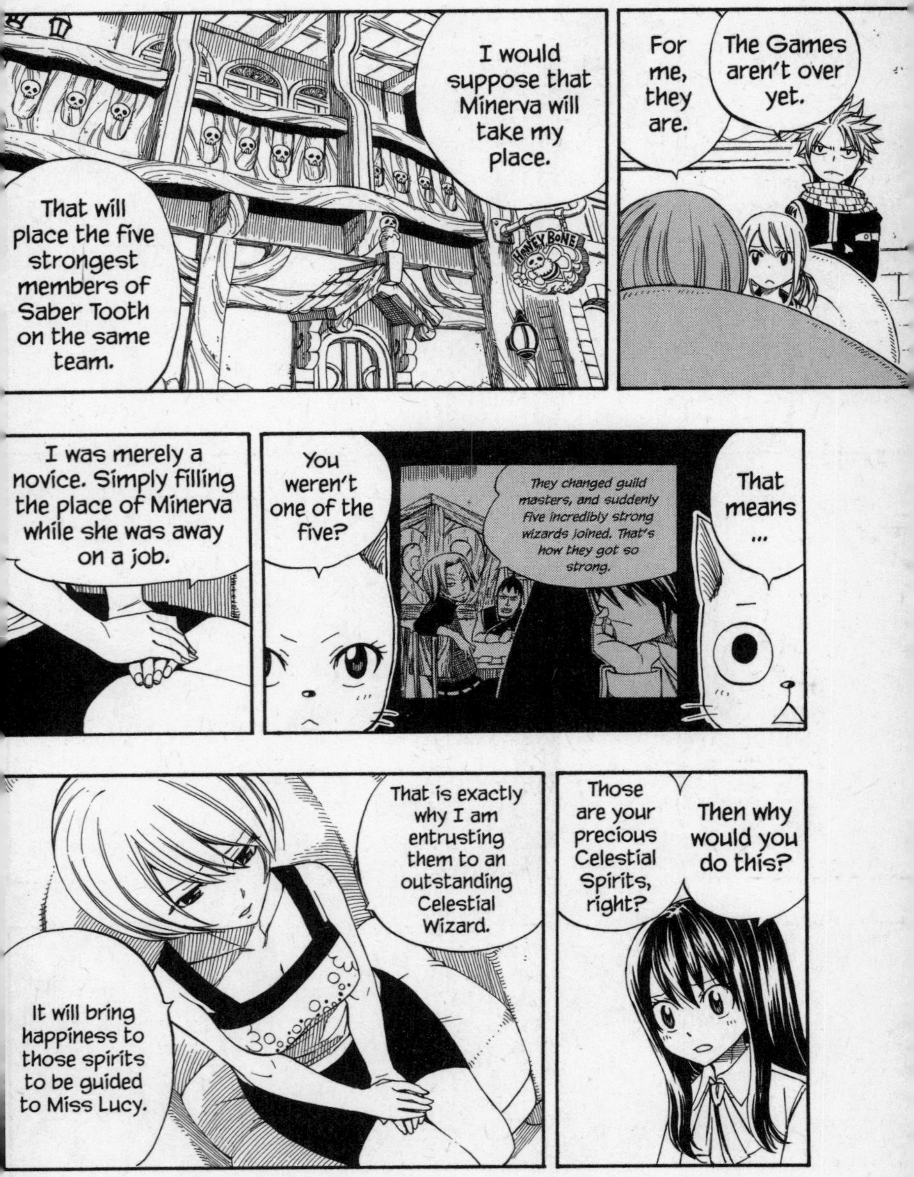

The Games aren't over yet.
For me, they are.
I would suppose that Minerva will take my place.
That will place the five strongest members of Saber Tooth on the same team.
That means ...
They changed guild masters, and suddenly five incredibly strong wizards joined. That's how they got so strong.
You weren't one of the five?
I was merely a novice. Simply filling the place of Minerva while she was away on a job.
Then why would you do this?
Those are your precious Celestial Spirits, right?
That is exactly why I am entrusting them to an outstanding Celestial Wizard.
It will bring happiness to those spirits to be guided to Miss Lucy.

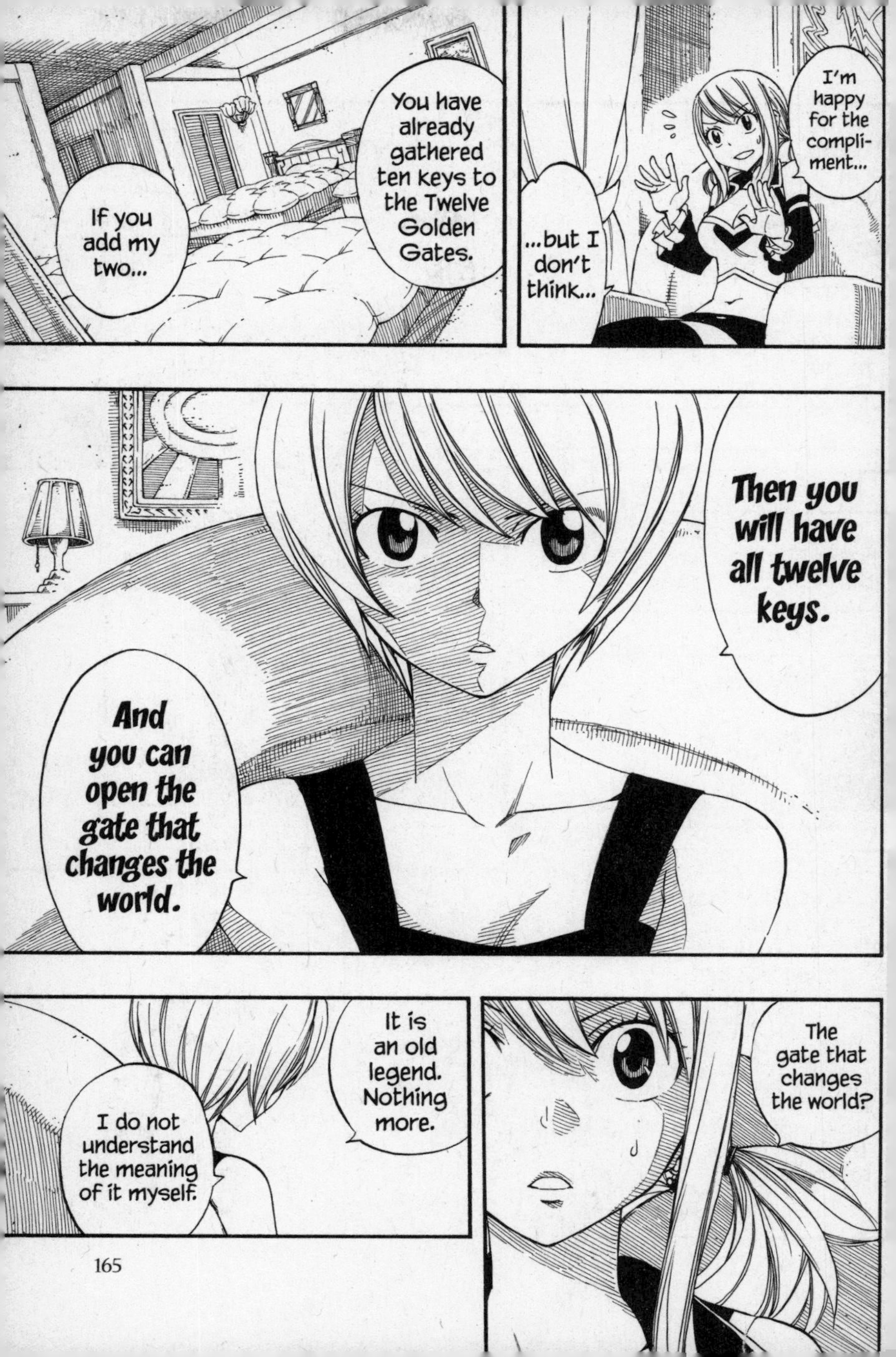
I'm happy for the compliment...
...but I don't think...
You have already gathered ten keys to the Twelve Golden Gates.
If you add my two...
Then you will have all twelve keys.
And you can open the gate that changes the world.
The gate that changes the world?
It is an old legend. Nothing more.
I do not understand the meaning of it myself.

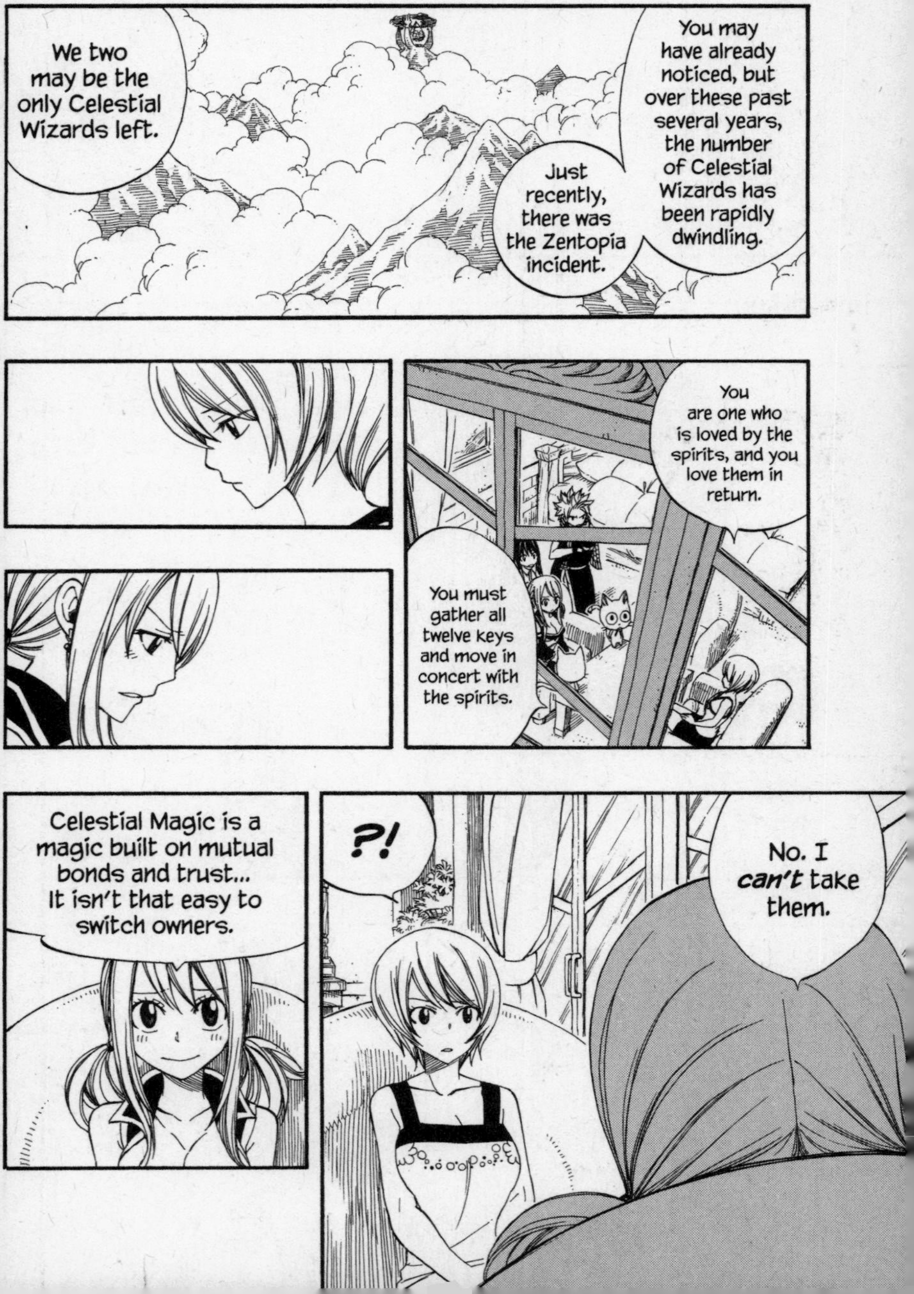
You may have already noticed, but over these past several years, the number of Celestial Wizards has been rapidly dwindling.
Just recently, there was the Zentopia incident.
We two may be the only Celestial Wizards left.
You are one who is loved by the spirits, and you love them in return.
You must gather all twelve keys and move in concert with the spirits.
No. I *can't* take them.
?!
Celestial Magic is a magic built on mutual bonds and trust... It isn't that easy to switch owners.

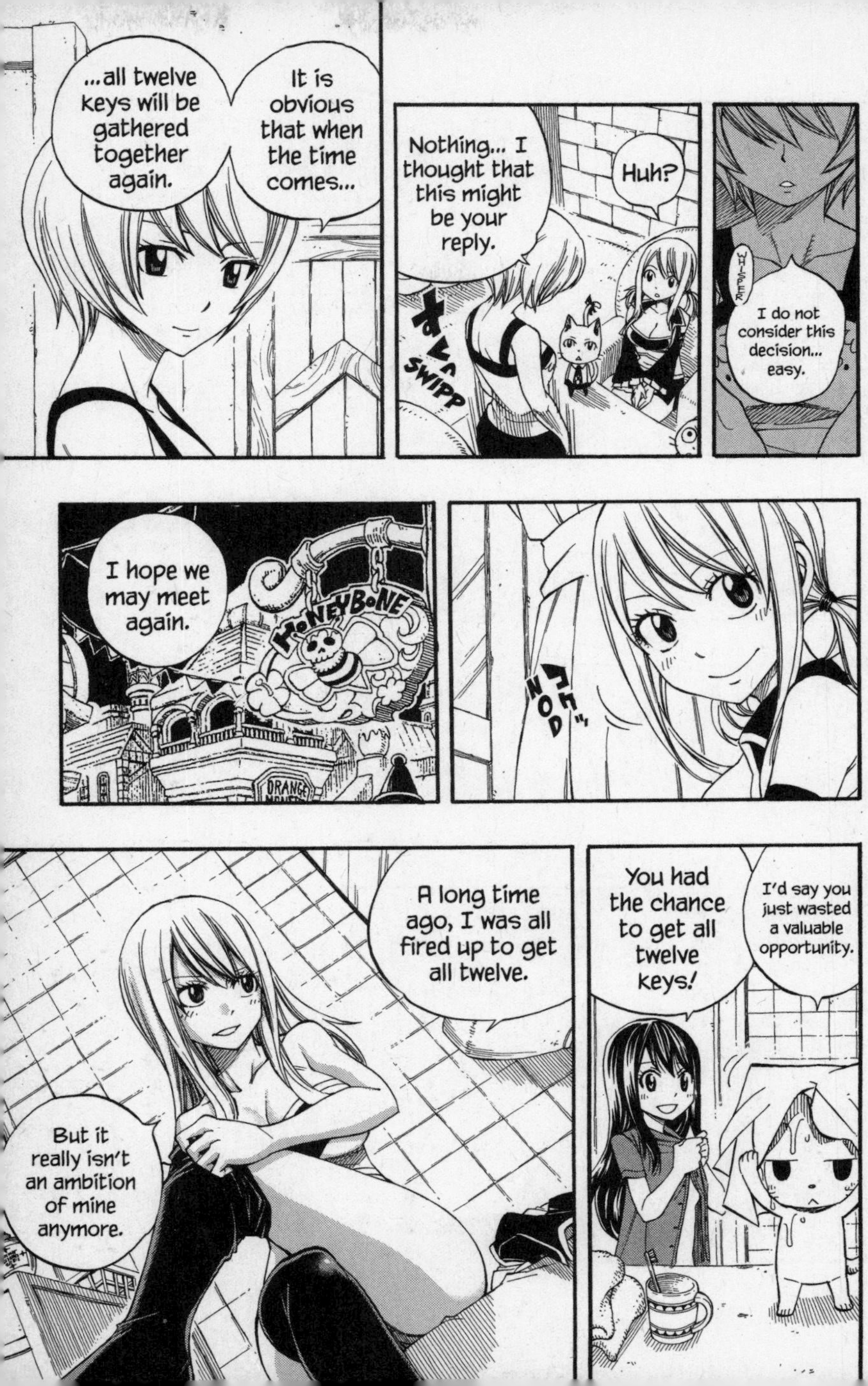

WHISPER
I do not consider this decision... easy.
Huh?
Nothing... I thought that this might be your reply.
SWIPP
It is obvious that when the time comes...
...all twelve keys will be gathered together again.
NOD
I hope we may meet again.
HONEYBONE
ORANGE
I'd say you just wasted a valuable opportunity.
You had the chance to get all twelve keys!
A long time ago, I was all fired up to get all twelve.
But it really isn't an ambition of mine anymore.

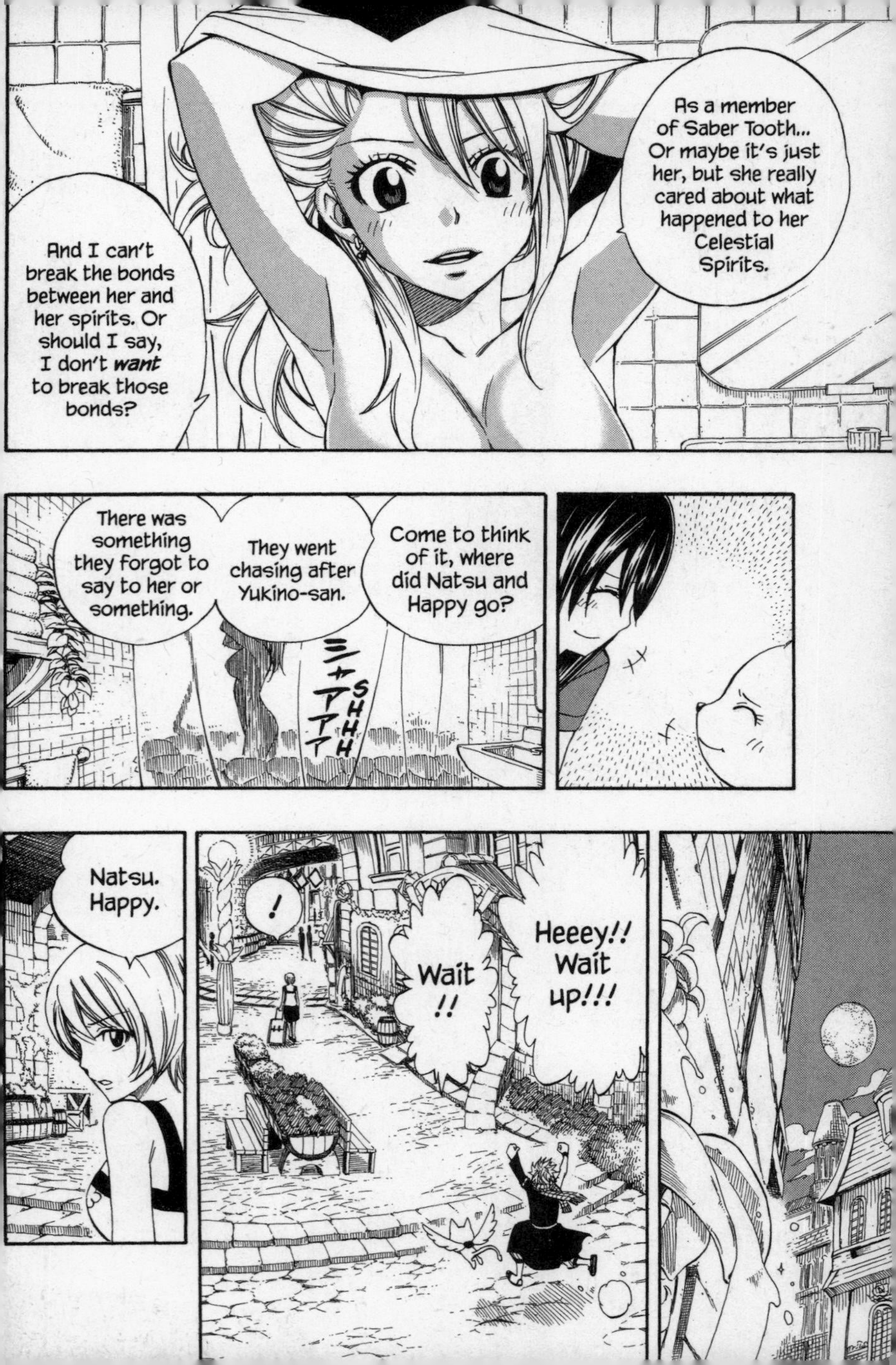
As a member of Saber Tooth... Or maybe it's just her, but she really cared about what happened to her Celestial Spirits.
And I can't break the bonds between her and her spirits. Or should I say, I don't *want* to break those bonds?
Come to think of it, where did Natsu and Happy go?
They went chasing after Yukino-san.
There was something they forgot to say to her or something.
SHHH
Heeey!! Wait up!!!
Wait !!
!
Natsu. Happy.

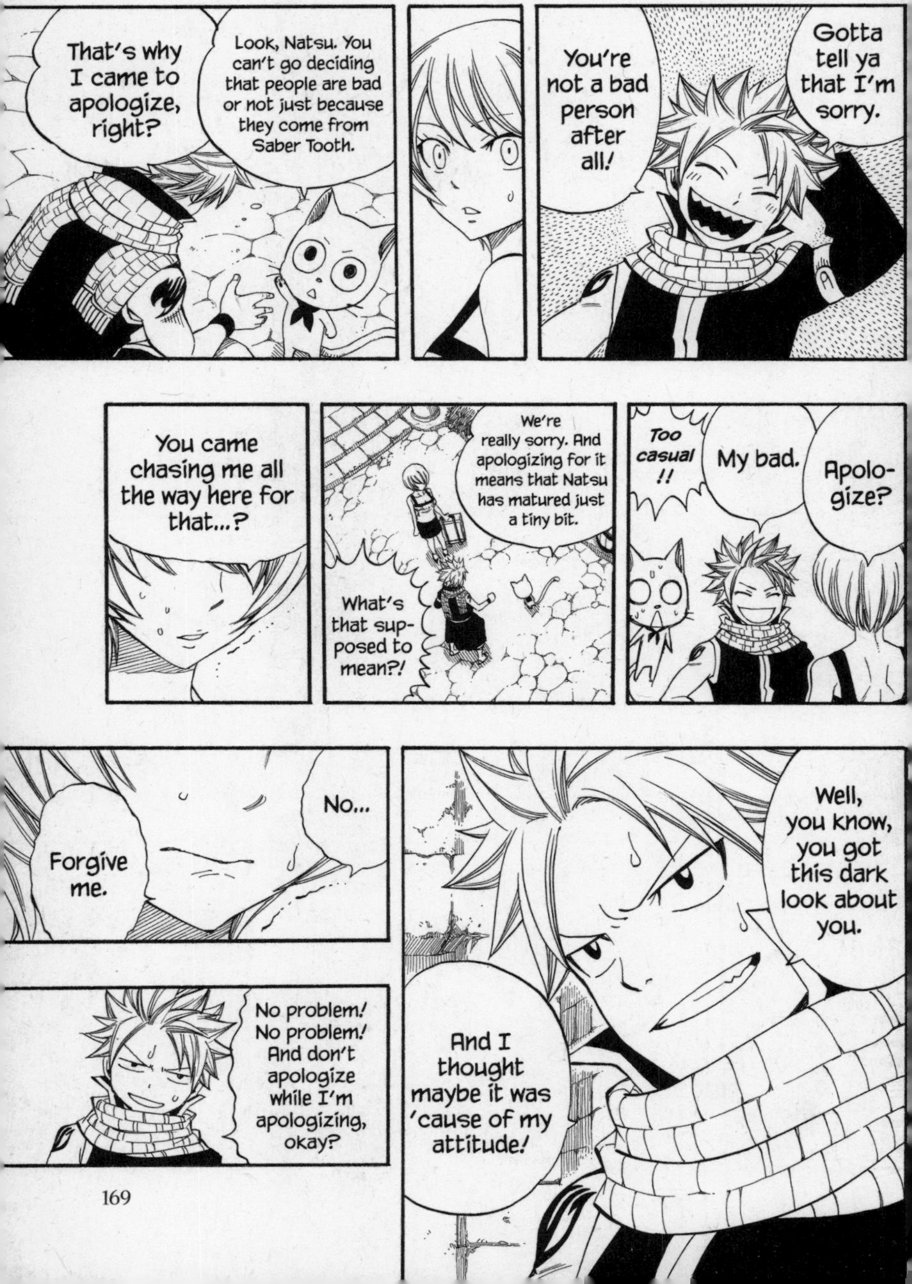

Gotta tell ya that I'm sorry.
You're not a bad person after all!
Look, Natsu. You can't go deciding that people are bad or not just because they come from Saber Tooth.
That's why I came to apologize, right?
Apologize?
My bad.
Too casual!!
We're really sorry. And apologizing for it means that Natsu has matured just a tiny bit.
What's that supposed to mean?!
You came chasing me all the way here for that...?
Well, you know, you got this dark look about you.
And I thought maybe it was 'cause of my attitude!
No...
Forgive me.
No problem! No problem! And don't apologize while I'm apologizing, okay?

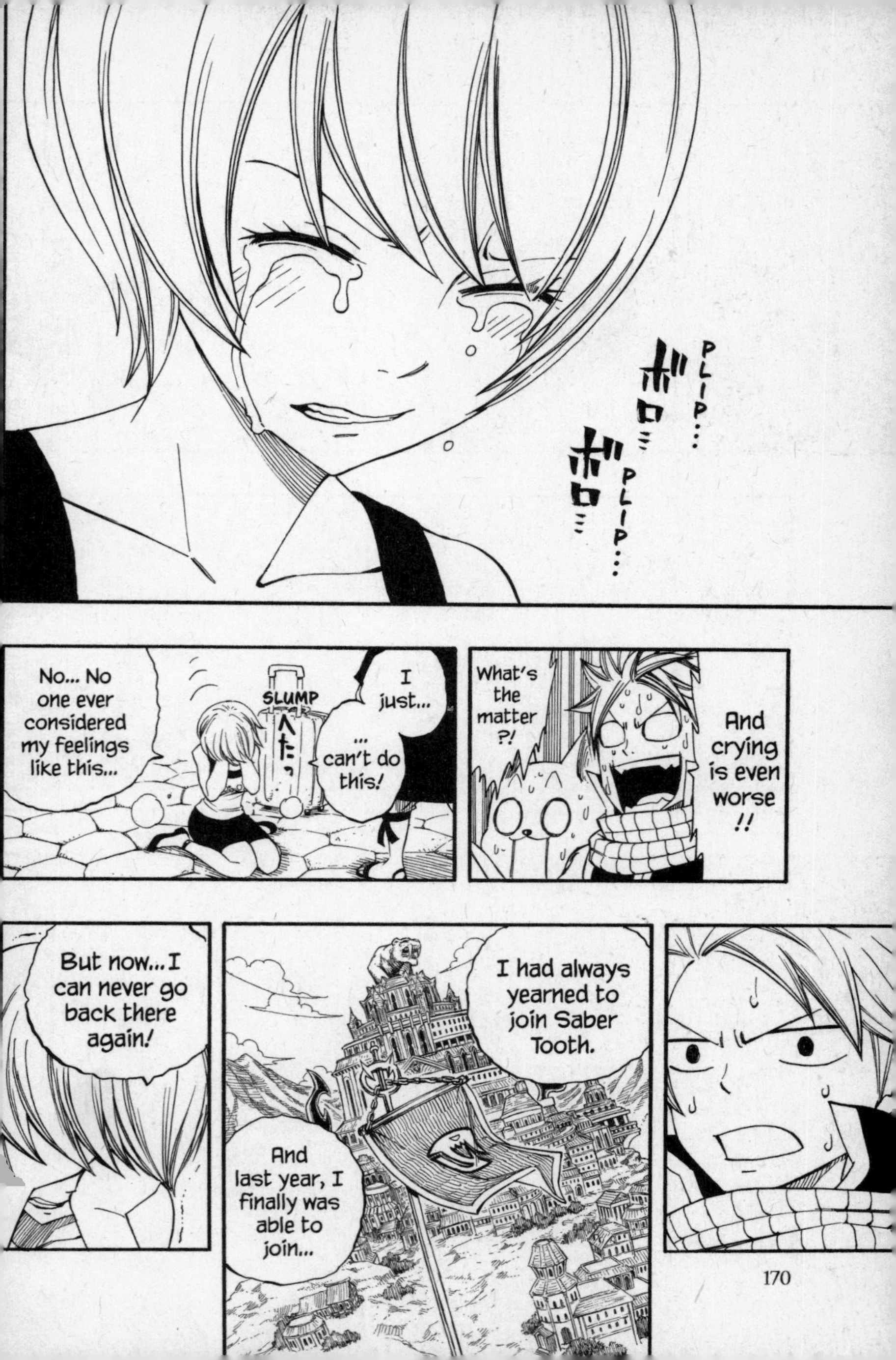
ボロ
PLIP...
ボロ
PLIP...
What's the matter ?!
And crying is even worse !!
I just...
... can't do this!
SLUMP
へたっ
No... No one ever considered my feelings like this...
I had always yearned to join Saber Tooth.
And last year, I finally was able to join...
But now... I can never go back there again!

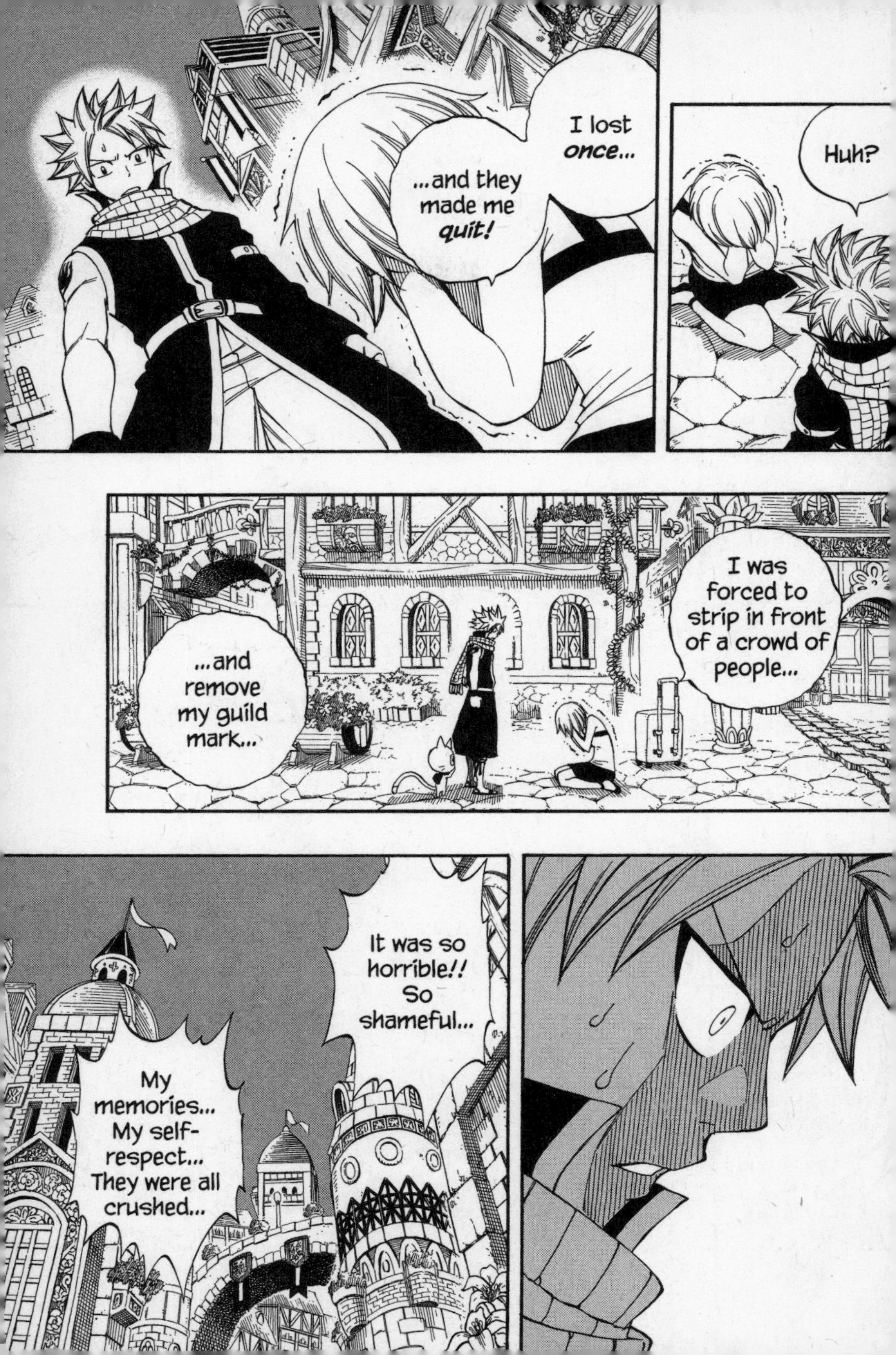

Huh?
I lost once...
...and they made me quit!
I was forced to strip in front of a crowd of people...
...and remove my guild mark...
It was so horrible!! So shameful...
My memories... My self-respect... They were all crushed...

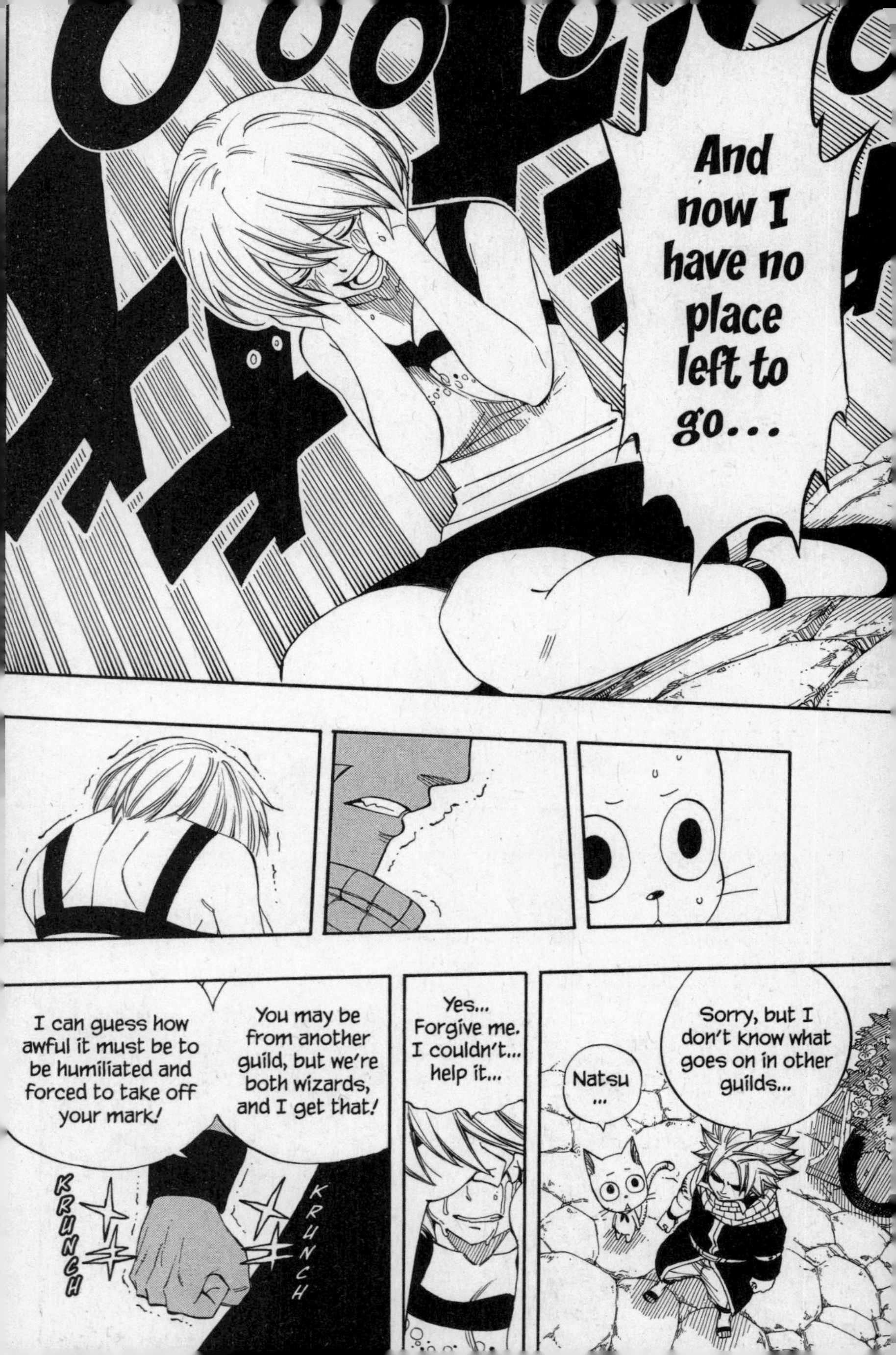
And now I have no place left to go...
Sorry, but I don't know what goes on in other guilds...
Natsu ...
Yes... Forgive me. I couldn't... help it...
You may be from another guild, but we're both wizards, and I get that!
I can guess how awful it must be to be humiliated and forced to take off your mark!
KRUNCH
KRUNCH

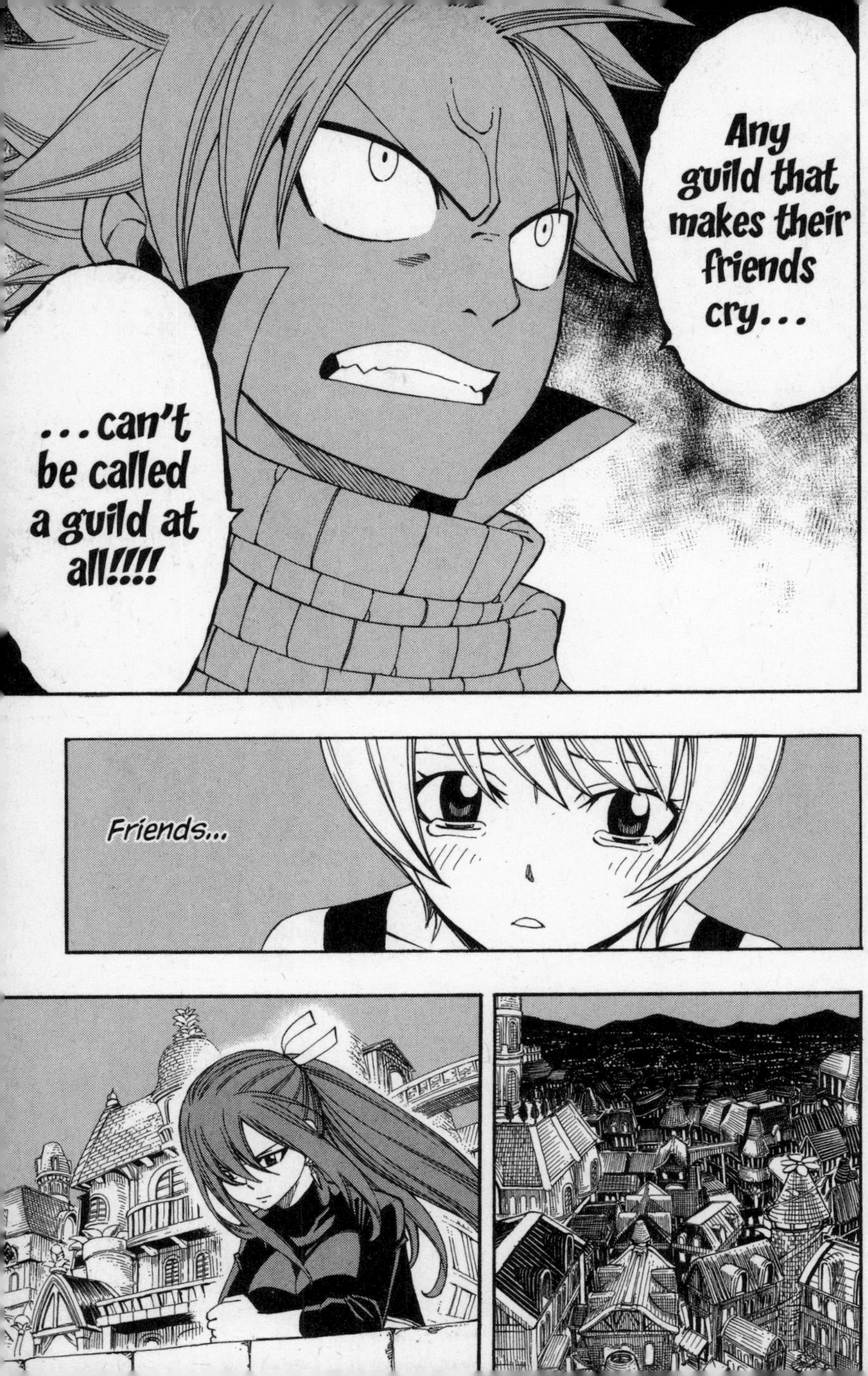
Any guild that makes their friends cry...
...can't be called a guild at all!!!!
Friends...

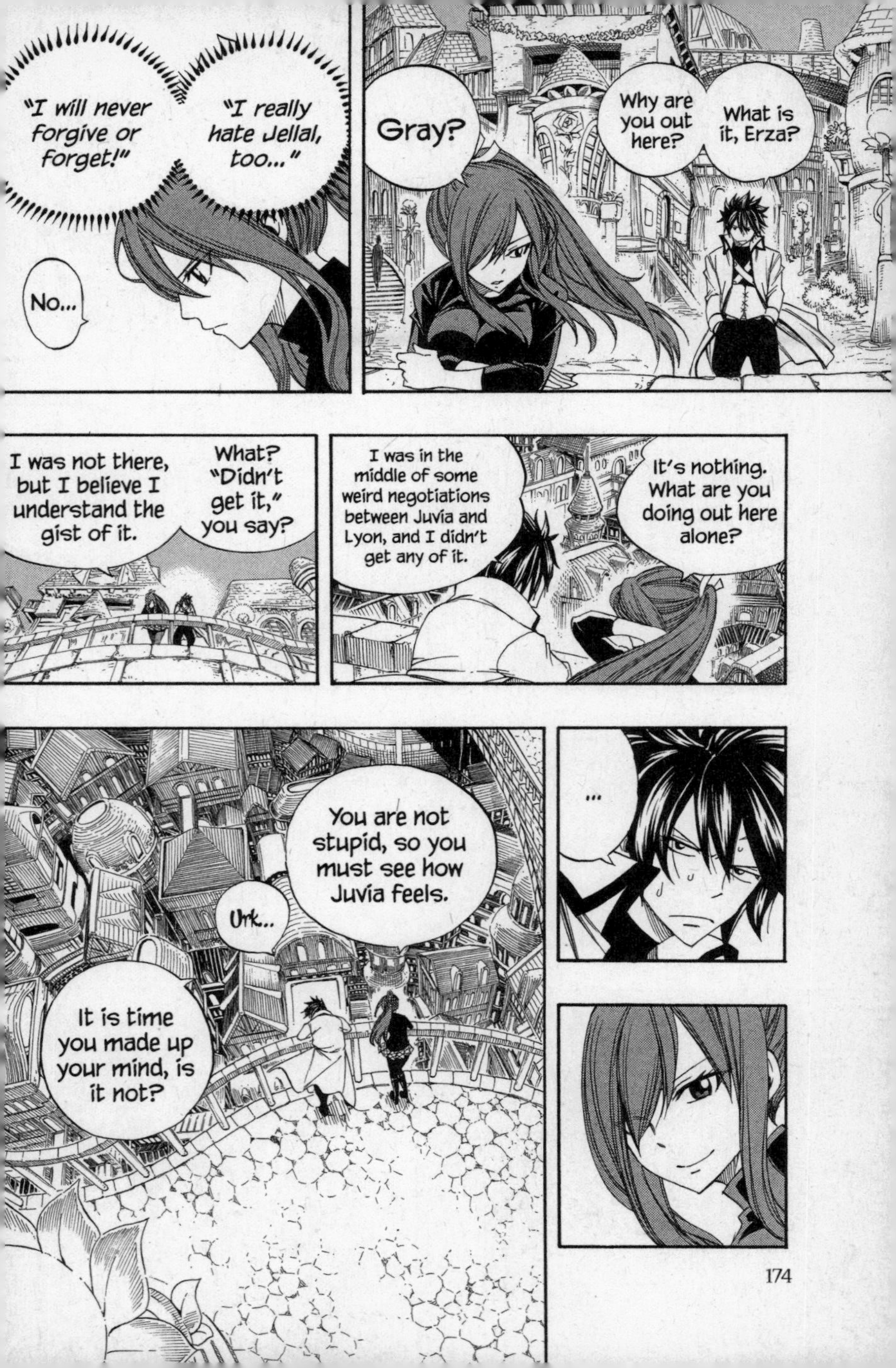
What is it, Erza?
Why are you out here?
Gray?
"I really hate Jellal, too..."
"I will never forgive or forget!"
No...
It's nothing. What are you doing out here alone?
I was in the middle of some weird negotiations between Juvia and Lyon, and I didn't get any of it.
What? "Didn't get it," you say?
I was not there, but I believe I understand the gist of it.
...
You are not stupid, so you must see how Juvia feels.
Urk...
It is time you made up your mind, is it not?

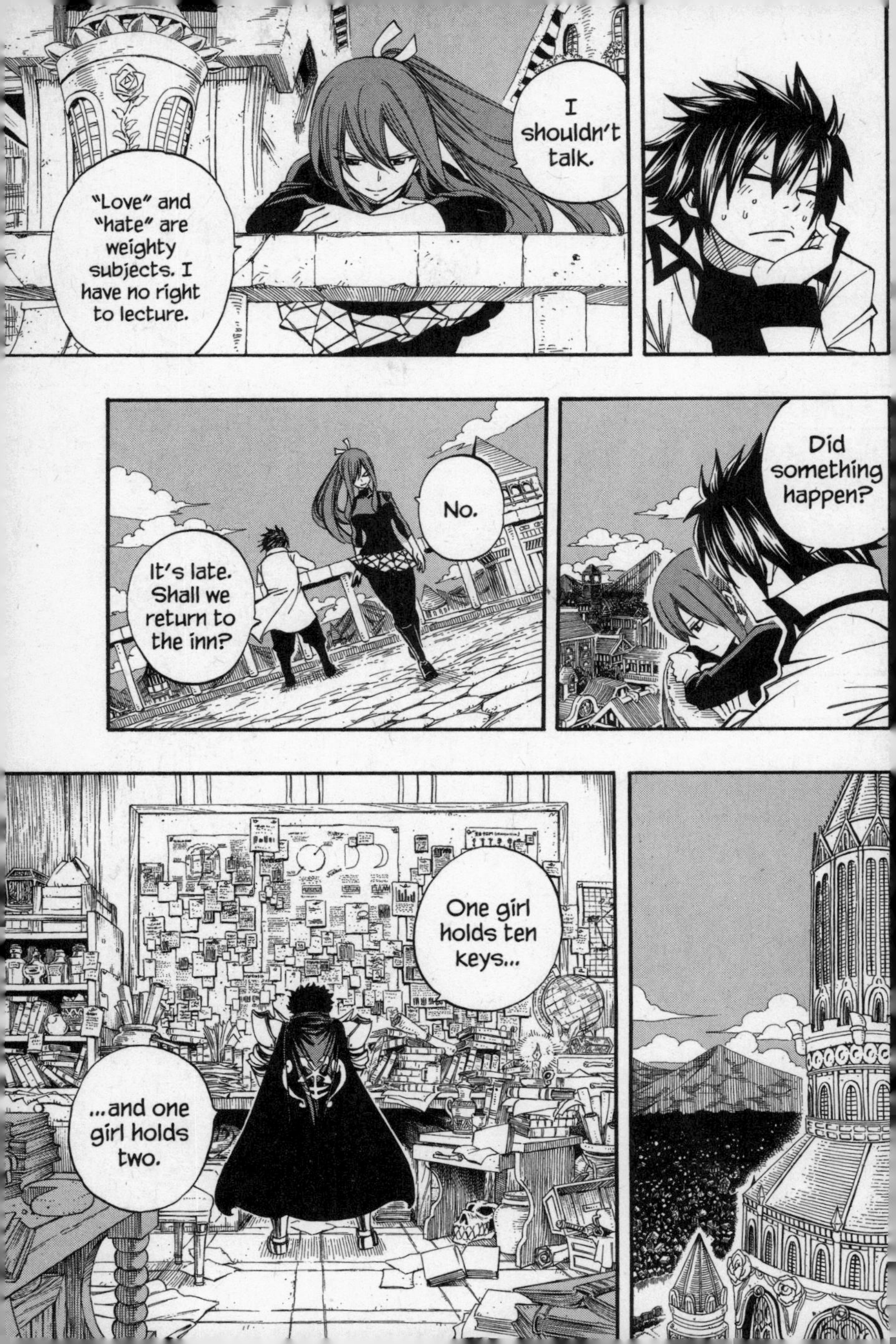
I shouldn't talk.
"Love" and "hate" are weighty subjects. I have no right to lecture.
Did something happen?
No.
It's late. Shall we return to the inn?
One girl holds ten keys...
...and one girl holds two.

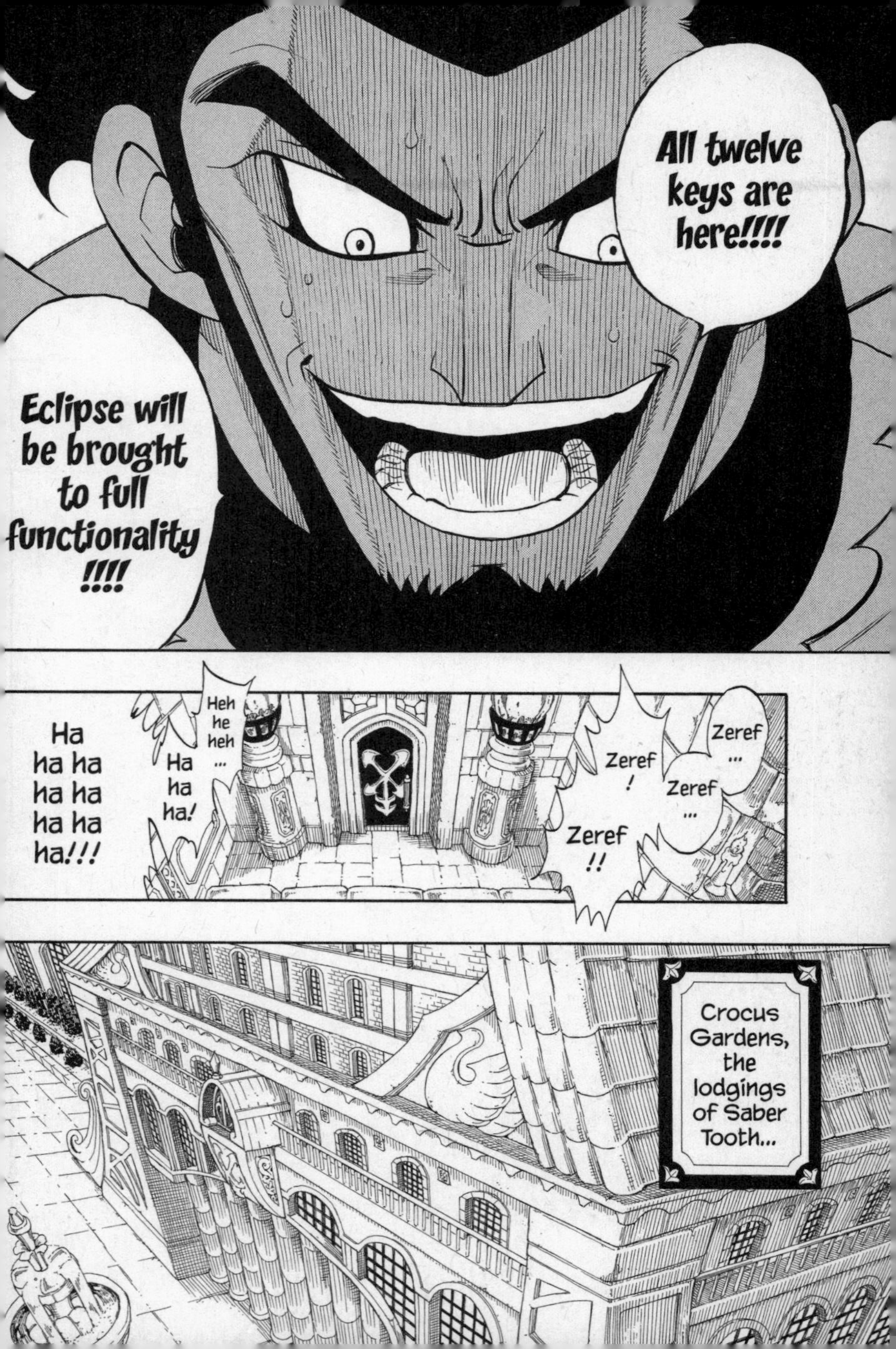
All twelve keys are here!!!!
Eclipse will be brought to full functionality !!!!
Zeref ...
Zeref !
Zeref ...
Zeref !!
Heh he heh ...
Ha ha ha!
Ha ha ha ha ha ha ha ha!!!
Crocus Gardens, the lodgings of Saber Tooth...

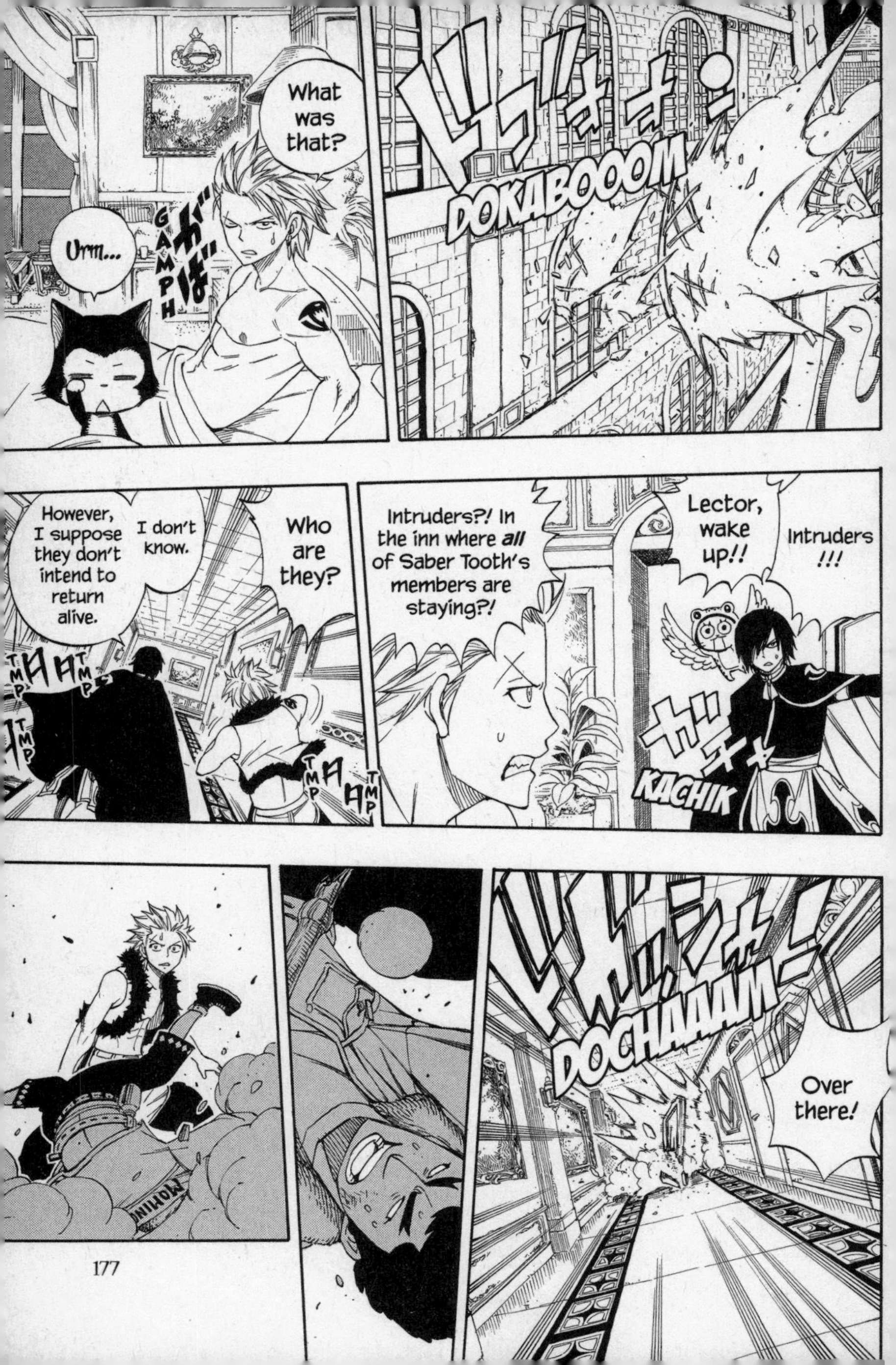
DOKABOOOM
What was that?
GAMPH
Urm...
Intruders!!!
Lector, wake up!!
KACHIK
Intruders?! In the inn where *all* of Saber Tooth's members are staying?!
Who are they?
I don't know.
However, I suppose they don't intend to return alive.
TMP TMP
TMP TMP
TMP
DOCHAAAM
Over there!

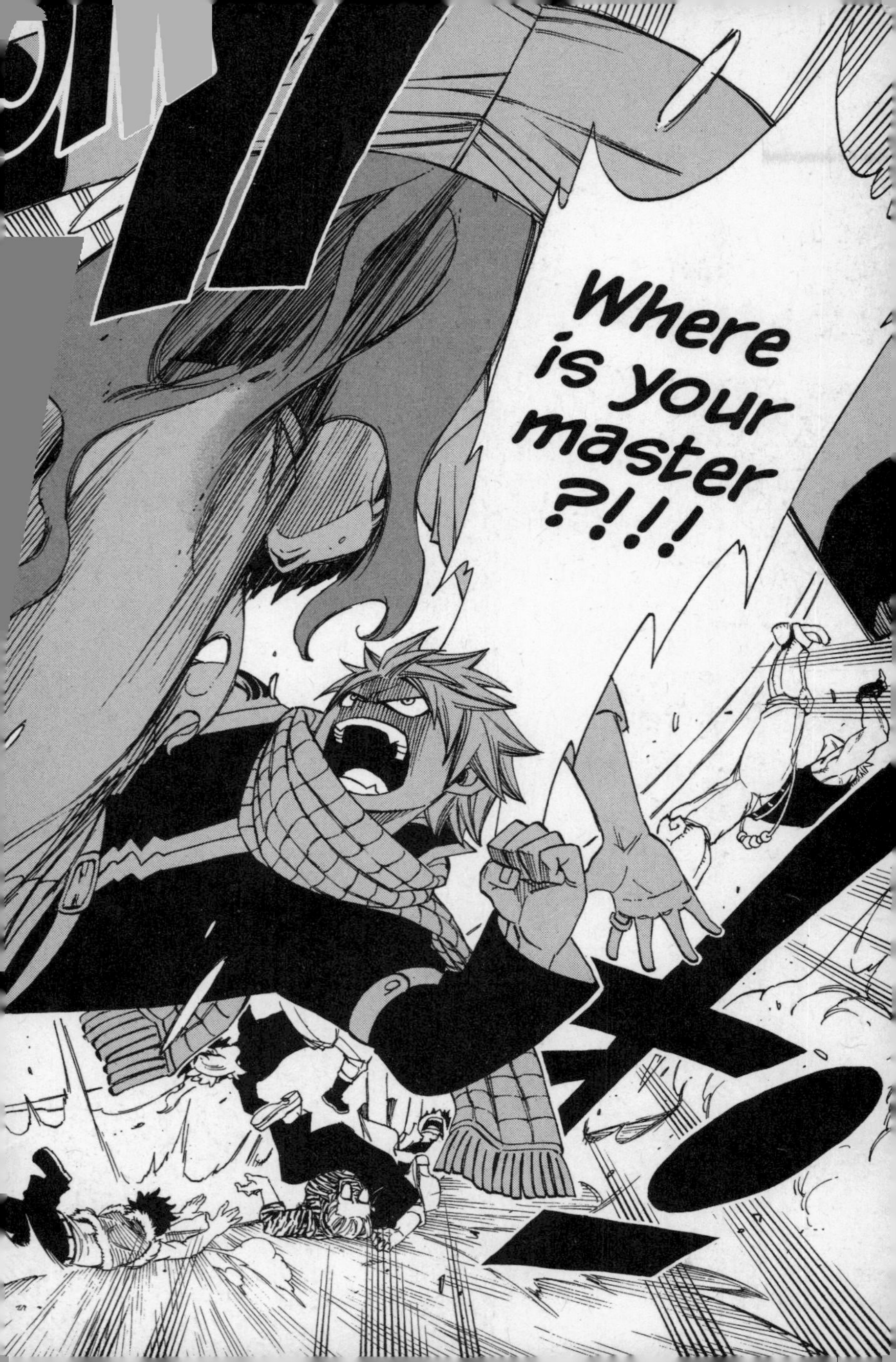
Where is your master ?!!!

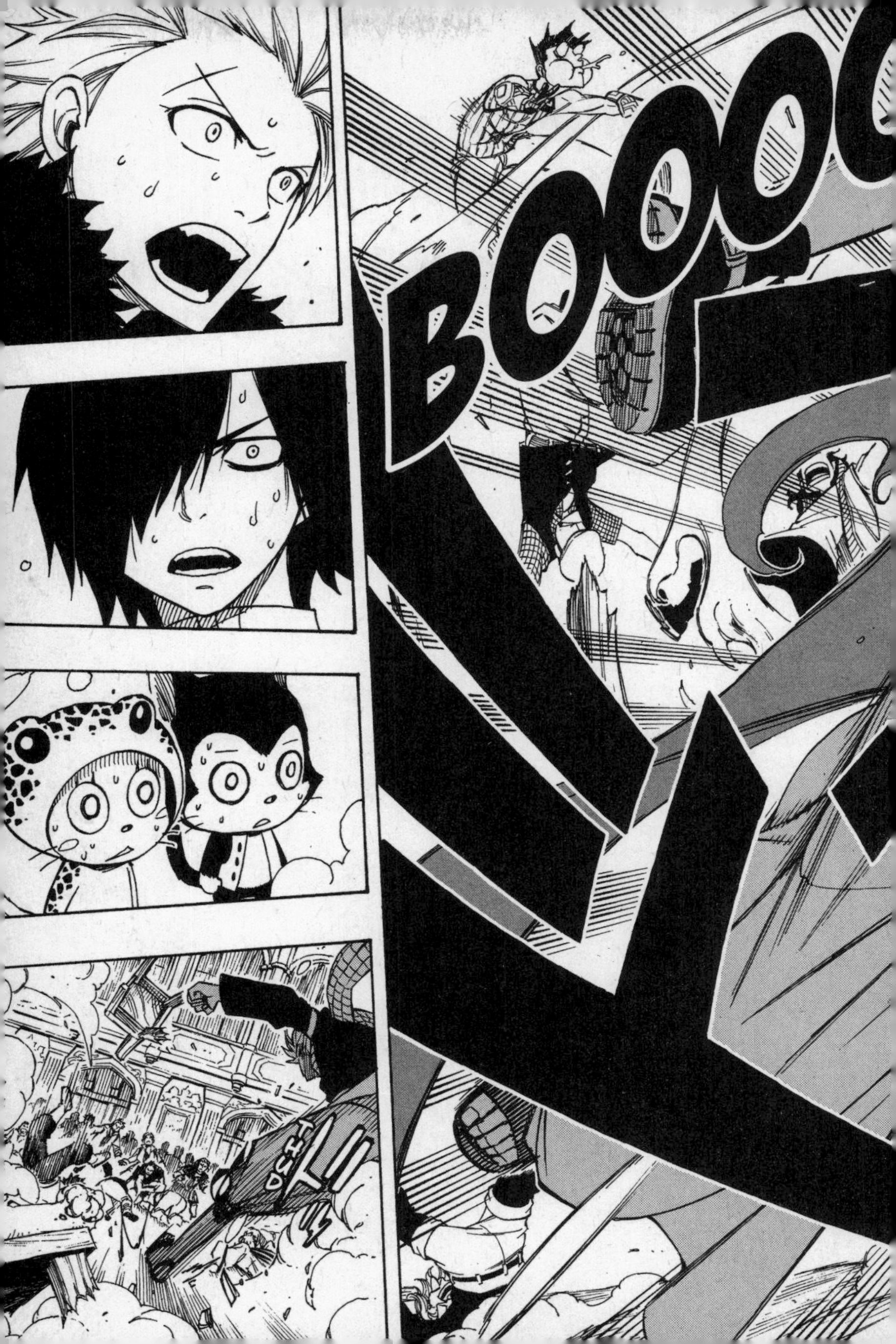
BOOOO
THUD

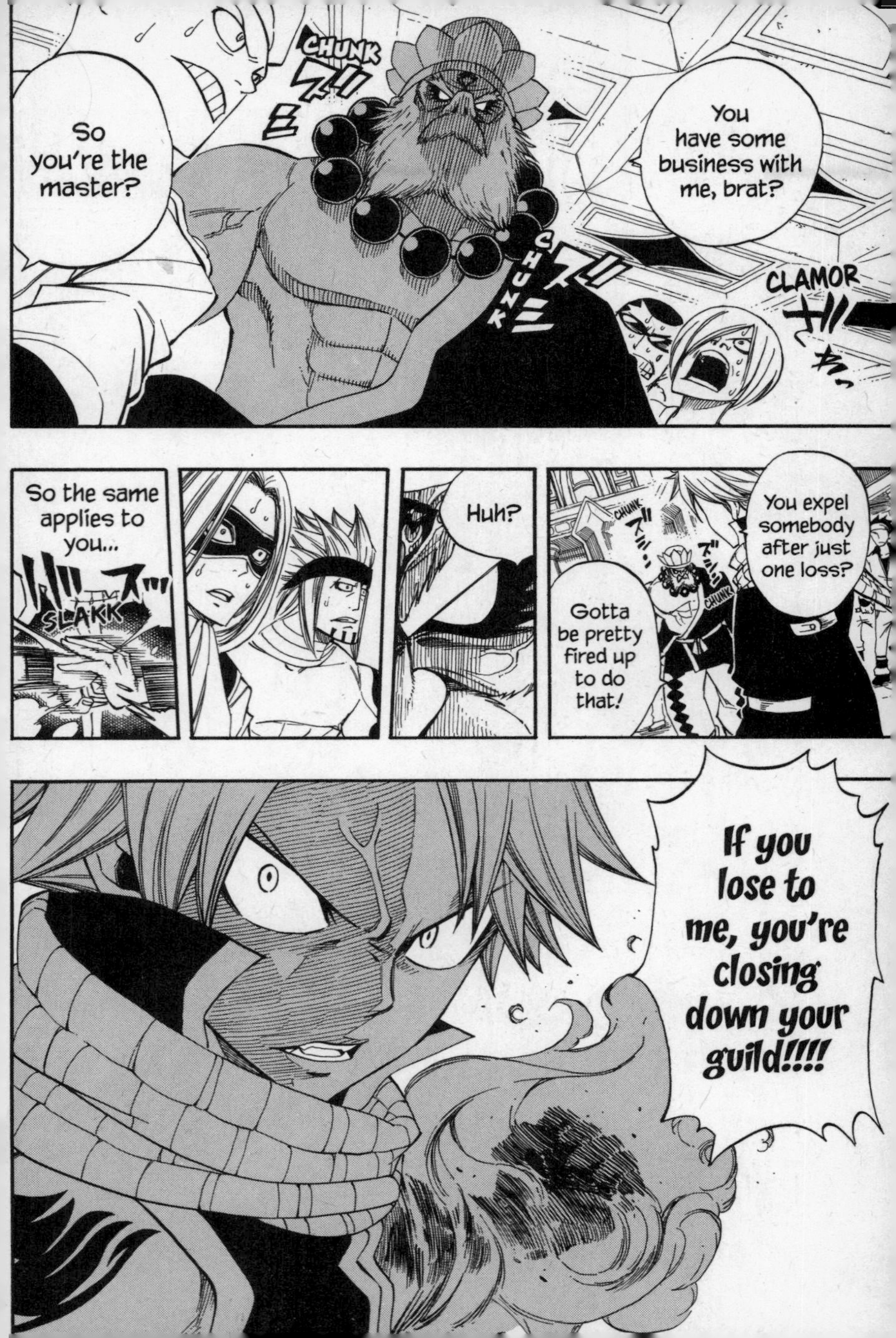
CHUNK
You have some business with me, brat?
So you're the master?
CHUNK
CLAMOR
You expel somebody after just one loss?
CHUNK
CHUNK
Gotta be pretty fired up to do that!
Huh?
So the same applies to you...
SLAKK
If you lose to me, you're closing down your guild!!!!

Bonus pages of FAIRY TAIL

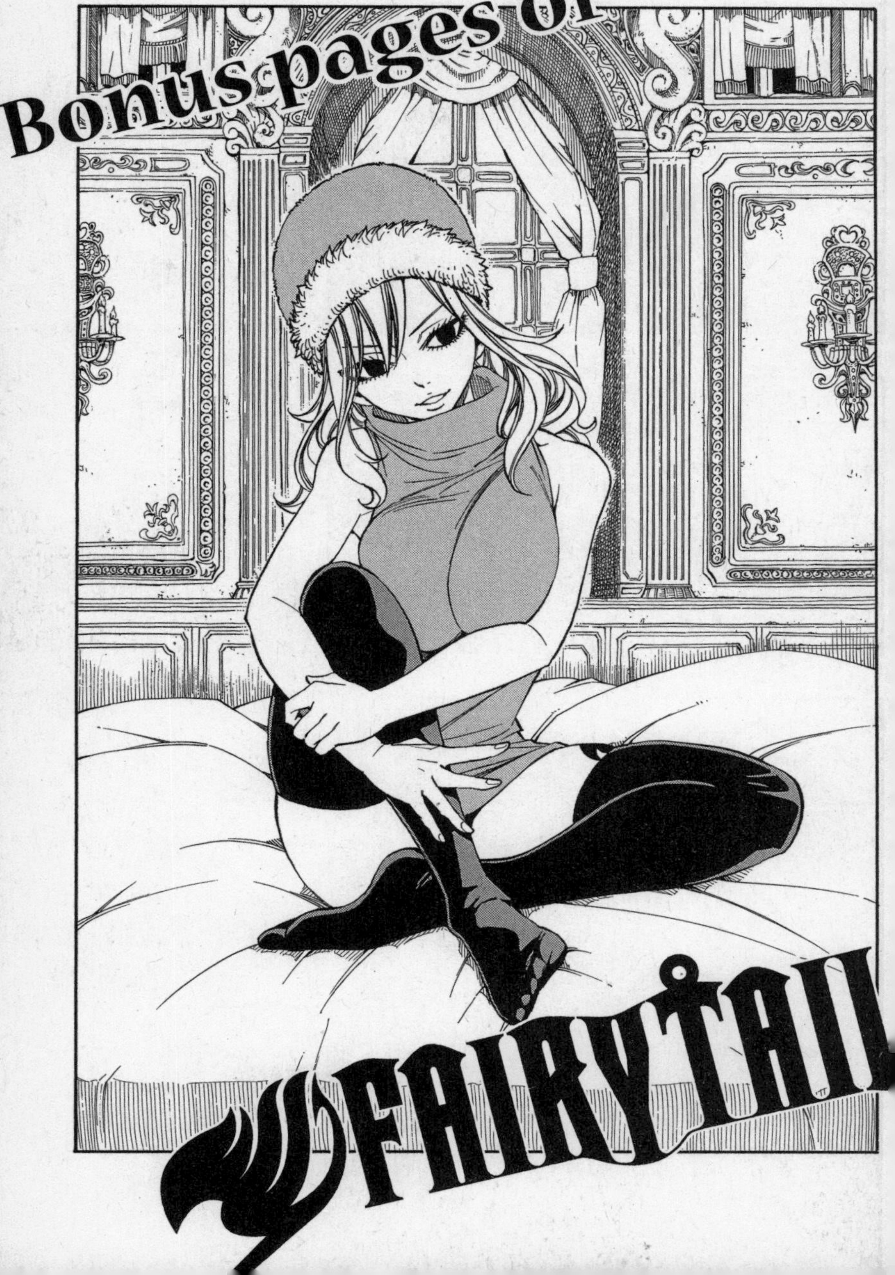

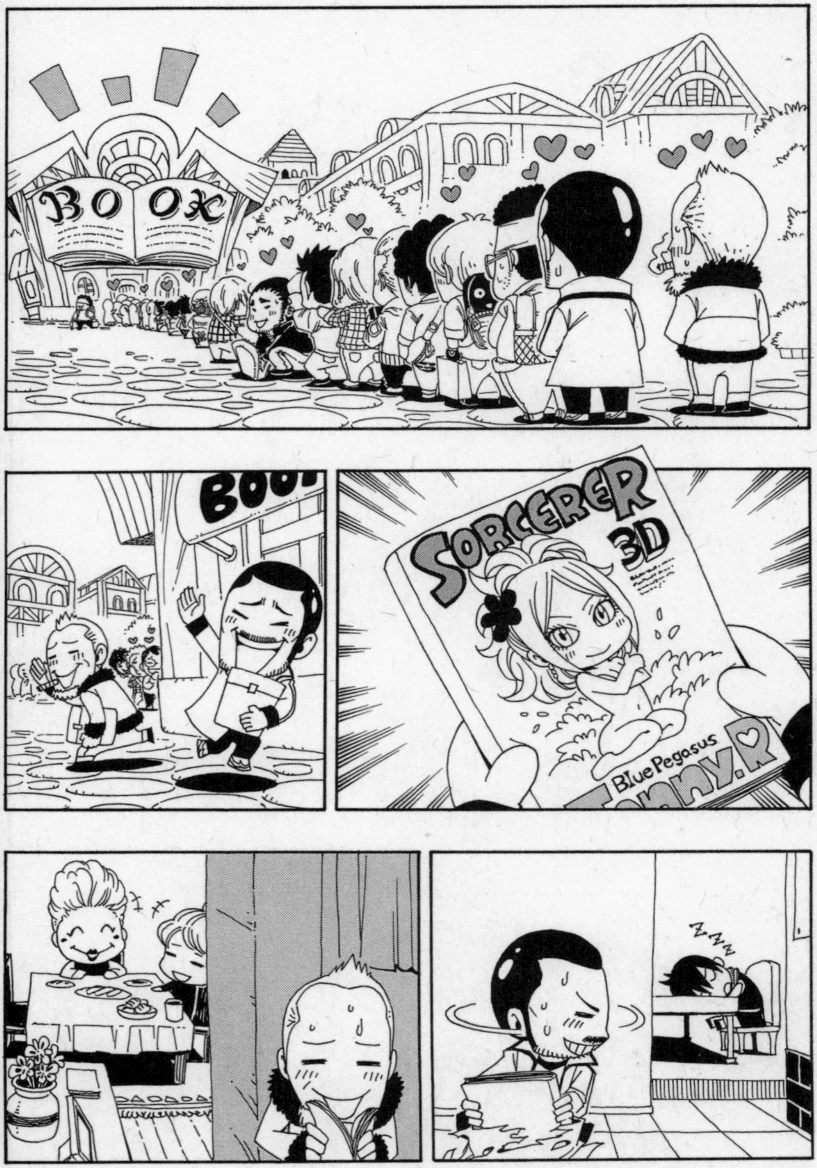
BOOK
SORCERER 3D
Blue Pegasus

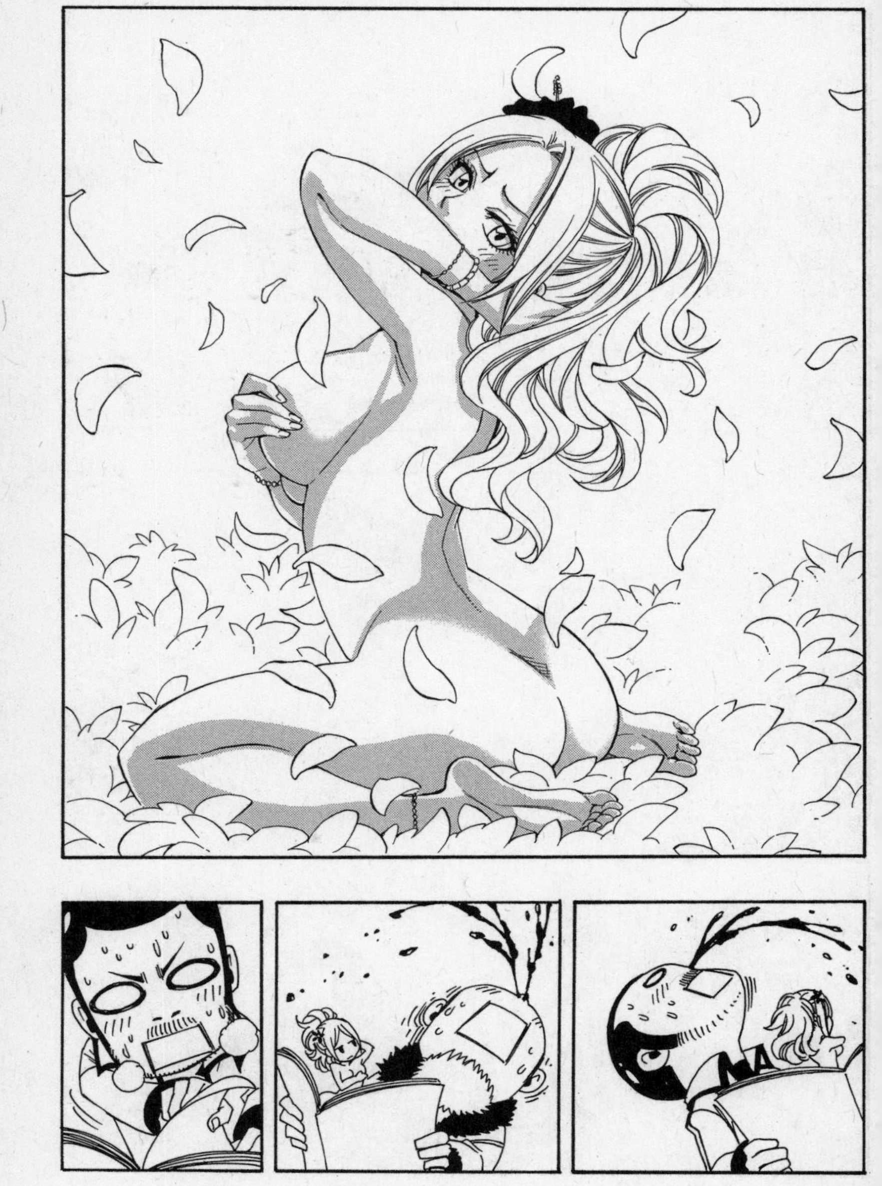
MA

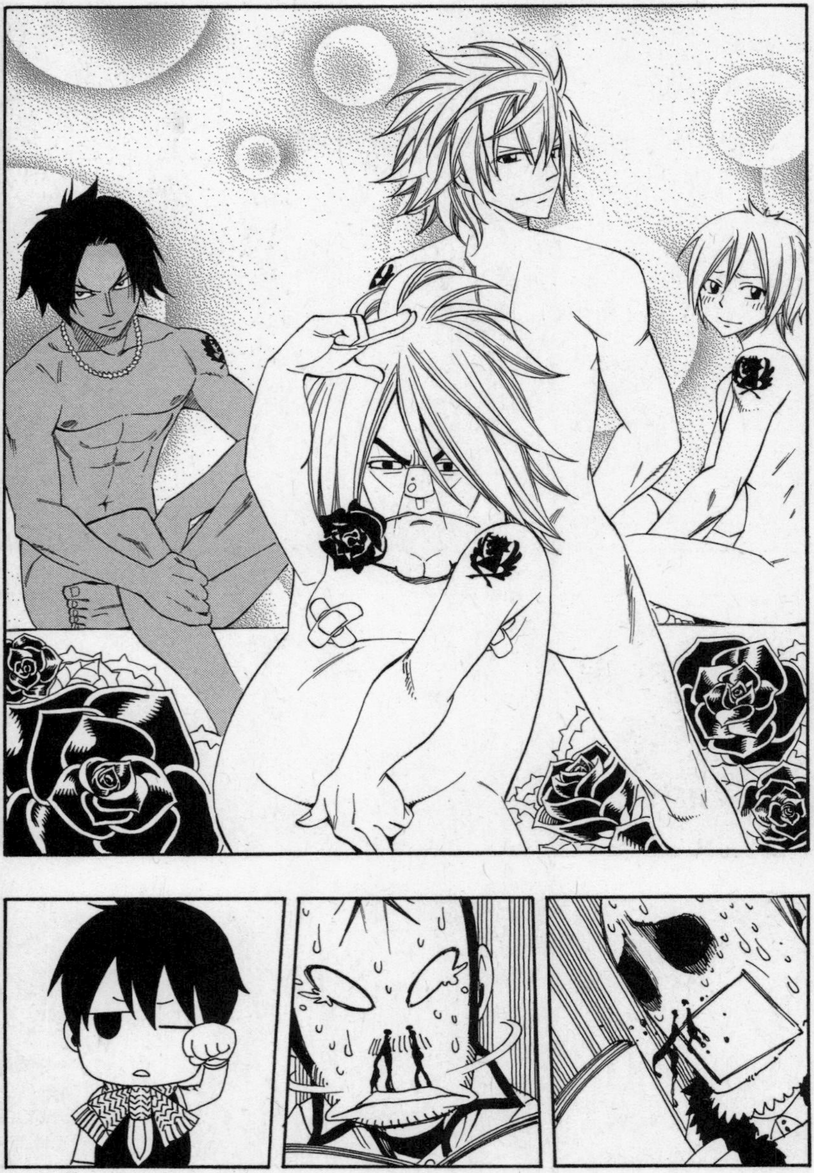

Rejected Splash Page

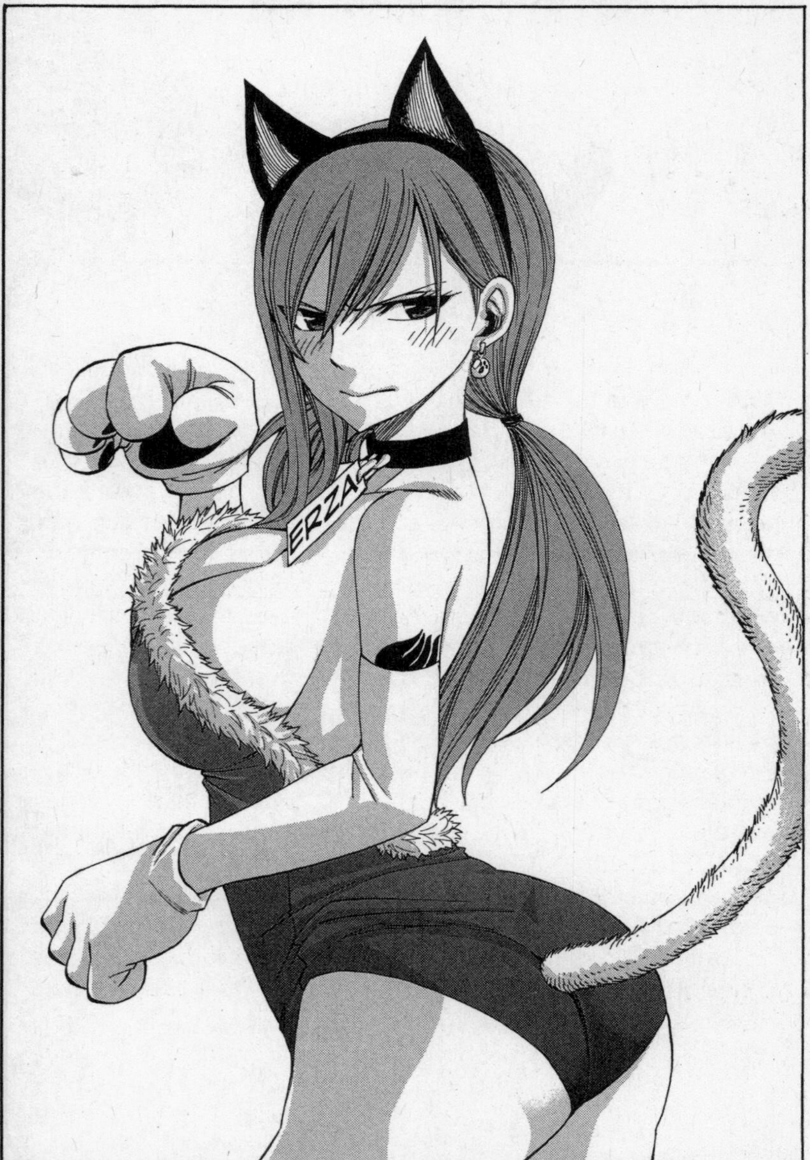
ERZA

It was too much of a pain to draw in the background, so I just didn't, and it was rejected.

Afterword
あとがき

I participated in the recording of Fairy Tail Web's radio show. Hosting were Tetsuya Kakihara-san (who plays Natsu) and Mai Nakahara-san (who plays Juvia), and the guests were Aya Hirano-san (who plays Lucy), Rie Kugimiya-san (who plays Happy) and myself. All sorts of people showed up, so it was really fun! Still, no matter how often it happens, I still get nervous when talking in front of people... After the recording, we were supposed to have a drawing to give away some presents to the fans who were there in attendance, but somehow it turned into a surprise birthday party for me. That seems to happen at times on TV, you know? When someone says, "And before we go on, we'd just like to say that it's X-san's birthday, and we've got a cake prepared!" Then X-san says, "Are you serious? I never suspected a thing!" Only that happened to me for real. Afterwards I heard that the entire cast and staff were in on it, and they prepared everything for me in secret. To have a birthday party that includes the entire staff (all of whom are really very kind and considerate) and the cast and all the fans... I knew this was an official event, and I was supposed to be professional, but I couldn't help but tear up. That's what happiness is, huh? So I'd like to take this opportunity to say thank you to everyone involved! And that cake tasted totally awesome!

Continued from the left-hand page.

Lucy: Yeah, well, I can't say I'd turn that stuff down. Fried meats and such.

Mira: And for me, it'd be **a sardine.**

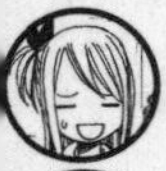

: You're going to use that for every answer, aren't you?

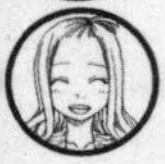

: Just kidding. For me, it's actually kuzumochi. I just love the texture in my mouth! ♡

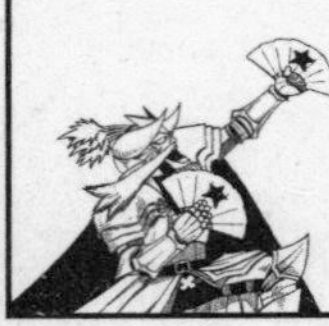

Could you two describe something interesting that you've experienced recently?

Lucy: "Something interesting"?

Mira: Got anything?

Lucy: I don't know... I can't say if it's interesting or not, but recently I (actually my Daddy) paid my landlord ***5.88 million jewels*** for seven years of back rent.

Mira: For the time we were on Sirius Island?

Lucy: But we disappeared in December of X784 and we returned in March of X791. So I did a bit of calculating, and what I actually owed her was ***5.32 million!***

Mira: Ah! You were overcharged!

Lucy: So when I asked the landlord about it, she said, "I kept your room sparkling clean! Quit sweating the small stuff!!"

Mira: Oh, dear.

Lucy: But after, I did some more digging, and it seems that from X786-X790, the rent on the apartment was raised to ***80 thousand per month!!***

Mira: ... Which means?

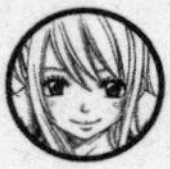

: That in reality, the full amount I should have paid was ***5.92 million jewels.*** So I got a bit of a break from the landlord.

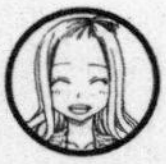

: A borderline interesting story, huh?

Lucy: What about you, Mira?

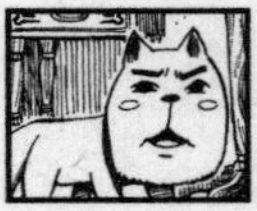

Mira: Me? Well, you know about Alexandria, right?

Lucy: Oh, yeah. That dog with the weird bark!

Mira: Well a little while ago, it went missing in the park.

Lucy: Yeah, yeah?

Mira: And it went away somewhere.

Lucy: Oh?! Okay, and?

Mira: The end.

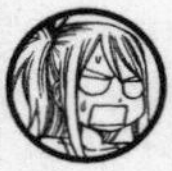

: What?! What's so interesting about that story?!

Mira: Well, it started out as a stray, right? So I'm sure it found its original owner and is now living with that person happily ever after!♡

Lucy: Urk... How do you come by such an optimistic vision of what happened?

Mira: Either that or it was adopted by a dark guild, became its greatest wizard-dog, and will show up at some point in the future to take us on.

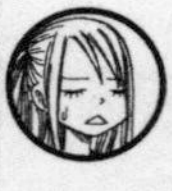

: Optimism and extreme, scary pessimism in the same story.

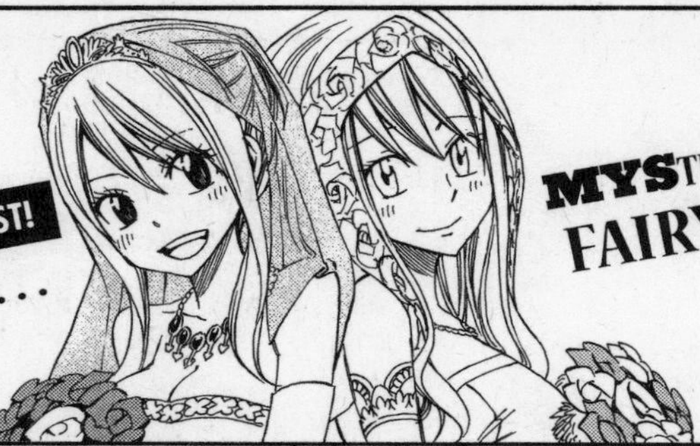

EMERGENCY REQUEST! explain the . . .

MYSTERIES OF FAIRY TAIL

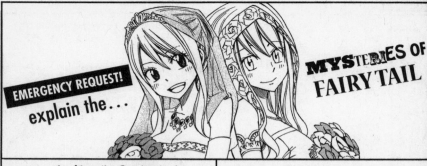

At Kardia Cathedral...

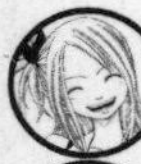
: Hellooo!!

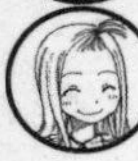
: Hello, everybody!

Lucy: I was thinking we'd change up what we're always doing a bit.

Mira: That's pretty sudden. Why?

Lucy: You know... Because this time, again, there are a lot of questions about the Grand Magic Games that we can't answer yet.

Mira: You're talking a bit more "real world" than usual, huh?

Lucy: Well, under the dust covers of the recent volumes (included as bonus pages in the English version), Mashima had all this awful stuff under there!

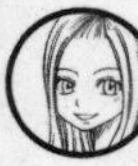
: Ah! That original scheme he had for the plot?

Lucy: So there were a *ton* of letters trying to predict the future. And we can't answer those!

Mira: Okay, then for this time, we'll do some very odd questions that we've been asked.

If you were to take the people of the guild and think of them as animals, what animals would they be?

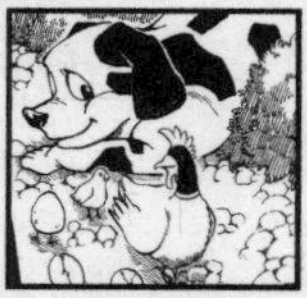

Lucy: That's a tough one... But I'm sure Natsu would be a lizard!

Mira: Gray would be a wolf. Erza would be...

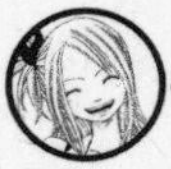
: A black panther!

Mira: Elfman would be a gorilla, and Lisanna a kitten.

Lucy: Wendy would be a puppy.

Mira: She *does* seem the type to put out her hand when you say, "Shake."

Lucy: By the way, what about me?

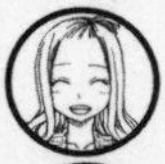
: Lucy...hm. You'd be a raccoon.

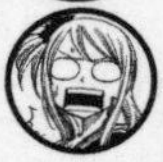
: Huh?! I think a bunny would be better!

Mira: And for me, it'd be **a sardine.**

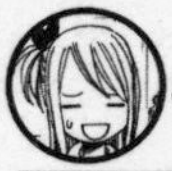
: A sardine...

What are Lucy's and Mira's favorite foods?

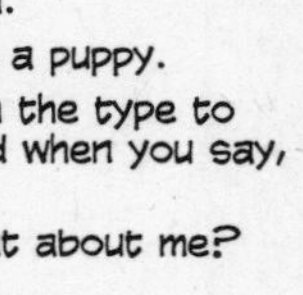

Lucy: I really love yogurt!!

Mira: Really? I never knew. I thought for sure you'd like fried foods best!

Continued on the right-hand page.

TAIL d'ART

The Fairy Tail Guild is looking for illustrations! Please send in your art on a postcard or at postcard size, and do it in black pen, okay? Those chosen to be published will get a signed mini poster! ♪ Make sure you write your real name and address on the back of your illustration!

Okinawa Prefecture, Orange

FAIRY TAIL

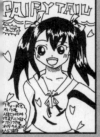

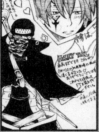

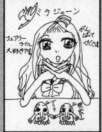

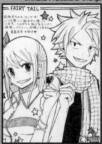

▲ Nice composition on this! I like how they're bumping the backs of their hands.

Gifu Prefecture, Yûki Minakami

ミラジェーン
フェアリーテイル大好きです
がんばってください

▲ Mira-san! She had a big part this volume!

Ishikawa Prefecture, Arisa Kojima

FAIRY TAIL

▲ Jellal still has a lot of work to do in the future too!

Shizuoka Prefecture, I Love Dragon Slayers 3

FAIRY TAIL

▲ This one has a lot of energy that really comes through! Wendy!

Tokyo, Jubin.

FAIRY TAIL
祝・劇場版アニメ化!

Three types of Juvia. Which one do you like best? ▶

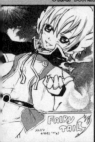

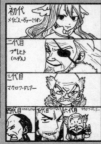

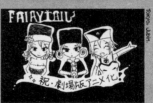

Fukushima Prefecture, Nyanko Love

FAIRY TAIL
~エクシード達~

Exceed Combine!! Which cat is your favorite? ▶

Aichi Prefecture, Silver

初代
メイビス・ヴァーミリオン
二代目
プレヒト
(ハデス)
三代目
マカロフ・ドレアー
四代目
五代目
六代目

▲ When you line them all up like that, it hits you that Macao... Heh heh heh...

Osaka, Scofield

FAIRY TAIL

▲ That's so nostalgic! This is Merudy from seven years ago, huh?

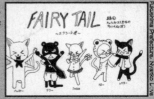

Send to Hiro Mashima, Kodansha Comics
451 Park Ave. South, 7th Floor New York, NY 10016

FAIRY GUILD

Yamanashi Prefecture, Peace

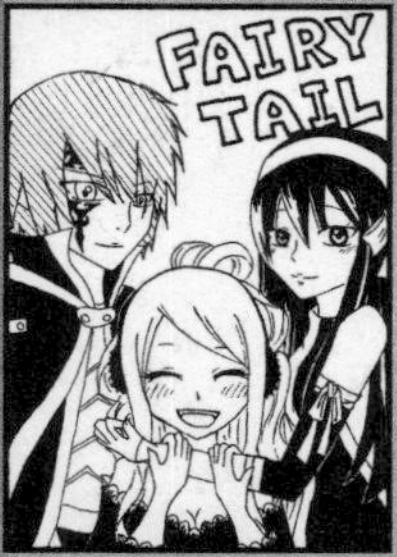
FAIRY TAIL

▲The three members of Crime Sorcière. Their main job is still to come.

Nara Prefecture, Tsukasa

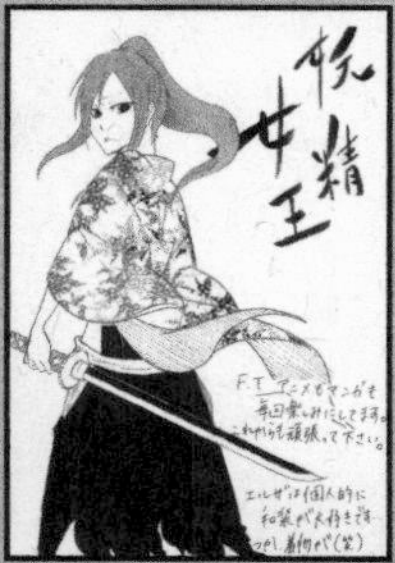
妖精女王

▲Yes, Japanese style looks great on Erza. I agree.

Hyogo Prefecture, Mao Furubayashi

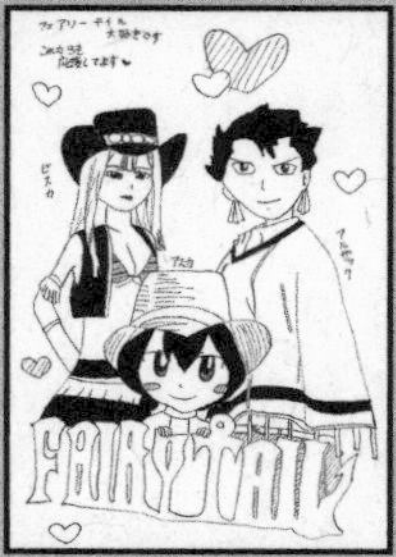
FAIRY TAIL

▲The Connel family. Asuka is so cute!

Aichi Prefecture, Celery

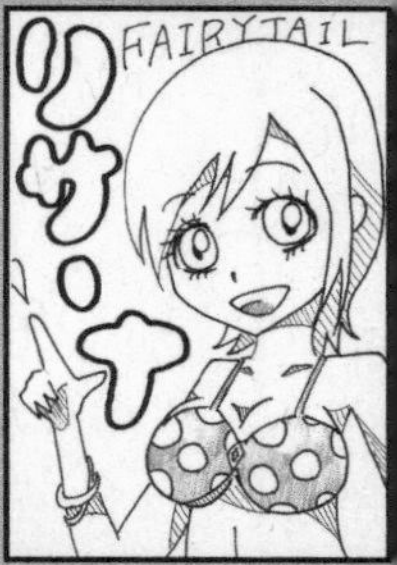
FAIRY TAIL

▲What a bouncy image! Lisanna's so cute!

REJECTION CORNER

Hooold on! That's scary!!▶

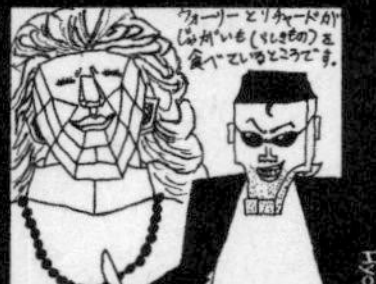

Hyogo Prefecture, Yoppy

Mie Prefecture, Mei Nakazawa

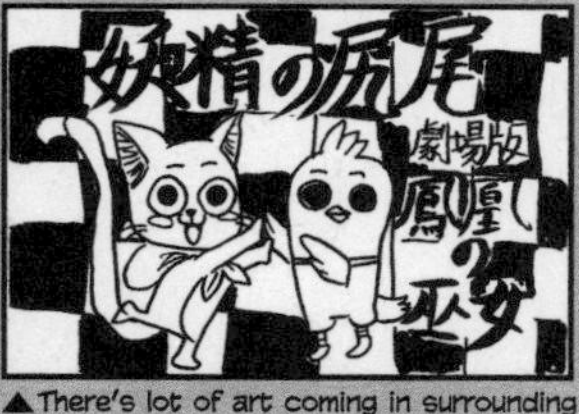
妖精の尻尾
劇場版
鳳凰の巫女

▲There's lot of art coming in surrounding the movie. I guess it has a lot of good buzz!

By sending in letters or postcards, you give us permission to give your name, address, postal code, and any other information you include to the artist as-is. Please keep that in mind.

Tokyo, Riu

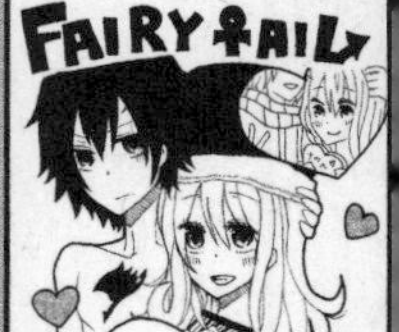
FAIRY TAIL
Gray & Juvia + Natsu & Lucy

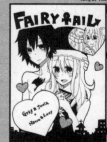

▲Look at how cute this is! And it's good too!

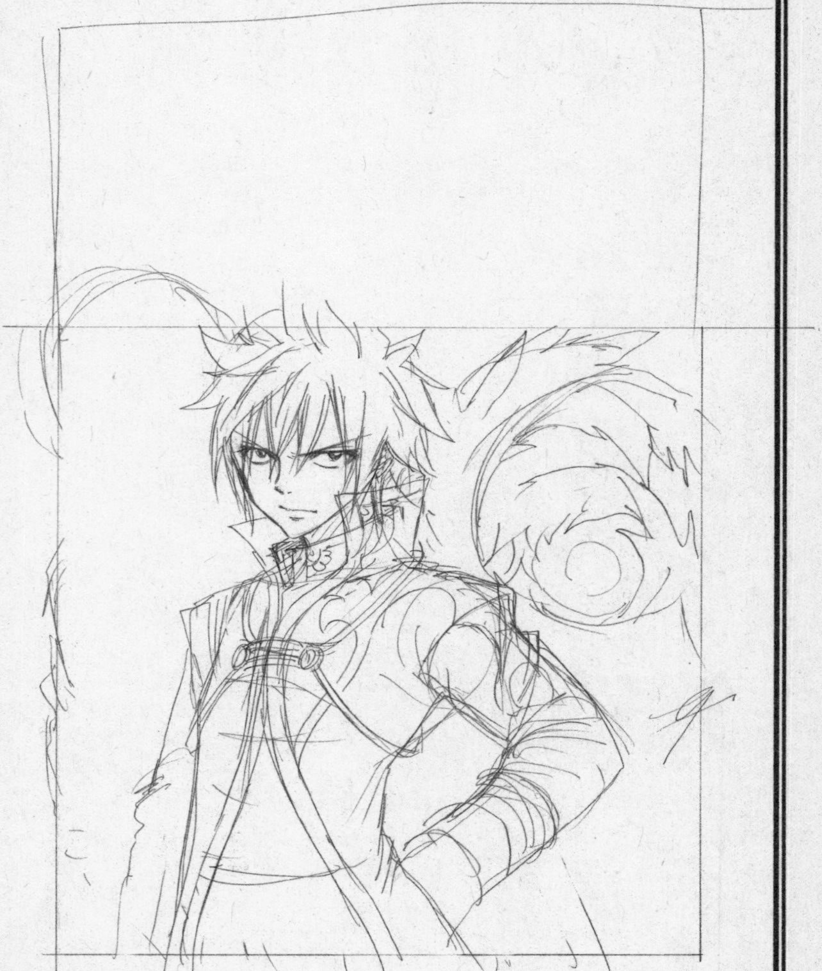

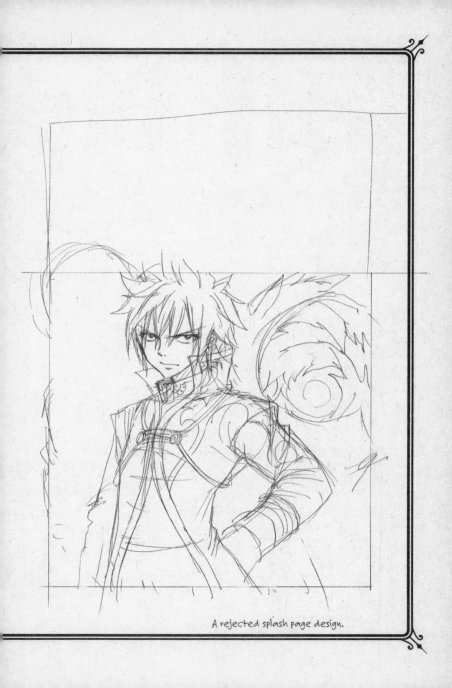

A rejected splash page design.

FAIRY TAIL
フェアリーテイル
33

HIRO MASHIMA

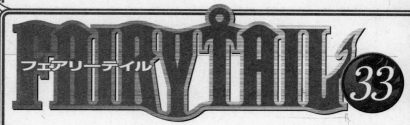

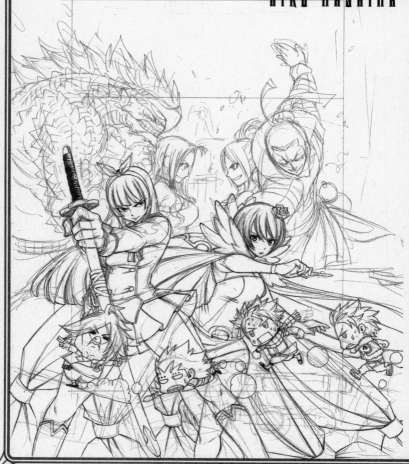

FROM HIRO MASHIMA

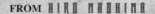

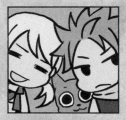

Fairy Tail is going to be a movie!! All right!! Everyone out there who wished for it, it's come true! I think it's going to be a passionate, fun story! We're hard at work on it now, so look forward to it!

Original Jacket Design: Hisao Ogawa

Translation Notes:

Japanese is a tricky language for most Westerners, and translation is often more art than science. For your edification and reading pleasure, here are notes on some of the places where we could have gone in a different direction with our translation of the work, or where a Japanese cultural reference is used.

Page 6, Cana's Whisky Bottle
The label of Kana's whiskey bottle has two phrases. The one in large print is *Takama-ga-Hara* ("The Plains of High Heaven") which is the place of the Gods in the Japanese Shinto religion, and the line in small type is *Tenjo Tenge Yuiga Dokuson*, which is the Japanese translation of a quote from the Buddha Sakyamuni, meaning, "In heaven and earth, respect only me."

Page 19, Wild Fwooh
I do not definitively know the origin of this phrase, "Wild," followed by, "Fwoo," but my guess is that it comes from a combination of Japanese comedians. The comedian known as Razor Ramon HG used the, "Fwoo," call often in his early-to-mid 2000s media success, and more recently the comedian Sugi-chan brought the English word, "Wild," back into the Japanese pubic consciousness with his catchphrase, "Wild darou?" ("Wild, right?")

Page 20, Pigua Quan
Bacchus's martial art, Pigua Quan (meaning "hanging chop fist," also called Piguaquan, Pi Kua, Piguazhang, and, in Japanese, *hikasho*) is a real-world martial art that emphasizes palm techniques. It is said to get its power from subtle hip movements and rotation of the arms.

The Drunken Hawk... Bacchus of the Drunken Pigua Quan School.

We've fought many times, but neither of us has ever had a decisive win.

Page 60, Bacchus's Liquor Bottle

The *kanji* on Bacchus's liquor bottle is *Kikokusui.* The first part, *kikoku,* is a word relating to ghosts who cry because they are left on this world and cannot depart to the next one. The final *kanji, sui,* means "drunkenness." It may be a reference to the sake brand "Kikusui," though that *sui* means "water."

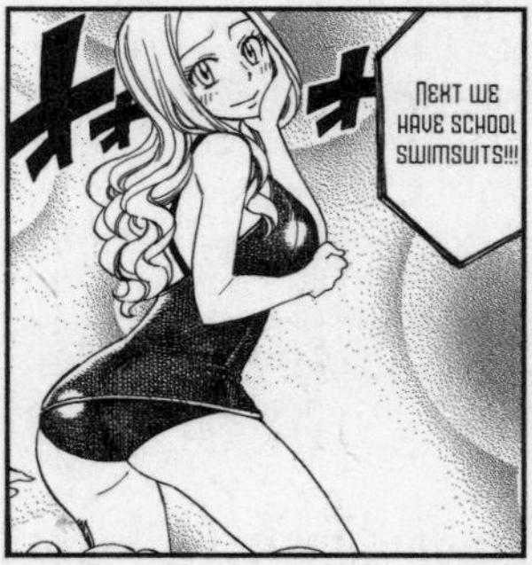
NEXT WE HAVE SCHOOL SWIMSUITS!!!

Page 105, School Swimsuits

Most of Japanese junior highs and high schools not only have school uniforms, but also uniform swimwear for physical education classes. And like the school uniforms, the school swimsuits have also become fetishized.

Page 132, Gyo

The Pisces fish say *"gyo"* in the first panel of this page, which is appropriate because it is one of the pronunciations of the Japanese *kanji* for fish.

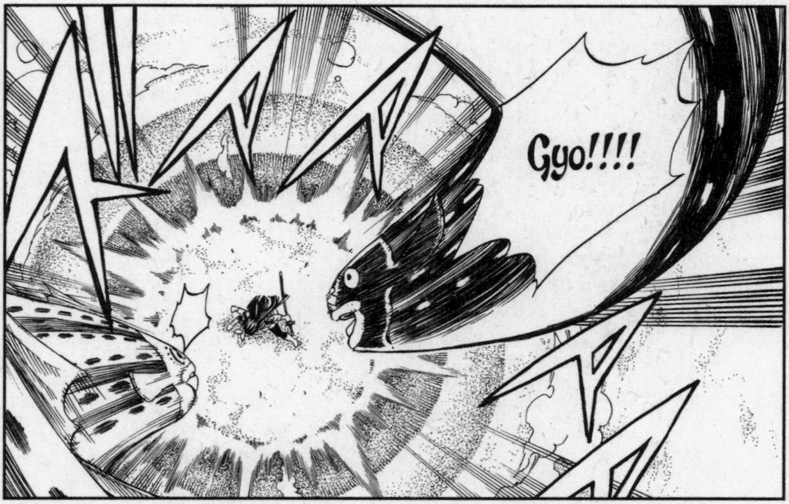
Gyo!!!!

Page 188, Kuzumochi

Kuzumochi is a block of soft *mochi* that is covered in the molasses-like *kuromitsu* and *kinako,* a common soybean flour covering for sweets. Kuzumochi gets its name because unlike most *mochi,* which is made from rice, this is made from the roots of the *kuzu* (kudzu) plant.

Preview of *Fairy Tail*, volume 34

We're pleased to present you with a preview from Fairy Tail, volume 34, now available on digital devices and coming to print in January 2014. See our Web site (www.kodanshacomics.com) for more details!

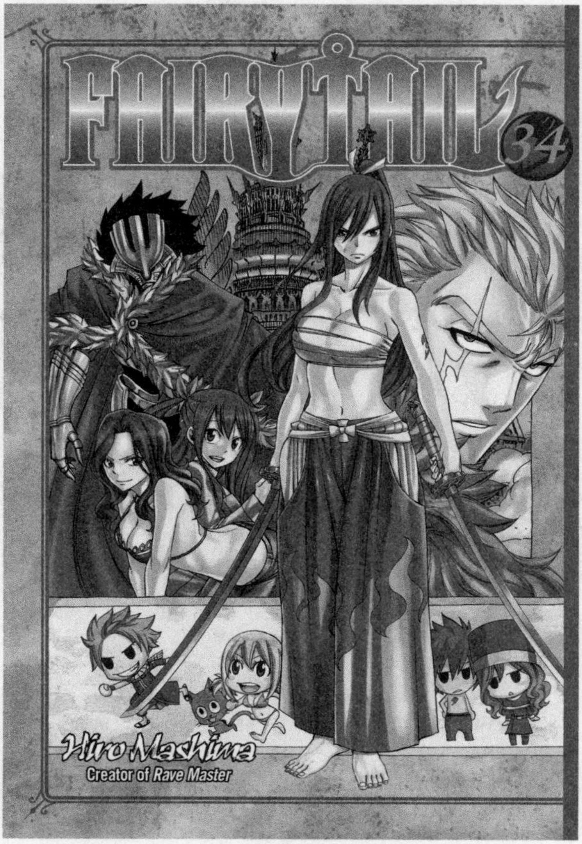
FAIRY TAIL
34
Hiro Mashima
Creator of Rave Master

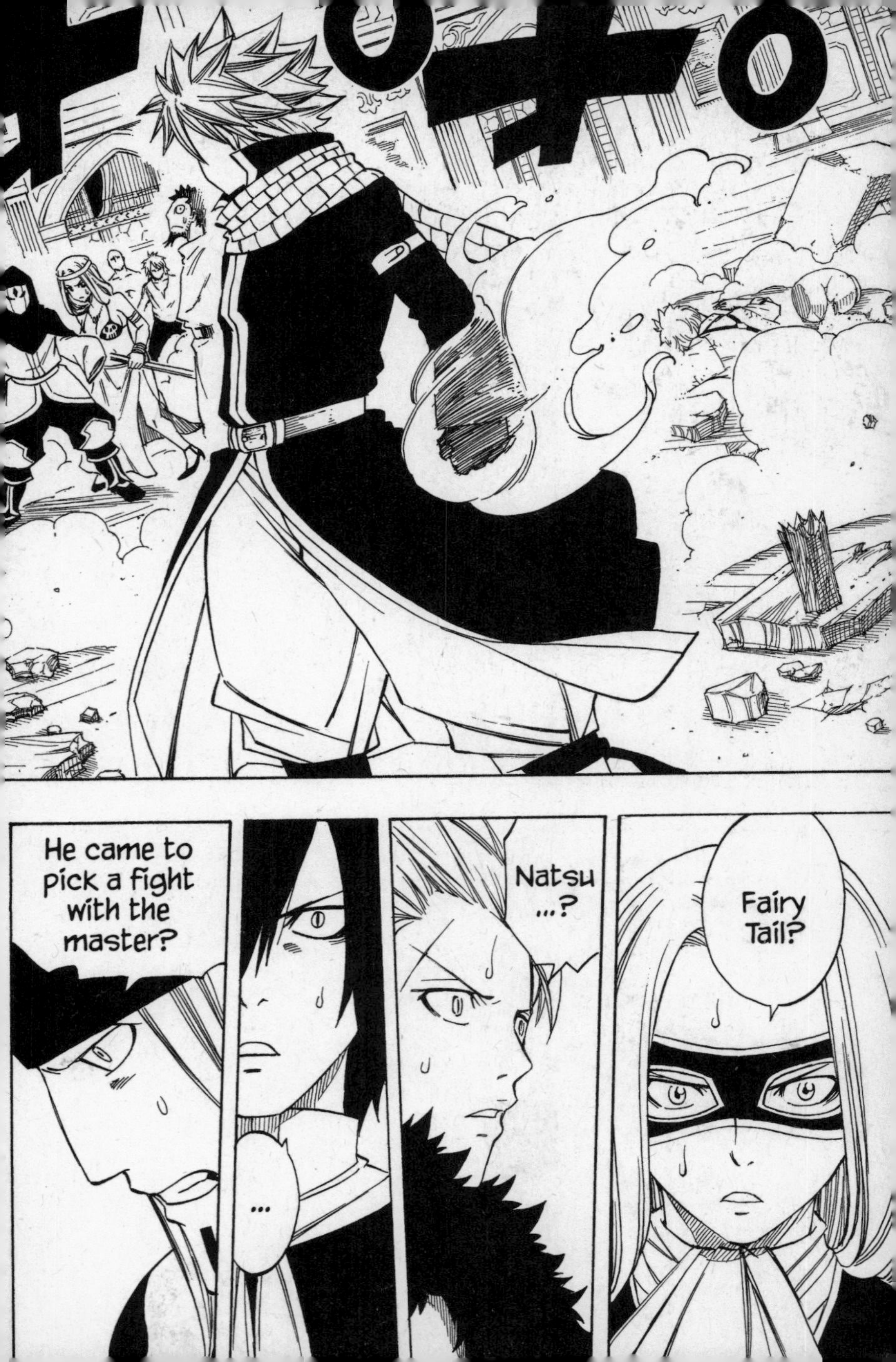
Fairy Tail?
Natsu ...?
...
He came to pick a fight with the master?

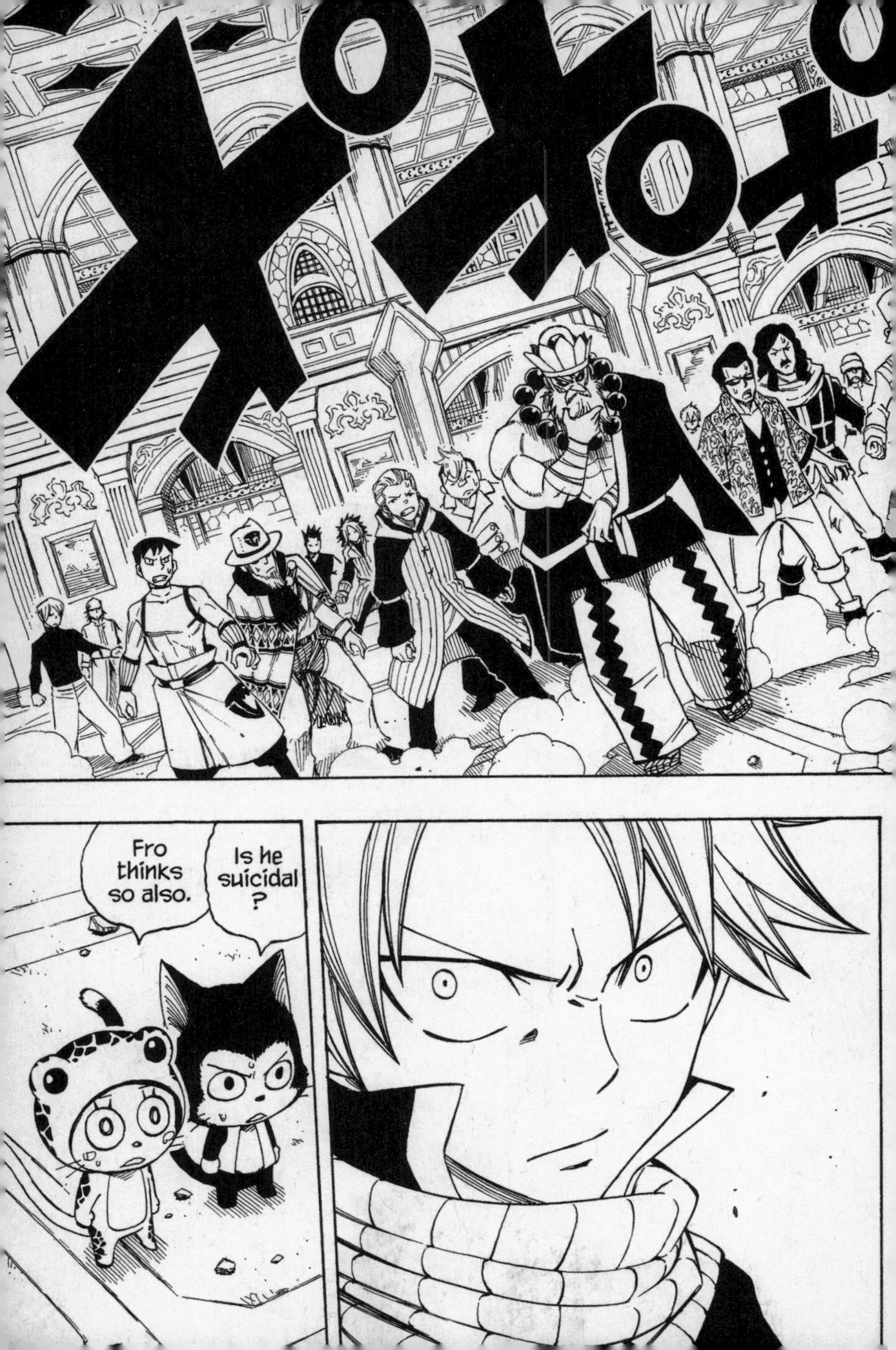
Is he suicidal?
Fro thinks so also.

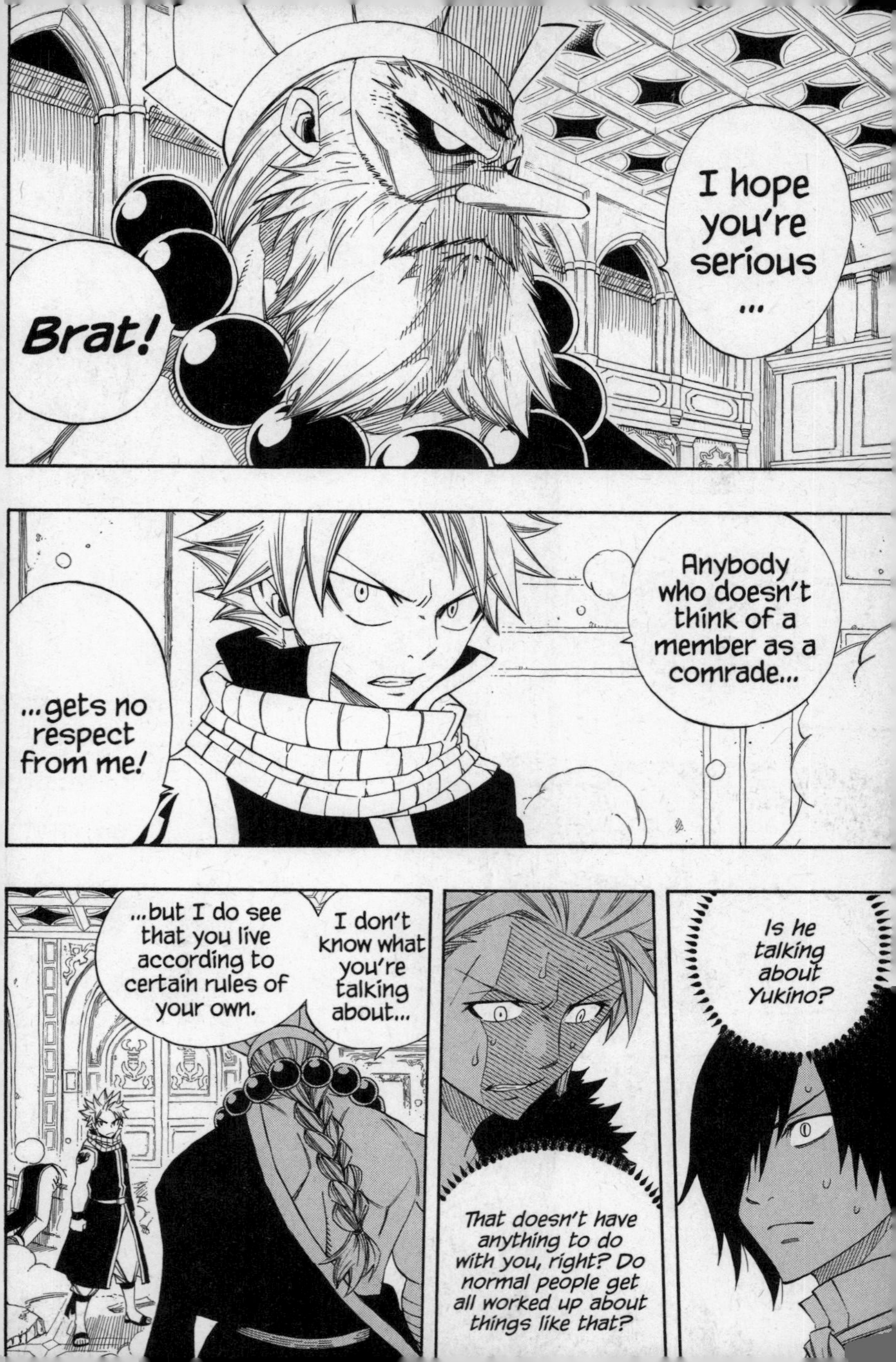
I hope you're serious ...
Brat!
Anybody who doesn't think of a member as a comrade...
...gets no respect from me!
Is he talking about Yukino?
That doesn't have anything to do with you, right? Do normal people get all worked up about things like that?
I don't know what you're talking about...
...but I do see that you live according to certain rules of your own.

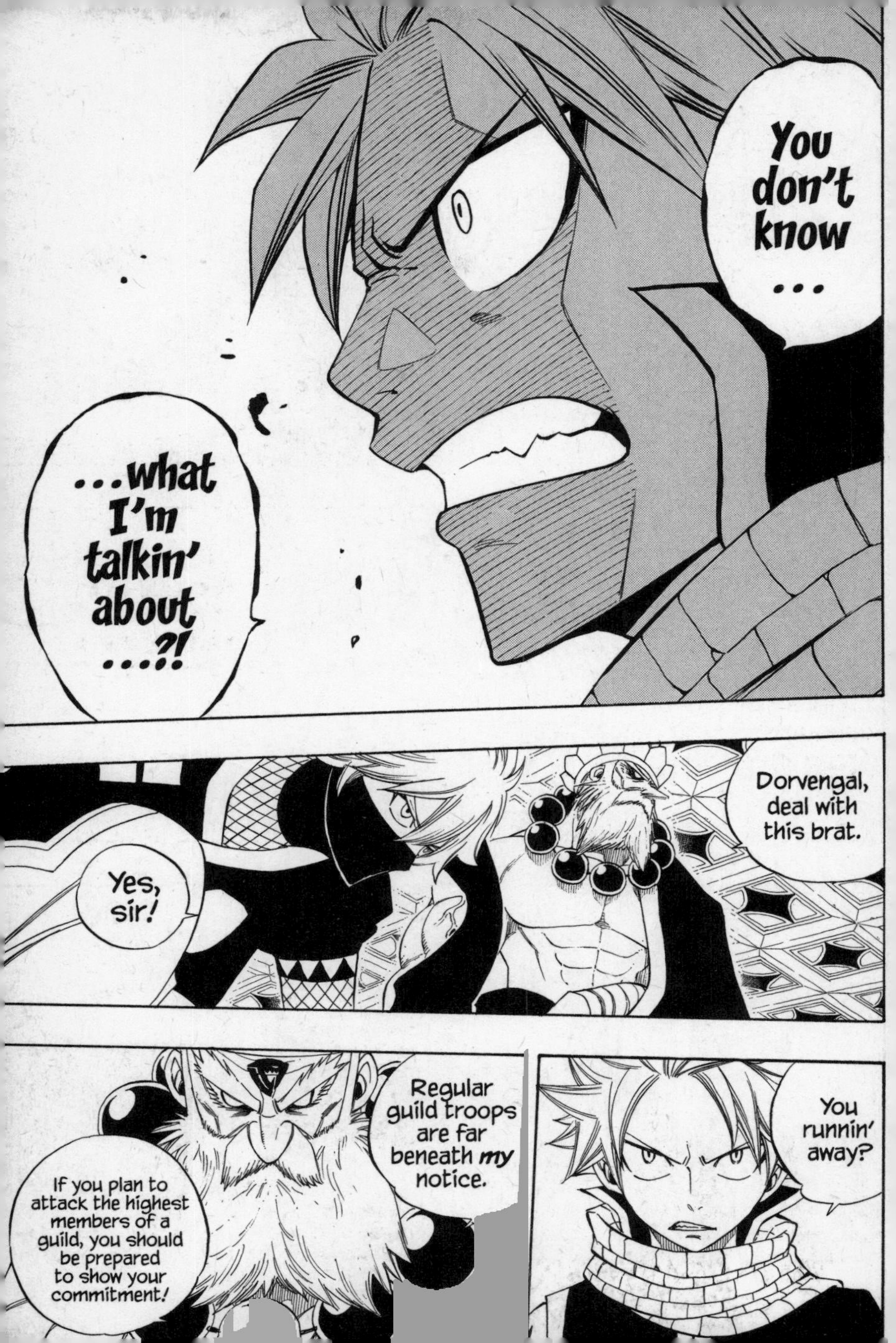
You don't know...
...what I'm talkin' about...?!
Dorvengal, deal with this brat.
Yes, sir!
You runnin' away?
Regular guild troops are far beneath *my* notice.
If you plan to attack the highest members of a guild, you should be prepared to show your commitment!

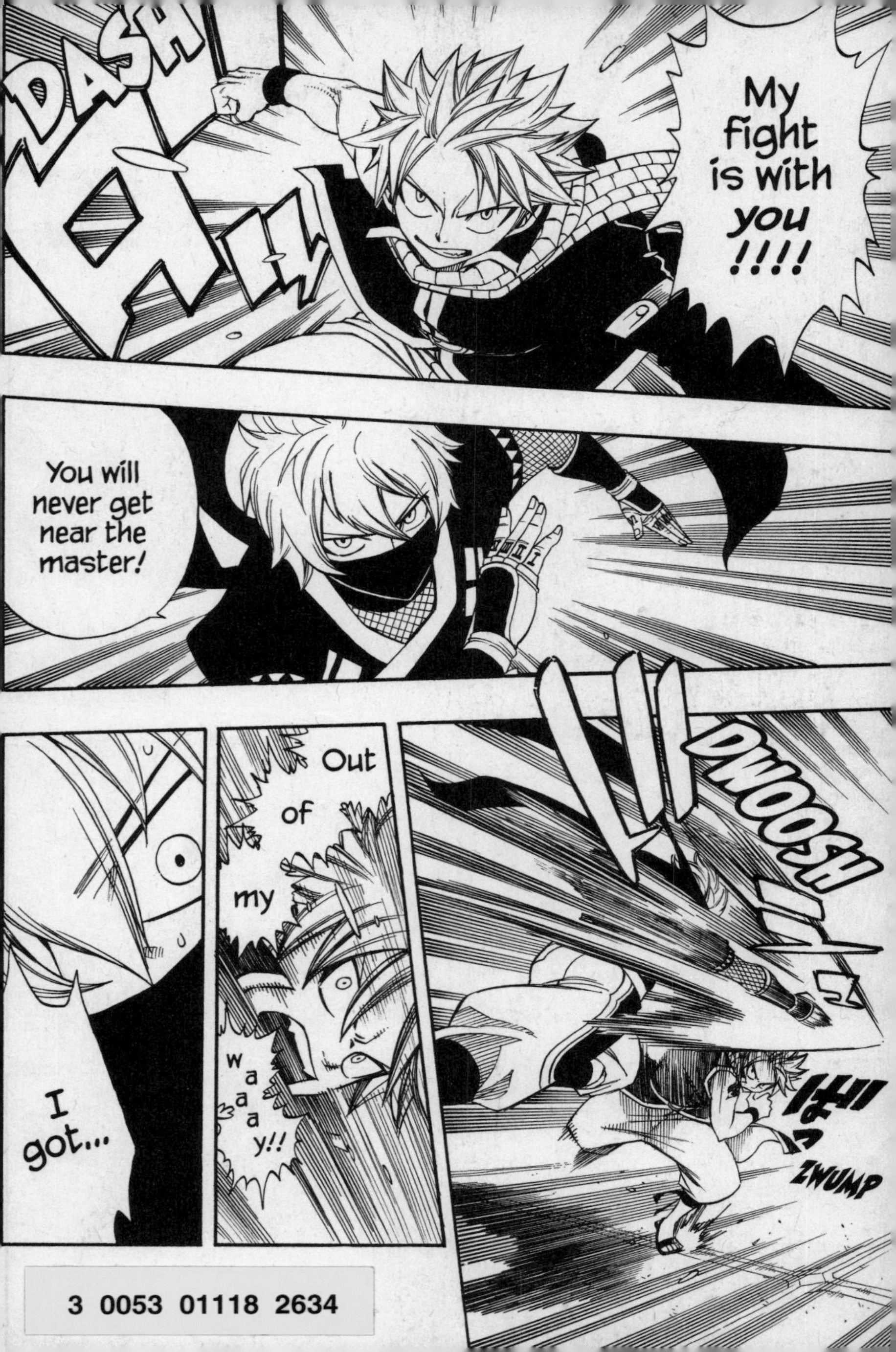
DASH
My fight is with you!!!!
You will never get near the master!
DWOOSH
ZWUMP
Out of my waaaay!!
I got...

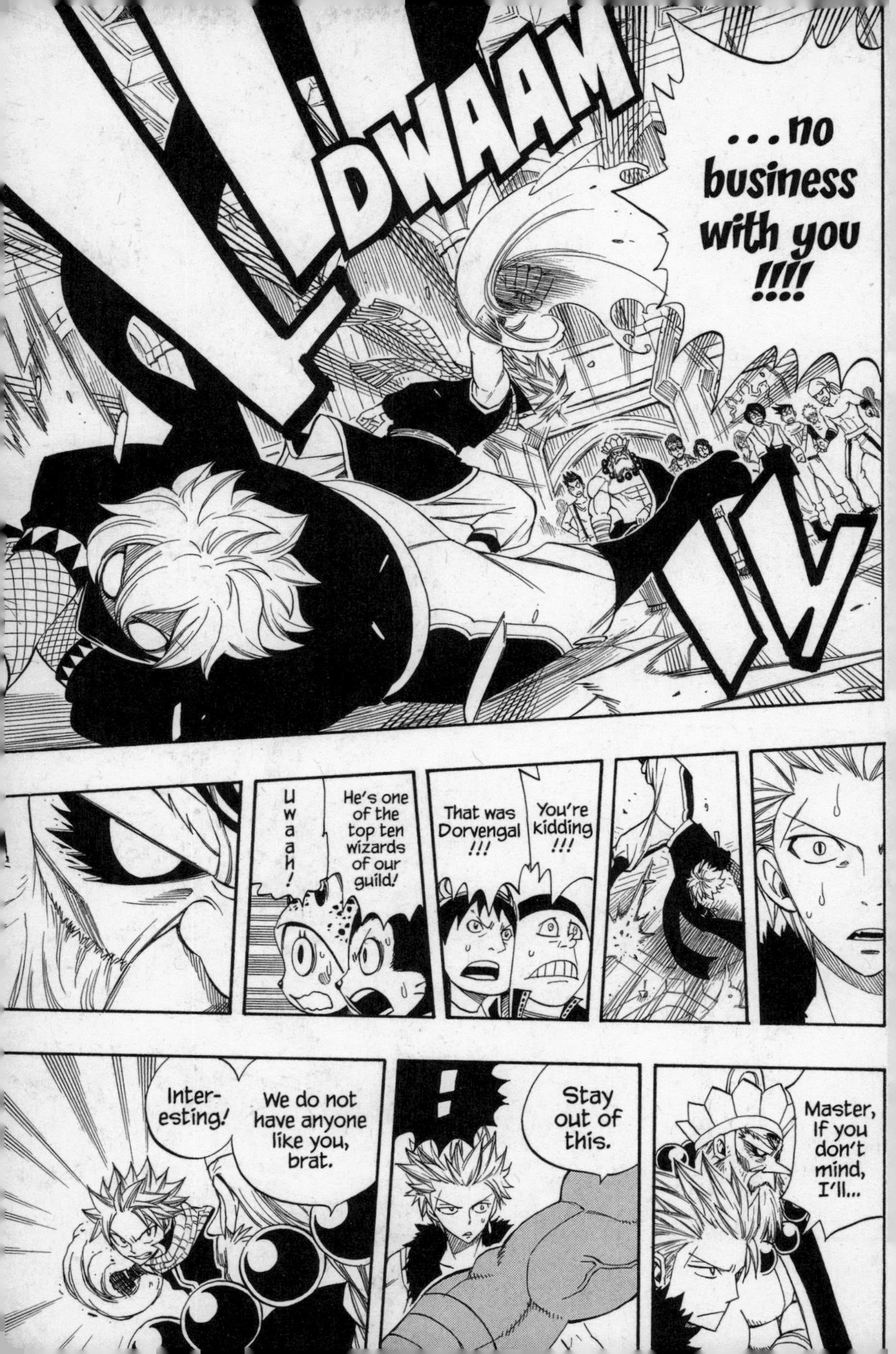
...no business with you !!!!
DWAAM
You're kidding !!!
That was Dorvengal !!!
He's one of the top ten wizards of our guild!
Uwaah!
Master, If you don't mind, I'll...
Stay out of this.
!
Inter-esting!
We do not have anyone like you, brat.

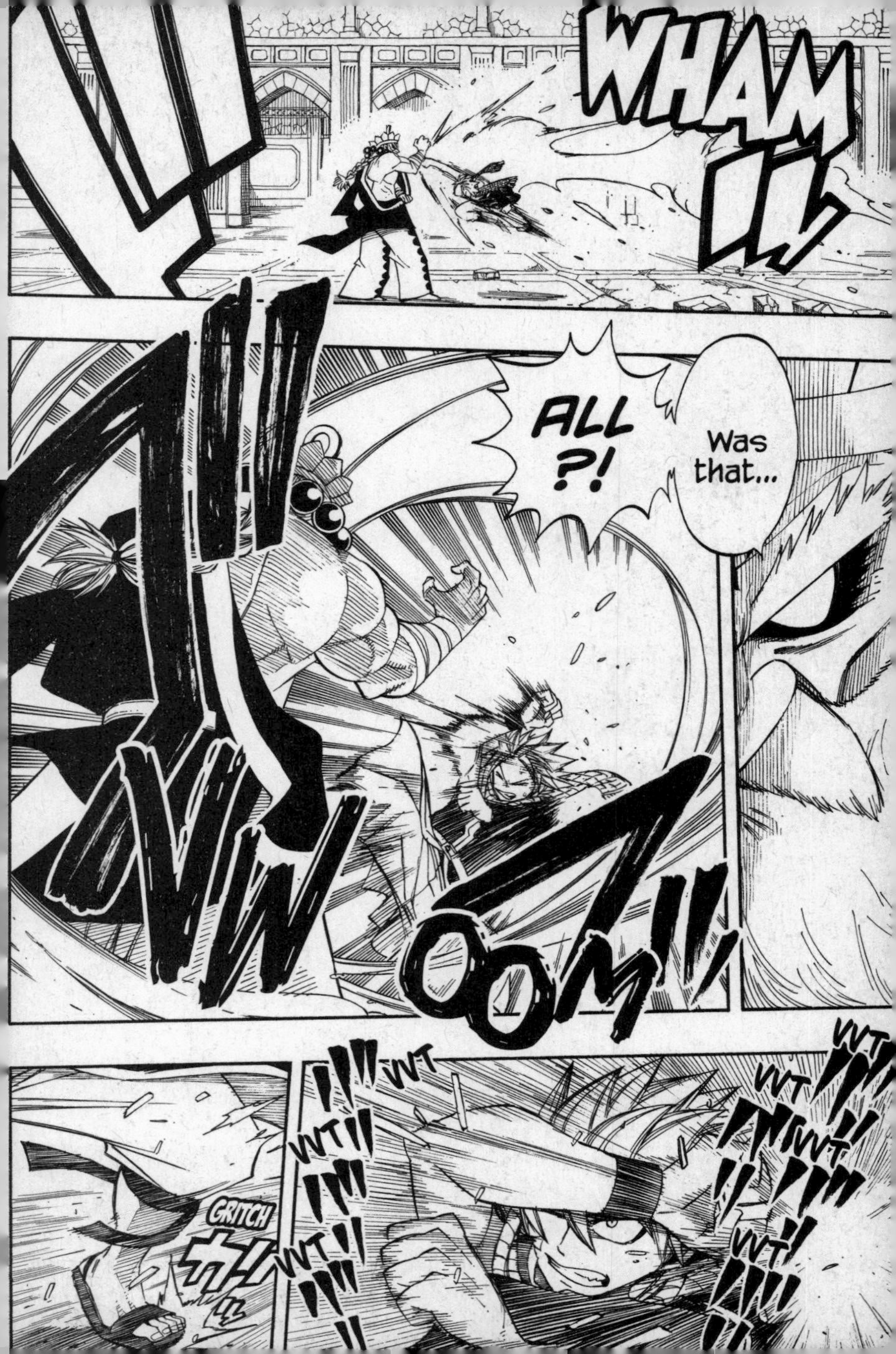
WHAM!!
Was that...
ALL ?!
VWOOM!!
VVT
VVT
VVT
VVT
VVT
VVT
GRITCH

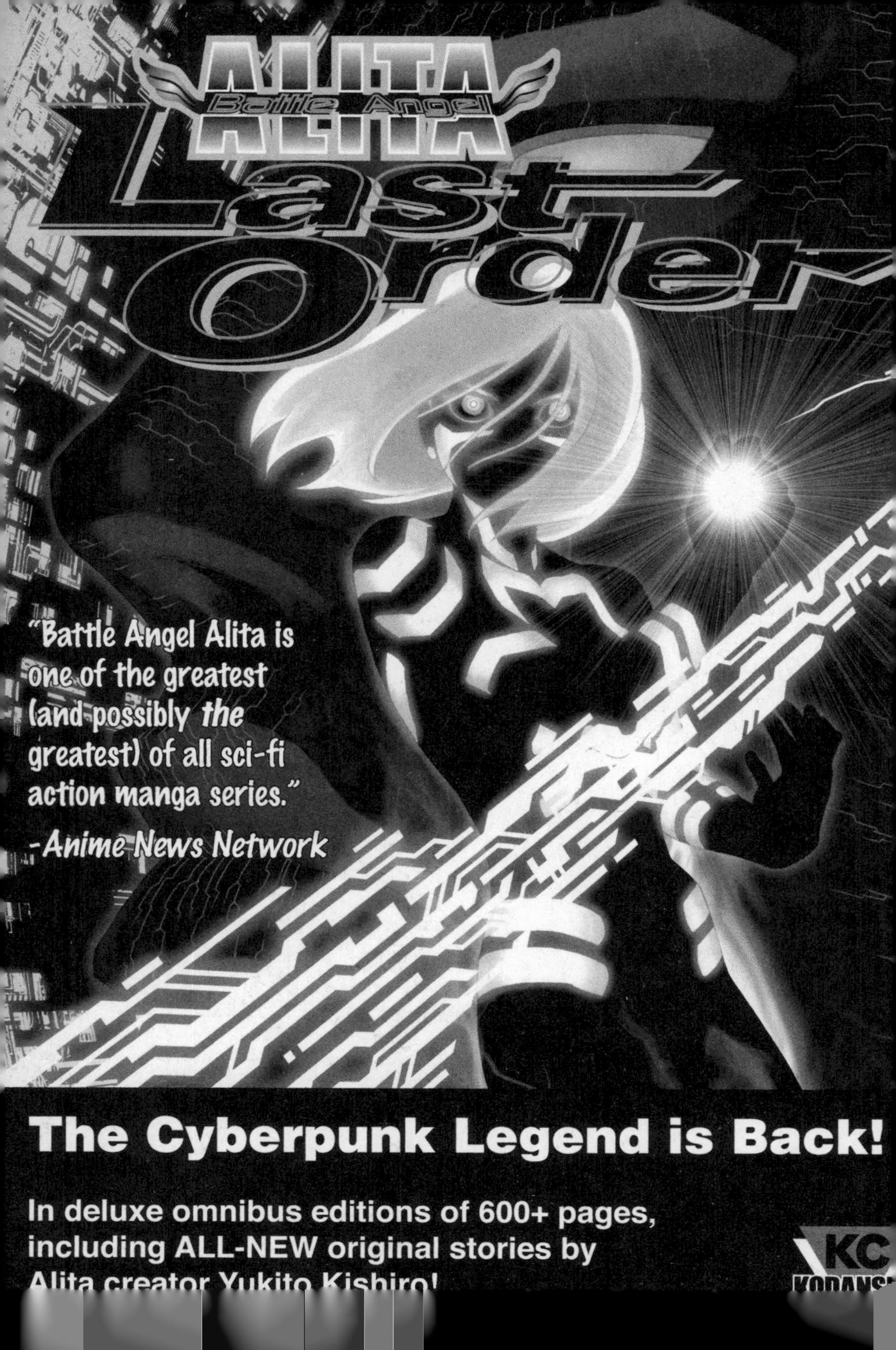
ALITA
Battle Angel
ALITA
Last Order
"Battle Angel Alita is one of the greatest (and possibly *the* greatest) of all sci-fi action manga series."
-Anime News Network

ATTACK ON TITAN

Humanity
has been decimated!

A century ago, the bizarre creatures known as Titans devoured most of the world's population, driving the remainder into a walled stronghold. Now, the appearance of an immense new Titan threatens the few humans left, and one restless boy decides to seize the chance to fight for his freedom, and the survival of his species!

Fairy Tail volume 33 is a work of fiction. Names, characters, places, and incidents are the products of the author's imagination or are used fictitiously. Any resemblance to actual events, locales, or persons, living or dead, is entirely coincidental.

A Kodansha Comics Trade Paperback Original.

Published in the United States by Kodansha Comics, an imprint of Kodansha USA Publishing, LLC, New York.

Publication rights for this English edition arranged through Kodansha Ltd., Tokyo.

First published in Japan in 2012 by Kodansha Ltd., Tokyo
ISBN 978-1-61262-410-5

Printed in the United States of America.

www.kodanshacomics.com

9 8 7 6 5 4 3 2 1

Translator: William Flanagan
Lettering: AndWorld Design

TOMARE!

止まれ
[STOP!]

You're going the wrong way!

Manga is a completely different type of reading experience.

To start at the *beginning,* go to the *end!*

That's right! Authentic manga is read the traditional Japanese way— from right to left, exactly the *opposite* of how American books are read. It's easy to follow: Just go to the other end of the book and read each page—and each panel—from right side to left side, starting at the top right. Now you're experiencing manga as it was meant to be!